上大法学文库
非洲法律系列之一

投资埃塞俄比亚法律必读

(中英对照)

Required Readings of Laws on Investment in Ethiopia

(In Chinese & English)

李 智　蔡建宇　[埃塞]戴维德·希梅莱斯(Dawit Shimeles)　等编译

上海大学出版社
·上海·

图书在版编目(CIP)数据

投资埃塞俄比亚法律必读:汉英对照/李智,蔡建宇,(埃塞)戴维德·希梅莱斯(Dawit Shimeles)编译.—上海:上海大学出版社,2021.10
ISBN 978-7-5671-4275-6

Ⅰ.①投… Ⅱ.①李… ②蔡… ③戴… Ⅲ.①法律—基本知识—埃塞俄比亚—汉、英 Ⅳ.①D942.1

中国版本图书馆 CIP 数据核字(2021)第 188249 号

责任编辑 王悦生
封面设计 缪炎栩
技术编辑 金 鑫 钱宇坤

投资埃塞俄比亚法律必读(中英对照)
Required Readings of Laws on Investment in Ethiopia
(In Chinese & English)
李 智 蔡建宇 [埃塞]戴维德·希梅莱斯(Dawit Shimeles) 等编译
上海大学出版社出版发行
(上海市上大路99号 邮政编码200444)
(http://www.shupress.cn) 发行热线 021-66135112
出版人 戴骏豪

*

南京展望文化发展有限公司排版
上海普顺印刷包装有限公司印刷 各地新华书店经销
开本 787mm×1092mm 1/16 印张 25.5 字数 653千
2021年12月第1版 2021年12月第1次印刷
ISBN 978-7-5671-4275-6/D·241 定价 88.00元

版权所有 侵权必究
如发现本书有印装质量问题请与印刷厂质量科联系
联系电话:021-36522998

本书是上大法学文库"非洲法律系列"之一,受上海大学法学院和泰和泰(上海)律师事务所资助,特此表示感谢!

前　言

2020年新冠疫情席卷全球,全民共克时艰,中国同国际社会一道,共同维护地区和全球公共卫生安全。新冠疫情于中国企业家而言,是"不期";后疫情时代,在以国内大循环为主体、国内国际双循环相互促进的新发展格局中,"一带一路"沿线国家的经济潜力再度吸引了人们的眼球。投资者该如何把握时代机遇,在后疫情时代的"而遇"中成为弄潮儿呢?

埃塞俄比亚(以下简称"埃塞")位于非洲东部,有"非洲屋脊"之称。作为"一带一路"倡议的重要合作伙伴和中非产能合作先行先试的示范国家,埃塞在经济发展中处处都展现着中国企业的风采。埃塞在过去10年里实现了年均10%以上的经济增速,是中国在非洲投资的样板国家。

进入21世纪以来,埃塞公共投资显著增加。该国在社会和经济基础设施方面进行了大量的投资,如道路、学校、医疗设施以及铁路和能源投资,这些软硬基础设施方面的建设有利于改善埃塞的投资环境。劳动力成本低廉是外资企业选择埃塞的另一原因。在埃塞的1亿多人口中,劳动力人口约为4 500万人,埃塞是非洲的第二大劳动力市场。

近年来,中国对埃塞的直接投资也保持着快速增长,由投资集中在农业、资源等方面,现已经扩展到第二产业及第三产业。据商务部2020年8月份统计数据显示,2020年1—6月,我国与埃塞双边贸易额12.6亿美元,同比增长16.9%[①]。且中国已与埃塞建立东方工业园,工业园区已成为中埃经贸合作的成功典型。

世界银行《2020年营商环境报告》中显示,埃塞的营商环境便利度在190个国家中名列后茅,排位第159名,与2019年维持同样的排位。

在这样的背景下,在埃塞投资的不少中国企业家,依然对投资埃塞持有耐心和信心。埃塞俄比亚,一个求商若渴的时代已经来临,这将对中国的投资者意味着什么呢?中国的投资者要如何应对?针对中国投资者的疑虑,本书可从法律层面指引中国投资者应对在埃塞投资的挑战与机遇。

第一编介绍投资法律制度。在《投资公告》中通过确保投资者在进行投资时的竞争力来促进和加强各区域之间的投资公平分配,规定了"外国投资者的投资形式和资本要求""投资许可证的取得";强调了"与国内投资者签订的技术转让和合作协议的登记"和"投资激励、担保和保护";规范了"投资管理"及"外派人员的雇用"。《为国内投资者保留的投资激励措施和投资领域》为埃塞国内投资者保留"国内投资者专有的投资领域",另为外国投

---

① 商务部西亚非洲司:中国-埃塞俄比亚经贸合作简况[EB/OL].(2020-08-18)(2021-01-11). http://www.mofcom.gov.cn/article/tongjiziliao/sjtj/xyfztjsj/202008/20200802993313.shtml.

资者设计了"允许外国投资者投资的领域";制定了"投资激励",如:"免除所得税"或"免征关税"。

第二编呈现劳动法律制度。《劳动公告》为保证工人与雇主的关系受权利和义务的基本原则支配,以使工人和雇主能够确保生产力的可持续发展与竞争力的提高,就"就业关系""工资""工作时间、每周休息和公共假日""休假"作了明确的规定;为保护特殊人群并营造健康安全的职业环境,规定了"妇女和低龄工人的工作条件""职业安全与健康及工作环境";为制定工作系统以保证工人与雇主成立他们各自的协会并参与的权利,以及拟定迅速解决工人与雇主之间的劳动纠纷的程序,特别设计了"集体关系"与"劳动纠纷"两部分;制定"时效期限和优先受偿权""劳动法的执行"和"行政措施和其他规定",以建立合理的劳动行政管理制度。

第三编勾画税收法律制度。《联邦税收管理公告》为规范埃塞全国内税收管理系统,以确保税收体系的有效性、效率性和可衡量性,明确了"税收法律的管理""纳税人"和"税收文件";在税收流程环节具体了"税收申报""税收评估""收缴税款和其他款项"和"抵免、退款、免除税务责任";通过"税收纠纷""信息收集和执行""事前裁定""通讯、表格和通知""税务上诉委员会""税收代理许可"和"行政、刑事处罚和奖励",来适用税收纠纷及其解决机制。

第四编涉猎工业园区制度。《工业园区公告》鉴于有必要通过在战略要地建立工业园区来加速国家的经济转型和发展,从而提升工业水平并创造就业机会,专门设计了"工业园区开发商和工业园区运营商的权利义务"及"工业园区企业与投资"两个准入制度;为给予园区企业及其员工优惠待遇,规定了"工业园区工作许可证和居住证"与"保障和保护国民待遇";通过"土地使用和环境保护"及"监管机构和申诉程序"保证园区的正常运转。

为了给中国企业家投资埃塞提供更多的便利,本书译者梳理了埃塞近十年有关投资的法律法规,挑选了对投资者最具价值的9部法规,通过广泛搜集、精心挑选、巧妙编排、贴切翻译,使得本书能如期与读者见面。在此特别感谢埃塞留学生戴维德·希梅莱斯(Dawit Shimeles)在法规搜集与筛选中做出的特殊贡献。

需要说明的是,我们是从2020年9月确定翻译的书名,10月组建翻译团队并着手筛选法规,11月着手翻译,时间非常紧张。由于翻译的内容涵盖法学多个学科,即使经过几轮校对,翻译不当或错误仍在所难免,在此,恳请各位专家与读者不吝赐教。

本书一为已在埃塞发展的企业与个人更好地投资提供法律参考,二为打算去埃塞投资的企业与个人提供法律指南,三为政府的决策者提供法律索引,四为相关研究的学者提供法律铺陈。

本书的翻译分工如下:

1.《投资公告》——蔡建宇、张乐

2.《投资法修正案公告》——朱瑞航、陈志

3.《为国内投资者保留的投资激励措施和投资领域部长理事会条例》——李智、蔡建宇

4.《修订为国内投资者保留的投资激励措施和投资领域部长理事会第270/2012号条例》——张乐、戴维德·希梅莱斯(Dawit Shimeles)

5.《劳动公告》——李智、张冰、陈子涵

6.《联邦税收管理公告》——李智、庄笑笑、刘渊园

7.《部长理事会联邦税收管理条例》——刘渊园、陈子涵
8.《部长理事会联邦所得税条例》——张冰、庄笑笑
9.《工业园区公告》——陈志、戴维德·希梅莱斯（Dawit Shimeles）

全文译校统稿：李智

校对：魏林强、朱瑞航

翻译团队介绍：

李　智，女，民商法博士，上海大学法学院教授、博士生导师。

蔡建宇，男，泰和泰（上海）律师事务所高级合伙人。

[埃塞]戴维德·希梅莱斯（Dawit Shimeles），男，埃塞俄比亚 A 照律师、上海大学法学院 2019 级研究生。

张　冰，女，上海大学法学院 2019 级民商法研究生。

刘渊园，女，上海大学法学院 2019 级民商法研究生。

庄笑笑，女，上海大学法学院 2019 级民商法研究生。

陈子涵，男，上海大学法学院 2019 级法律硕士研究生。

陈　志，男，上海大学法学院 2019 级法律硕士研究生。

朱瑞航，女，上海大学法学院 2018 级民商法研究生。

张　乐，男，上海大学法学院 2018 级法律硕士研究生。

魏林强，男，上海大学法学院 2017 级本科生。

本书定稿于 2021 年 1 月 29 日

上海大学东区法学院

目 录

第一编 投资法规

第一部 投资公告（第 769/2012 号公告）

- 第一部分　总则 ··· 2
  - 1. 简称 ·· 2
  - 2. 定义 ·· 2
  - 3. 适用范围 ·· 3
  - 4. 管辖权 ·· 3
- 第二部分　投资目标和投资领域 ··· 4
  - 5. 投资目标 ·· 4
  - 6. 应预留给政府或与政府联合投资的相关领域 ·································· 4
  - 7. 为国内投资者预留的投资领域 ·· 4
  - 8. 允许外国投资者投资的领域 ·· 4
  - 9. 与政府共同投资 ·· 4
- 第三部分　外国投资者的投资形式和资本要求 ······································· 4
  - 10. 投资形式 ··· 4
  - 11. 外国投资者的最低资本要求 ··· 5
- 第四部分　投资许可证 ··· 5
  - 12. 投资许可要求 ··· 5
  - 13. 国内投资者的投资许可证申请 ··· 6
  - 14. 外国投资者的投资许可证申请 ··· 6
  - 15. 扩建或升级投资许可证申请 ··· 7
  - 16. 出具投资许可证 ··· 7
  - 17. 续签投资许可证 ··· 7
  - 18. 正在实施阶段的投资项目转让 ··· 7
  - 19. 暂停或撤销投资许可证 ··· 8
  - 20. 报告和合作的责任 ··· 8
- 第五部分　与国内投资者签订的技术转让和合作协议的登记 ··························· 8
  - 21. 技术转让协议 ··· 8

22. 以出口为导向,不以股权为基础的外国企业合作协议 ·················· 8

第六部分　投资激励、担保和保护 ·················· 9
　　23. 投资激励 ·················· 9
　　24. 不动产所有权 ·················· 9
　　25. 投资担保与保护 ·················· 9
　　26. 资金的汇款 ·················· 9

第七部分　投资管理 ·················· 10
　　27. 投资管理机构 ·················· 10
　　28. 投资局的权力和职责 ·················· 10
　　29. 投资理事会的权力和职责 ·················· 10
　　30. 一站式服务 ·················· 11
　　31. 投资相关信息 ·················· 12
　　32. 投诉处理 ·················· 12

第八部分　工业开发区 ·················· 12
　　33. 建立工业开发区 ·················· 12
　　34. 工业开发区管理 ·················· 12
　　35. 关于工业开发区的规定 ·················· 12

第九部分　其他规定 ·················· 13
　　36. 外币贷款和利用 ·················· 13
　　37. 外派人员的雇用 ·················· 13
　　38. 遵守其他法律和环境保护的义务 ·················· 13
　　39. 发布条例的权力 ·················· 13
　　40. 废除和不适用的法律 ·················· 13
　　41. 生效日期 ·················· 13

第二部　投资修正案公告(第849/2014号公告)

　　1. 简称 ·················· 15
　　2. 修正案 ·················· 15
　　3. 生效日期 ·················· 16

第三部　为国内投资者保留的投资激励措施和投资领域部长理事会条例(部长理事会第270/2012号条例)

第一部分　总则 ·················· 18
　　1. 简称 ·················· 18
　　2. 定义 ·················· 18
　　3. 为国内投资者保留的投资领域 ·················· 18
　　4. 允许外国投资者投资的领域 ·················· 19

第二部分　投资激励 ·················· 19
　　第一节　免征所得税 ·················· 19

5. 新企业免征所得税 ··· 19
6. 扩大或升级现有企业的所得税免税部分 ··· 19
7. 出口产品或服务的投资者可享受额外的所得税豁免 ································ 19
8. 减少激励的条件 ·· 19
9. 提交信息的义务 ·· 19
10. 所得税免税期的开始 ··· 20
11. 所得税免税期内的收入申报 ·· 20
12. 亏损结转 ·· 20
第二节 免征关税 ··· 20
13. 资本货物和建筑材料免征关税 ·· 20
14. 机动车辆免征关税 ··· 20
15. 免税进口货物的转让 ··· 20
第三部分 其他规定 ··· 20
16. 废除和不适用的法律 ··· 20
17. 暂行规定 ·· 21
18. 生效日期 ·· 21
投资领域和所得税免税表 ·· 21

第四部 修订为国内投资者保留的投资激励措施和投资领域部长理事会第270/2012号条例（部长理事会第312/2014号条例）

1. 简称 ··· 29
2. 修订内容 ··· 29
3. 生效日期 ··· 30

第二编 劳动法规

第五部 劳动公告（第1156/2019号公告）

第一部分 总则 ·· 32
　1. 简称 ·· 32
　2. 定义 ·· 32
　3. 适用范围 ·· 33
第二部分 雇佣关系 ·· 34
　第一章 雇佣合同 ··· 34
　　第一节 雇佣合同的形式 ·· 34
　　　4. 雇佣合同的要素 ·· 34
　　　5. 形式 ·· 34
　　　6. 书面雇佣合同 ·· 34

7. 非书面形式的雇佣合同 ·· 34
　　　8. 违约 ·· 34
　　第二节　雇佣合同期限 ·· 34
　　　9. 无固定期限雇佣合同 ·· 34
　　　10. 定期或计件雇佣合同 ··· 35
　　　11. 试用期 ··· 35
　　第三节　双方的义务 ··· 35
　　　12. 雇主的义务 ·· 35
　　　13. 工人的义务 ·· 36
　　　14. 禁止行为 ··· 36
　　第四节　雇佣合同的修改 ·· 37
　　　15. 修改条件 ··· 37
　　　16. 企业所有权的合并、分割和转让 ······························· 37
　　第五节　临时中止雇佣合同产生的权利义务 ··························· 37
　　　17. 一般原则 ··· 37
　　　18. 中止的理由 ·· 37
　　　19. 报告的义务 ·· 37
　　　20. 劳动与社会事务部或有关当局的决定 ·························· 37
　　　21. 中止的确认或核准的效力 ··· 38
　　　22. 中止期到期的效力 ··· 38

第二章　雇佣关系的终止 ·· 38
　　23. 一般原则 ·· 38
　　第一节　通过法律或协议终止雇佣合同 ································· 38
　　　24. 通过法律终止雇佣合同 ·· 38
　　　25. 通过协议终止雇佣合同 ·· 38
　　第二节　缔约双方终止雇佣合同 ··· 38
　　　附款一　由雇主提出的终止雇佣合同 ······························· 38
　　　26. 一般原则 ··· 38
　　　27. 没有预先通知而终止雇佣合同 ··································· 39
　　　28. 预先通知终止雇佣合同 ·· 39
　　　29. 裁员 ·· 40
　　　30. 例外情况 ··· 40
　　　附款二　由工人提出的终止雇佣合同 ······························· 40
　　　31. 预先通知而终止的雇佣合同 ······································ 40
　　　32. 无须预先通知就可终止的雇佣合同 ···························· 40
　　　33. 时效期限 ··· 41

第三章　关于终止雇佣合同的一般规定 ····································· 41
　　第一节　终止雇佣合同的通知 ·· 41
　　　34. 发出通知的程序 ·· 41

  35. 通知期限 ·· 41
 第二节 终止雇佣合同时支付的工资和其他款项 ·· 41
  36. 付款期限 ·· 41
  37. 争议金额 ·· 41
  38. 延迟的影响 ·· 41
 第三节 解雇费和补偿 ·· 41
  39. 一般原则 ·· 41
  40. 解雇费数额 ·· 42
  41. 无通知而终止雇佣合同的赔偿费 ·· 42
 第四节 非法终止雇佣合同的后果 ·· 42
  42. 一般原则 ·· 42
  43. 非法终止中对工人的恢复和补偿 ·· 42
  44. 例外情况 ·· 43
  45. 工人的赔偿责任 ··· 43
 第四章 特别合同 ·· 43
 第一节 家庭工作合同 ·· 43
  46. 订立合同 ·· 43
  47. 备案 ··· 44
 第二节 学徒合同 ·· 44
  48. 订立合同 ·· 44
  49. 合同内容 ·· 44
  50. 缔约方的义务 ·· 44
  51. 合同终止 ·· 44
  52. 证书 ··· 45
第三部分 工资 ·· 45
 第一章 工资的确定 ·· 45
  53. 一般原则 ·· 45
  54. 空闲时间的付款条件 ·· 45
 第二章 付款方式和执行 ·· 45
  55. 一般原则 ·· 45
  56. 付款执行 ·· 45
  57. 亲自付款 ·· 45
  58. 付款时间 ·· 46
  59. 工资扣除 ·· 46
  60. 保留付款记录 ·· 46
第四部分 工作时间、每周休息和公共假日 ·· 46
 第一章 工作时间 ·· 46
 第一节 正常工作时间 ·· 46
  61. 每日或每周最长工作时间 ·· 46

62. 减少正常工作时间 …… 46
63. 每周工作时间的安排 …… 46
64. 平均正常工作时间 …… 46
65. 例外 …… 46

第二节 加班

66. 一般原则 …… 47
67. 允许加班的情形 …… 47
68. 加班费 …… 47

第二章 每周休息

69. 一般原则 …… 47
70. 每周特殊休息日 …… 47
71. 每周休息日完成的工作 …… 48
72. 适用 …… 48

第三章 公共假期

73. 一般原则 …… 48
74. 公共假期不减少工资 …… 48
75. 公共假期工作的报酬 …… 48

第五部分 休假

第一章 年休假

76. 一般原则 …… 48
77. 年休假的天数 …… 48
78. 准予休假 …… 49
79. 年休假的分休和延期 …… 49
80. 召回休假的工人 …… 49

第二章 特殊情况休假

81. 家庭事务休假 …… 49
82. 工会休假 …… 49
83. 特殊目的休假 …… 49
84. 通知 …… 50

第三章 病假

85. 休假期限 …… 50
86. 支付 …… 50

第六部分 妇女和低龄工人的工作条件

第一章 妇女的工作条件

87. 一般原则 …… 50
88. 产假 …… 51

第二章 低龄工人的工作条件

89. 一般原则 …… 51
90. 工作时间限制 …… 51

  91. 夜间和加班工作 ………………………………………………………… 51

第七部分　职业安全和健康及工作环境 ……………………………………… 51
第一章　预防措施 ……………………………………………………………… 51
  92. 雇主的义务 …………………………………………………………… 51
  93. 工人的义务 …………………………………………………………… 52
  94. 禁止行为 ……………………………………………………………… 52
第二章　职业伤害 ……………………………………………………………… 52
第一节　责任 …………………………………………………………………… 52
  95. 一般原则 ……………………………………………………………… 52
  96. 无过错责任 …………………………………………………………… 52
  97. 职业事故 ……………………………………………………………… 53
  98. 职业病 ………………………………………………………………… 53
第二节　残疾程度 ……………………………………………………………… 53
  99. 一般原则 ……………………………………………………………… 53
  100. 暂时性残疾 ………………………………………………………… 54
  101. 永久性部分或完全残疾 …………………………………………… 54
  102. 残疾评估 …………………………………………………………… 54
第三章　工伤赔偿 ……………………………………………………………… 54
第一节　一般原则 ……………………………………………………………… 54
  103. 付款和付款责任 …………………………………………………… 54
  104. 特殊义务 …………………………………………………………… 54
第二节　医疗服务 ……………………………………………………………… 54
  105. 医疗服务类型 ……………………………………………………… 54
  106. 医疗服务期限 ……………………………………………………… 55
第三节　各种方式的现金救济 ………………………………………………… 55
  107. 一般原则 …………………………………………………………… 55
  108. 定期报酬 …………………………………………………………… 55
  109. 伤残赔偿金 ………………………………………………………… 55
  110. 家属抚恤金 ………………………………………………………… 55
  111. 举证责任 …………………………………………………………… 56
  112. 不缴税补助金 ……………………………………………………… 56

第八部分　集体关系 …………………………………………………………… 56
第一章　工会和雇主协会 ……………………………………………………… 56
  113. 结社权 ……………………………………………………………… 56
  114. 协会的成立 ………………………………………………………… 56
  115. 协会的职能 ………………………………………………………… 57
  116. 联合会和联盟的职能 ……………………………………………… 57
  117. 禁止行为 …………………………………………………………… 57
  118. 协会章程 …………………………………………………………… 57

- 119. 协会注册 ··· 58
- 120. 拒绝注册 ··· 58
- 121. 撤销注册 ··· 58
- 122. 取消协会注册的通知 ··· 59
- 123. 上诉 ··· 59
- 124. 协会要求取消注册或解散的后果 ································· 59

第二章 集体协议 ··· 59

第一节 一般原则 ··· 59
- 125. 定义 ··· 59
- 126. 谈判 ··· 59
- 127. 代表权 ·· 59
- 128. 顾问 ··· 59
- 129. 集体协议的主题 ··· 60
- 130. 集体协议的内容 ··· 60
- 131. 集体谈判的程序 ··· 60
- 132. 集体协议的登记 ··· 60
- 133. 集体协议的加入 ··· 60

第二节 集体协议的有效条件 ··· 60
- 134. 集体协议的有效期限 ·· 60

第三节 集体协议的适用范围 ··· 61
- 135. 适用范围 ··· 61
- 136. 例外 ··· 61

第九部分 劳动纠纷 ··· 61

第一章 一般原则 ··· 61
- 137. 定义 ··· 61

第二章 劳动法庭 ··· 62
- 138. 建立劳动法庭 ·· 62
- 139. 初审法院劳动分庭 ··· 62
- 140. 上诉法院劳动分庭 ··· 62

第三章 与劳工问题有关的替代性争端解决机制 ························· 63
- 141. 社会对话 ··· 63
- 142. 调解员的任命 ·· 63
- 143. 调解员的职责和责任 ·· 63
- 144. 调解与仲裁 ··· 63

第四章 劳动关系委员会 ··· 63
- 145. 委员会的设立 ·· 63
- 146. 常设委员会或临时委员会的组成 ································ 64
- 147. 常设委员会或临时委员会的会议程序 ························· 64
- 148. 常设委员会或临时委员会的权力 ································ 64

  149. 议事规则 ··· 65
  150. 案件听证会 ··· 65
  151. 审议事项 ··· 65
  152. 裁决 ·· 65
  153. 决议的效果 ··· 66
  154. 委员会对事实的最后裁决 ··· 66
  155. 上诉 ·· 66
  156. 违反常设委员会或临时委员会的行为 ·· 66
  157. 年度报告 ··· 66
 第五章 罢工和停工 ··· 66
  158. 一般原则 ··· 66
  159. 需要满足的条件 ··· 66
  160. 通知程序 ··· 67
  161. 禁止行为 ··· 67
 第六章 费用 ·· 67
  162. 费用豁免 ··· 67
第十部分 时效期限和优先受偿权 ·· 67
 第一章 时效期限 ··· 67
  163. 时效期限 ··· 67
  164. 时效期限的计算 ··· 67
  165. 时效期限的中断 ··· 67
  166. 时效期限的放弃 ··· 68
  167. 主管当局的自由裁量权 ··· 68
 第二章 优先受偿权 ··· 68
  168. 优先于其他债务 ··· 68
  169. 赔偿支付的程序 ··· 68
  170. 家庭工人的留置权 ··· 68
第十一部分 劳动法的执行 ··· 68
 第一章 劳动管理 ··· 68
  171. 劳动与社会事务部的权力 ··· 68
  第一节 就业服务 ··· 69
   172. 一般原则 ··· 69
   173. 职业介绍所 ··· 69
   174. 私营职业介绍所参与提供本地职业介绍服务的条件 ··············· 69
   175. 私营职业介绍所的许可证 ··· 69
   176. 外籍人士的就业 ··· 70
  第二节 劳动监察机构 ·· 70
   177. 劳动监察机构 ··· 70
   178. 劳动监察员的权力和义务 ··· 70

179. 劳动监察应采取的措施	71
180. 上诉	71
181. 对劳动监察员的职能和责任的限制	71
182. 禁止行为	71
183. 私营监察机构	71

第十二部分　行政措施和其他规定 … 72

第一章　行政措施 … 72
184. 一般原则	72
185. 对雇主的措施	72
186. 常用措施	72
187. 针对私营职业介绍所的措施	73
188. 提出诉讼的权力	73

第二章　其他规定 … 73
189. 时效期限	73
190. 暂行规定	73
191. 残疾程度的确定	73
192. 废除法律	73
193. 生效日期	74

第三编　税　收　法　规

第六部　联邦税收管理公告（第 983/2016 号公告）

第一部分　总则 … 76
1. 简称	76
2. 定义	76
3. 公允市场价值	80
4. 关联人员	80

第二部分　税收法律的管理 … 81
5. 管理部门的职责	81
6. 税务人员的职责和义务	81
7. 合作义务	81
8. 税收信息的保密	81

第三部分　纳税人 … 82

第一章　登记 … 82
| 9. 纳税人登记 | 82 |
| 10. 变更通知 | 83 |

11. 注销登记 …… 83

第二章 纳税人识别号

12. 纳税人识别号 …… 83
13. TIN 的签发 …… 83
14. TIN 的使用 …… 84
15. 取消 TIN …… 84

第三章 税收代表

16. 税收代表的义务 …… 84

第四部分 文件

17. 记录保留义务 …… 85
18. 文件检查 …… 85
19. 收据 …… 85
20. 销售登记机 …… 85

第五部分 税收声明

21. 申报纳税 …… 86
22. 持照税务代理人纳税申报证明 …… 86
23. 预先纳税声明 …… 87
24. 正式提交的纳税声明 …… 87

第六部分 税收评估

25. 自我评估 …… 87
26. 综合评估 …… 88
27. 危险评估 …… 88
28. 修订评估 …… 89
29. 申请对自我评估作出修订 …… 90

第七部分 征收和追缴税款和其他款项

第一章 缴纳税款及其他款项

30. 税收作为政府的债务 …… 90
31. 次要债务和税收追回费用 …… 90
32. 延长纳税时间 …… 90
33. 税收优先权和扣押额 …… 91
34. 纳税顺序 …… 91
35. 纳税担保 …… 91
36. 保护 …… 92

第二章 逾期纳税利息

37. 逾期纳税利息 …… 92

第三章 未缴税款的追回

38. 税收评估的执行 …… 92
39. 优先求偿权 …… 93

    40. 接管人的职责 ……………………………………………………… 93
    41. 扣押财产 …………………………………………………………… 94
    42. 金融机构保留的资金和资产 …………………………………… 95
    43. 向第三方追缴未缴税费 ………………………………………… 95
    44. 离境禁止令 ………………………………………………………… 96
    45. 暂停营业 …………………………………………………………… 97
    46. 税收责任转移 ……………………………………………………… 97
    47. 机构应缴税款 ……………………………………………………… 97
    48. 欺诈或逃税的税收责任 ………………………………………… 98

第八部分　抵免、退款、免除税务责任 …………………………………… 98
    49. 税收抵免 …………………………………………………………… 98
    50. 退还多缴的税款 ………………………………………………… 98
    51. 遇到严重困难时的减免 ………………………………………… 99

第九部分　税收纠纷 ………………………………………………………… 99
    52. 声明的原因 ………………………………………………………… 99
    53. 税收终结和上诉决定 …………………………………………… 99
    54. 反对税收决定的通知 …………………………………………… 100
    55. 做出异议决定 …………………………………………………… 100
    56. 向税务上诉委员会提出上诉 …………………………………… 101
    57. 向联邦高等法院上诉 …………………………………………… 101
    58. 向联邦最高法院上诉 …………………………………………… 101
    59. 举证责任 …………………………………………………………… 102
    60. 执行委员会或法院的决定 ……………………………………… 102

第十部分　信息收集和执行 ………………………………………………… 102
    61. 完税清单 …………………………………………………………… 102
    62. 公司组织章程的备案 …………………………………………… 102
    63. 公共审计师 ………………………………………………………… 102
    64. 与非居民的服务合同通知 ……………………………………… 102
    65. 取得信息或证据的通知 ………………………………………… 103
    66. 进入和搜索的权力 ……………………………………………… 103
    67. 行政互助协议的执行 …………………………………………… 104

第十一部分　事前裁定 ……………………………………………………… 104
  第一章　公开裁定 ………………………………………………………… 104
    68. 具有约束力的公开裁定 ………………………………………… 104
    69. 作出公开裁定 …………………………………………………… 104
    70. 撤销公开裁定 …………………………………………………… 104
  第二章　私人裁定 ………………………………………………………… 105
    71. 具有约束力的私人裁定 ………………………………………… 105

72. 拒绝私人裁定申请 ································· 105
　　73. 作出私人裁定 ······································· 106
　　74. 撤销私人裁定 ······································· 106
　　75. 公布私人裁定 ······································· 106
　第三章　本部的其他建议 ································· 106
　　76. 管理局提供的其他建议 ·························· 106
第十二部分　通讯、表格和通知 ····························· 106
　77. 工作语言 ··· 106
　78. 表格和通知 ··· 107
　79. 批准表格 ··· 107
　80. 向管理局提交文件的方式 ·························· 107
　81. 送达通知书 ··· 107
　82. 电子税收系统的适用 ······························· 107
　83. 提交文件或缴纳税款的截止日期 ················ 108
　84. 不影响通知书有效性的瑕疵 ······················ 108
　85. 错误更正 ··· 108
第十三部分　税务上诉委员会 ······························· 109
　86. 成立税务上诉委员会 ······························· 109
　87. 任命委员会委员 ····································· 109
　88. 上诉通知书 ··· 109
　89. 有权向委员会提交文件 ···························· 110
　90. 委员会诉讼程序 ····································· 110
　91. 委员会的决定 ·· 110
　92. 委员会的行政事项 ·································· 111
　93. 财政 ··· 111
　94. 委员会的年度报告 ·································· 111
第十四部分　税收代理许可 ·································· 111
　95. 申请税务代理人执照 ······························· 111
　96. 税务代理人的执照 ·································· 111
　97. 税务代理人执照的续期 ···························· 112
　98. 提供税务代理服务的限制 ························· 112
　99. 取消税务代理人执照 ······························· 112
第十五部分　行政、刑事处罚和奖励 ······················ 113
　第一章　一般规定 ·· 113
　　100. 行政和刑事责任的一般规定 ·················· 113
　第二章　行政处罚 ·· 113
　　101. 有关登记及取消登记的处罚 ·················· 113
　　102. 未能保存文件的处罚 ··························· 113

103. 关于 TIN 的处罚 ……………………………………………………… 114

104. 逾期提交的处罚 ……………………………………………………… 114

105. 逾期付款的处罚 ……………………………………………………… 114

106. 预扣税处罚 …………………………………………………………… 114

107. 增值税处罚 …………………………………………………………… 115

108. 未能开具税务发票 …………………………………………………… 115

109. 少报税款的处罚 ……………………………………………………… 115

110. 避税处罚 ……………………………………………………………… 115

111. 不遵守电子税收制度的处罚 ………………………………………… 115

112. 税务代理人的处罚 …………………………………………………… 115

113. 与销售登记机有关的罚款 …………………………………………… 116

114. 其他处罚 ……………………………………………………………… 117

115. 行政处罚评估 ………………………………………………………… 117

第三章 税收犯罪 …………………………………………………………… 117

116. 税收犯罪案件的程序 ………………………………………………… 117

117. 有关 TIN 的犯罪 ……………………………………………………… 117

118. 虚假或误导性陈述和欺诈性文件 …………………………………… 118

119. 欺诈或非法开具发票 ………………………………………………… 118

120. 与发票有关的一般罪行 ……………………………………………… 118

121. 要求非法退款或超额信贷 …………………………………………… 119

122. 增值税犯罪 …………………………………………………………… 119

123. 印花税犯罪 …………………………………………………………… 119

124. 与追税有关的犯罪 …………………………………………………… 119

125. 逃税 …………………………………………………………………… 120

126. 妨碍税收管理法 ……………………………………………………… 120

127. 未经授权的税收 ……………………………………………………… 120

128. 协助或教唆税收犯罪 ………………………………………………… 120

129. 与税务上诉委员会有关的犯罪 ……………………………………… 120

130. 税务代理人的犯罪 …………………………………………………… 121

131. 与销售登记机有关的罪行 …………………………………………… 121

132. 机构犯罪 ……………………………………………………………… 122

133. 公布名称 ……………………………………………………………… 122

第四章 奖励 ………………………………………………………………… 122

134. 提供可核实的逃税信息的奖励 ……………………………………… 122

135. 杰出表现奖 …………………………………………………………… 122

第十六部分 其他规定 ……………………………………………………… 122

136. 颁布法规和指令的权力 ……………………………………………… 122

137. 过渡性规定 …………………………………………………………… 122

| 138. 不适用的法律 | 123 |
| 139. 生效日期 | 123 |

第七部 部长理事会联邦税收管理条例(部长理事会第407/2017号条例)

第一部分 总则
- 1. 简称 ... 125
- 2. 定义 ... 125

第二部分 税法管理
- 3. 提供机密信息 ... 125

第三部分 注册
- 4. 身份证明文件 ... 125
- 5. 生物识别信息 ... 126

第四部分 税务代表
- 6. 非居民税务代表 ... 126

第五部分 困难情形
- 7. 减免税收债务的限额 ... 126

第六部分 通知和纳税
- 8. 提交申报表和缴税的方式 ... 126

第七部分 税务上诉委员会

第一章 委员会在听证会中的权力
- 9. 委员会的权力 ... 127

第二章 委员会的决定
- 10. 中止、驳回或者恢复上诉申请 ... 127
- 11. 当事人协议 ... 127
- 12. 发回管理局的决定 ... 127
- 13. 决定更正 ... 128

第三章 委员会的管理
- 14. 听证地点 ... 128
- 15. 费用 ... 128
- 16. 向委员会提交文件 ... 128
- 17. 文件送达地址 ... 128

第八部分 税务代理许可
- 18. 提供税务代理服务的合适人选 ... 128

第九部分 其他部分
- 19. 过渡条款 ... 129
- 20. 发出指令的权力 ... 129
- 21. 生效日期 ... 129

第八部　部长理事会联邦所得税条例（部长理事会第 410/2017 号条例）

第一部分　一般原则 ·· 131
  1. 简称 ··· 131
  2. 定义 ··· 131

第二部分　《公告》术语的适用 ·· 131
  3. 利息 ··· 131
  4. 常设机构 ··· 131
  5. 居民个人 ··· 131
  6. 股份与债券 ·· 132

第三部分　附表"A"收入 ·· 132
第一节　附加福利 ·· 132
  7. 第三部分定义的第一节 ··· 132
  8. 附加福利 ··· 132
  9. 债务免除附加福利 ··· 133
  10. 家政人员附加福利 ··· 133
  11. 住房或者住宿附加福利 ·· 133
  12. 贴息贷款附加福利 ··· 134
  13. 餐点或者茶点附加福利 ·· 134
  14. 车辆附加福利 ··· 134
  15. 私人支出附加福利 ··· 134
  16. 财产或者服务附加福利 ·· 134
  17. 雇员股份计划权益 ··· 135
  18. 其他附加福利 ··· 135
  19. 附加福利的税收责任限制 ··· 135

第二节　境外人员就业收入 ·· 135
  20. 境外人员就业收入 ··· 135

第四部分　附表"B"收入 ·· 136
  21. 超过一年的租金收入 ·· 136
  22. 企业资产租赁 ··· 136
  23. 租赁建筑物、家具和设备的折旧 ······························· 136
  24. 租金收入损失 ··· 136
  25. 境外人员租金收入 ··· 136
  26. 租赁新建筑物的通知 ·· 137

第五部分　附表"C"收入 ·· 137
第一节　扣除额 ··· 137
  27. 代表费用 ··· 137

28. 支付给国外贷款人的利息扣除额 ………………………………………… 137
29. 雇员医疗费用 …………………………………………………………… 137
30. 从事餐饮服务的机构提供的餐饮服务 ……………………………………… 137
31. 业务推广费用 …………………………………………………………… 137
32. 承租人自费维护、修理或者改善企业资产 ………………………………… 138
33. 慈善捐赠 ………………………………………………………………… 138
34. 资本货物租赁协议中允许扣除的业务资产 ………………………………… 138
35. 总公司费用 ……………………………………………………………… 138

第二节 折旧扣除
36. 折旧资产和企业无形资产的折旧扣除 ……………………………………… 138
37. 直线折旧 ………………………………………………………………… 138
38. 价值递减折旧扣除 ……………………………………………………… 139
39. 折旧扣除率 ……………………………………………………………… 139
40. 部分用作商业资产建筑物允许的折旧 ……………………………………… 139
41. 维修和改进 ……………………………………………………………… 139

第三节 亏损结转
42. 亏损结转 ………………………………………………………………… 139
43. 亏损向后结转 …………………………………………………………… 140

第四节 外汇兑换损益
44. 外汇兑换损益 …………………………………………………………… 140

第五节 银行和保险公司
45. 银行损失准备金 ………………………………………………………… 140
46. 普通保险公司未到期风险准备金 ………………………………………… 140
47. 人寿保险业务应税所得额 ……………………………………………… 141

第六节 微型企业
48. 微型企业记账的义务 …………………………………………………… 141

第七节 "C"类纳税人
49. "C"类纳税人的推定营业税 …………………………………………… 141

第六部分 附表"C"收入 ………………………………………………… 142
50. 资产临时租赁收益 ……………………………………………………… 142
51. 常设机构的返还利润 …………………………………………………… 142
52. 业务利润调整对派息的影响 …………………………………………… 142
53. 以捐赠方式处置投资资产应缴纳的资本收益税 ………………………… 142

第七部分 免税收入 ……………………………………………………… 142
54. 免税收入 ………………………………………………………………… 142

第八部分 资产 …………………………………………………………… 143
55. 资产处置与收购 ………………………………………………………… 143
56. 成本 ……………………………………………………………………… 143

57. 股权转让 ··· 143
第九部分　行政和程序规则 ·· 143
58. "B"类纳税人保管的账簿 ··· 143
59. "C"类纳税人应保留的账簿和文件 ··· 143
60. 按"C"类纳税人缴纳税款 ··· 143
61. 预扣税的不适用 ··· 144
62. 国内支付的预扣税 ··· 144
63. 向扣缴义务人提供商业许可证的要求 ··· 144
64. 扣缴义务人的责任 ··· 144
65. 账簿的延迟提交 ··· 144
66. 停业后所得收入 ··· 144
第十部分　其他规定 ·· 144
67. 合并折旧资产 ··· 144
68. 业务亏损结转 ··· 145
69. 指令豁免 ··· 145
70. 已废止和不适用的法律 ··· 145
71. 生效日期 ··· 145

第四编　工业园区法规

第九部　工业园区公告（第886/2015号公告）

第一部分　总则 ·· 147
1. 简称 ··· 147
2. 定义 ··· 147
3. 适用范围 ··· 149
4. 目标 ··· 149
第二部分　工业园区开发商和工业园区经营者的权利和义务 ························· 149
5. 工业园区开发商的权利 ··· 149
6. 工业园区开发商的义务 ··· 149
7. 工业园区经营者的权利 ··· 150
8. 工业园区经营者的义务 ··· 150
第三部分　工业园区企业与投资 ·· 150
9. 工业园区企业的权利 ··· 150
10. 工业园区企业的义务 ·· 151
11. 理事会处罚投机活动的行政措施 ·· 151
12. 商业登记与合规 ·· 151
第四部分　工业园区工作许可证和居住证 ·· 151
13. 工业园区外籍人员入境、工作许可和居留权 ································· 151

  14. 工业园区居住证 ··· 151
  15. 工业园区居民权利 ··· 152
  16. 工业园区居民义务 ··· 152
  17. 工业园区居民投机管理办法 ································· 152
  18. 撤销工业园区居民证 ·· 152
 第五部分 保障和保护国民待遇 ·· 152
  19. 国民待遇 ··· 152
  20. 担保与保护 ·· 153
  21. 适用的外汇规则 ··· 153
 第六部分 土地使用和环境保护 ·· 153
  22. 收购工业园区动产和不动产 ································· 153
  23. 建筑规范 ··· 153
  24. 环境条例 ··· 153
  25. 工业园区设计与改造 ·· 154
  26. 工业园区开发商选拔要求 ···································· 154
  27. 一站式商店 ·· 154
  28. 劳工事务 ··· 154
 第七部分 监管机构和申诉程序 ·· 154
  29. 监管机构 ··· 154
  30. 处罚、暂停及撤销许可证 ···································· 155
  31. 投诉渠道 ··· 155
 第八部分 其他规定 ·· 156
  32. 颁布法规和指令的权力 ······································· 156
  33. 临时规定 ··· 156
  34. 不适用的法律 ·· 156
  35. 生效日期 ··· 156

Contents

GROUP ONE INVESTMENT LAWS AND REGULATIONS

TITLE ONE A PROCLAMATION ON INVESTMENT
(Proclamation No. 769/2012)

PART ONE GENERAL 158
   1. Short Title 158
   2. Definitions 158
   3. Scope of Application 160
   4. Jurisdiction 160

PART TWO INVESTMENT OBJECTIVES AND AREAS OF INVESTMENT 160
   5. Investment Objectives 160
   6. Areas of Investment Reserved for the Government or Joint Investment with
      the Government 161
   7. Areas of Investment Reserved for Domestic Investors 161
   8. Areas of Investment Allowed for Foreign Investors 161
   9. Investments to be Undertaken Jointly with the Government 161

PART THREE FORMS OF INVESTMENT AND CAPITAL REQUIREMENT FOR
                 FOREIGN INVESTORS 161
   10. Forms of Investment 161
   11. Minimum Capital Requirements for Foreign Investors 162

PART FOUR INVESTMENT PERMIT 162
   12. Requirement of Investment Permit 162
   13. Application for Investment Permit by a Domestic Investor 163
   14. Application for Investment Permit by a Foreign Investor 163
   15. Application for Investment Permit for Expansion or Upgrading 164
   16. Issuance of Investment Permit 165
   17. Renewal of Investment Permit 165

18. Transfer of an Investment Project Under Implementation Phase 165
19. Suspension or Revocation of Investment Permit 166
20. Duty to Report and Cooperate 166

PART FIVE REGISTRATION OF TECHNOLOGY TRANSFER AND COLLABORATION AGREEMENTS WITH DOMESTIC INVESTERS 166

21. Technology Transfer Agreement 166
22. Export-Oriented Non-Equity Based Foreign Enterprise Collaboration Agreement 167

PART SIX INVESTMENT INCENTIVES, GUARANTEES AND PROTECTION 167

23. Investment Incentives 167
24. Ownership of Immovable Property 167
25. Investment Guarantees and Protection 168
26. Remittance of Funds 168

PART SEVEN INVESTMENT ADMINISTRATION 168

27. Investment Administration Organs 168
28. Powers and Duties of the Agency 168
29. Powers and Duties of the Investment Board 169
30. One-Stop Shop Service 170
31. Investment Related Information 171
32. Lodging of Complaints 171

PART EIGHT INDUSTRIAL DEVELOPMENT ZONES 171

33. Establishment of Industrial Development Zones 171
34. Administration of Industrial Development Zones 172
35. Regulations Related to Industrial Development Zones 172

PART NINE MISCELLANEOUS PROVISIONS 172

36. Loans and Utilization of Foreign Currency 172
37. Employment of Expatriates 172
38. Duty to Observe Other Laws and Protection of Environment 173
39. Power to Issue Regulation 173
40. Repealed and Inapplicable Laws 173
41. Effective Date 173

TITLE TWO A PROCLAMATION TO AMEND THE INVESTMENT PROCLAMATION (Proclamation No. 849/2014)

1. Short Title 175
2. Amendment 175
3. Effective Date 176

TITLE THREE COUNCIL OF MINISTERS REGULATION ON INVESTMENT INCENTIVES AND INVESTMENT AREAS RESERVED FOR DOMESTIC INVESTORS (Proclamation No. 270/2012)

PART ONE GENERAL 178
    1. Short Title 178
    2. Definitions 178
    3. Investment Areas Reserved for Domestic Investors 178
    4. Investment Areas Allowed for Foreign Investors 179

PART TWO INVESTMENT INCENTIVES 179
    SECTION ONE EXEMPTION FROM INCOME TAX 179
    5. Income Tax Exemption for New Enterprise 179
    6. Income Tax Exemption for Expansion or Upgrading of Existing Enterprise 179
    7. Additional Income Tax Exemption for Investors Exporting Products or Services 180
    8. Condition for Reducing Incentive 180
    9. Duty to Submit Information 180
    10. Commencement of Period of Income Tax Exemption 180
    11. Declaration of Income During Income Tax Exemption Period 180
    12. Loss Carry Forward 180
    SECTION TWO EXEMPTION FROM CUSTOMS DUTY 180
    13. Exemption of Capital Goods and Construction Materials from Customs Duty 180
    14. Exemption of Motor Vehicles from Customs Duties 181
    15. Transfer of Duty-Free Imported Goods 181

PART THREE MISCELLANEOUS PROVISIONS 181
    16. Repealed and Inapplicable Laws 181
    17. Transitory Provisions 181
    18. Effective Date 182

TITLE FOUR COUNCIL OF MINISTERS REGULATION TO AMEND THE INVESTMENT INCENTIVES AND INVESTMENT AREAS RESERVED FOR DOMESTIC INVESTORS REGULATION No. 270/2012 (Council of Ministers Regulation No. 312/2014)

    1. Short Title 192
    2. Amendment 192
    3. Effective Date 193

GROUP TWO   LABOR LAWS AND REGULATIONS

TITLE FIVE   LABOUR PROCLAMATION (Proclamation No. 1156/2019)

PART ONE   GENERAL ·· 195
    1. Short Title ·· 195
    2. Definitions ·· 195
    3. Scope of Application ··· 197
PART TWO   EMPLOYMENT RELATIONS ·· 197
  CHAPTER ONE   CONTRACT OF EMPLOYMENT ································· 197
    SECTION ONE   FORMATION OF CONTRACT OF EMPLOYMENT ········ 197
      4. Element of a Contract of Employment ··· 197
      5. Form ·· 198
      6. Contract of Employment made in Writing ······································ 198
      7. Contract of Employment not made in Writing ································ 198
      8. Failure to Comply Condition ··· 198
    SECTION TWO   DURATION OF CONTRACT OF EMPLOYMENT ········· 198
      9. Contract of Employment for an Indefinite Period ·························· 198
      10. Contract of Employment for Definite Period or Piecework ·········· 198
      11. Probation Period ··· 199
    SECTION THREE   OBLIGATIONS OF THE PARTIES ···························· 199
      12. Obligations of an Employer ·· 199
      13. Obligations of Workers ··· 200
      14. Prohibited Acts ··· 201
    SECTION FOUR   MODIFICATION OF CONTRACT OF EMPLOYMENT ··· 201
      15. Conditions of Modification ·· 201
      16. Amalgamation, Division or Transfer of Ownership ······················ 202
    SECTION FIVE   TEMPORARY SUSPENSION OF RIGHTS AND OBLIGATIONS
                    ARISING FROM CONTRACT OF EMPLOYMENT ··············· 202
      17. General ·· 202
      18. Grounds for Suspension ··· 202
      19. Duty to Inform ··· 202
      20. Decisions of the Ministry or the Appropriate Authority ················ 202
      21. Effect of Confirmation or Authorization of Suspension ················ 203
      22. Effects of Expiry of the Period of Suspension ····························· 203
  CHAPTER TWO   TERMINATION OF EMPLOYMET RELATIONS ·········· 203
      23. General ·· 203

SECTION ONE   TERMINATION OF CONTRACT OF EMPLOYMENT BY THE OPERATIONS OF THE LAW OR BY AGREEMENT ·············· 203

 24. Termination of contract of Employment by the Operations of the Law ············ 203

 25. Termination of Contract of Employment by Agreement ······························ 203

SECTION TWO   TERMINATION OF CONTRACT OF EMPLOYMENT UPON THE INITIATION OF THE PARTIES ································ 204

SUB-SECTION ONE   TERMINATION OF CONTRACT OF EMPLOYEMENT BY THE EMPLOYER ··· 204

 26. General ·· 204

 27. Termination of Contract of Employment without Prior Notice ······················ 204

 28. Termination of contract of Employment with Prior Notice ·························· 205

 29. Reduction of Workforce ··· 206

 30. Exceptions ··· 206

SUB-SECTION TWO   TERMINATION OF CONTRACT OF EMPLOYEMENT BY THE WORKER ·· 206

 31. Termination of Contract of Employment with Prior Notice ·························· 206

 32. Termination of Contract of Employment without prior notice ······················ 206

 33. Period of Limitation ·· 207

CHAPTER THREE   COMMON PROVISIONS WITH RESPECT TO TERMINATION OF CONTRACT OF EMPLOYMENT ······························ 207

 SECTION ONE   NOTICE TO TERMINATE A CONTRACT OF EMPLOYMENT ······ 207

  34. Procedure for Giving Notice ··· 207

  35. Period of Notice ··· 207

 SECTION TWO   PAYMENT OF WAGES AND OTHER PAYMENTS ON TERMINATION OF CONTRACT OF EMPLOYMENT ·············· 208

  36. Period of Payment ·· 208

  37. Amount in Dispute ··· 208

  38. Effects of Delay ·· 208

 SECTION THREE   SEVERANCE PAY AND COMPENSATION ························ 208

  39. General ·· 208

  40. Amount of Severance Pay ·· 209

  41. Compensation for Termination of Contract of Employment without Notice ········ 209

 SECTION FOUR   CONSEQUENCES OF UNLAWFUL TERMINATION OF CONTRACT OF EMPLOYMENT ······································ 209

  42. General ·· 209

  43. Reinstatement or Compensation of *a* Worker in the Case of unlawful termination ·· 210

  44. Exceptions ·· 210

  45. Liability of the Worker to Pay Compensation ·································· 210

CHAPTER FOUR SPECIAL CONTRACTS 211
SECTION ONE HOME WORK CONTRACT 211
46. Formation of Contract 211
47. Keeping of Records 211
SECTION TWO CONTRACT OF APPRENTICESHIP 211
48. Formation of Contract 211
49. Contents of the Contract 211
50. Obligations of the Parties 211
51. Termination of a Contract 212
52. Certificate 212

PART THREE WAGES 212
CHAPTER ONE DETERMINATION OF WAGES 212
53. General 212
54. Conditions of Payments for Idle Time 213
CHAPTER TWO MODE AND EXECUTION OF PAYMENT 213
55. General 213
56. Execution of Payments 213
57. Payment in Person 213
58. Time of Payment 213
59. Deduction from Wages 213
60. Keeping Record of Payment 214

PART FOUR HOURS OF WORK, WEEKLY REST AND PUBLIC HOLIDAYS 214
CHAPTER ONE HOURS OF WORK 214
SECTION ONE NORMAL HOURS OF WORK 214
61. Maximum Daily or weekly Hours of Work 214
62. Reduction of Normal Hours of Work 214
63. Arrangement of Weekly Hours of Work 214
64. Averaging of Normal Hours of Work 214
65. Exclusion 214
SECTION TWO OVERTIME WORK 215
66. General 215
67. Circumstances in which Overtime Work is Permissible 215
68. Overtime Payment 215
CHAPTER TWO WEEKLY REST 215
69. General 215
70. Special Weekly Rest Day 216
71. Works Done on Weekly Rest Days 216
72. Application 216

CHAPTER THREE   PUBLIC HOLIDAYS ... 216
   73. General ... 216
   74. Non-Reduction of Wages for Public Holidays ... 216
   75. Payment for Working on Public Holidays ... 217

PART FIVE   LEAVE ... 217
CHAPTER ONE   ANNUAL LEAVE ... 217
   76. General ... 217
   77. Amount of Annual Leave ... 217
   78. Granting of Leave ... 217
   79. Dividing and Postponing Annual Leave ... 218
   80. Recalling of Worker on Leave ... 218
CHAPTER TWO   SPECIAL LEAVES ... 218
   81. Leave for family events ... 218
   82. Union Leave ... 218
   83. Leave for special purpose ... 218
   84. Notification ... 219
CHAPTER THREE   SICK LEAVE ... 219
   85. Duration of Leave ... 219
   86. Payment ... 219

PART SIX   WORKING CONDITIONS OF WOMEN AND YOUNG WORKERS ... 219
CHAPTER ONE   WORKING CONDITIONS OF WOMEN ... 219
   87. General ... 219
   88. Maternity Leave ... 220
CHAPTER TWO   WORKING CONDITIONS OF YOUNG WORKERS ... 220
   89. General ... 220
   90. Limits of Hours of Work ... 221
   91. Night and Over time Work ... 221

PART SEVEN   OCCUPATIONAL SAFETY AND HEALTH AND WORKING ENVIRONMENT ... 221
CHAPTER ONE   PREVENTIVE MEASURES ... 221
   92. Obligations of an Employer ... 221
   93. Obligations of Worker ... 222
   94. Prohibited Acts ... 222
CHAPTER TWO   OCCUPATIONAL INJURIES ... 222
SECTION ONE   LIABILITY ... 222
   95. General ... 222
   96. Liability Irrespective of Fault ... 222
   97. Occupational Accident ... 223

98. Occupational Disease 223
SECTION TWO DEGREE OF DISABLEMENT 224
99. General 224
100. Temporary Disablement 224
101. Permanent Partial or Total Disablement 224
102. Assessment of Disablement 224
CHAPTER THREE BENEFITS IN THE CASE OF EMPLOYMENT INJURIES 225
SECTION ONE GENERAL 225
103. Payment and Responsibility to Pay 225
104. Special Obligation 225
SECTION TWO MEDICAL SERVICES 225
105. Types of medical services 225
106. Duration of medical services 225
SECTION THREE VARIOUS KINDS OF CASH BENEFITS 225
107. General 225
108. Periodical Payment 226
109. Disablement Payments 226
110. Dependents' Benefits 226
111. Burden of Proof 227
112. Benefits not Taxable 227
PART EIGHT COLLECTIVE RELATIONS 227
CHAPTER ONE TRADE UNIONS AND EMPLOYERS' ASSOCIATIONS 227
113. The Right to Form associations 227
114. Formation of Associations 228
115. Function of Associations 228
116. Function of Federations and Confederations 229
117. Prohibited Act 229
118. By Laws of Association 229
119. Registration of Associations 229
120. Refusal to Register 230
121. Cancellation of Registration 230
122. Notice to Cancel Registration of Association 231
123. Appeal 231
124. Consequence of Cancellation of Registration or Dissolution on Request of Association 231
CHAPTER TWO COLLECTIVE AGREEMENT 231
SECTION ONE GENERAL 231
125. Definition 231

- 126. Bargaining 231
- 127. Representation 231
- 128. Advisors 232
- 129. Subject Matter of a Collective Agreement 232
- 130. Contents of the Collective Agreement 232
- 131. Procedure for Collective Bargaining 232
- 132. Registration of Collective Agreement 233
- 133. Accession of Collective Agreement 233

  SECTION TWO   CONDITIONS OF VALIDITY OF COLLECTIVE AGREEMENT 233
- 134. Duration of Validity of Collective Agreement 233

  SECTION THREE   SCOPE OF APPLICATION OF A COLLECTIVE AGREEMENT 233
- 135. Scope of Application 233
- 136. Exception 234

PART NINE   LABOUR DISPUTE 234

CHAPTER ONE   GENERAL 234
- 137. Definitions 234

CHAPTER TWO   LABOUR COURTS 235
- 138. Establishment of Labour Divisions 235
- 139. Labour Division First Instance Court 235
- 140. The Labour Division of Appellate court 235

CHAPTER THREE   ALTERNATIVE DISPUTE SETTLEMENT MECHANISM PERTAINING TO LABOUR ISSUES 236
- 141. Social Dialogue 236
- 142. Assigning of Conciliator 236
- 143. Duty and Responsibility of Conciliator 236
- 144. Conciliation and Arbitration 237

CHAPTER FOUR   THE LABOUR RELATIONS BOARD 237
- 145. Establishment of the Board 237
- 146. Composition of Permanent or Ad Hoc Board 237
- 147. Meeting Procedures of Permanent or Ad Hoc Boards 238
- 148. Powers of Permanent or Ad Hoc Board 238
- 149. Rules of Procedure 239
- 150. Hearings of cases 239
- 151. Consideration of Matters 239
- 152. Decisions 240
- 153. Effects of Decisions 240

- 154. Finality of Board's Findings of Fact ⋯⋯ 240
- 155. Appeal ⋯⋯ 240
- 156. Offences against Permanent or Ad Hoc *Board* ⋯⋯ 240
- 157. Annual Report ⋯⋯ 241
- CHAPTER FIVE　STRIKE AND LOCK-OUT ⋯⋯ 241
  - 158. General ⋯⋯ 241
  - 159. Conditions to be Fulfilled ⋯⋯ 241
  - 160. Procedure for Notice ⋯⋯ 241
  - 161. Prohibited Acts ⋯⋯ 241
- CHAPTER SIX　FEES ⋯⋯ 242
  - 162. Exemption from Fees ⋯⋯ 242
- PART TEN　PERIOD OF LIMITATION AND PRIORITY OF CLAIMS ⋯⋯ 242
  - CHAPTER ONE　PERIOD OF LIMITATION ⋯⋯ 242
    - 163. Period of Limitation ⋯⋯ 242
    - 164. Calculation of Period of Limitation ⋯⋯ 242
    - 165. Interruption of a Period of Limitation ⋯⋯ 242
    - 166. Waiver of Limitation ⋯⋯ 243
    - 167. Discretion of the Competent Authority ⋯⋯ 243
  - CHAPTER TWO　PRIORITY OF CLAIMS ⋯⋯ 243
    - 168. Priority over other Debts ⋯⋯ 243
    - 169. Procedure of Payment of Claims ⋯⋯ 243
    - 170. Lien of Home Workers ⋯⋯ 243
- PART ELEVEN　Enforcement of Labour law ⋯⋯ 244
  - CHAPTER ONE　Labour Administration ⋯⋯ 244
    - 171. Powers of the Ministry ⋯⋯ 244
    - SECTION ONE　EMPLOYMENT SERVICE ⋯⋯ 244
      - 172. General ⋯⋯ 244
      - 173. Employment Exchange ⋯⋯ 245
      - 174. Conditions for the Private Employment Agencies to Participate in Provision of Local Employment Service ⋯⋯ 245
      - 175. Licensing of Private Employment Agencies ⋯⋯ 245
      - 176. Employment of Foreign Nationals ⋯⋯ 245
    - SECTION TWO　LABOUR INSPECTION SERVICE ⋯⋯ 245
      - 177. LABOUR INSPECTION SERVICE ⋯⋯ 245
      - 178. Power and Duty of Labour Inspectors ⋯⋯ 246
      - 179. Measures to be taken by Labour Inspection ⋯⋯ 246
      - 180. Appeal ⋯⋯ 247
      - 181. Restriction on the Functions and Responsibility of Labour Inspectors ⋯⋯ 247

    182. Prohibited Acts ··· 247
    183. Private Inspection Service ································· 248
PART TWELVE   Administrative Measures and Miscellaneous Provisions ················ 248
  CHAPTER ONE   Administrative Measures ··· 248
    184. General ··· 248
    185. Measures Against Employer ································· 248
    186. Common Measures ··· 249
    187. Measures Against Private Employment Agency ····················· 249
    188. The Power to Institute Cases ································· 250
  CHAPTER TWO   MISCELLANEOUS PROVISIONS ··························· 250
    189. Period of Limitation ··· 250
    190. Transitory Provisions ··· 250
    191. Determination of Degree of Disablement ····················· 250
    192. Repeal Laws ··· 250
    193. Effective Date ··· 250

GROUP THREE   TAX LAWS AND REGULATIONS

TITLE SIX   FEDERAL TAX ADMINISTRATION PROCLAMATION
(Proclamation No. 983/2016)

PART ONE   GENERAL ·· 253
    1. Short Title ··· 253
    2. Definitions ··· 253
    3. Fair Market Value ··· 258
    4. Related Persons ··· 258
PART TWO   ADMINISTRATION OF THE TAX LAWS ························ 259
    5. Duty of the Authority ··· 259
    6. Obligations and Responsibilities of Tax Officers ····················· 259
    7. Duty to Co-operate ··· 259
    8. Confidentiality of Tax Information ································· 260
PART THREE   TAXPAYERS ··· 260
  CHAPTER ONE   REGISTRATION ··· 260
    9. Registration of Taxpayers ····································· 260
    10. Notification of Changes ··· 262
    11. Cancellation of Registration ································· 262
  CHAPTER TWO   TAXPAYER IDENTIFICATION NUMBER ··················· 263
    12. Taxpayer Identification Number ································· 263

    13. Issue of a TIN ·· 263
    14. Use of a TIN ·· 263
    15. Cancellation of a TIN ·· 263
  CHAPTER THREE TAX REPRESENTATIVES ··································· 264
    16. Obligations of Tax Representatives ·· 264
PART FOUR DOCUMENTS ·· 264
    17. Record-keeping Obligations ·· 264
    18. Inspection of Documents ·· 265
    19. Receipts ·· 265
    20. Sales Register Machines ·· 265
PART FIVE TAX DECLARATIONS ·· 266
    21. Filing of Tax Declarations ··· 266
    22. Licensed Tax Agent Certification of Tax Declaration ····················· 266
    23. Advance Tax Declarations ·· 267
    24. Tax Declaration Duly Filed ·· 267
PART SIX TAX ASSESSMENTS ·· 268
    25. Self-assessments ··· 268
    26. Estimated Assessments ··· 268
    27. Jeopardy Assessments ·· 269
    28. Amended Assessments ·· 270
    29. Application for Making an Amendment to a Self-assessment ············ 271
PART SEVEN COLLECTION AND RECOVERY OF TAX AND OTHER AMOUNTS
  ·· 271
  CHAPTER ONE PAYMENT OF TAX AND OTHER AMOUNTS ············ 271
    30. Tax as a Debt Due to the Government ······································· 271
    31. Secondary Liabilities and Tax Recovery Costs ······························ 272
    32. Extension of Time to Pay Tax ·· 272
    33. Priority of Tax and Garnishee Amounts ······································ 272
    34. Order of Payment ··· 273
    35. Security for Payment of Tax ··· 273
    36. Protection ·· 273
  CHAPTER TWO LATE PAYMENT INTEREST ··································· 274
    37. Late Payment Interest ·· 274
  CHAPTER THREE RECOVERY OF UNPAID TAX ····························· 274
    38. Enforcement of Tax Assessments ·· 274
    39. Preferential Claim to Assets ·· 275
    40. Duties of Receivers ··· 276
    41. Seizure of Property ··· 276

42. Preservation of Funds and Assets Deposited with Financial Institutions ············ 278
43. Recovery of Unpaid Tax From Third Parties ··· 279
44. Departure Prohibition Order ··· 280
45. Temporary Closure of Business ··· 280
46. Transferred Tax Liabilities ··· 281
47. Tax Payable by a Body ··· 281
48. Liability for Tax in the Case of Fraud or Evasion ····································· 281

PART EIGHT   CREDIT, REFUND, AND RELEASE FROM TAX LIABILITY ······ 282
49. Credit for Tax Payments ··· 282
50. Refund of Overpaid Tax ··· 282
51. Relief in Cases of Serious Hardship ··· 283

PART NINE   TAX DISPUTES ··· 284
52. Statement of Reasons ··· 284
53. Finality of Tax and Appealable Decisions ··· 284
54. Notice of Objection to a Tax Decision ··· 284
55. Making Objection Decisions ··· 285
56. Appeal to Tax Appeal Commission ··· 286
57. Appeal to the Federal High Court ··· 286
58. Appeal to the Federal Supreme Court ··· 287
59. Burden of Proof ·· 287
60. Implementation of Decision of Commission or Court ······························· 287

PART TEN   INFORMATION COLLECTION AND ENFORCEMENT ····················· 287
61. Tax Clearance ·· 287
62. Filing of Memorandum and Articles of Association ································· 288
63. Public Auditors ·· 288
64. Notification of Services Contract with Non-resident ································· 288
65. Notice to Obtain Information or Evidence ··· 288
66. Power to Enter and Search ··· 289
67. Implementation of Mutual Administrative Assistance Agreements ··················· 289

PART ELEVEN   ADVANCE RULINGS ·· 290
CHAPTER ONE   PUBLIC RULINGS ·· 290
68. Binding Public Rulings ·· 290
69. Making a Public Ruling ··· 290
70. Withdrawal of a Public Ruling ··· 291
CHAPTER TWO   PRIVATE RULINGS ·· 291
71. Binding Private Rulings ··· 291
72. Refusing an Application for a Private Ruling ·· 292
73. Making a Private Ruling ·· 292

74. Withdrawal of a Private Ruling 292
75. Publication of Private Rulings 293

CHAPTER THREE OTHER ADVICE OF THE MINISTRY 293

76. Other Advice Provided by the Authority 293

PART TWELVE COMMUNICATIONS, FORMS, AND NOTICES 293

77. Working Language 293
78. Forms and Notice 293
79. Approved Form 294
80. Manner of Filing Documents with the Authority 294
81. Service of Notices 294
82. Application of Electronic Tax System 294
83. Due Date for Filing a Document or Payment of Tax 295
84. Defect Not to Affect Validity of Notices 295
85. Correction of Errors 296

PART THIRTEEN TAX APPEAL COMMISSION 296

86. Establishment of Tax Appeal Commission 296
87. Appointment of Members to the Commission 296
88. Notice of Appeal 297
89. Authority to File Documents with the Commission 297
90. Proceedings of the Commission 298
91. Decision of the Commission 298
92. Administration of the Commission 299
93. Finances 299
94. Annual Report of the Commission 299

PART FOURTEEN LICENSING OF TAX AGENTS 299

95. Application for Tax Agent's Licence 299
96. Licensing of Tax Agents 300
97. Renewal of Tax Agent's Licence 300
98. Limitation on Providing Tax Agent Services 300
99. Cancellation of Tax Agent's Licence 301

PART FIFTEEN ADMINISTRATIVE, CRIMINAL PENALTIES, AND REWARDS
.... 301

CHAPTER ONE GENERAL PROVISIONS 301

100. General Provisions Relating to Administrative and Criminal Liabilities 301

CHAPTER TWO ADMINISTRATIVE PENALTIES 302

101. Penalties Relating to Registration and Cancellation of Registration 302
102. Penalty for Failing to Maintain Documents 302
103. Penalty in Relation to TINs 303

 104. Late Filing Penalty 303
 105. Late Payment Penalty 303
 106. Withholding Tax Penalties 304
 107. Value Added Tax Penalties 304
 108. Failure to Issue Tax Invoice 304
 109. Tax Understatement Penalty 305
 110. Tax Avoidance Penalty 305
 111. Penalty for Failing to Comply with Electronic Tax System 305
 112. Tax Agent Penalties 305
 113. Penalties Relating to Sales Register Machines 305
 114. Miscellaneous Penalties 307
 115. Assessment of Administrative Penalties 308

CHAPTER THREE TAX OFFENCES 308
 116. Procedure in Tax Offence Cases 308
 117. Offences Relating to TINs 308
 118. False or Misleading Statements and Fraudulent Documents 308
 119. Fraudulent or Unlawful Invoices 309
 120. General Offences Relating to Invoices 309
 121. Claiming Unlawful Refunds or Excess Credits 310
 122. Value Added Tax Offences 310
 123. Stamp Duty Offences 310
 124. Offences Relating to Recovery of Tax 311
 125. Tax Evasion 311
 126. Obstruction of Administration of Tax Laws 312
 127. Unauthorised Tax Collection 312
 128. Aiding or Abetting a Tax Offence 312
 129. Offences Relating to the Tax Appeal Commission 312
 130. Offences by Tax Agents 313
 131. Offences Relating to Sales Register Machines 313
 132. Offences by Bodies 314
 133. Publication of Names 314

CHAPTER FOUR REWARDS 314
 134. Reward for Verifiable Information of Tax Evasion 314
 135. Reward for Outstanding Performance 315

PART SIXTEEN MISCELLANEOUS PROVISIONS 315
 136. Power to Issue Regulations and Directives 315
 137. Transitional Provisions 315
 138. Inapplicable Laws 316

139. Effective Date ··· 316

TITLE SEVEN COUNCIL OF MINISTERS FEDERAL TAX ADMINISTRATION REGULATION (Council of Ministers Regulation No. 407/2017)

PART ONE GENERAL ··· 318
    1. Short Title ··· 318
    2. Definition ··· 318

PART TWO ADMINISTRATION OF TAX LAWS ································· 318
    3. Supply of Confidential Information ································· 318

PART THREE REGISTRATION ··· 318
    4. Documentary Evidence of Identity ··································· 318
    5. Biometric Information ··· 319

PART FOUR TAX REPRESENTATIVES ··· 319
    6. Tax Representative of a Non-Resident ····························· 319

PART FIVE HARDSHIP CASES ··· 320
    7. Limit to Remission of Tax Debt ······································ 320

PART SIX NOTICES AND PAYMENT OF TAX ································· 320
    8. Manner of Filing Documents and Paying Tax ····················· 320

PART SEVEN TAX APPEAL COMMISSION ····································· 320
CHAPTER ONE POWERS OF THE COMMISSION ON A HEARING ······ 320
    9. Powers of the Commission ·· 320
CHAPTER TWO DECISION OF THE COMMISSION ························· 320
    10. Discontinuance, Dismissal, or Reinstatement of Appeal Application ······ 320
    11. Agreement Between the Parties ···································· 321
    12. Decision to be Remitted to the Authority ······················· 321
    13. Correction of Decision ··· 321
CHAPTER THREE ADMINSTRATION OF THE COMMISSION ············ 322
    14. Place of Hearing ·· 322
    15. Costs ·· 322
    16. Filing of Documents with Commission ···························· 322
    17. Address for Service of Documents ································· 322

PART EIGHT LICENSING OF TAX AGENTS ··································· 322
    18. Fit and Proper Person to Provide Tax Agent Services ······· 322

PART NINE MISCELLANEOUS ··· 323
    19. Transitional Provisions ··· 323
    20. Power to Issue Directives ·· 323
    21. Effective Date ··· 323

TITLE EIGHT COUNCIL OF MINISTERS REGULATION ON THE FEDERAL INCOME TAX (Council of Ministers Regulation No. 410/2017)

SECTION ONE   GENERAL PROVISIONS 325
   1. Short Title 325
   2. Definition 325
SECTION TWO   APPLICATION OF TERMS USED IN THE PROCLAMATION 325
   3. Interest 325
   4. Permanent Establishment 325
   5. Resident Individual 326
   6. Shares and Bonds 326
SECTION THREE   SCHEDULE "A" INCOME 326
SUB-SECTION ONE FRINGE BENEFITS 326
   7. Sub-Section One of Section Three Definition 326
   8. Fringe Benefits 327
   9. Debt Waiver Fringe Benefit 328
   10. Household Personnel Fringe Benefit 328
   11. Housing or Accommodation Fringe Benefit 328
   12. Discounted Interest Loan Fringe Benefit 328
   13. Meal or Refreshment Fringe Benefit 328
   14. Vehicle Fringe Benefit 328
   15. Private Expenditure Fringe Benefit 329
   16. Property or Services Fringe Benefit 329
   17. Employees' Share Scheme Benefit 330
   18. Residual Fringe Benefit 330
   19. Limitation of Tax Liability on Fringe Benefits 330
SUB-SECTION TWO   FOREIGN EMPLOYMENT INCOME 331
   20. Foreign Employment Income 331
SECTION FOUR   SCHEDULE "B" INCOME 331
   21. Rental Payment Covering More Than One Year 331
   22. Lease of Business Assets 331
   23. Depreciation of a Rental Building, Furniture, and Equipment 332
   24. Rental Income Losses 332
   25. Foreign Rental Income 332
   26. Notification of Rental of New Building 332
SECTION FIVE   SCHEDULE "C" INCOME SUB-SECTION ONE DEDUCTIONS 333

27. Representation Expenditures ········· 333
28. Deductibility of Interest Paid to a Foreign Lender ········· 333
29. Medical Expense Incurred for Employees' ········· 333
30. Food and Beverage Services Provided by Establishments Engaged in the Provision of Food and Beverage Services ········· 333
31. Business Promotion Expenditure ········· 333
32. A Lessee Maintaining or Repairing or Improving a Business Asset at his own Expense ········· 333
33. Charitable Donation ········· 333
34. Deduction allowed for Business Asset held under Capital Goods Lease Agreement ········· 334
35. Head Office Expense ········· 334

SUB-SECTION TWO DEPRECIATION DEDUCTION ········· 334
36. Depreciation Deduction of Depreciable Assets and Business Intangibles ········· 334
37. Straight-line Depreciation ········· 334
38. Diminishing Value Depreciation Deduction ········· 335
39. Rates of Depreciation Deduction ········· 335
40. Depreciation allowed on a Building used Partially as a Business Asset ········· 335
41. Repairs and Improvements ········· 335

SUB-SECTION THREE LOSS CARRY FORWARD ········· 336
42. Loss Carry Forward ········· 336
43. Loss Carry Backward ········· 336

SUB-SECTION FOUR FOREIGN CURRENCY EXCHANGE GAINS AND LOSSES ········· 336
44. Foreign Currency Exchange Gains and Losses ········· 336

SUB-SECTION FIVE BANKS AND INSURANCE COMPANIES ········· 337
45. Loss Reserve of Banks ········· 337
46. Reserve for Unexpired Risks of General Insurance Companies ········· 337
47. Taxable Income from Life Insurance Business ········· 337

SUB-SECTION SIX MICRO ENTERPRISES ········· 338
48. Obligation of Micro Enterprises to Maintain Books of Account ········· 338

SUB-SECTION SEVEN CATEGORY "C" TAX PAYERS ········· 338
49. Presumptive Business Tax of Category "C" Tax Payers ········· 338

SECTION SIX SCHEDULE "D" INCOME ········· 339
50. Income from Casual Rental of Asset ········· 339
51. Repatriated Profit of a Permanent Establishment ········· 339
52. The Effect of Adjustment of Business Profit on Paid out Dividends ········· 339
53. Capital Gains Tax Payable on the Disposal of Certain Investment Assets by

Donation ··· 339
  SECTION SEVEN   EXEMPT INCOME ·· 340
    54. Exempt Income ·· 340
  SECTION EIGHT   ASSETS ·· 340
    55. Disposal and Acquisition of Asset ·· 340
    56. Cost ·· 340
    57. Transfer of share ·· 341
  SECTION NINE   ADMINISTRATIVE AND PROCEDURAL RULES ················ 341
    58. Books of Account to be kept by Category "B" Tax Payers ··············· 341
    59. Books of Account and Documents to be Kept by Category "C" Tax Payers ······ 341
    60. Payment of Tax by Category "C" Tax Payers ································ 341
    61. Non- Applicability of Withholding Tax ·· 341
    62. Withholding of Tax from Domestic Payments ··································· 341
    63. Requirement to provide Trade License to a Withholding Agent ······· 341
    64. The Liability of a Withholding Agent ·· 342
    65. Delayed Submission of Books of Account ··· 342
    66. Income Derived after Ceasing of Business ····································· 342
  SECTION TEN   MISCELLANEOUS ··· 342
    67. Pooled Depreciable Assets ··· 342
    68. Business Loss Carried Forward ··· 342
    69. Exemptions under Directives ·· 342
    70. Repealed and Inapplicable Laws ··· 343
    71. Effective Date ·· 343

GROUP FOUR   INDUSTRIAL PARK CODE

TITLE NINE   A PROCLAMATION ON INDUSTRIAL PARKS
(Proclamation No. 886/2015)

PART ONE   GENERAL ··· 345
    1. Short Title ·· 345
    2. Definition ·· 345
    3. Scope of application ·· 347
    4. Objectives ·· 347
**PART TWO   RIGHTS AND OBLIGATIONS OF INDUSTRIAL PARK DEVELOPER
                  AND INDUSTRIAL PARK OPERATOR** ································ 348
    5. Rights of an Industrial Park Developer ·· 348
    6. Obligations of an Industrial Park Developer ··· 348

    7. Rights of an Industrial Park Operator ································ 349

    8. Obligations of an Industrial Park Operator ······················· 349

PART THREE   INDUSTRIAL PARK ENTERPRISE AND INVESTMENT ············· 349

    9. Rights of Industrial Park Enterprise ································ 349

    10. Obligation of the Industrial Park Enterprise ·················· 350

    11. Administrative Measures of the Board against Speculation ·············· 350

    12. Business Registration and Compliance ························· 350

PART FOUR   INDUSTRIAL PARK WORK PERMITS AND RESIDENCE ············ 351

    13. Industrial Park Expatriate Entry, Work Permits and Residency ··············· 351

    14. Eligibility for a Certificate of Industrial Park Residency ············· 351

    15. Industrial Park Resident Rights ································· 351

    16. Industrial Park Resident Obligations ························· 351

    17. Speculation by Industrial Park Residents Administrative Measures of the Commission ··· 352

    18. Revocation of Certificate of Industrial Park Residency ············· 352

PART FIVE   GUARANTEES AND PROTECTION, AND NATIONAL TREATMENT ·· 352

    19. National Treatment ··· 352

    20. Guarantee and Protection ·· 352

    21. Applicable Foreign Exchange Rules ···························· 353

PART SIX   ACCESS TO LAND AND ENYJRONMENTAL PROTECTION ············ 353

    22. Acquisition of Industrial Park Land Moveable and Immoveable Asset ············· 353

    23. Building Norms ··· 353

    24. Environmental Regulations ······································ 354

    25. Industrial Park Designation and Modification ················ 354

    26. Requirements for Selection of Industrial Park Developer ··············· 354

    27. One-Stop Shop ··· 354

    28. Labor Affairs ·· 354

PART SEVEN   REGULATORY ORGANS AND GRIEYANCE PROCEDURE ········· 355

    29. Regulatory Organs ··· 355

    30. Issuance of Reprimand, Suspension and Revocation of Permit ············· 355

    31. Complaint Handing ··· 356

PART EIGHT   MISCELIANEOUS PROVISIONS ··································· 356

    32. Powers to Issue Regulation and Directive ····················· 356

    33. Transitory Provision ·· 357

    34. Inapplicable Laws ··· 357

    35. Effective Date ·· 357

第一编
投 资 法 规

第一部
投资公告(第 769/2012 号公告)

埃塞俄比亚联邦民主共和国联邦政府公报

第 18 年 63 号 2012 年 9 月 17 日,亚的斯亚贝巴

第 769/2012 号公告
投资公告

鉴于,鼓励和扩大投资,特别是在制造业方面,有必要加强国内生产能力,从而加速我国的经济发展并改善人民的生活水平;

鉴于,有必要进一步促进资本的流入,并加速技术向本国的转让;

鉴于,有必要通过确保投资者在进行投资时的竞争力来促进和加强各区域之间的投资公平分配,并使社会受益;

鉴于,有必要建立监督制度,以确保给予投资者的激励措施用于预期目的;

鉴于,投资管理制度必须透明和有效;

鉴于,设立工业开发区有助于创造有利的竞争条件,使以创造价值为基础的制造部门相互联系,并吸引和扩大投资;

鉴于,为此目的,有必要修改现行的投资法;

因此,根据《埃塞俄比亚联邦民主共和国宪法》第 55 条第(1)款,现公告如下:

第一部分
总　　则

1. 简称

本公告可称为《第 769/2012 号投资公告》。

2. 定义

在本公告中,除非上下文另有规定,否则:

1/ "投资"是指投资者以现金或实物或两种兼有方式进行的资本支出,以建立新企业或者扩大或升级已有企业;

2/ "企业"是指为营利目的而成立的企业;

3/ "资本"是指本币或外币、可转让的票据、器械或设备、建筑物、营运资金、产权、专利权或其他商业资产;

4/ "投资者"是指在埃塞俄比亚投资的国内或外国投资者;

5/ "国内投资者"是指按照有关法律被视为国内投资者的埃塞俄比亚国民或外国公民,包括根据有关法律建立的政府、公共企业以及合作社;

6/ "外国投资者"是指在埃塞俄比亚投资了外国资本的外国人或外国人全资拥有的企业、与国内投资者联合投资的外国人或由外国人拥有的埃塞俄比亚注册企业,其中包括永久居住在国外并希望将其作为外国投资者对待的埃塞俄比亚人;

7/ "外国资本"是指来源于外国的资本,包括外国投资者的再投资利润和股息;

8/ "扩展"或"升级"包括通过引进新的生产或服务提供线,使现有企业可达到的生产或

服务提供能力在量上至少增加 50%,或在品种上至少增加 100%,或者两者同时增加;

9/ "公共企业"是指联邦或地方政府全资或部分出资拥有的企业;

10/ "技术转让"是指为制造产品、应用或改进工艺或者提供服务而进行的系统知识的转让,包括管理和技术秘密以及营销技术,但不得扩展至仅涉及商品销售或租赁的交易;

11/ "以出口为导向的,基于非股权的外国企业合作"是指国内投资者与外国企业之间的100%以出口为导向的合同协议,其中外国企业需满足以下全部或部分条件:

a) 保证外部市场准入;

b) 出口市场产品的生产技术秘密;

c) 出口营销的商业秘密;

d) 出口业务管理知识;

e) 出口产品所需的原材料和中间投入物的供应战略;

12/ "政府"是指联邦政府或地方政府;

13/ "地区"是指《埃塞俄比亚联邦民主共和国宪法》第 47 条第(1)款所指定的任何州,包括亚的斯亚贝巴和德雷达瓦市;

14/ "投资局"是指根据部长理事会的规定设立的埃塞俄比亚投资局;

15/ "投资理事会"是指投资局的最高管理机构;

16/ "有关投资机构"是指有权签发投资许可证的投资局或地区执行机构;

17/ "工业开发区"是指由有关机关划定有明显界线的区域,以道路、电、水等基础设施为依托,有计划地发展相同的、相似的、相互关联的产业,或者按照规划发展多层次的产业,实行以产业发展、减轻环境污染影响、有计划、系统地管理城市用地为目的的奖励计划;

18/ 男性性别中的任何表达都包括女性。

3. 适用范围

本公告的规定不适用于矿产和石油资源的勘探和开发投资。

4. 管辖权

1/ 下列投资的管理应在投资局的管辖范围内:

a) 外商独资的投资;

b) 国内外投资者的共同投资;

c) 根据本公告第 2 条第(5)款,外国国民(非埃塞俄比亚人)作为国内投资者进行的投资;

d) 国内投资者在有资格获得奖励的领域进行的投资,但该国内投资者必须从有关联邦机构获得营业执照。

2/ 尽管有本条第(1)款的规定,埃塞俄比亚民航局和埃塞俄比亚电力局应分别代表投资局签发、续签、更换和注销航空运输服务投资许可证以及发电、输电或配电投资许可证。

3/ 埃塞俄比亚民航局和埃塞俄比亚电力局应:

a) 根据本公告以及根据本公告所颁布的条例和指示,执行本条第(2)款赋予他们的职能;

b) 向投资局提供有关他们以授权方式提供服务的信息。

4/ 本条第(1)款和第(2)款所述投资以外的投资交由地区投资机构管辖。

第二部分
投资目标和投资领域

5. 投资目标

埃塞俄比亚联邦民主共和国的投资目标旨在通过实现可持续的经济和社会发展来改善埃塞俄比亚人民的生活水平,其特点如下:

1/ 加快国家经济发展;

2/ 开发和利用本国丰富的自然资源;

3/ 通过生产、生产力水平和服务的增长来发展国内市场;

4/ 通过鼓励扩大本国出口产品和服务的数量、种类和质量来增加外汇收入,并通过在当地生产进口产品的替代品来节省外汇;

5/ 鼓励各地区之间的平衡发展和综合经济活动,并加强部门间经济上的联系;

6/ 加强私营部门在促进国家经济发展中的作用;

7/ 使外国投资在国家经济发展中发挥作用;

8/ 为埃塞俄比亚人创造充足的就业机会,并推动国家发展所需的技术转让。

6. 应预留给政府或与政府联合投资的相关领域

1/ 以下投资领域应专门留给政府:

a) 通过国家综合电网系统传输和分配电能;

b) 邮政服务、快递服务除外;

c) 使用可容纳 50 名以上乘客的飞机进行的航空运输服务。

2/ 以下领域只允许投资者与政府共同进行投资:

a) 制造武器和弹药;

b) 电信服务。

3/ 部长理事会认为必要时,可通过发布条例确定为政府专门保留或向私人投资者开放与政府共同投资的投资领域。

7. 为国内投资者预留的投资领域

为国内投资者专门保留的投资领域应由部长理事会发布的条例规定。

8. 允许外国投资者投资的领域

允许外国投资者投资的领域应由部长理事会发布的条例确定。

9. 与政府共同投资

私营化和公共企业监督局应接受任何私人投资者与政府联合投资的投资建议,并将建议提交工业部决定,经批准后指定一家公共企业作为合营企业的合伙人进行投资。

第三部分
外国投资者的投资形式和资本要求

10. 投资形式

1/ 投资可以下列形式其中之一进行:

a）独资经营；

b）在埃塞俄比亚或国外注册的商业组织；

c）根据相关法律设立的公共企业；

d）根据相关法律设立的合作社。

2／以本条第(1)款规定的形式进行的任何投资，均应根据《商法典》或其他法律进行注册。

11. 外国投资者的最低资本要求

1／根据本公告允许投资的任何外国投资者，必须为单个投资项目分配最低20万美元的资本。

2／尽管有本条第(1)款的规定，外国投资者与国内投资者共同投资的最低资本要求为15万美元。

3／投资于建筑、工程或相关技术咨询服务、技术测试与分析或出版工作的外国投资者的最低资本应为：

a）如果投资完全由本人进行，则为10万美元；

b）如果与国内投资者共同投资，则为5万美元。

4／外国投资者将其从现有企业获得的利润或股息再投资时，可以不必要求分配最低资本。

5／外国投资者携带资金进境的，应当经投资局登记，取得登记证书。投资局将向埃塞俄比亚国家银行发送证书副本。

第四部分
投 资 许 可 证

12. 投资许可要求

1／以下投资者必须要求获得投资许可证：

a）外国投资者；

b）合伙投资的国内和外国投资者；

c）根据本公告第2条第(5)款被视为国内投资者的非埃塞俄比亚原籍的外国公民；

d）在有资格获得激励措施的领域进行投资并正在寻求成为该激励措施受益者的国内投资者。

2／尽管有本条第(1)款的规定，但国内投资者（不包括非埃塞俄比亚原籍的外国公民）在以下情况中有权根据本国的相关法律进行投资，而无须获得国家的投资许可：

a）在不符合激励措施的地区；或者

b）在有资格获得激励的领域放弃他们的权利。

3／虽有本条第(1)款的规定，外国投资者购买现有企业经营或购买现有企业股份，应事先征得贸易部的批准。

4／贸易部应在收到根据本条第(3)款提出的请求后，应查明在上述两种转让情况下，该企业经营的是允许对外国投资者投资的领域，符合本公告规定的最低资本要求以及《商业登记和经营许可公告》规定的其他要求。

5/ 贸易部在根据本条第(4)款对请求进行审查后,应:

a) 在收到适当费用后,如果认为申请可以接受,则更换营业执照或注册股份转让;或者

b) 如果发现申请不可接受,应书面通知投资者其决定及其原因。

13. 国内投资者的投资许可证申请

国内投资者的投资许可证申请应采用为此目的设计的格式提出,并连同以下文件一式一份一并提供给相应的投资机构:

1/ 如该申请是由代理人签字确认的,则应提供其委托书的复印件;

2/ 如果投资是由个人进行的,则应提供其有效护照相关页的复印件或证明其国内投资者身份的身份证复印件,以及护照尺寸的近照两张;

3/ 如果投资是由商业组织进行的,应当提供其组织章程大纲和组织章程的复印件,如果是将要新成立的商业组织,还应提交股东身份证复印件或影印本以证明其国内投资者身份;

4/ 如果投资是由公共企业进行的,则应为该投资所依据的法规的复印件或其组织章程的复印件;

5/ 如果由合作社进行投资的,应提供其组织章程的复印件。

14. 外国投资者的投资许可证申请

1/ 外国投资者的投资许可证申请应采用为此目的设计的格式提出,并连同以下文件一并提供给相关机构:

a) 如该申请是由代理人签字确认的,则应提供其委托书的复印件;

b) 如果投资是由个人进行的,则应出示其有效护照相关页的复印件以显示其身份,以及护照尺寸的近照两张;

c) 如果投资是由长期居住在国外的埃塞俄比亚人进行的,且该人更愿意被作为外国投资者对待,则应提供证明其居住在国外的文件的复印件;

d) 在埃塞俄比亚注册成立的商业组织进行投资的,则应提供:

(1) 公司章程复印件,如果是将要新成立的商业组织,还应提交每位股东有效护照相关页的复印件以显示其身份,以及总经理护照尺寸的近照两张;

(2) 在企业组织中有外国公民但被视为国内投资者的,还应出示证明其具有国内投资者身份的身份证复印件;

(3) 商业组织中有法人或者外国法人的分支机构的,应提供其公司章程或者母公司类似文件的复印件,商业登记证或母公司的有权机构授权法人或分支机构在埃塞俄比亚投资的决议案的复印件。

e) 如果投资是由在国外成立的外国商业组织的埃塞俄比亚分支机构进行的,则应提供:

(1) 公司章程或其母公司的类似文件的复印件;

(2) 分支机构经理的聘任文件复印件及护照尺寸的近照两张、分支机构代理人有效护照或身份证相关页复印件及营业机构的商业登记证复印件;

(3) 母公司授权机构授权在埃塞俄比亚设立分公司的决议的复印件。

f) 如果投资是国内外投资者共同投资的,除本条第(1)款(d)项规定的文件外,还应当提交身份证复印件或者证明其国内投资者国内身份的身份证复印件(视情况而定);

g) 投资局认为适当的证明投资者的财务状况或身份或资料的文件。

2/ 根据本条第(1)款的规定,所有出自埃塞俄比亚境外的文件均应由国外和国内公证人公证。

3/ 如因工程项目的延期而取消许可证的人,向投资局提出申请恢复,投资局须查明延期和取消许可证的原因已得到纠正。

15. 扩建或升级投资许可证申请

申请投资许可证以扩大或升级现有企业,应采用为此目的设计的格式提出,连同下列文件一式一份一并提供给投资局:

1/ 申请书是由代理人签字确认的,则应提供其委托书的复印件;

2/ 如果投资是由独资所有人进行的,则应提供其有效护照相关页的复印件或其国内投资者身份证的复印件以及护照尺寸的近照两张(视情况而定);

3/ 如果投资是由企业组织进行的,则需提供公司章程复印件以及总经理护照尺寸的近照两张;

4/ 现有企业有效营业执照的复印件;和

5/ 项目可行性研究的复印件。

16. 出具投资许可证

1/ 收到根据本公告第13条、第14条或第15条提出的申请后,相应的投资机构应在根据本公告以及本公告下发布的条例和指令之后检查预定的投资活动:

a) 如果该申请被接受,则应在收到适当费用后签发投资许可证;或者

b) 在不接受申请的情况下,书面通知投资者该决定及其原因。

2/ 有关投资机构应在签发投资许可证后通知相关部门,以便相关部门可以进行必要的后续行动。

3/ 投资许可证持有人在其项目完成后开始生产或提供服务之前,不得要求其获得营业执照。

4/ 未经有关投资机构的事先书面批准,不得将投资许可证转让给他人。

5/ 将投资许可证转让给他人或对其内容进行任何更改时,应将其提交给有关投资机构批准。

6/ 在任何时候,任何投资者均不得同时持有国内和外国投资许可证。

17. 续签投资许可证

1/ 自投资者开始销售其产品或提供服务,须每年续签投资许可证。

2/ 投资许可证的续期申请,应当在许可证一年有效期满后的一个月内提出并续期。

3/ 相关投资机构应在有充分理由延误其项目实施的开始或完成时,续签投资许可证。

4/ 虽有本条第(1)款的规定,但投资者自投资许可证签发之日起两年内未开始实施其项目的,应在没有任何先决条件的情况下取消其许可。

18. 正在实施阶段的投资项目转让

1/ 任何希望将其项目(正在实施阶段且尚未签发营业执照)转让给另一投资者的投资者,应通过向相关投资机构提交其填写的为此目的设计的申请表,并得到该机构的批准。

2/ 投资者应在提交本条第(1)款规定的申请书时一并提交以下文件:

a）一份新的投资许可证复印件；

b）一份经公证人认证的销售协议复印件；

c）一份转让给买方的土地租赁协议复印件（视情况而定）。

19. 暂停或撤销投资许可证

1/ 如果投资者违反本公告的规定或为执行本公告而颁布的条例或指令，则相关投资机构可以暂停其投资许可，直到投资者采取适当的纠正措施为止。

2/ 如确有以下情况，有关投资机构可以撤销投资许可证：

a）投资者以欺诈手段或通过提供虚假信息或陈述获得许可的；

b）激励措施被滥用或非法转让给他人的；

c）投资者无正当理由没有根据本公告第17条续签许可证的；

d）投资者连续两期未提交项目进度报告的；

e）该项目无法在此期间开始运营，并且投资局认为该项目将无法运行的。

3/ 相关投资机构应将根据本条采取的撤销措施通知有关部门。撤销投资许可证后，投资者立即丧失所有权利。

4/ 投资者被吊销投资许可证的，应当自被吊销之日起一个月内，返还埃塞俄比亚税务海关总署和其他有关当局给予其的全部利益。

5/ 除已签发投资许可证的相关投资机构外，任何机构均不得暂停或吊销投资许可证。

6/ 被吊销投资许可证的投资者在吊销之日起一年之内，不得获得新的投资许可。

20. 报告和合作的责任

持有投资许可证的任何投资者应该：

1/ 每三个月末向相关投资机构提交有关其项目执行情况的进度报告；

2/ 在相关投资机构要求时，提供有关其投资活动的信息。

第五部分
与国内投资者签订的技术转让和合作协议的登记

21. 技术转让协议

1/ 投资者签订与其投资有关的技术转让协议的，须将该文件提交投资局登记。

2/ 根据本条提交的技术转让协议的注册申请应满足以下条件：

a）由技术接受者签字确认的完整的申请表；

b）技术的接受者与提供者之间的认证协议的复印件；

c）技术接受者的有效营业执照或投资许可证的复印件；

d）技术提供者的注册证书或营业执照。

3/ 投资局应在收到本条第（2）款规定的完整注册申请后，向投资者签发注册证书。

4/ 根据本条未在投资局注册的技术转让协议不具有法律效力。

5/ 投资局应将根据本条签订的技术转让协议的注册事项通知有关联邦行政机关。

22. 以出口为导向，不以股权为基础的外国企业合作协议

1/ 任何与以出口为导向的非股权外国企业达成合作协议的国内投资者，均应在投资局注册。

2/ 根据本条提出的合作协议的注册申请应满足以下条件:

a) 由国内投资者签字确认的完整的申请表;

b) 国内投资者与外国企业之间经认证的合作协议的复印件;

c) 国内投资者的有效营业执照或投资许可证的复印件;

d) 外国企业的商业登记证或营业执照。

3/ 投资局应在收到本条第(2)款规定的完整注册申请后,向投资者签发注册证书。

4/ 根据本条未在投资局注册的合作协议不具有法律效力。

5/ 投资局应将根据本条订立的合作协议的注册事项通知相关联邦行政机关。

第六部分
投资激励、担保和保护

23. 投资激励

1/ 由部长理事会根据本公告第 5 条规定的投资目标发布的法规规定的投资领域应符合投资激励条件。

2/ 根据本条第(1)款将要发布的条例应确定激励权利的类型和程度。

24. 不动产所有权

1/ 尽管有《民法典》第 390 条至第 393 条的规定,外国投资者或被视为国内投资者的外国人有权拥有其投资所必需的房屋和其他不动产。

2/ 本条第(1)款的规定还应包括在本公告发布之前进行投资的人。

25. 投资担保与保护

1/ 除为了公共利益外,只有在符合法律要求的情况下,才可以征收或国有化任何投资。

2/ 为了公共利益而对一项投资进行征收或国有化时,应预先支付与现行市场价值相对应的适当赔偿。

3/ 就本条而言,"国有化"一词应与"征收"一词互换使用,并对由此造成的损失支付适当或充分的补偿金。

26. 资金的汇款

1/ 任何外国投资者均有权就其批准的投资,以汇款之日的现行汇率从埃塞俄比亚以可兑换外币汇出下列汇款:

a) 投资产生的利润和股息;

b) 对外贷款的本金和利息;

c) 与根据本公告第 21 条注册的技术转让协议相关的款项;

d) 与根据本公告第 22 条注册的合作协议相关的款项;

e) 将企业股份或部分所有权转让给国内投资者的收益;

f) 企业出售或清算所得;

g) 根据本公告第 25 条第(2)款支付给投资者的补偿。

2/ 尽管有本条第(1)款的规定,也不得允许合资企业的本地合伙人将资金汇出埃塞俄比亚。

3/ 受雇于企业的外籍人士可以按照国家的外汇法,以可兑换外币汇出其受雇时的薪金和其他款项。

第七部分
投 资 管 理

27. 投资管理机构

投资管理机构包括投资局和根据各自地区法律定义的地区投资机构。

28. 投资局的权力和职责

投资局应:

1/ 充当投资事务的核心,并促进、协调和加强有关投资的活动;

2/ 提出必要的政策和实施措施,以创造有利和竞争性的投资环境,并在批准后跟进实施;

3/ 与可能吸引潜在投资流入该国的其他国家就双边投资促进和保护条约进行谈判,并在部长理事会批准下签字确认该条约;

4/ 准备并分发小册子、宣传册、电影和其他材料,并酌情在本地或国外组织诸如展览、讲习班和研讨会之类的活动,参加类似的活动并进行培训,以鼓励和促进投资并树立良好的国家形象;

5/ 实现投资者、政府机关、地区政府和其他有关当局之间的联络与协调,以期增加投资;

6/ 收集、汇编、分析、更新和传播任何与投资有关的信息;

7/ 准备并促进具体的投资机会,根据要求提供可能的联合投资伙伴的配对服务;

8/ 颁发、续签和注销其管辖范围内的投资许可,并对外国投资者带入该国的投资资本进行注册;

9/ 注册与投资有关的技术转让协议;

10/ 对国内投资者和外国企业之间以出口为导向的非股权合作协议进行注册;

11/ 监督已签发许可证的投资项目的执行情况,确保投资许可证的条款得到遵守,并给予投资者用于预期目的的奖励。

12/ 向投资者提供咨询服务、信息和技术支持,并协助提供信息,以确保投资项目之间存在供应链;

13/ 与为此目的设立的机构合作,开展投资后支持和监测服务;

14/ 提供咨询服务和技术支持,以帮助加强区域投资机构;举办联合咨询论坛;

15/ 提高投资者对本公告内容以及下文发布的条例和指令的认识;

16/ 联合相关政府机构合作解决投资瓶颈。

29. 投资理事会的权力和职责

投资理事会应:

1/ 监督并跟进本公告的执行情况和投资局的活动;

2/ 决定与执行本公告有关的政策问题;

3/ 必要时建议对本公告和发布的相关条例进行修订;

4/ 为实施本公告和相关条例发布必要的指令;

5/ 决定投资者对投资局局长的决定提出的上诉；

6/ 必要时,提出建议,以征得部长理事会的批准,给予新的或额外的激励措施,而不是现行条例规定的激励措施；

7/ 如有必要,提出由国内投资者专用的投资领域应向外国投资者开放的建议,以供部长理事会批准。

30. 一站式服务

1/ 投资局应根据相关法律,为其根据本公告第 4 条颁发的获得制造业领域投资许可的投资者提供本条所述的一站式服务。

2/ 投资局应酌情代表联邦或地区行政主管机关提供以下服务：

a) 允许免征关税的优惠；

b) 颁发施工许可证；

c) 公证公司章程及其修正案；

d) 商业注册,以及对其进行续期、修改、替换或注销；

e) 进行商号或公司名称的注册,以及对其进行修改、替换或注销；

f) 向外籍雇员签发工作许可证,以及对其进行续签、更换、暂停或注销；

g) 签发营业执照；

h) 进行建筑承包商的评级；

i) 签发税务识别号(TIN)。

3/ 与本条第(2)款(c)项至(f)项所指服务有关的修改、续期、更换和注销,只有在向投资者颁发营业执照之后,投资局才能进行。

4/ 投资局应代表投资者提供以下服务：

a) 执行投资者对其投资项目所需土地的要求；

b) 执行投资者的贷款请求；

c) 执行外国投资者的居留许可请求；

d) 执行投资者要求批准对其投资项目进行的环境影响评估研究的请求；

e) 执行投资者获取水、电和电信服务的请求。

5/ 为实施本条第(4)款,有关联邦行政机关应设立投资服务部门,以加快并促进满足投资者提出的要求。地区行政机关应接受此做法并相应地设立投资服务部门。

6/ 在不损害本条第(5)款规定的前提下,有关联邦或地区行政机关应采取必要的措施,以帮助投资局适当履行本条第(4)款规定的职责。

7/ 收到根据本条第(2)款提出的申请后,投资局根据有关法律对请求进行审查后,应：

a) 在申请可接受的情况下,在收到适当费用后签发必要的文件,并促使投资者承诺遵守国家相关法律；

b) 在发现申请不可接受的情况下,书面通知投资者其决定及不接受的原因。

8/ 投资局应在提供本条第(2)款规定的服务后,通知有关联邦和地区行政机关采取必要的后续行动。

9/ 投资者向投资局申请领取营业执照的,应当提交项目可行性研究报告,但不得违反依照有关法律应当履行的要求。

10/ 地区投资机构可根据联邦和地区有关法律,向已获得投资许可的投资者提供本条规定的一站式服务。

31. 投资相关信息

1/ 有关联邦和地区执行机构应将有关投资项目所需土地,带入该国的投资资金以及其他必要的投资相关信息的完整版和最新信息提交给投资局和地区投资机构,以帮助他们适当履行本公告规定的权力和义务。

2/ 每个地区投资机构均应向投资局提交有关该地区的资源潜力和投资机会的信息以及有关该地区投资活动的定期报告。

3/ 有关投资机构应根据需要汇编、分析和分发其根据本条第(2)款获得的信息。

4/ 任何联邦或地区执行机构都有责任在有关投资机构要求时提供与投资有关的信息。

32. 投诉处理

1/ 投资者有权向有关投资机构提出与其投资有关的投诉。

2/ 对有关投资机构的决定有不满的投资者,可以在收到决定后的 30 天内,酌情向投资理事会或有关地区机构提出上诉。

第八部分
工业开发区

33. 建立工业开发区

1/ 为了使工业部门在国家经济中发挥领导作用,联邦政府应在各地区建立工业开发区。

2/ 在不影响本公告第 6 条规定的情况下,工业区的开发应由联邦政府进行,或者在认为必要时,由政府和私营部门共同投资。

34. 工业开发区管理

1/ 负责工业开发区管理和监督的机构应由部长理事会发布的规定确定。

2/ 根据本条第(1)款由部长理事会指定的机关,应依照本公告及其条例所规定的程序,以及国家批准的计划和协议,向部长理事会提交减少或扩大工业开发区的建议。

3/ 如果本条第(2)款所指的建议获得批准,则出于以下目的,可以通过协商拥有工业开发区内或附近的租赁土地:

a) 将土地与现有工业开发区合并;

b) 获得进入工业开发区的通道;

c) 维护法律要求保护的自然资源、遗产和场所。

35. 关于工业开发区的规定

1/ 从事工业开发区联邦政府开发活动的机关,应由部长理事会的规定来设立。

2/ 有关工业开发区的指定、分配标准、边界划定、投资者的权利和义务、政府预期和监督部门提供的服务、建筑活动的完成及其监督,除本公告规定以外的激励措施以及本公告本部分的执行等事项,由部长理事会条例确定。

3/ 除非特殊部分另有规定,特殊部分和基于本特殊部分规定的条例适用于工业开发区,根据本公告发布的相关公告和条例的规定适用于工业开发区。

第九部分
其 他 规 定

36. 外币贷款和利用

1/ 获得外部贷款的投资者应按照该银行的指示在埃塞俄比亚国家银行注册该贷款。

2/ 就其投资活动而言,应允许任何外国投资者按照埃塞俄比亚国家银行的指示在经授权的当地银行开设和经营外币账户。

37. 外派人员的雇用

1/ 任何投资者均可聘请经营其业务所需的正式合格的外籍专家。

2/ 依照本条第(1)款雇用外籍人员的投资者,应在有限的时间内负责安排必要的培训,由埃塞俄比亚人替换此类外籍人员。

3/ 尽管有本条第(1)款和第(2)款的规定,外国投资者仍可无任何限制地雇用外籍雇员担任其企业的最高管理职位。

38. 遵守其他法律和环境保护的义务

任何投资者在进行投资活动时都有义务遵守国家法律。尤其应适当注意环境保护。

39. 发布条例的权力

部长理事会可发布执行本公告所必需的条例。

40. 废除和不适用的法律

1/ 特此废除第 280/2002 号投资公告(经修正)。

2/ 只要法律或惯例与本公告不一致,就对本公告中规定的事项无效。

41. 生效日期

该公告自其在《联邦政府公报》上颁布之日起生效。

2012 年 9 月 17 日在亚的斯亚贝巴签署

吉尔马·沃尔德·乔治斯

埃塞俄比亚联邦民主共和国总统

第二部
投资修正案公告(第 849/2014 号公告)

埃塞俄比亚联邦民主共和国联邦政府公报

第 20 年 52 号
2014 年 7 月 22 日,亚的斯亚贝巴

第 849/2014 号公告
投资修正案公告

鉴于有必要修改第 769/2012 号投资公告,因此,根据《埃塞俄比亚联邦民主共和国宪法》第 55 条第(1)款,现宣布如下:

1. 简称

本公告可以称为"第 849/2014 号投资(修订)公告"。

2. 修正案

现将第 769/2012 号投资公告修改如下:

1/ 删除了《公告》第 2 条第(14)、(15)和(17)款,并以以下新的条款代替第(14)、(15)和(17)条:

"14/ '委员会'是指根据部长理事会的条例设立的埃塞俄比亚投资委员会;

15/ '投资理事会'是指根据部长理事会的条例设立的埃塞俄比亚投资理事会;

17/ '工业开发区'是指由有关当局指定的一个有明确边界的区域,在计划实施基础设施和各种服务(如道路、电力和水)的基础上,共同发展相同、相似或相关的产业,或发展多方面的产业,并有特别激励计划,以期广泛地、有计划、有系统地发展工业、减轻环境污染的影响和发展城市中心,包括经济特区、工业园区、技术园区、出口加工区,投资理事会指定的自由贸易区等;"

2/ 由"委员会"取代原公告中任何地方的"投资局";

3/ 公告第 27 条被删除,并由以下新的第 27 条代替:

"**27. 投资管理机关**

投资管理机关应包括投资理事会、委员会和各地区法律所定义的地方投资机关;"

4/ 删除了《公告》第 29 条第(5)、(6)和(7)款,并以下列新的第(5)、(6)和(7)款代替:

"5/ 就投资者对委员会的决定向委员会提出的上诉作出决定;

6/ 必要时,授权给予新的或额外的激励措施,而不是现行法规所规定的激励措施;

7/ 在必要的情况下,在不影响本公告第 6 条规定的情况下,才可以授权为外国投资者开放投资区域,否则仅向国内投资者开放。"

5/ 第 33 条第(2)款宣布被删除,并由以下新的第(2)款代替:

"2/ 在不影响本公告第 6 条规定的情况下,工业区的开发应由联邦政府或在必要时由政府与私人投资者或私人投资者共同投资进行。"

6/ 删除了《公告》第 34 条第(1)和(2)款,并以下列新的第(1)和(2)款代替:

"1/ 投资理事会应对工业开发区进行监督和管理;

2/ 投资理事会应按照本公告和按本公告颁布的条例以及国家已批准的投资计划和协定的规定,决定缩小或扩大工业开发区的边界。"

7/ 删除公告第 34 条第 3 款开头的内容:"本条第(2)款规定的建议获得批准时,为下列目的,可通过协商占有工业开发区内或毗邻的租赁土地",改为"根据本条第 2 款决定减少或扩大工业开发区边界的,为下列目的,可以协商占有工业开发区内或毗邻的租赁土地"。

8/ 删除了《公告》第 35 条第(2)和第(3)款,并以下列新的第(2)和(3)款代替:

"2/ 关于工业开发区的指定、分配标准和划界、投资方的权利和义务、政府应提供的服务及其监督、建筑活动的实施和监督、除本公告给予的激励和本部分规定的执行以外的其他激励措施,均应根据投资理事会的指示确定。

3/ 在不损害本部分规定和根据本条第(2)款发布的投资理事会指令的例外的情况下,本公告的其他规定和以下发布的法规应适用于工业开发区。"

3. 生效日期

该公告自其在《联邦政府公报》上颁布之日起生效。

2014 年 7 月 22 日在亚的斯亚贝巴签署

穆拉图·特肖姆(博士)

埃塞俄比亚联邦民主共和国总统

第三部
为国内投资者保留的投资激励措施和投资领域部长理事会条例(部长理事会第 270/2012 号条例)

埃塞俄比亚联邦民主共和国联邦政府公报

第 19 年 4 号
2012 年 12 月 29 日,亚的斯亚贝巴

部长理事会第 270/2012 号条例
为国内投资者保留的投资激励措施和投资领域部长理事会条例

本条例由部长理事会根据《埃塞俄比亚联邦民主共和国第 691/2010 号公告》第 5 条行政机关的权力和责任的定义和《第 769/2012 号投资公告》的第 39 条发布。

第一部分
总　　则

1. 简称

本条例可称为《为国内投资者保留的投资激励措施和投资领域部长理事会第 270/2012 号条例》。

2. 定义

在本条例中，除非上下文另有规定，否则：

1/ "公告"是指《第 769/2012 号投资公告》；

2/《公告》第 2 条规定的定义也应适用于本条例；

3/ "投资局"是指根据《部长理事会第 269/2012 号条例》重新设立的埃塞俄比亚投资局；

4/ "理事会"是指《部长理事会第 269/2012 号条例》第 6 条第（1）款所指的投资理事会；

5/ "生产资料"，是指生产货物或提供服务所需的机器、设备及其配件，包括生产货物或提供服务所必需的车间和实验室生产资料所需的机器和设备；

6/ "建筑材料"包括建设投资项目所需的基本投入；

7/ "关税"包括对进口货物征收的间接税；

8/ "所得税"指对企业的利润征收的税，属于联邦政府、地方政府的收入或作为其共同的收入。

3. 为国内投资者保留的投资领域

1/ 以下投资领域专为埃塞俄比亚国民保留：

a）银行、保险以及小额信贷和储蓄服务；

b）包装货运代理服务；

c）广播服务；

d）大众传媒服务；

e）律师和法律咨询服务；

f）本地传统药物制备；

g）广告、促销和翻译作品；

h）可容纳 50 名乘客的飞机的航空运输服务。

2/ 就本条第(1)款而言,商业组织可以具有埃塞俄比亚国籍,但其总资本必须由埃塞俄比亚国民拥有。

4. 允许外国投资者投资的领域

1/ 外国投资者可以投资于附表所列的投资领域,但附表 1.3.3、1.4.2、1.7、1.11.3、1.11.4、5.3、6.2、8.2、9.2、9.3 和 12 规定的领域除外。

2/ 尽管有本条第(1)款的规定,委员会仍可允许外国投资者在附表中指定的领域以外的领域进行投资,但公告第 6 条第(1)和(2)款以及本条例第 3 条第(1)款规定的领域除外。

3/ 外国投资者依照本条第(1)款或第(2)款投资的,为其经营所需可以购买一辆私人商业道路运输车辆。

第二部分
投 资 激 励

第一节 免 征 所 得 税

5. 新企业免征所得税

1/ 投资者投资兴办新企业的,可按本条例附表的规定免征所得税。

2/ 投资兴办新企业的投资者在:

a) 甘贝拉人民州;

b) 本尚古勒-古马兹州;

c) 阿法尔州(阿瓦施河左右两侧 15 千米以内的地区除外);

d) 索马里州;

e) 奥罗米亚州的古吉和博雷纳区;

f) 南方各族州的南奥莫区、塞根(德拉谢、阿马罗、孔索和布吉)地区民族区班其-马吉区、道罗区、卡夫区或康塔和布莱博特区;

在本条例附表规定的免税期届满后,可连续 3 年享受 30% 的所得税减免。

6. 扩大或升级现有企业的所得税免税部分

根据公告第 2 条第(8)款对现有企业进行扩建或升级的任何投资者,根据扩建或升级产生的额外收入,享有本条例附表规定的所得减免。

7. 出口产品或服务的投资者可享受额外的所得税豁免

投资者向出口商出口或者提供产品或者服务时,除本条例附表规定的免税外,其产品或者服务的 60% 以上可以享受 2 年的所得税减免。

8. 减少激励的条件

尽管有本条例第 5 条、第 6 条和第 7 条的规定,在未建造自己的生产或服务建筑物的情况下,给予从事制造业或信息通信技术开发领域的投资者免征所得税,比本条例附表所规定的少 1 年。

9. 提交信息的义务

投资者只要向有关税务机关提交所有必要的信息,就有权享受本条例第 5 条、第 6 条和第 7 条规定的税收豁免。

10. 所得税免税期的开始

1/ 免除所得税的期限应自投资者开始生产或提供服务之日起。

2/ 为实施本条第(1)款,有关投资机构应将投资者生产或提供服务的开始日期告知有关征税机关。

11. 所得税免税期内的收入申报

有权获得所得税免税的投资者应每年将其在免税期内获得的收入向有关征税机关申报。

12. 亏损结转

1/ 在所得税免税期内有亏损倾向的投资者,可在免税期期满后将亏损结转一半。

2/ 尽管有本条第(1)款的规定,为了计算结转亏损的期限,应将半年期限视为完整的所得税期限。

3/ 虽有本条第(1)款、第(2)款的规定,投资者在所得税免税期内发生亏损的,在5个以上的所得税免税期内不得结转亏损。

第二节 免 征 关 税

13. 资本货物和建筑材料免征关税

1/ 除附表第7号、第11号、第14号和第15号所指明的投资领域外,凡投资于本附表所列投资领域之一的投资者,均可进口开办新企业或者扩建或升级现有企业所需的免税资本货物和建筑材料。

2/ 为实施本条第(1)款,投资者应提前提交免税进口的资本货物和建筑材料清单,并获得有关投资机关的批准。

3/ 享受免税奖励的投资者从当地制造业购进资本货物或者建筑材料的,应当退还用于生产资本货物或者建筑材料的原材料或者零配件的进口关税。

4/ 符合本条规定的免税奖励条件的投资者,自项目投产之日起5年内,可以进口不超过资本货物总值15%的零部件。

14. 机动车辆免征关税

机动车辆全部或部分免征关税应由理事会根据投资项目的类型和性质发布的指示确定。

15. 免税进口货物的转让

1/ 免征关税进口的资本货物或建筑材料或机动车辆可转让给享有类似免税待遇的人。

2/ 尽管有本条第(1)款的规定,免征关税进口的资本货物、建筑材料或机动车辆在缴纳适当的关税后,仍可以转让给不享有类似免税待遇的人。

3/ 投资者可以将免税进口的资本货物或建筑材料或机动车辆再出口。

4/ 投资者违反本条规定的,应根据海关公告的有关规定予以处罚。

第三部分
其 他 规 定

16. 废除和不适用的法律

1/ 兹废除《为国内投资者保留的投资激励措施和投资领域部长理事会第84/2003号条例》(经修订)。

2/ 在与本条例相抵触的范围内,任何条例、指示或惯例均不适用于本条例规定的事项。

17. 暂行规定

1/ 尽管有本条例第 16 条的规定,但根据《为国内投资者保留的投资激励措施和投资领域部长理事会第 84/2003 号条例》(经修订)和根据该条例发布的指示给予的激励措施将继续有效。

2/ 凡有资格根据《为国内投资者保留的投资激励措施和投资领域部长理事会第 84/2003 号条例》(经修订)以及根据该条例发布的指令获得激励但尚未行使其权利的投资者,可以通知相关的投资机关并有权自主选择成为本条例规定的激励措施的受益人。

18. 生效日期

本条例自其在《联邦政府公报》上颁布之日起生效。

2012 年 11 月 29 日在亚的斯亚贝巴签署

海尔马里亚姆·德萨莱尼

埃塞俄比亚联邦民主共和国总理

附表　投资领域和所得税免税表

编号	投资领域		在亚的斯亚贝巴和亚的斯亚贝巴附近的奥罗米亚特区	在其他地区
1	制造业			
	1.1　食品工业			
		1.1.1　肉和肉制品加工 1.1.2　鱼和鱼制品加工 1.1.3　水果和/或蔬菜加工 1.1.4　食用油的制造 1.1.5　牛奶加工和/或乳制品生产 1.1.6　淀粉和淀粉制品的制造 1.1.7　豆类、油料或谷物的加工,不包括面粉生产 1.1.8　其他食品的制造	豁免 3 年所得税	豁免 5 年所得税
		1.1.9　糖的制造	豁免 5 年所得税	豁免 6 年所得税
		1.1.10　巧克力、糖果、饼干和其他糖果(冰激凌和蛋糕除外)的制造	豁免 1 年所得税	豁免 2 年所得税
		1.1.11　通心粉、面食和/或类似产品的制造	豁免 3 年所得税	豁免 5 年所得税
		1.1.12　婴儿食品、烘焙与研磨咖啡、可溶性咖啡、茶、酵母、醋、蛋黄酱、人造蜂蜜、碘盐或类似食品的生产 1.1.13　动物饲料加工	豁免 2 年所得税	豁免 4 年所得税
	1.2　饮料行业			

续 表

编号	投资领域	在亚的斯亚贝巴和亚的斯亚贝巴附近的奥罗米亚特区	在其他地区
1	1.2.1 酒精饮料的制造	豁免 1 年所得税	豁免 2 年所得税
	1.2.2 葡萄酒的制造	豁免 3 年所得税	豁免 4 年所得税
	1.2.3 啤酒和/或啤酒麦芽的制造	豁免 2 年所得税	豁免 3 年所得税
	1.2.4 软饮料、矿泉水或其他瓶装水的制造	豁免 1 年所得税	豁免 2 年所得税
	1.3 纺织及纺织制品业		
	1.3.1 棉、毛、丝绸和类似纺织纤维的制备和纺丝	豁免 4 年所得税	豁免 5 年所得税
	1.3.2 纺织品的编织、整理和印花	豁免 5 年所得税	豁免 6 年所得税
	1.3.3 织物、纱线、经纱、纬纱、服装和其他纺织品的整理、漂白、染色、收缩、消毒、丝光处理或修整	豁免 3 年所得税	豁免 4 年所得税
	1.3.4 其他纺织品整理活动	豁免 2 年所得税	豁免 3 年所得税
	1.3.5 针织和钩编织物的制造 1.3.6 纺织制成品(除服装外)的制造 1.3.7 地毯制造	豁免 4 年所得税	豁免 5 年所得税
	1.3.8 服装(包括运动服)的生产 1.3.9 纺织品配饰的制造	豁免 5 年所得税	豁免 6 年所得税
	1.4 皮革及皮革制品业		
	1.4.1 成品水平的皮革鞣制	豁免 5 年所得税	豁免 6 年所得税
	1.4.2 低于成品水平的皮革鞣制	不符合免税条件	不符合免税条件
	1.4.3 皮革制品(箱包、手提袋、皮球和类似产品)的生产 1.4.4 皮鞋制造 1.4.5 皮革制品配饰的制造	豁免 5 年所得税	豁免 6 年所得税
	1.5 木制品业(不包括锯木制造和半组装的木制品) 木制品的制造(不包括锯、磨木加工和半成品木制品的组装)	豁免 2 年所得税	豁免 3 年所得税
	1.6 造纸及纸制品业		

续 表

编号	投资领域		在亚的斯亚贝巴和亚的斯亚贝巴附近的奥罗米亚特区	在其他地区
1	1.6.1 1.6.2	纸浆制造 造纸	豁免 5年所得税	豁免 6年所得税
	1.6.3	纸包装的制造	豁免 3年所得税	豁免 4年所得税年份
	1.6.4	其他纸制品的制造	豁免 1年所得税	豁免 2年所得税
	1.7	印刷业	不符合免税条件	不符合免税条件
	1.8	化学及化工制品业		
	1.8.1 1.8.2	基本化学品(包括乙醇)的制造 化肥和/或氮化合物的制造	豁免 5年所得税	豁免 6年所得税
	1.8.3 1.8.4	初级形式的塑料和/或合成橡胶的制造 农药、除草剂或杀菌剂的制造	豁免 3年所得税	豁免 5年所得税
	1.8.5 1.8.6	油漆、清漆或类似涂料;印刷、书写和绘画油墨和乳胶的制造 肥皂和洗涤剂,清洁和抛光制剂,香水和厕所制剂的制造	豁免 2年所得税	豁免 4年所得税
	1.8.7	人造纤维的制造	豁免 5年所得税	豁免 6年所得税
	1.8.8	其他化学产品(推进剂粉末、炸药、摄影胶片和类似产品)的制造	豁免 2年所得税	豁免 3年所得税
	1.9	基本药品和药物制剂行业		
	1.9.1	基本药品和药物制剂的制造	豁免 5年所得税	豁免 6年所得税
	1.9.2	药品的制造或配制	豁免 4年所得税	豁免 5年所得税
	1.10	橡胶和塑料制品业		
	1.10.1	橡胶制品的制造	豁免 3年所得税	豁免 5年所得税
	1.10.2	用作建筑、车辆或其他工业产品的投入品的塑料产品,用于灌溉和饮用水供应以及污水处理系统的塑料管或配件的制造	豁免 4年所得税	豁免 5年所得税
	1.10.3	其他塑料制品(不包括塑料购物袋)的制造	豁免 1年所得税	豁免 2年所得税
	1.11	其他非金属矿物制品业		

续表

编号	投资领域		在亚的斯亚贝巴和亚的斯亚贝巴附近的奥罗米亚特区	在其他地区
1	1.11.1 1.11.2	玻璃和/或玻璃制品的制造 陶瓷产品制造	豁免 4年所得税	豁免 5年所得税
	1.11.3	水泥的制造	不符合免税条件	豁免 4年所得税
	1.11.4	黏土和水泥制品的生产	不符合免税条件	不符合免税条件
	1.11.5	大理石和石灰石的切割、整形和精加工(不包括采石)	豁免 1年所得税	豁免 2年所得税
	1.11.6	石灰、石膏和/或类似涂层的生产	不符合免税条件	豁免 2年所得税
	1.11.7	磨石、玻璃纸或吸音或隔热材料的制造	豁免 1年所得税	豁免 2年所得税
	1.12	基础金属行业(不包括矿产开采)		
	1.12.1	基础钢铁的生产	豁免 5年所得税	豁免 6年所得税
	1.12.2	基础贵金属及其他有色金属的制造	豁免 3年所得税	豁免 4年所得税
	1.12.3	钢铁铸造	豁免 4年所得税	豁免 5年所得税
	1.13	金属制品业(不包括机械及设备)		
	1.13.1	金属结构件、罐、储存器和容器或蒸汽发生器的制造	豁免 3年所得税	豁免 4年所得税
	1.13.2	除屋顶用的波纹金属板和钉子外,其他金属制品(手动工具、物品和类似产品)的制造	豁免 1年所得税	豁免 2年所得税
	1.14	计算机、电子和光学产品行业		
	1.14.1	电子元器件和电路板的制造	豁免 4年所得税	豁免 5年所得税
	1.14.2 1.14.3 1.14.4	计算机和外部设备的制造 通信设备的制造 消费类电子产品(电视、DVD、收音机和类似设备)的制造	豁免 3年所得税	豁免 4年所得税
	1.14.5 1.14.6	测量、测试、导航、控制设备或钟表的制造 医疗设备(放射、电子医疗或电疗设备)的制造	豁免 3年所得税	豁免 4年所得税
	1.14.7 1.14.8	光学仪器或摄影器材的制造 磁性和光学介质的制造	豁免 2年所得税	豁免 3年所得税

续 表

编号	投资领域		在亚的斯亚贝巴和亚的斯亚贝巴附近的奥罗米亚特区	在其他地区
1	1.15	电气产品行业		
	1.15.1	电动机、发电机、变压器或配电或控制设备的制造	豁免 4年所得税	豁免 5年所得税
	1.15.2 1.15.3 1.15.4 1.15.5 1.15.6	蓄电池或电池的制造 电线或电缆(包括光纤)及相关产品的制造 电子照明设备的制造 家用电器的制造 其他电气设备的制造	豁免 2年所得税	豁免 4年所得税
	1.16	机械/设备行业		
	1.16.1	通用机械(电动机,起重和装卸设备,泵及类似设备)的制造	豁免 5年所得税	豁免 6年所得税
	1.16.2	专用(用于农业、食品加工;饮料、纺织和采矿生产及类似活动)机械的制造		
	1.17	车辆、拖车和半拖车行业		
	1.17.1	机动车的制造	豁免 2年所得税	豁免 3年所得税
	1.17.2 1.17.3	汽车、拖车和/或半拖车的车身、组件的制造 汽车零配件的制造	豁免 3年所得税	豁免 4年所得税
	1.17.4	铁路机车和车辆的制造	豁免 5年所得税	豁免 6年所得税
	1.17.5	其他运输设备(船、自行车、摩托车和类似设备)的制造	豁免 2年所得税	豁免 3年所得税
	1.18 1.19	办公和家用家具(不包括陶瓷家具)的制造 其他设备(珠宝及相关物品、乐器、运动器材、游戏和玩具及类似产品)的制造	豁免 1年所得税	豁免 2年所得税
	1.20	农业相关的集成制造业	豁免 4年所得税	免税 5年所得税
2	农业			
	2.1	作物生产		
	2.1.1	一年生作物生产		
	2.1.1.1	谷类、豆类作物和/或油料作物和水稻的种植	不符合免税条件	豁免 3年所得税
	2.1.1.2	蔬菜和/或草药的种植	豁免 3年所得税	豁免 4年所得税
	2.1.1.3	纤维作物的种植	不符合免税条件	豁免 5年所得税

续 表

编号	投资领域	在亚的斯亚贝巴和亚的斯亚贝巴附近的奥罗米亚特区	在其他地区
2	2.1.1.4 其他一年生作物(动物饲料、药用作物、芳香作物、香料和类似作物)的种植	豁免 2年所得税	豁免 3年所得税
	2.1.1.5 已认证种子的生产	豁免 3年所得税	豁免 4年所得税
	2.1.2 中期生长作物的种植		
	2.1.2.1 鲜花的种植 2.1.2.2 中期生长水果(草莓,蓝莓和类似农作物)的种植	豁免 3年所得税	豁免 4年所得税
	2.1.2.3 中期生长香料、芳香或药用作物(葫芦、姜黄、黑胡椒和类似作物)的种植	不符合免税条件	豁免 4年所得税
	2.1.3 多年生作物生产		
	2.1.3.1 多年生水果(芒果、鳄梨、香蕉、橘子、木瓜、葡萄、百香果和类似农作物)的种植 2.1.3.2 饮料作物(咖啡、茶和类似作物)的种植	不符合免税条件	豁免 5年所得税
	2.1.3.3 其他多年生作物(橡胶树、棕榈树、麻风树和类似作物)的种植	不符合免税条件	豁免 6年所得税
	2.2 动物产品		
	2.2.1 家畜饲养以及牛奶、鸡蛋、生羊毛和类似产品的生产	豁免 3年所得税	豁免 4年所得税
	2.2.2 野生动物饲养以及奶、蛋和类似产品的生产	不符合免税条件	豁免 3年所得税
	2.2.3 蜜蜂养殖/蜂蜜生产	豁免 2年所得税	豁免 4年所得税
	2.2.4 丝绸生产 2.2.5 人工池塘养鱼(水产养殖)	豁免 3年所得税	豁免 4年所得税
	2.3 (农作物和畜牧业)混合种殖	豁免 3年所得税	豁免 4年所得税
	2.4 林业	豁免 8年所得税	豁免 9年所得税
3	根据通信和信息技术部指令确定的信息和通信技术发展领域	豁免 4年所得税	豁免 5年所得税
4	发电、输电和配电	豁免 4年所得税	豁免 5年所得税
5	酒店和旅游		
	5.1 星级酒店(包括度假酒店)、汽车旅馆、旅馆和餐厅	不符合免税条件	不符合免税条件

续 表

编号	投 资 领 域	在亚的斯亚贝巴和亚的斯亚贝巴附近的奥罗米亚特区	在其他地区
5	5.2 一级旅游业务	不符合免税条件	不符合免税条件
	5.3 一级以下旅游业务	不符合免税条件	不符合免税条件
6	施工承包 6.1 一级施工承包(包括水井和矿产勘探钻探) 6.2 一级以下的施工承包(包括水井和矿产勘探钻探)	不符合免税条件	不符合免税条件
7	房地产开发	不符合免税条件	不符合免税条件
8	教育和培训 8.1 通过建造自有建筑物提供中等和高等教育 8.2 通过建造自有建筑物提供幼儿园、小学和初中教育 8.3 提供技术和职业(包括体育)培训服务	不符合免税条件	不符合免税条件
9	健康服务 9.1 通过建造自有建筑物提供医院服务 9.2 通过建造自有建筑物来提供诊断中心服务 9.3 通过建造自有建筑物提供临床服务	不符合免税条件	不符合免税条件
10	建筑工程、技术测试和分析 10.1 建筑工程及相关技术咨询服务 10.2 技术测试和分析	不符合免税条件	不符合免税条件
11	出版	不符合免税条件	不符合免税条件
12	资本货物租赁,不包括机动车辆租赁	不符合免税条件	不符合免税条件
13	进口贸易 进口液化石油气和沥青	不符合免税条件	不符合免税条件
14	出口贸易 出口贸易,不包括出口从市场购买的生咖啡、茶、油籽、豆类、贵重矿物和兽皮;天然林产品和非投资者饲养的活羊、山羊、骆驼、牛和马。	不符合免税条件	不符合免税条件
15	批发贸易 石油及其副产品的供应以及自营产品的批发	不符合免税条件	不符合免税条件

第四部
修订为国内投资者保留的投资激励措施和投资领域部长理事会第 270/2012 号条例
（部长理事会第 312/2014 号条例）

埃塞俄比亚联邦民主共和国联邦政府公报

第 20 年 62 号
2014 年 8 月 13 日，亚的斯亚贝巴

部长理事会第 312/2014 号条例
修订为国内投资者保留的投资激励措施和投资领域部长理事会第 270/2012 号条例

本条例由部长理事会根据《埃塞俄比亚联邦民主共和国第 691/2010 号公告》第 5 条行政机关的权力和责任的定义和《第 769/2012 号投资公告》第 39 条发布。

1. 简称

本条例可称为《为国内投资者保留的投资奖励和投资领域部长理事会第 312/2014 号条例》(经修订)。

2. 修订内容

现将《为国内投资者保留的投资鼓励措施和投资领域部长理事会第 270/2012 号条例》作如下修订:

1/ 在条例第 2 条下增加了以下新的第(9)款:

"9/ '现有企业'是指具有营业执照或任何其他适当执照的从事生产或提供服务的企业。"

2/ 该条例所附附表第 1.20 款之后增加了以下第 1.21 款:

1.21 工业开发区(包括私人工业开发区投资,和在公告发布前与政府商定投资方向的)	豁免 10 年所得税	豁免 15 年所得税

3/ 条例第 7 条的现有规定重新编号为第(1)款,并增加了以下新的第(2)和(3)款:

"2/ 在工业开发区内投资的投资者,除本条第(1)款规定和附表所附的权利外,在亚的斯亚贝巴或亚的斯亚贝巴周围奥罗莫特区的工业区投资的,可免缴 2 年所得税;在其他地区的工业区投资的,可免缴 4 年所得税,但条件是其生产的工业产品出口 80% 或以上或产品供应给出口其产品的投资者。

3/ 投资者已投资或拟投资于民营工业开发区,且在公告发布前已与政府商定设立的,在满足本条第(2)款规定的前提条件后,可获得本条第(2)款规定的奖励。"

4/ 条例第 8 条被删除,第 9 条至第 18 条分别重新编号为第 8 条至第 17 条。

5/ 根据条例第 12 条,增加了以下新的第(5)款(根据本条第(3)款重新编号):

"5/ 在不损害本条第(1)款的规定的前提下,从事以下活动的任何投资者:

a) 在制造业或农业投资至少 200 000 美元或依现行汇率等值的埃塞俄比亚比尔,并为至少 50 名埃塞俄比亚公民创造长期就业机会,有权在任何时候进口其现有的企业必要的免税资本货物;

b) 另一个符合免税条件的投资领域,已投资了至少 200 000 美元或按现行汇率等值的埃塞俄比亚比尔,并为至少 50 名长期雇员创造了长期就业机会的,应允许其从获得营业执照或其他适当执照之日起 5 年内进口现有企业所需的免税资本货物。"

3. 生效日期

本条例自其在《联邦政府公报》上颁布之日起生效。

2014 年 8 月 13 日在亚的斯亚贝巴签署

海尔马里亚姆·德萨莱尼

埃塞俄比亚联邦民主共和国联邦总理

第二编
劳动法规

第五部
劳动公告(第1156/2019号公告)

埃塞俄比亚联邦民主共和国

联邦政府公报

第25年89号
2019年9月5日,亚的斯亚贝巴

第 1156/2019 号公告
劳动公告

鉴于,有必要保证工人与雇主的关系受权利和义务的基本原则的支配,以使工人和雇主能够通过合作参与实现国家的全面发展,确保持久的产业和平、生产力的可持续发展与竞争力的提高;

鉴于,有必要制定一个工作系统,以保障工人与雇主成立他们各自的协会,并通过他们正式授权的代表参与社会对话和集体谈判,以及拟定迅速解决工人与雇主之间的劳资纠纷的程序的权利;

鉴于,有必要通过建立合理的劳动行政管理制度,创造有利于投资和实现国民经济目标的良好环境,同时又不损害基本的工作场所权利;并明确被赋予监督劳动条件权的政府机关的职责和责任,营造健康安全的职业环境;保护环境依靠联合建立双方或三方社会对话机制;以及制定相应的国家政治、经济和社会政策;

鉴于,有必要重新制定现行的劳动法,以实现上述目标,并符合埃塞俄比亚加入的国际公约和其他法律承诺;

因此,根据《埃塞俄比亚联邦民主共和国宪法》第55条第(1)款和第(3)款,现宣布如下:

第一部分
总　　则

1. 简称

本公告可称为《第1156/2019号劳动公告》。

2. 定义

在本公告中,除非文中另有规定:

1/ "雇主"是指根据本公告第4条的规定,雇佣一个或多个自然人的个人或企业。

2/ "企业"是指在联合管理下成立的,为开展任何商业、工业、农业、建筑或任何其他合法活动的实体。开展单独指定的,享受业务上或组织上自主权的企业活动的任何分支机构,将被视为是一个独立的企业。

3/ "工人"是指根据本公告第4条的规定,与雇主有雇佣关系的个人。

4/ "部"或"部长"分别指劳动与社会事务部和劳动与社会事务部部长。

5/ "有关当局"是指拥有执行劳动法的权力的地方性国家机关。

6/ "工作规则"是指从属于本公告和其他相关法律,对工作时间、休息时间、薪水支付以及工作量计算方式、安全维护和事故防范措施、劳动纪律及实施以及其他工作条件做出规定的一种内部规定。

7/ "工作条件"是指工人与雇主之间整个劳动关系,包括工作时间、工资、休假、解雇费、工人健康与安全、对工伤受害者的赔偿、因裁员而导致的解雇、申诉程序及其他类似情况。

8/"区域"是指《埃塞俄比亚联邦民主共和国宪法》第47条第(1)款所指的任何州,其中包括亚的斯亚贝巴和德雷达瓦行政区域。

9/"社会对话"是指雇主与雇员之间的信息交流、双边或三方性质的对话或谈判,或让政府参与共同关心的经济和社会问题以达成共识的过程。

10/"管理雇员"是指根据法律或雇主的授权,有权制定和执行管理政策的雇员,并根据企业的活动类型,不管有没有上述权力的雇员都拥有雇佣、调动、中止、裁员、解雇或分配雇员的权力,以及包括法律服务负责人,该法律服务负责人根据自己的独立判断,为雇主的利益建议雇主应针对此类管理问题采取的措施。

11/"性骚扰"是指未经他人同意,通过言语、手势或任何其他方式劝说或说服他人接受性帮助。

12/"性暴力"是指伴随暴力或企图暴力的性骚扰。

13/"私营职业介绍所"(以下简称"职业介绍所")是指任何具有合法执照的个人,提供以下一种或两种本地职业介绍服务,而无须直接或间接向工人收取任何费用。

a) 没有加入雇佣关系的当地就业交流服务;或者

b) 通过与此类雇员签订雇佣合同,或将两种服务结合起来,将其授权的员工部署到服务用户企业的服务中。

14/"许可证"是指由主管机关签发的证明该实体有资格从事私人职业交换服务的证书。

15/"歧视"是指任何基于民族种族、肤色、性别、宗教、政治观点、国籍、社会出身、艾滋病毒/艾滋病状况、残疾和其他而造成的区别、排斥或偏爱,其结果是使就业或职业中的机会或待遇平等无效或受到损害。

16/"雇佣私人服务"是指为雇主及其家庭消费雇用非营利性的清洁监护、园艺、驾驶和其他相关服务。

17/"商业旅行者和代表"应具有商业法规规定的含义。

18/"人"是指任何自然人或法人。

19/ 本公告中以男性性别规定的规定也应适用于女性性别。

3. 适用范围

1/ 在不影响本条第(2)款的前提下,本公告适用于基于工人与雇主之间存在雇佣合同(包括招聘过程)的雇佣关系。

2/ 本公告不适用于以下雇佣关系:

a) 以养育、治疗、护理或康复为目的的合同;

b) 以学徒以外的目的进行教育或培训的合同;

c) 员工为管理人员;

d) 个人服务合同;

e) 与诸如武装部队成员、警察部队成员、国家行政部门雇员、法院法官、检察官以及其他受特殊法律约束的雇佣关系的人有关的合同;

f) 与履行自己的业务或职业责任的人有关的合同。

3/ 尽管有本条第(1)款的规定:

a）除非部长理事会通过条例决定，或埃塞俄比亚与之达成国际协议另有规定，埃塞俄比亚国民与在埃塞俄比亚境内经营的外国外交使团或国际组织之间的雇佣关系应受本公告管辖；

b）部长理事会可以通过条例决定，基于宗教和慈善组织建立的雇佣关系不受本公告制约；

c）部长理事会可以颁布条例来规范个人服务工作条件。

第二部分
雇 佣 关 系

第一章　雇 佣 合 同

第一节　雇佣合同的形式

4. 雇佣合同的要素

1/ 如果自然人直接或间接同意并在雇主的授权范围内做定期或不定期或临时工作并获得酬劳的，则应视为已订立雇佣合同；

2/ 雇佣合同应明确规定，以使关于双方权利和义务的条款没有异议。

3/ 雇佣合同应规定雇佣类型、工作地点、工资率、工资计算方法、支付方式和期限以及合同期限；

4/ 不得为实施非法或不道德行为而订立雇佣合同；

5/ 雇佣合同不该为受雇人提供比由法律、集体协议或工作准则拟定的更不利的条件。

5. 形式

除非法律另有规定，雇佣合同不得采用任何特殊形式。

6. 书面雇佣合同

根据相关法律规定，书面雇佣合同应明确规定以下内容：

1/ 雇主的姓名和地址；

2/ 工人的姓名、年龄、地址和工作卡号（如果有）；

3/ 缔约方根据本公告第 4 条第(3)款达成的协议；和

4/ 缔约方的签字。

7. 非书面形式的雇佣合同

1/ 如果没有签订书面雇佣合同，雇主应在合同缔结的 15 天内，根据本公告第 6 条明确要求的内容，向工人提供一份附签字的书面文件。

2/ 如果工人在收到涉及上述本条第(1)款的书面文件 15 天内没有任何异议，那么将认为工人与雇主之间的雇佣合同成立。

8. 违约

不遵守本公告第 6 条或第 7 条规定的要求，本公告下规定的工人的权利不应被剥夺。

第二节　雇佣合同期限

9. 无固定期限雇佣合同

除下述条款第 10 条中规定的条款外，任何无固定期限的雇佣合同必须视为已缔结。

10. 定期或计件雇佣合同

1/ 在下列情形下,可以签订定期或计件合同:

a) 雇员受雇从事的指定件工作;

b) 替代因休假、疾病或其他原因暂时缺勤的工人;

c) 工作压力异常时的施工;

d) 为防止危及生命财产安全的损坏或灾害,排除故障或工程材料、建筑物或企业厂房的倒塌所进行的紧急工作作业;

e) 涉及雇主的永久性工程部分,但在非正常间隔时间内出现的不定期工作;

f) 涉及雇主的永久性工程部分,仅在本年的规定期所进行的,然而又是这几年中有规律的反复的季节性工程;

g) 不构成雇主的永久性工程部分,但断断续续的临时性工作;

h) 临时安置的工人,突然并永久性离开具有无限期合同的职位;

i) 在组织机构的准备至实施期间,临时安置工人以填补空缺。

2/ 根据本条第(1)款(h)项或(i)项签订的雇佣合同不得超过45个工作日,且只能签订一次。

11. 试用期

1/ 可以雇佣试用期的工人,以测试其是否适合预期担任的职位。

2/ 再次受雇于同一雇主进行同一工种的工人可免去试用期。

3/ 双方同意有试用期,需达成书面协议;在这种情况下,试用期从首次受雇之日起不得超过60个工作日。

4/ 除非法律、工作准则或集体协议另有规定,试用期内工人应具有与试用期结束的工人同样的权利和义务。

5/ 如果工人在试用期内被证明不适合担任该职位的,雇主可以在不另行通知的情况下终止雇佣合同,并且没有义务支付解雇费或补偿金。

6/ 试用期工人也可以在不另行通知的情况下终止其雇佣合同。

7/ 试用期届满后,劳动者继续工作的,应当视为从试用期之初起签订预定期限或者工种的劳动合同。

第三节 双方的义务

12. 雇主的义务

除非合同有特殊规定外,雇主有如下义务:

1/ a) 根据雇佣合同,向工人提供工作;和

b) 除非雇佣合同另有规定,向工人提供执行工作必要的工具和材料;

2/ 根据本公告或集体协议,向工人支付工资和其他福利;

3/ 在工人书面要求扣除的情况下,从工人的正常工资中扣除工会会费,并将现金转入工会的银行账户;

4/ 尊重工人的人格尊严;

5/ 采取一切必要的职业安全和卫生措施,并遵守有关当局就这些措施制定的标准和指示;

6/ 在法律或有关当局要求进行医疗检查时,支付工人体检费用;

7/ 保留一份包含本细则第 6 条规定的相关详细信息,以及每周休息日、公众假期和工人的带薪休假、员工的健康状况(艾滋病毒/艾滋病除外)、工伤记录和劳动与社会事务部或有关当局要求的其他详细信息的登记表;

8/ 在雇佣合同终止或工人要求时,可免费向工人提供工作类型、服务年限和工资水平的证明;

9/ 遵守本公告、集体协议、工作准则、指示和根据法律所颁布的规定;

10/ 记录并保留本公告所要求的信息,以及相关机构执行其职权所必需的任何其他信息,并在主管当局要求的合理时间内提交;

11/ 根据劳动与社会事务部准备的表格,登记关于工作地点和工作相关数据的信息;和

12/ 每当企业制定工作准则时,都应为有关工人安排提高水平的计划。

13. 工人的义务

每个工人应承担以下义务:

1/ 亲自执行其雇佣合同中规定的工作;

2/ 遵循雇主根据合同条款和工作准则给出的指示;

3/ 妥善保管托付给他的所有设备和工具;

4/ 在身心健康的情况下汇报工作;

5/ 在不危及其安全与健康的前提下,当他所在的工作场所发生事故或紧急的危险威胁到生命或财产时,提供一切适当的援助;

6/ 任何危害自己、同事或损害企业利益的情况发生时,立即通知雇主;

7/ 遵守本公告的规定、集体协议、依法发布的工作规则和指示。

14. 禁止行为

1/ 如果雇主或管理雇员有以下任何行为,则对雇主而言是非法的:

a) 以任何方式限制工人行使权利或因其行使权力而采取报复行为;

b) 以其性别为由,在酬劳方面歧视女工;

c) 违反本公告的规定终止雇佣合同;

d) 胁迫或以任何方式强迫任何工人加入或不加入工会;或继续或停止加入工会;或要求工人退出一个工会的会员资格,并要求他加入另一个工会;或要求他在工会职务选举中投票给某个候选人或不投票给某个候选人;

e) 强迫任何工人执行任何危害其生命的任务;

f) 以民族、性别、宗教、政治观点、感染艾滋病毒/艾滋病致残或伤残等任何其他理由区别对待工人;

g) 通过隐瞒谈判的有关信息或进行任何其他违反诚信的行为而过分拖延集体谈判的;

h) 在工作场所进行性骚扰或性侵犯;

i) 在工作场所虐待任何人;

j) 以任何方式胁迫工人工作或履行义务。

2/ 工人以下行为是非法的:

a) 故意在工作场所实施任何危害生命或财产的行为;

b) 未经雇主明确授权,从工作场所带走财产;
c) 使用伪造的文件或企图使用伪造的文件;
d) 在工作场所使用法律禁止的药物或使用酒精饮料,并损害其身心健康;
e) 除艾滋病毒/艾滋病测试外,在法律或雇主出于正当理由要求时,拒绝接受身体检查;
f) 拒绝遵守安全和事故防范规则,并拒绝采取必要的安全预防措施;
g) 无视集体协议规定的时间或未得到雇主的允许在工作时间内举行会议;
h) 在工作场所进行性骚扰或性暴力;
i) 在工作场所虐待任何一个人。

第四节 雇佣合同的修改

15. 修改条件

本公告未确定的雇佣合同条款可以通过以下方式修改:

1/ 集体协议;

2/ 按本公告发布的工作准则;或者

3/ 双方的书面协议。

16. 企业所有权的合并、分割和转让

在不损害本公告第 15 条的前提下,企业所有权的合并、分割和转让不影响雇佣合同的修改。

第五节 临时中止雇佣合同产生的权利义务

17. 一般原则

1/ 雇佣合同产生的权利和义务可以按照本节规定的方式暂时中止。

2/ 由于雇佣合同引起的权利和义务的暂时中止,并不意味着该合同的终止或中断。但是雇佣合同的中止将中断下列义务:

a) 工人的作业职责;

b) 雇主支付工资、其他福利和津贴,本公告或集体协议另有规定的除外。

18. 中止的理由

根据本公告第 17 条,下列各项应为中止的有效理由:

1/ 经工人要求并经雇主同意的不带薪休假;

2/ 因在工会或其他社会服务机构任职为目的而请假;

3/ 拘留期限不超过 30 天;但雇主应于 10 天内获得通知或得知有关拘留信息;

4/ 国家需要;

5/ 由于不可抗力,雇主的活动被全部或部分中止,连续不超过 10 天;

6/ 并非由雇主的过错引起的财务问题,要求雇主停止活动连续不超过 10 天。

19. 报告的义务

根据第 18 条第(5)款或第(6)款,当由于雇佣合同引起的权利和义务暂时中止时,雇主必须在暂时中止理由发生 3 日内,向劳动与社会事务部或主管当局作书面报告。

20. 劳动与社会事务部或有关当局的决定

1/ 劳动与社会事务部或有关当局应在收到上述第 19 条规定的书面通知后的 3 个工作日内,确定存在中止的正当理由。如果本部或有关当局在 3 天内未通知其决定,则该组织被视为同意中止。

2/ 如果劳动与社会事务部或有关当局发现没有正当理由暂停工作,应指令恢复工作,并支付工人被暂停工作的工资。

3/ 如果一方不服根据本条第(1)款或第(2)款作出的决定,可以在5个工作日内,向主管劳动法院提出上诉。

21. 中止的确认或核准的效力

1/ 如果劳动与社会事务部或有关当局确认或证明存在中止的充分理由,则应确定中止的期限;但是,中止的期限不得超过90天。

2/ 如果主管当局或有关当局确信雇主无法在本条第(1)款规定的期限内恢复活动,则应终止雇佣合同,工人有权享有本公告第39条和第44条规定的利益。

22. 中止期到期的效力

工人应在停职期满之日后的工作日报到工作;在不影响其工作岗位和工资的情况下,雇主应当恢复报到的工人从事与其职业有关的工作。

第二章 雇佣关系的终止

23. 一般原则

1/ 雇佣合同只有在雇主或工人根据法律规定或集体协议或当事方协议时方可提起终止。

2/ 企业所有权的合并、分立或转化不影响雇佣合同的终止。

第一节 通过法律或协议终止雇佣合同

24. 通过法律终止雇佣合同

发生下列情形,雇佣合同终止:

1/ 雇佣合同是针对特定工作的情况下,完成特定的工作;

2/ 工人死亡;

3/ 根据有关法律规定,工人退休;

4/ 当企业由于破产或任何其他原因永久终止经营时;

5/ 当工人因暂时或永久失去劳动能力而无法工作时。

25. 通过协议终止雇佣合同

1/ 双方可以通过协议终止其雇佣合同,但是工人自动放弃法律规定的权利将不产生法律效力。

2/ 只有书面形式的终止协议才对工人发生效力。

第二节 缔约双方终止雇佣合同
附款一 由雇主提出的终止雇佣合同

26. 一般原则

1/ 只有基于工人的行为或工作的能力或承担组织的或业务上的要求,而产生的客观情况,才可终止雇佣合同。

2/ 以下内容不应被视为构成终止雇佣合同的合法理由:

a) 因工人成为工会会员或其参加工会的合法活动;

b）因工人寻求或担任工人代表的职务；

c）工人对雇主或其参加司法或其他程序提出的申诉；

d）因工人的国籍、性别、宗教、政治观、婚姻状况、种族、肤色、家庭责任、怀孕、残疾或社会地位。

27. 没有预先通知而终止雇佣合同

1/ 除非集体协议另有规定,雇佣合同仅在下列情况下可以不通知而终止：

a）除非因集体协议,工作规则或雇佣合同的正当理由,在6个月内迟到八次并被书面警告；

b）在6个月内总共缺勤5天,并被书面警告该问题且缺勤不能列入公告规定的任何请假范围的；

c）在执行职务时采取欺骗或弄虚作假的行为；

d）盗用雇主的财产或资金,意图为自己或第三人谋取非法财产；

e）尽管工人有潜力,但其绩效成绩始终低于集体协议规定或双方协议所确定的质量和数量；

f）应对工作中的斗殴或争吵负责,但需考虑到事件的严重性程度；

g）因犯罪而不能胜任其所担任的职务；

h）因故意或重大过失对雇主的任何财产或与其企业工作直接相关的其他财产造成损害负责的；

i）实施本公告第14条第(2)款中的任何禁止行为；

j）由于法院判刑,该工人缺勤超过30天；

k）发生集体协议中规定的其他违反雇佣合同的行为,可以作为不经通知终止雇佣合同的理由。

2/ 根据本条款,雇主终止雇佣合同,应当书面说明合同终止的原因及日期。

3/ 根据本条款,自雇主得知存在解雇理由之日起30个工作日后,将失去其终止雇佣合同的权利。

4/ 根据本条款,在雇佣合同终止之前,工人工作中止的原因由集体协议决定,但是中止期限最多不能超过30个工作日。

28. 预先通知终止雇佣合同

1/ 下列有关工人能力的丧失和形势影响的理由,均构成预先通知而终止雇佣合同的正当原因：

a）工人明显丧失执行其被指派的工作的能力,或缺乏继续其工作的技能,由于拒绝接受雇主准备的以提高其技能的培训机会,或经培训后仍无力获得必要的技能；

b）工人因健康或残疾原因,永久性无法履行雇佣合同中规定的义务；

c）工人不愿搬到企业搬去的地方；

d）工人的工作岗位因正当理由被取消,该工人又不能被调任到其他的工作岗位。

2/ 本条第(1)款(a)项所指的任何工作能力丧失,除集体协议另有规定外,均应通过定期工作绩效评估予以核实。

3/ 下列有关企业组织或运营要求的理由,应构成预先通知而终止雇佣合同的正当理由：

a）任何导致工人部分或全部直接或永久停止活动的事件,导致有必要终止雇佣合同;

b）在不损害第 18 条第(5)款和第(6)款的规定的情况下,对雇主产品或服务的需求下降,导致工作量或企业利润减少,从而需要终止雇佣合同;

c）因改变工作方法或引进新技术以提高生产率为目的的决定导致终止雇佣合同。

4/ 根据本公告第 29 条第(1)款的规定,如果取消一个工作岗位影响到该劳动者,则应按照第 29 条第(3)款的规定终止雇佣。

29. 裁员

1/ 在本公告中,"裁员"是指按本公告第 28 条第(3)款中规定的任何原因而终止企业的劳动力,从而影响到至少占雇佣人数的 10%的工人;如果企业雇佣工人人数在 20 人到 50 人之间,在连续 10 天内解雇至少 5 名雇员。

2/ 本条第(1)款所指的"工人人数",是指用人单位采取裁员措施之日前 12 个月内被雇主雇佣的平均工人人数。

3/ 根据本公告第 28 条第(3)款裁员时,雇主应与工会或工人代表进行协商,以保留具有技能和较高生产率的工人。如果技能和生产率相同,首先受裁员影响的工人应按下列顺序:

a）在企业中工作时间最短者;

b）抚养人较少者;

c）裁员应影响第一批工人,但本小节(d)项至(e)项所列人员除外;

d）残疾雇员;

e）在企业中遭受工伤者;

f）工人代表;和

g）孕妇和产后 4 个月内的母亲。

30. 例外情况

1/ 本公告中规定的程序不适用于因连续完工而造成的施工工程量正常减少而导致的裁员,除非裁员影响到在其受雇工作完成之前受雇于该部分工作的工人。

2/ 就本条第(1)款而言,"施工工程"包括建筑物、道路、铁路、水坝和桥梁的建造、翻新、升级、维护和修理,机械设备的安装和其他类似工程。

附款二 由工人提出的终止雇佣合同

31. 预先通知而终止的雇佣合同

在不违背本公告第 32 条规定的前提下,已完成试用期的工人,可以提前 30 天通知雇主终止其雇佣合同。

32. 无须预先通知就可终止的雇佣合同

1/ 下列是预先不通知即终止雇佣合同的正当理由:

a）雇主做出任何违反人的尊严和道德的行为或其他根据《刑法》应受惩罚的行为;

b）工人是遭受雇主或管理人员性骚扰或性暴力的受害者;

c）在紧急的危险威胁工人安全或健康的情况下,雇主已经意识到这种危险,但未按照主管当局或有关工会或工人发出的预警在限期内采取行动、避免危险的;

d）雇主多次未能履行本公告、集体协议、工作准则或其他相关法律规定的基本义务。

2/ 工人因本条第(1)款所述的原因终止其雇佣合同,应书面通知雇主终止的原因和终止合同生效的日期。

33. 时效期限

根据本公告第32条第(1)款的规定,工人终止雇佣合同的权利,自该行为发生或停止该行为之日起15个工作日内终止。

第三章　关于终止雇佣合同的一般规定

第一节　终止雇佣合同的通知

34. 发出通知的程序

1/ 本公告规定要求的终止通知应采用书面形式。通知应明确合同终止的原因和终止生效的日期。

2/ 雇主解雇通知应亲自交付给工人。若不能找到该工人或其拒绝接收通知,必须将该通知张贴在工人工作地点的告示板上,为期连续十天。

3/ 工人提出的终止雇佣合同的通知书应移交给雇主或其代表,或交付给其登记处。

4/ 根据本公告第17条,在雇佣合同被中止期间,雇主向工人发出的终止雇佣合同的通知无效。

35. 通知期限

1/ 雇主发出的通知期限如下:

a) 试用期届满且服务期限不超过1年的工人,通知期限为一个月;

b) 服务期在一年至九年之间的工人,通知期限为两个月;

c) 服务期超过九年的工人,通知期限为三个月;

d) 已完成试用期且雇佣合同由于裁员而终止的工人,通知期限为两个月。

2/ 尽管有本条第(1)款的规定,固定期限工作或计件工作中,雇佣合同的通知期限应由合同双方商定。

3/ 本公告规定的通知期应自正式发出通知之日起的第一个工作之日起算。

4/ 在通知期内,双方因雇佣合同而承担的义务应保持不变。

第二节　终止雇佣合同时支付的工资和其他款项

36. 付款期限

终止雇佣合同的,应在解除雇佣合同之日起7个工作日内支付与解除雇佣合同有关的工资和其他报酬;但是,由于工人自身的过失,未及时将属于雇主的财物归还雇主,支付期间可以延长。

37. 争议金额

工人对支付的金额产生异议时,雇主应按本公告第36条的规定,将双方认可的金额在规定限期内支付给工人。

38. 延迟的影响

如果雇主未能在本公告第36条规定的期限内支付应付给工人的款项,主管法院的劳动庭可裁定支付最多三个月工资的违约金,但因雇主无法控制的原因而延期的除外。

第三节　解雇费和补偿

39. 一般原则

1/ 结束试用期的工人且不符合领取退休金资格的,在下列情况下有权从雇主那里获得解雇费：

a）因破产或其他原因而永久性停业，造成雇佣合同终止的；

b）因雇主违反法律规定，造成雇佣合同终止的；

c）根据本公告规定的条款，被裁减的；

d）因其雇主或管理人员的性骚扰或性暴力而辞职的工人；或同事有此行为，并已向雇主举报，但雇主未能采取适当措施的工人；

e）因其雇主的虐待而有损工人人格尊严、心理健康或构成《刑法》规定的刑事犯罪，而终止雇佣合同的；

f）因雇主被告知威胁工人安全或健康的因素存在，但未采取措施，导致工人辞职的；

g）因工人被医院确诊部分或完全残疾，造成雇佣合同终止的；

h）工人为雇主提供了至少5年的服务，并且由于生病或死亡而终止其雇佣合同，或者工人的雇佣合同是主动终止的，前提是其没有与之相关的接受培训以向雇主提供服务的合同义务；

i）因感染艾滋病毒/艾滋病，工人主动终止雇佣合同的。

2/ 如果工人在领取解雇费之前死亡，则应将其支付给本公告第110条第（2）款所述的家属。

3/ 向死者家属分配解雇费的方式应与本公告第110条相同。

40. 解雇费数额

1/ 参照本公告第39条规定，解雇费应是：

2/ 服务一年的，按最后一周的日平均工资的30倍支付，服务不足一年的，按服务期间的比例计算。

3/ 服务一年以上的工人，每增加一年的服务，其报酬应参照本条第（1）款所述金额的三分之一增加；但是，总金额不得超过工人12个月的工资。

4/ 若雇佣合同根据本公告第24条第（4）款和第29条终止，工人应得到报酬。除本条第（1）款和第（2）款中的报酬外，还应向工人支付等同于工作最后一周的每日平均工资60倍的金额。

41. 无通知而终止雇佣合同的赔偿费

1/ 根据本公告第32条第（1）款终止雇佣合同的工人，除有权享有本公告第40条中规定的解雇费外，还应享有等同于服务最后一周日平均工资30倍的赔偿金。该规定也适用于享受相关退休金法所涵盖的工人。

2/ 但是，如果终止是基于第32条第（1）款（b）项，则除解雇费外，工人还应有权获得等同于其日平均工资90倍的补偿。该规定也适用于享受相关退休金法所涵盖的工人。

第四节 非法终止雇佣合同的后果

42. 一般原则

若雇主或工人未遵守本公告或其他有关终止雇佣合同的法律规定的，则其终止是非法的。

43. 非法终止中对工人的恢复和补偿

1/ 如果由于本公告第26条第（2）款提及的理由而终止雇佣合同，雇主有义务恢复该工人的职位;如果工人想辞职,应获得补偿金。

2/ 在不损害本条第(1)款的情况下,如果雇佣合同违反本公告第 24 条、第 25 条、第 27 条、第 28 条和第 29 条的规定而终止的,劳动争议解决法庭可以让工人复职或支付工人赔偿金。

3/ 尽管有本文第(2)款的规定,即使工人要求重新复职,而法庭认为维持特定的工人和雇主关系,由于其性质或可能导致恐慌的争议,可能会引起严重的困难,劳动法庭可能确认在支付赔偿后终止该工人的雇佣合同。同样地,如果工人在获得恢复原职的判决后拒绝恢复原职,法庭可根据工作的性质和案件的其他情况,在支付了对工人所受的不便的赔偿金后,下令终止其工作。

4/ 根据本条第(1)款、第(2)款或第(3)款向未恢复工作的工人支付的补偿金,除本公告第 40 条所述的解雇费外,还应为:

a) 如果是无限期的雇佣合同,根据本公告第 44 条规定,支付日平均工资的 180 倍工资和等于其在适当通知期内工资的金额;

b) 如果是固定期限或计件雇佣合同,如雇佣合同持续至合约期满或工程完成时,支付其所获得的工资;但其报酬不得超过日平均工资的 180 倍;本条第(4)款的规定也应适用于有关退休金法所涵盖的工人。

5/ 根据本条第(1)款或第(2)款的规定,若一审判决指令工人复职,法院应下令支付不超过 6 个月工资金额的赔偿金。若复职决定经上诉法院确认,应责令补发不超过一年的工资。

44. 例外情况

尽管有第 43 条的规定,用人单位不遵守第 35 条所规定的通知要求的情况,将会导致雇主支付报酬或工资以代替通知期。

45. 工人的赔偿责任

1/ 终止其雇佣合同的工人,违背本公告第 31 条或第 35 条第(2)款的规定,应向雇主支付赔偿金。

2/ 但是,根据本条第(1)款,工人支付的赔偿金不得超过该工人 30 天的工资,从应付给该工人的剩余款项中支付。

第四章 特别合同

第一节 家庭工作合同

46. 订立合同

1/ 当自然人在雇主自己的房屋或在由其自由选择的任何其他地方为雇主从事工作,不受任何直接监视或雇主的指导而获得工资时,应订立一份家庭工作合同。

2/ 如果雇主同意将原材料或工具出售给家庭工人,并将产品出售给雇主,或雇主与家庭工人之间作出的任何其他类似安排,应被视为家庭工作合同。

3/ 家庭工人和雇主之间订立的合同,应视为固定期限或计件合同。

4/ 劳动与社会保障部部长应会同有关机构,下达本公告规定的适合家庭工人及其运用方式的指示。

47. 备案

根据家庭工作合同雇佣工人的雇主应建立登记册,记载下列事项和其他有关情况:

1/ 工人的全名、年龄、婚姻状况和地址;

2/ 将要开展工作的地址;

3/ 雇主向工人提供的材料的类型、价格、质量和数量;

4/ 工作类型、订购的质量和数量;

5/ 产品或材料的交付时间和地点;

6/ 付款金额和方式。

第二节 学 徒 合 同

48. 订立合同

1/ 雇主同意在某一特定职业中,按照该行业的技能,对学徒进行与其所从事的工作有关的全面而系统的培训,而该人又同意遵守关于在该职业中开展培训和相关工作的指示,即为学徒合同。

2/ 学徒合同应与年龄不小于15周岁的人签订。

3/ 学徒合同及其变更,必须以书面形式订立,并经劳动与社会事务部或有关当局批准,方为有效。

49. 合同内容

学徒合同应至少规定以下内容:

1/ 学徒培训的性质和期限;

2/ 培训期间应支付的津贴;

3/ 工作条件。

50. 缔约方的义务

1/ 学徒应认真接受培训,努力完成培训任务。

2/ 雇主不得安排学徒从事与其培训无关且无助于其培训的职业。

51. 合同终止

1/ 学徒合同应基于以下理由终止:

a) 在确定的学徒期届满时;

b) 合同任意一方发出通知;

c) 学徒未事先通知而终止合同。

2/ 有下列情形之一的,雇主可根据本条第(1)款(b)项的规定发出通知,终止学徒合同:

a) 因工作变动或其他无法控制的原因而不能履行其义务;

b) 学徒违反该企业的纪律规则;

c) 学徒永久性的无法在规定的期限内继续接受培训或完成培训。

3/ 有下列情形之一的,学徒可根据本条第(1)款(b)项发出终止通知,终止学徒合同:

a) 雇主未遵守合同或本公告规定的义务;

b) 学徒有与其健康或家庭或其他类似的正当理由。

4/ 有下列情形之一的,学徒可终止学徒合同,而无须根据本条第(1)款(c)项发出通知:

(a) 学徒通过适当的医疗证明,证明在不严重危害其健康的情况下不能履行其义务;

(b) 雇主单方面更改了合同条款。

5/ 本公告关于解雇费、赔偿金和复职的规定不适用于学徒合同。

52. 证书

在学徒合同终止时,雇主应向学徒出具证明,说明其接受培训的职业、培训时间和其他有关情况。

第三部分
工　资

第一章　工资的确定

53. 一般原则

1/ "工资"是指工人按雇佣合同履行其工作而有权获得的定期报酬。

2/ 就本公告而言,以下报酬不应视为工资:

a) 加班费;

b) 以每日津贴、辛劳津贴、交通津贴、搬迁费用收到的款项以及在工人外出旅行或居住地变更时发给该工人的类似津贴;

c) 奖金;

d) 佣金;

e) 因额外工作成果而支付的其他奖励;

f) 从客户处收取的服务费。

54. 空闲时间的付款条件

1/ 除非本公告或相关法律另有规定,工资仅应为完成的工作支付。

2/ 不符合本条第(1)项规定的,工人在准备工作时,因工具或原材料供应中断或其他不可归责于本人的原因而不能工作的,有权领取工资。

第二章　付款方式和执行

55. 一般原则

1/ 工资应以现金支付,但经雇主和工人约定,工资可以以实物形式支付的除外。以实物形式支付的工资不得超过所在地区的实物的市场价值,并不得超过以现金形式支付工资的30%。

2/ 部长理事会条例应确定工资委员会的权力和责任,该委员会由政府代表、雇员和工会代表以及其他利益相关者组成,综合考虑国家的经济发展、劳动力市场和其他因素,定期修订最低工资。

56. 付款执行

1/ 除另有协议外,工资应在工作日和工作地点支付。

2/ 本条第(1)款所述的支付日为每周休息日或公共假日时,支付日应为前一个工作日。

57. 亲自付款

除法律、集体协议或工作规则另有规定外,工资应直接支付给工人或其授权的人。

58. 付款时间
工资应按法律、集体协议、工作规则或雇佣合同规定的时间间隔支付。

59. 工资扣除
1/ 除法律、集体协议、工作规则、法院的指令或有关工人的书面协议另有规定外,雇主不得从工人的工资中扣除、扣减、附加或抵扣其工资。

2/ 除工人以书面形式表示同意,任何情况下单次从工人工资中扣除的金额均不得超过其月工资的三分之一。

60. 保留付款记录
1/ 除非有特殊安排,雇主应保存一份付款记录表,列明工资总额、工资计算方法以及其他不定报酬、扣除金额及类别、净工资和其他相关细节,且需工人在此记录表上签字。

2/ 雇主有义务应工人的要求向工人提供该记录表并向其解释其条目。

3/ 工人收到了记录表上注明的数额而未提出异议的事实,不表明其放弃应得工资任何部分。

第四部分
工作时间、每周休息和公共假日

第一章 工作时间

第一节 正常工作时间

61. 每日或每周最长工作时间

1/ 在本公告中,"正常工作时间"是指工人实际工作或根据法律、集体协议或工作准则规定从事工作的时间。

2/ 正常工作时间每天不得超过8小时,每周不得超过48小时。

62. 减少正常工作时间

1/ 对于有特殊工作条件的经济部门、行业和职业,劳动与社会事务部可以发布减少正常工作时间的指令。

2/ 根据本公告,减少正常工作时间并不意味着减少工人的工资。

63. 每周工作时间的安排

工作时间应在一周的工作日内平均分配,但如工作性质需要,可以缩短其中任何一个工作日的工作时间,在每日8小时工作时间延长不得超过2小时的情况下,将差额分配给该周其余工作日。

64. 平均正常工作时间

在必须进行工作的情况下,正常工作时间无法在一周内平均分配的,正常工作时间可以按超过一周的时间平均计算,但这一段时间内的平均小时数不得超过每天8小时或每周48小时。

65. 例外

除集体协议或雇佣合同中另有规定外,本公告中有关工作时间的规定不适用于商业旅行者或商业代表。

第二节 加 班

66. 一般原则

1/ 超出本公告规定的正常每日工作时间的工作,应视为加班。

2/ 在本公告第61条、第63条和第64条所述范围内完成的工作不应视为加班。

3/ 仅在第67条明确规定的情况以及在雇主的明确指示下,才能视为加班。

4/ 根据本条第(3)款给出的指示,每个工人的实际加班时间应由雇主记录。

67. 允许加班的情形

1/ 工人不得被强迫加班,但是,如果雇主不能采取其他措施,只有在下列情况下,工人才可以加班:

a) 实际或者重大的事故;

b) 不可抗力;

c) 紧急工作;

d) 替换被分配从事连续无间断工作的缺席工人。

2/ 尽管有本条第(1)款的规定,但工人每天加班不得超过4小时,每周不得超过12小时。

68. 加班费

1/ 除标准工资外,加班的工人还应至少享有以下报酬:

a) 在早上6:00至晚上10:00之间完成的工作,按正常每小时工资额的1.5倍计算;

b) 在晚上10:00至次日早上6:00之间的夜间工作,按正常每小时工资额的1.75(一又四分之三)倍计算;

c) 在每周休息日完成工作的情况下,按正常每小时工资额的2倍计算;

d) 在公共假日工作的情况下,按正常每小时工资额的2倍计算。

2/ 加班费应在规定的工资支付日连同工资一起支付。

第二章 每 周 休 息

69. 一般原则

1/ 在每7天的期间内,工人有权享有每周不少于24小时的不间断休息时间。

2/ 除集体协议或工作规则另有规定外,每周休息日应尽可能:

a) 在星期日;

b) 同时该企业的所有工人都享有。

3/ 每周休息时间应从早上6:00到次日早上6:00进行计算。

4/ 尽管有本条第(1)款的规定,但由于工作性质,工人无法利用每周的休息日,雇主应当给予工人一个月4个工作日的休息时间。

70. 每周特殊休息日

1/ 如果雇主提供的工作或服务的性质使工人每周的休息时间不能在星期日进行,则可以选择另外一天代替。

2/ 本条第(1)款的规定应适用于以下活动和其他类似活动:

a) 必须提供生活必需品以满足公众健康、娱乐或文化需求的工作;

b) 本公告第137条第(2)款规定的基本公共服务;

c）由于其性质或技术原因，若中断或推迟可能导致遭遇困难或损失的工作。

71. 每周休息日完成的工作

1/ 仅在以下情况下，才有必要要求工人在每周的休息日工作以避免严重干扰其正常工作：

a）实际或潜在威胁的事故；

b）不可抗力；

c）紧急工作。

2/ 在不影响本公告第 68 条第（1）款（c）项规定的情况下，根据本章规定在每周休息日工作的工人有权享有补偿性休息时间；但是，如果工人在使用补偿性休息期之前被终止雇佣合同，则其将以现金形式获得补偿。

72. 适用

本章的规定不适用于商业旅行者或商业代表。

第三章 公共假期

73. 一般原则

根据有关法律规定的公共假日为带薪公共假期。

74. 公共假期不减少工资

1/ 按月领薪的工人，不得因未在公共假日工作而减少其工资。

2/ 除本条第（1）款所指工人以外的其他工人在公共假日获得的工资，应由雇佣合同或者集体协议确定。

75. 公共假期工作的报酬

1/ 在公共假期，工人每工作 1 小时，必须支付工人正常小时工资的 2 倍。

2/ 如果公共假日与另一个公共假日同时发生或在法律规定的休息日内，工人在这一天工作仅有权获得一天的公共假日工作报酬。

第五部分
休　　假

第一章　年　休　假

76. 一般原则

1/ 工人以任何方式放弃其年休假权利的协议无效。

2/ 除本公告另有规定外，禁止以支付工资代替年休假。

77. 年休假的天数

1/ 根据本条规定，工人有权享受带薪年休假。这种假期在任何情况下均不得少于：

a）工作第一年，年休假为 16 个工作日；

b）每多工作 2 年，年休假增加 1 天。

2/ 工人在年休假期间所领取的工资，应当与正常工作时的工资相等。

3/ 为了确定有权享受年休假的工作年限，在企业中服务 26 天应被视为等同于受雇一个月。

4/ 根据本公告终止雇佣合同的工人有权获得其未休假的工资。

5/ 如果工人的服务年限少于1年,则该工人有权享受与其服务年限成比例的年假。

78. 准予休假

1/ 在工作满一年后,应准予工人第一次年休假,并在每个公历年内准予下一次及随后的年休假。

2/ 雇主应当在公历年即将终止时,按照休假计划给予工人休假。

3/ 本条第(2)款所指的休假表应由雇主草拟,并应适当考虑:

a) 工人的利益;

b) 维持企业正常运行的需要。

79. 年休假的分休和延期

1/ 尽管有本公告第77条第(1)款规定,但如果工人提出要求并且雇主同意,则可以分两次休假。

2/ 当工人提出要求并且雇主同意时,年休假可以推迟。

3/ 由于企业的经营需求,雇主可以推迟工人的假期。

4/ 根据本条第(2)款和第(3)款推迟的假期,不得超过2年。

5/ 休年假的工人生病并需要住院治疗时,应暂停其年休假,并应根据本公告第85条和第86条的规定开始休病假。

80. 召回休假的工人

1/ 只有在意外情况要求休年假的工人在岗时,才可以召回休年假的工人。

2/ 从休假中被召回的工人有权要求支付其剩余休假时间的报酬,但不包括旅行所损失的时间。

3/ 雇主应承担工人因被召回而直接产生的交通费用并按日计酬。

第二章 特殊情况休假

81. 家庭事务休假

1/ 在下列情况下,工人有权获得3个工作日的带薪休假:

a) 缔结婚姻;或者

b) 其配偶、子女、祖父母、外祖父母、兄弟姐妹、叔叔、阿姨等,不论是直系亲属还是旁系亲属死亡,均有权获得3个工作日的带薪假期。

2/ 男性雇员应享有连续3天的全薪陪产假。

3/ 如果发生特殊和严重事件,工人有权获得连续5天的无薪休假。但是,这样的假期在一个预算年度中只能给予2次。

82. 工会休假

工会负责人有权带薪休假,以处理劳动纠纷案件、谈判集体协议、参加工会会议、参加研讨会或培训课程。授予这种假期的方式可以通过集体协议确定。

83. 特殊目的休假

1/ 在工人出现在审理劳动纠纷或执行劳动法的机构的听证会上时可获得带薪休假,但仅限于因上述目的所占用的时间。

2／ 为行使其投票权或履行其作为证人的义务供司法或准司法机关使用,应准予工人享受带薪休假。

3／ 可在集体协议或工作规则中确定准予教育或培训假的方式以及提供财政援助的形式和范围。

84. 通知

工人依照本章规定休假的,应当事先通知雇主,并在雇主提出要求时,提供必要的证明材料。

第三章 病 假

85. 休假期限

1／ 工人在试用期结束后由于疾病并非工伤而无法工作的,将有权享受病假。

2／ 本条第(1)款所指的假期,在任何情况下,自患病之日起连续或分别计算的时间,12个月内均不得超过6个月。

3／ 工人因病缺勤的,应当在缺勤的次日通知雇主,但雇主知道该疾病或者无法被通知的除外。

4／ 在不影响集体协议或工作规则规定的前提下,工人只要出示由正式认可的医疗机构签发的有效医疗证明,即有权请病假。

86. 支付

第85条规定病假期间,应以下列方式支付工人:

1／ 第一个月,支付其全月的工资;

2／ 在接下来的2个月,支付其工资的一半;

3／ 接下来的3个月,不支付其工资。

第六部分
妇女和低龄工人的工作条件

第一章 妇女的工作条件

87. 一般原则

1／ 妇女不应在任何方面因性别受到歧视。

2／ 在不损害本条第(1)款的一般前提下,如果妇女在竞争就业、晋升或获取任何其他利益时与男子同等的结果,应优先考虑妇女。

3／ 禁止指派妇女从事劳动与社会事务部上列出的可能特别危险或危害妇女健康的工作。

4／ 不得在晚上10:00至次日早上6:00之间安排孕妇夜班工作或加班工作。

5／ 如果由医生确定妇女的工作对其健康或胎儿有害,则应将其转移到另一个工作地点。

6／ 雇主不得在女性雇员怀孕期间和其分娩后4个月内终止雇佣合同。

7／ 尽管有本条第(6)款的规定,雇佣合同可因第27条(b)项~(k)项和第29条第(3)款的规定终止,但不得因妇女怀孕和分娩而终止。

88. 产假

1/ 雇主应给予怀孕工人带薪休假,让其做怀孕体检,但她须出示检查的医疗证明书。

2/ 根据医生的建议,怀孕女工应有权享有带薪休假。

3/ 怀孕的女工应当享受连续产前 30 天的带薪休假和连续 90 天的产后休假。

4/ 怀孕工人如未能在产前假期的 30 个工作日内分娩,其可根据本条第(2)款的规定享有额外假期,直至分娩。但在产前假期满前生育的,产后假从分娩日开始计算,为 90 个工作日。

5/ 对经医生证明已终止妊娠的怀孕女工,不得执行第 86 条规定的无薪休假。

第二章 低龄工人的工作条件

89. 一般原则

1/ 就本公告而言,"低龄工人"是指 15 周岁以上、18 周岁以下的自然人。

2/ 禁止雇用年龄小于 15 周岁的自然人。

3/ 禁止指派低龄工人从事工作性质或工作条件危害其生命或健康的工作。

4/ 劳动与社会事务部可规定禁止低龄工人从事的活动清单,其中应特别包括:

a) 从事公路、铁路、航空、内河、码头、仓库等运送旅客、货物的,包括重物搬运、拖拉、推挤或者其他有关劳动的;

b) 与发电厂、变压器或传输线有关的工作;

c) 地下作业,例如,矿山和采石场;

d) 下水道和隧道开挖方面的工作。

5/ 本条第(4)款之规定,不适用于经主管当局核定的职业学校中的低龄工人为完成课程要求而进行的工作。

90. 工作时间限制

低龄工人的正常工作时间每天不得超过 7 个小时。

91. 夜间和加班工作

严禁雇佣低龄工人在以下时间工作:

1/ 晚上 10:00 至次日早上 6:00 之间的夜间工作;

2/ 加班;

3/ 每周休息日;

4/ 公共假期。

第七部分
职业安全和健康及工作环境

第一章 预防措施

92. 雇主的义务

雇主应当采取必要措施,充分保障工人的健康和安全,必须做到:

1/ 遵守本公告中规定的职业健康和安全要求。

2/ 采取适当措施,以确保工人得到有关各自相关行业危害的正确指导和通知;指派安全员并且建立职业健康与安全委员会。

3/ 向工人提供防护装备、衣服和其他材料,并指导他们如何使用。

4/ 记录工伤事故和职业病,并向劳动监察部门报告。

5/ 根据工作性质,出资安排对新雇佣的工人和从事危险工作的工人进行身体检查,除检查感染艾滋病毒/艾滋病状况外,雇主必须遵守国际条约的义务。

6/ 确保企业的工作处所和场所不对工人的健康和安全构成威胁。

7/ 采取适当的预防措施,确保工人在所从事的所有工作过程中不会产生对其健康和安全造成物理、化学、生物、人体和心理危害。

8/ 执行主管当局根据本公告发出的指示。

93. 工人的义务

工人应当遵守下列规定:

1/ 协同制定并实施保障工人健康和安全的规章制度;

2/ 立即通知雇主其在经营过程中意识到的与使用的器具有关的任何缺陷以及对工人健康和安全造成伤害的事件;

3/ 向雇主报告其有理由认为可能构成危险并且无法单独预防的任何情况,以及在工作过程中或与工作有关的任何损害健康的事件;

4/ 正确使用所有为保护其健康和安全或保护他人的健康和安全而配备的安全装置和其他用具;

5/ 遵守雇主或主管当局发布的一切健康和安全指示。

94. 禁止行为

禁止工人:

1/ 干扰、移动、取代、损坏或毁坏为保护其本人或他人而提供的任何安全装置或其他设备;或者

2/ 妨碍为减少任何职业危害所采取的任何方法或程序。

第二章 职业伤害

第一节 责任

95. 一般原则

1/ 就本公告而言,"职业伤害"是指职业事故或职业病。

2/ 遵守有关退休金法的规定,本章的规定适用于工人在工作期间或在从事与其工作相关的工作内容时遭受工伤的情况。

96. 无过错责任

1/ 雇主对工人遭受的工伤,不考虑工人过失,均应当承担赔偿责任,并依照本章规定确定赔偿责任。

2/ 雇主对工人故意伤害自己的行为不承担任何责任。特别是,以下行为造成的任何伤害均应视为由工人故意造成的:

a) 不遵守雇主给出的明确安全指令或事故预防规则的规定;

b) 因服用含酒精的饮料或药物而导致中毒的工作状态,使其无法正常地调节自己的身体或理解力。

3/ 根据本条第(1)款的规定,如果由于雇主的过失造成工人职业伤害,则不得影响工人依据有关法律要求赔偿的权利。

97. 职业事故

就本公告而言,"职业事故"是指工人因与受伤工人无关的任何原因或在其工作期间或执行与工作有关的任何工作所导致的任何器官损伤或功能障碍:

1/ 工人在执行其雇主指令时遭受的任何伤害,即使是在工作地点或在正常工作时间以外;

2/ 工人在工作之前或之后或在任何工作中断期间遭受的任何伤害,但前提是该工人由于其职责而在工作场所或经营场所内工作;

3/ 工人乘坐企业提供的企业工人普遍使用的运输车辆,或乘坐由企业租用并直接指定的车辆,往返于工作地而遭受的任何受伤;

4/ 工人在工作期间由于雇主或第三方的行为而遭受的任何伤害。

98. 职业病

1/ 就本公告而言,"职业病"是指以下任何疾病:

a) 工人从事的工作类型;或者

b) 由物理、化学或生物因素引起的病理状态,这种病理状态是由于工人在疾病明显之前的一定时期内不得不在其工作的环境工作所造成的。

2/ 职业病不包括在工作场所流行和接触的地方性、流行性疾病,但因职业原因专门从事防治此类疾病的工人除外。

3/ 劳动与社会事务部应会同有关当局发布指示,列出职业引起疾病的目录,上述目录至少每五年修订一次。

4/ 从事相关工种的工人,如发生了有关目录中所列的任何疾病,必须充分证明该疾病因职业而引起。

5/ 尽管有本条第(4)款的规定,应接受任何证据以确定未列入有关附表的疾病的职业来源,以及当这些疾病在不同于确定其职业性质推定的条件出现时所列疾病的职业来源。

6/ 在缺少相反证明时,如果从事某些职业的工人频繁发生某种疾病,且患病工人从事这种职业,并由医生查明存在该病,均应推断该病具有职业起因。

7/ 一种职业病明显发生的日期是指劳动者丧失劳动能力的第一日、首次诊断患病的第一日或者工伤人员死亡的第一日,为职业病发生的日期。

8/ 工人患列入相应目录的职业病治愈后,从事上述目录中规定的相关工作,再次患该疾病,视为重新患职业病。

第二节 残 疾 程 度

99. 一般原则

1/ "职业残疾"是指任何因工作能力下降或丧失而导致的工伤。

2/ 残疾应具有以下影响:

a) 暂时性残疾;

b) 永久性部分残疾；
c) 永久性完全残疾；
d) 死亡。

100. 暂时性残疾
暂时性残疾是由于工人在有限的时间内降低了部分或全部工作的能力。

101. 永久性部分或完全残疾
1/ "永久性部分残疾"是指无法治愈的工伤降低了受伤工人的能力。

2/ "永久性完全残疾"是指无法治愈的工伤使受伤的工人无法从事任何有偿工作。

3/ 虽然没有导致丧失工作能力的伤害，但造成受伤者严重伤残或者毁容的，为补偿或者其他利益的目的，应将其视为永久性部分残废。

102. 残疾评估
1/ 永久性完全或部分残疾的程度应根据劳动与社会事务部发布的指令所规定的残疾评估表确定。

2/ 残疾程度应由医疗委员会根据本条第（1）款规定的评估表进行评估。医疗委员会应自工人受伤之日起的12个月内，尽可能确定残疾程度。

3/ 如果工人的病情恶化或改善或被错误诊断，则可以根据本条第（1）款和第（2）款对残疾等级评估进行审查：

a) 在有关当局发起时；或者
b) 根据有关工人或雇主的要求，可以根据本条第（1）款和第（2）款对问题进行修订。

4/ 审查结果证明确有必要的，应当确认或者撤销工人获得伤残保险金的权利，或视情况增加或者减少给付的数额。

5/ 遭受工伤的工人再次遭受其他工伤的，应根据新情况重新评估其残疾程度。

第三章　工　伤　赔　偿

第一节　一　般　原　则

103. 付款和付款责任
伤害赔偿金应按照本章的规定支付。

104. 特殊义务
1/ 雇主必须履行以下义务：

a) 及时为受伤工人提供救助；
b) 通过适当的运输方式将伤者送往最近的医疗机构；
c) 向有关机关通报工伤事故的发生情况。

2/ 雇主有义务负担本公告第110条第（1）款（b）项规定的丧葬费。

第二节　医　疗　服　务

105. 医疗服务类型
工人因工受伤的，雇主应当负担下列医疗费用：

1/ 普通和专门内外科检查；

2/ 医院和药学服务；

3/ 任何必要的假肢或矫形器具。

106. 医疗服务期限
医疗服务应根据医疗委员会的决定而停止。

第三节 各种方式的现金救济

107. 一般原则
1/ 受工伤的工人有权获得:
a) 在其暂时残疾时定期支付报酬;
b) 永久残疾时的残障抚恤金、酬金或补偿金;
c) 若工人死亡,给其家属的抚恤金、酬金或补偿金。

2/ 如果工人已经或正在领取定期付款,有以下情况的可以扣留定期付款:
a) 拒绝或忽视体检,或以任何方式故意阻碍或不必要地延误身体检查;
b) 故意拖延康复时间;
c) 违反有关主管机关发布的关于受伤工人行为的指示。

3/ 一旦中止支付的情况停止,定期付款应重新开始;但是,中止期间不应享有获得拖欠付款的权利。

108. 定期报酬
1/ 雇主应支付本公告第 107 条第(1)款(a)项所述的定期报酬,期限不超过一年。

2/ 本条第(1)款所述的定期支付标准为工人因工受伤之日起前 3 个月工人的平均年工资全额支付,在受伤后的第 4、第 5 和第 6 个月,按不少于工人先前年平均工资的 75% 支付,后 6 个月,按不少于先前年平均工资的 50% 支付。

3/ 发生下列任意一种情况,定期报酬都应停止:
a) 当该工人经医学证明不再残疾时;
b) 工人有权领取残疾抚恤金或酬金之日;
c) 从工人停止工作之日起 12 个月。

109. 伤残赔偿金
1/ 除非集体协议另有规定,应支付给本公告所涵盖的企业的残障救济金应符合退休金计划或保险计划。经营者未安排保险计划的,适用有关退休金计划。

2/ 虽有本条第(1)款的规定,但保险计划所涵盖的伤残赔偿金在任何情况下均不得少于本条第(4)款规定的金额。

3/ 雇主应向退休金法未涵盖的工人一次性支付伤残赔偿金。

4/ 雇主应支付的伤残赔偿金额为:
a) 如果工人遭受的伤害使其永久性完全残疾,赔偿金额等于其年薪的 5 倍;
b) 如果工人遭受的伤害低于永久性完全残疾,则应根据第 4 款(a)项规定的赔偿方法计算出与残疾程度成比例的赔偿金额。

5/ 当学徒遭受永久性残疾时,其致残津贴应参照其作为一名合格工人在学徒期结束后可能获得的工资来计算。

110. 家属抚恤金
1/ 如果工人或学徒因工伤死亡,其家属应享受以下抚恤金:

a) 根据本条第(2)款和第(3)款的规定支付家属补偿费;和

b) 除非集体协议或工作规则规定的金额更高,否则丧葬费的支付在任何情况下均不得少于工人两个月的工资。

2/ 以下人员应视为家属:

a) 寡妇或鳏夫;

b) 死者未满 18 周岁的子女;

c) 由死者赡养的父母。

3/ 未纳入退休金计划的工人的家属抚恤金应以死者年薪的 5 倍计算,并由雇主按以下比例一次性支付给死亡工人的被抚养人:

a) 寡妇或鳏夫者为 50%;

b) 死者未满 18 周岁的孩子各占 10%;

c) 由死者赡养的父母各占 10%。

4/ 如果根据本条第(3)款计算的被扶养人的工伤死亡赔偿总额超过应分摊总额的 100%,在不影响配偶份额的情况下,每个被扶养人的补偿金额应按比例减少,使各分摊比例之和达到 100%;少于应分摊总额 100% 的,应按比例增加每个被抚养人的补偿金额,使各分摊比例之和达到 100%。

111. 举证责任

如果自受伤之日起 12 个月后死亡,则不得支付本公告第 110 条所述的工伤死亡赔偿,除非已证明工伤是其死亡的主要原因。

112. 不缴税补助金

1/ 依照本节规定支付的工伤死亡赔偿,免征所得税。

2/ 不得通过抵销的方式转让、附加或扣除根据本节规定应支付的工伤死亡赔偿。

第八部分
集 体 关 系

第一章 工会和雇主协会

113. 结社权

1/ 工人和雇主有权分别成立和组织工会或雇主协会,并积极参与。

2/ 在本公告中:

a) "工会"是指由工人组成的协会;

b) "雇主协会"是指由雇主建立的协会;

c) "联合会"是指由多个工会或雇主协会建立的组织;

d) "联盟"是指由多个工会联合会或雇主联合会建立的组织。

114. 协会的成立

1/ 工会可以在工人人数为 10 人或更多人数的企业中建立;但是,规定工会会员人数不得少于 10 人。

2/ 在不同企业工作且从事类似活动但少于 10 名工人的可以组建总工会,但该工会会员人数不得少于10人。

3/ 多个工会可以共同组建工会联合会,而多个工会联合会也可以共同组建工会联盟。

4/ 多个雇主协会可以共同组建雇主联合会,而多个雇主联合会也可以共同组建雇主联盟。

5/ 任何工会或雇主协会如未组建工会联合会或雇主联合会,均不得组建联盟。

6/ 工会或雇主协会的任何联合会或联盟均可加入国际工会组织或国际雇主协会组织。

7/ 禁止工人在同一时间参加多个工会;如未遵守本规定,则以最新加入的工会成员资格为准;同时办理入会手续的,工会成员资格一律无效。

8/ 尽管有本条第(4)款的规定,但是任何雇主均可加入已建立的雇主联合会。

115. 协会的职能

协会应具有以下职能:

1/ 遵守工作条件,履行本公告中规定的义务,保护会员的权益,尤其是在会员要求或授权的情况下代表会员到主管机关参加集体谈判和劳动纠纷解决,但是,前提是:

a) 在某一企业存在多个工会的情况下,将成为独家谈判代理并与当局进行协商的工会应保护该企业50%以上的雇员的权益,且其中至少有一名雇员为该工会会员;

b) 如果一个组织获得多数工人成员,则该组织应得到劳动与社会事务部或有关当局的认证;

c) 如果一个组织后来未能获得多数工人成员,则多数工人入会的另一组织应替代其取得认证。

2/ 确保成员了解并遵守和执行法律、条例、指令和公告;

3/ 对与劳动关系有关的法律条例进行提案,并积极参与其制定和修正;

4/ 履行各自组织章程中规定的其他义务。

116. 联合会和联盟的职能

除本公告第115条所述的事项外,联合会和联盟还应具有以下职能:

1/ 加强工会成员之间的团结和合作精神;

2/ 参与决定或改善本行业或部门的工作条件;

3/ 鼓励成员加强对国家经济发展的参与;

4/ 在任何论坛中代表其成员;和

5/ 履行章程中分配给他们的其他任务。

117. 禁止行为

禁止雇主组织或工人组织违反诚信原则过度拖延集体谈判。

118. 协会章程

工会和雇主协会应当依法自主成立。协会章程可能包括但不限于以下内容:

1/ 协会名称;

2/ 协会总部地址;

3/ 协会的目标;

4/ 协会成立的日期;

5/ 协会会徽;

6/ 承担协会领导职务的要求;

7/ 适合会员的工会会费;

8／协会的财务和财产管理；

9／协会的会议和选举程序；

10／纪律处分程序；

11／解散协会的条件；和

12／协会解散时的财产状况。

119. 协会注册

1／每个协会均应由劳动与社会事务部或有关当局根据本公告规定进行注册。

2／每个协会应在申请注册后将以下文件提交给劳动与社会事务部或有关当局：

a）协会章程；

b）包含其成员和领导的姓名、地址和签名的文件；

c）如果是工会，则标明成员工作所在企业的名称；

d）如果是联合会或联盟，则需要其领导层和成员工会或雇主协会的名称、地址和签名；

e）协会名称和会徽。

3／劳动与社会事务部或有关当局应于收到申请之日起15个工作日内，审查文件，确认填写妥当后，核发注册证书。该部或有关当局未在规定期限内通知决定的，视为已注册。在这种情况下，应向协会发出注册证书。

4／未按照本条规定进行注册的协会不得履行本公告中规定的职能。

5／工会的首次注册免征印花税。

6／经劳动与社会事务部或主管当局根据本公告注册的工会或雇主协会，应具有法人资格，并具有以下权利：

a）签订合同；

b）起诉和被起诉；

c）占有、使用和转让财产；

d）代表任何层次的成员；和

e）采取任何必要的合法行动以实现其目标。

120. 拒绝注册

劳动与社会事务部或有关当局可基于以下理由拒绝协会注册：

1／如果协会不符合本公告、条例和根据本公告发布的指令中规定的要求；

2／协会的目的和章程是非法的；

3／该组织机构名称与已经注册的组织机构名称相同或相近，容易让成员或公众造成混淆的；或者

4／如果该协会一位或多位当选的领导人被法院限制享有某些公民权利，且该协会不愿更换他们。

121. 撤销注册

1／劳动与社会事务部或有关当局可基于以下任何理由向主管法院提出撤销协会注册证书的要求：

a）如果注册证书是通过欺诈、错误或欺骗手段获得的；

b）根据本公告，该协会的任何目标或章程被认定为非法，且该协会不愿意删除非法条款

或条件;或者

c) 如果发现该协会从事了本公告禁止的活动或进行了违反其目的和章程的活动,并且该协会不愿意停止、改正或取消这些活动的。

2/ 劳动与社会事务部或有关当局可以应协会的要求,确保该协会以其认为适当的方式解散。

122. 取消协会注册的通知

1/ 劳动与社会事务部或有关当局,依照本公告第121条第(1)款,提交申请取消注册协会的文件,并在给出撤销理由前一个月通知有关协会,以便该协会有机会申辩。除了本公告第121条第(1)款所列举的理由外,该部或有关当局不信赖任何其他理由。

2/ 如果本条第(1)款规定的通知期限已经到期,并且协会文件不反对该通知,或者劳动与社会事务部或主管当局不接受该答复,则可以向主管法院申请撤销注册。

3/ 在不损害本条第(2)款的前提下,劳动与社会事务部或有关当局可以同时中止该协会从事本公告禁止的行为或违反本公告第121条第1条(c)款所规定的目标和章程的行为。

123. 上诉

如果劳动与社会事务部或有关当局拒绝该协会的注册,该组织可在收到书面决定之日起15个工作日内向主管法院提出上诉,劳动与社会事务部或有关当局应有机会在法庭上捍卫其决定。

124. 协会要求取消注册或解散的后果

协会应视为自法院决定取消其注册之日起解散,或应协会要求由劳动与社会事务部或有关当局解散。

第二章 集体协议

第一节 一般原则

125. 定义

1/ "集体协议"是指一个或多个工会的代表与一个或多个雇主或雇主协会的代表或代理人就工作条件达成的书面协议。

2/ "集体谈判"是指雇主和工人组织或其代表之间就工作条件进行的谈判过程,以便达成集体协议或对其进行更新或修改。

126. 谈判

1/ 任何工会均有权就本公告第129条规定的事项与一个或多个雇主或其协会进行谈判。

2/ 任何雇主或雇主协会有权与工会组织的工人代表进行谈判。

127. 代表权

1/ 以下人员有权代表工人参加集体谈判:

a) 如果是工会,则为该工会领导人或根据工会章程被授权进行谈判并签字确认集体协议的工会成员;

b) 如果是总工会,则由根据该工会章程授权的总工会领导人进行谈判并签字确认集体协议。

2/ 相关雇主或雇主协会委派的人有权代表他们参加集体谈判。

128. 顾问

在谈判过程中,集体谈判的任何一方都可以得到提供专家意见的顾问的协助。

129. 集体协议的主题

有关雇佣关系和工人工作条件以及雇主与雇主协会和工会的关系的事项可以通过集体协议确定。

130. 集体协议的内容

在不损害本公告第 129 条的一般原则的前提下,以下各项可以通过集体协议确定:

1/ 本公告或其他法律规定由集体协议管理的事项;

2/ 维持职业安全与卫生的条件以及改善社会服务的方式;

3/ 工人的参与,特别是与晋升、工资、调动、裁员和纪律有关的事项;

4/ 工作条件、制定工作规则和申诉的程序;

5/ 工作时间和间隔休息时间的安排;

6/ 集体协议所涵盖的当事方及其有效期;

7/ 关于建立双方社会对话的机制和工作制度;

8/ 关于建立日托机制。

131. 集体谈判的程序

1/ 希望发起集体谈判的一方可以书面形式要求另一方参加,同时应该准备和提供谈判草案。

2/ 被请求方应在收到请求后的 10 个工作日内出面参与集体谈判。

3/ 各方应在开始集体谈判之前拟定议事程序规则。

4/ 谈判双方应秉持诚信原则。

5/ 基于诚信原则,双方谈判仍不能达成一致时,将提交到劳动争议法庭裁决。

6/ 集体协议的当事方应至少在集体协议有效期届满前 3 个月开始重新谈判,以修改或替代该协议。但是,如果重新谈判在其届满之日后的 3 个月内未完成,则集体协议中有关工资和其他利益的规定,除非经过谈判双方的书面协议予以延长,否则将不再适用。

132. 集体协议的登记

1/ 签字确认集体协议后,当事各方应将其足够的副本送交劳动与社会事务部或有关当局进行登记。

2/ 除非有正当理由拒绝登记,否则劳动与社会事务部或有关当局应在收到集体协议副本之日起 15 个工作日内对集体协议进行登记。

133. 集体协议的加入

其他谈判方可以加入已经由第三方签字确认和注册的集体协议。

第二节 集体协议的有效条件

134. 集体协议的有效期限

1/ 集体协议条款提供的工作条件和福利条件低于本公告或其他法律规定的,视为无效。

2/ 除非另有规定,否则集体协议自当事各方签字确认之日起具有法律效力。

3/ 除非集体协议中另有明确规定,否则任何一方均不得在其生效之日起的 3 年内对集体协议提出异议;但是出现下列情况:

a) 在发生重大经济变化之时,在集体协议失效之前,任何一方可以在固定的到期日之前向劳动与社会事务部或有关部门提出对集体协议的质疑;

b) 根据本条第 3 款(a)项,劳动与社会事务部或有关当局应在收到对集体协议提出的质疑后,指派一名调解人,以使各方能够通过协商解决问题。如果双方未能友好解决问题,则应适用本公告第 144 条;

c) 当事人可以随时变更或者修改集体协议;然而,在不损害本条(a)项和(b)项所规定的特殊条件的情况下,一方没有义务在集体协议到期之前参与变更或修改集体协议的谈判。

第三节 集体协议的适用范围

135. 适用范围

1/ 集体协议的规定应适用于其所涵盖的所有当事方。

2/ 如果集体协议在类似事项上比法律规定对工人更有利,则以集体协议的规定为准。但是,如果法律条款比集体协议更有利于工人,则以法律条款为准。

136. 例外

1/ 如果作为集体协议当事方的工会解散,则集体协议在雇主和工人之间仍然有效。

2/ 如果两个或多个企业合并,除非当事方另有规定,则:

a) 如果每个企业有各自的集体协议,职工人数较多的企业合并时的集体协议适用于合并后的企业;

b) 如果每个企业都有各自的集体协议,并且其工人人数相等,则总体上更有利于工人的集体协议适用于合并后的企业;

c) 如果只有一个企业有集体协议,则该协议应适用于合并后的其他企业。

3/ 如果一个企业被兼并或分解成多个企业,则本条第(2)款的规定应视情况适用。

第九部分
劳 动 纠 纷

第一章 一 般 原 则

137. 定义

在本公告中:

1/ "调解"是指由当事方任命或主管当局根据当事方的请求任命的一人或多人引导的活动,目的是使当事方聚集在一起并达到友好解决劳动纠纷的诉求,而这些纠纷是当事方凭借自己的努力无法解决的;

2/ "基本的公共服务事业"是指应在不中断情况下为公众提供的下列服务:

a) 航空运输服务;

b) 电力供给服务;

c) 供水和执行城市清洁与卫生的服务;

d) 城市轻轨运输服务;

e) 医院、诊所和药房;

f) 消防服务;和

g) 电信服务;

3/"劳动纠纷"是指工人与雇主或工会和雇主协会之间在法律、集体协议、工作规则、雇佣合同的适用方面发生的任何纠纷,以及在集体谈判期间或对有关集体协议的不同看法。

4/"停工"是指雇主通过关闭工作场所而采取的一项工业措施,目的是说服工人接受与劳动纠纷有关的或影响争端结果的某些劳动条件。

5/"罢工"意味着一定数量的工人放缓工作,减少正常工作量或临时停止工作,以说服雇主接受特定劳动纠纷相关的劳动条件或劳动纠纷的结果。

第二章 劳动法庭

138. 建立劳动法庭

1/ 应在联邦和区域一级设立劳动法庭。

2/ 劳动与社会事务部或有关当局应根据本条第(1)款,就有关将要设立的法庭数目提出建议,供有关当局决定。

139. 初审法院劳动分庭

1/ 联邦和区域初审法院的劳动分庭应有权裁决以下及其他类似的个人劳动纠纷:

a) 纪律性措施,包括解雇;

b) 与终止雇佣合同有关的索赔;

c) 有关工作时间、报酬、休假及休息日的索赔;

d) 与签发服务证书和结关有关的索赔;

e) 与工伤、调动、晋升、培训和其他类似问题有关的索赔;

f) 除非本公告另有规定,否则违反本公告规定的行为都适用诉讼。

2/ 区域初审法院劳动分庭应在提起诉讼之日起60天内作出裁决。

3/ 对初审法院的裁决感到不满的当事方可以在作出裁决之日起30天内,向联邦或区域上诉法院的劳动分庭提出上诉。

140. 上诉法院劳动分庭

1/ 上诉初审法院劳动分庭有权审理和裁决下列事项:

a) 根据本公告第139条从初审法院劳动分庭提出的上诉;

b) 关于管辖权问题的异议;

c) 劳动与社会事务部或有关当局根据本公告第123条针对拒绝注册提出的上诉;

d) 受劳工督察指令影响的雇主根据本公告第180条第(1)款提出的上诉;

e) 根据本公告第20条第(3)款,针对劳动与社会事务部或有关当局的决定提出的上诉;

f) 劳动与社会事务部或有关当局根据本公告第122条第(2)款提出的取消协会注册的请求;

g) 对劳动关系委员会根据本公告第155条关于法律问题的决定提出的反对意见。

2/ 上诉法院根据本条第(1)款做出的判决为终审判决。

3/ 联邦或区域上诉法院的劳动分庭应在根据本条第(1)款提出上诉之日起60天内作出判决。

第三章　与劳工问题有关的替代性争端解决机制

141. 社会对话

雇主和工人或其各自的协会可以进行社会对话,以友好地预防和解决劳动纠纷。

142. 调解员的任命

1/ 与第143条的规定相关的纠纷,由纠纷相关任何一方报告给劳动与社会事务部或有关当局,劳动与社会事务部或有关当局必须任命一名调解员以解决该问题。

2/ 劳动与社会事务部或有关当局可任命联邦级或区域级调解员,必要时可任命县级调解员。

143. 调解员的职责和责任

1/ 由劳动与社会事务部或有关当局任命的调解员应努力就以下及其他类似的集体劳动纠纷作出谈判裁决:

a) 未按工作规则或集体协议决定的工资和其他福利问题;

b) 建立新的工作条件;

c) 集体协议的缔结、修改、期限和废除;

d) 对本公告、集体协议或工作规则的任何规定的解释;

e) 雇佣和晋升工人的程序;

f) 影响工人和企业存续的一般问题;

g) 与雇主发布的有关晋升、调动和培训的诉讼程序;

h) 与裁员有关的问题。

2/ 调解员应努力以其认为适当的一切方式达成友好解决方案。

3/ 如果调解员在30天内未能解决劳动纠纷,则应将其意见一起向主管当局报告,并应将报告副本送达有关当事方。除本条第(1)款(a)项规定的事项外,任何一方均可将其提交劳动关系委员会。但是,如果本条第(1)款(a)项下的争端与本公告第137条第(2)款所规定的那些企业有关,则争议双方中的任意一方可将此问题提交至劳动关系临时委员会。

144. 调解与仲裁

1/ 尽管有本公告第142条的规定,纠纷各方仍可同意根据相关的法律自行选择将其案件提交仲裁员或调解员裁决。

2/ 依照本条第(1)款,当事人对提交调解的案件不能达成协议的,或者对仲裁裁决不满的,可以视情况提请劳动关系委员会或相关法院裁决。

第四章　劳动关系委员会

145. 委员会的设立

1/ 每个区域可能会根据需要设立一个或多个常设劳动关系委员会(以下简称"常设委员会")。但劳动与社会事务部应设立常设劳动关系委员会,受理涉及位于亚的斯亚贝巴和德雷达瓦市行政区域内且为联邦政府企业的案件。

2/ 可设立临时劳动关系委员会(以下简称"临时委员会"),就本公告第143条第(1)款(a)项所指明的事项及本公告第137条第(2)款所涉企业可能出现的纠纷,进行聆讯及作出裁决。同样,劳动与社会事务部应在必要时设立临时委员会,受理涉及位于亚的斯亚贝巴和德雷达瓦行政区域内且为联邦政府所有企业的案件。

3/ 每个常设或临时委员会必须由劳动与社会事务部或有关当局设立。

4/ 尽管有本条第(3)款的规定,但根据本条第(1)款和第(2)款的规定,应设立临时和常设委员会,负责审理和裁决位于亚的斯亚贝巴和德雷达瓦市行政区域内且为联邦政府所有企业的纠纷,并对劳动与社会事务部负责。

146. 常设委员会或临时委员会的组成

1/ 常设委员会或临时委员会将由劳动与社会事务部或有关当局任命的一名主席、两名拥有劳动关系知识和技能的成员、四名工会代表,两名雇主委员会代表,以及两名候补成员(一名来自工人方,一名来自雇主方)组成。

2/ 雇主代表应从雇主协会最具代表性的人中选出,工人代表应从工会最具代表性的人中选出。

3/ 劳动与社会事务部或有关当局需向委员会委派一名秘书和其他必要的工作人员。

4/ 委员会成员和候补成员应以无报酬的方式兼任,但劳动与社会事务部或有关当局应确定出席委员会会议的标准费用。

5/ 委员会成员和候补成员的任期为三年;但是,在进行初次任命时,应分别指定一年、两年和三年的任期,以便在随后的每一年中,任期在该公历年届满的成员和候补成员不超过三分之一。

6/ 如遇成员失职或渎职,劳动与社会事务部或有关当局将开除其成员资格,并安排其他成员接替其剩余的工作。

147. 常设委员会或临时委员会的会议程序

1/ 在主席缺席的情况下,由其指定的另一位委员会成员代理主席主持委员会会议。如果未指定任何此类成员,委员中资历最深的那一位成员将被视为主席。

2/ 委员会成员未出席会议,主席可以指定一名候补成员代替缺席者参加会议。该指定的候补委员应被视为指定会议的委员。

3/ 委员会的四名成员构成任何委员会会议的法定人数,其中至少有一名成员代表工人,一名成员代表雇主到会。

4/ 委员会的决定应以出席会议成员的多数票为准。如果票数相等,主席应投决定票。

5/ 委员会的每项决定均应由出席会议的所有成员签字确认。

6/ 经委员会批准后,会议记录应由秘书证明,以构成上述会议的正式记录。

148. 常设委员会或临时委员会的权力

1/ 常任理事会应具有以下权力:

a) 审理除第143条第(1)款(a)项规定之外的集体劳动纠纷,以调解双方并发布指令和决定;

b) 除本公告第(1)款(a)项规定的事项外,当事人未能按照本公告第143条第(3)款的规定达成协议时,应审理纠纷一方提交的案件;

c) 审理本公告第161条所述的禁止行为案件;

d) 要求任何个人或组织提交其履行职责所需的信息和文件;

e) 要求当事方和证人出庭;

f) 要求出庭的人宣誓或加以确认,并在宣誓或确认后对这些人进行审查;

g) 在工作时间内进入任何工作或企业的场所,以获取相关信息,听取证人的意见或要求在场的任何人提交文件或其他物品以供检查。

2/ 临时委员会有权审理依公告第143条第(1)款(a)项规定的劳动纠纷,调解当事各方并作出指令和决定。

3/ 除紧急情况外,在按照本条第(1)款(g)项的规定进入之前,应向经营场所或企业的负责人发出合理的事先通知。

4/ 常设委员会或临时委员会下达的指令和决定应视为民事法庭的裁决。

149. 议事规则

常设委员会或临时委员会可适用其自己的证据和程序规则。没有自己的诉讼程序的,适用《民事诉讼法》的规定。

150. 案件听证会

1/ 在处理此案之前,常设委员会或临时委员会应召集有关当事方,并为他们提供陈述的机会。应至少提前10个工作日通知当事各方,传票应注明听证的日期、时间和地点。

2/ 如果任何当事方或经过适当传唤的任何其他人未能在该时间和地点出庭,委员会可继续进行听证。如果未出庭不属当事人的过失,委员会必须给予此人第二次出庭的机会。

3/ 根据本条第(2)款的规定,对于委员会作出的裁决,不能提出任何上诉。

4/ 除非委员会出于正当理由另有决定,否则委员会的所有讨论均应公开。

5/ 常设委员会或临时委员会不适用于法院的证据规则和程序的约束,并可采用其认为适当的任何方法。

6/ 被召集参加听证会的工会、雇主协会和其他被传唤的各方可以由其正式授权的代表或法律顾问代表出庭。委员会可限制主动参加听证会的任何一方代表的人数。

151. 审议事项

1/ 常设委员会和临时委员会必须尽力通过协商解决提交的劳动纠纷,并应为此目的,采用和借用其认为适当的所有此类调解手段。

2/ 在适当的情况下,委员会不仅需要考虑各方当事人的利益,而且还要考虑其所属团体的利益,此时可由政府作为法官顾问来协助解决。

3/ 常设委员会或临时委员会在作出决定时应考虑到案件的主要优点,不必严格遵循民事法院所遵循的实体法原则。

152. 裁决

1/ 常设委员会或临时委员会应在提出要求之日起30天内作出裁决。

2/ 常设委员会或临时委员会的决定应以书面形式作出,并由持支持意见的委员会成员签字确认。反对意见(如果有)也应以书面形式提出,并由持反对意见的成员签字确认。

3/ 委员会的每项裁决均应包含以下内容:

a) 确定待决定的问题或争议;

b) 在诉讼过程中记录的相关证词和证据及其来源;

c) 委员会的调查结果以及对导致委员会作出此类调查结果的证据的评估;

d) 每个问题或纠纷的处理;

e) 根据该决定所采取的行动。

4/ 委员会裁决的副本应在作出裁决之日起 5 日内送达有关各方。

153. 决议的效果

1/ 在不影响本公告第 155 条的前提下,常设委员会或临时委员会的任何决定均应立即生效。

2/ 如果常设委员会或临时委员会的决定与工作条件有关,则应将其视为雇主和工人之间适用的雇佣合同的条款,并对合同进行相应调整。

154. 委员会对事实的最后裁决

委员会对所有事实的判定将是最终的和决定性的。

155. 上诉

1/ 在任何劳动纠纷中,裁决送达当事方后 30 天内,不服裁决的一方当事人可以就法律问题向高级法院提出上诉。

2/ 高级法院有权确认、推翻或修改委员会的决定。

3/ 高级法院应在提出上诉之日起 30 天内作出裁决。

156. 违反常设委员会或临时委员会的行为

1/ 凡在委员会询问或听证过程中以任何方式干扰审议的,应处以不超过 6 个月的监禁或不超过 1 000 比尔的罚款。

2/ 如果本条第(1)款所述的违反行为不是公开或在庭外进行的,则除较严重的情况外,处以不超过 500 比尔的罚款。

3/ 根据《刑法》第 449 条,委员会的程序应被视为准司法程序,委员会是合格的司法法庭,违反该法庭的行为应按《刑法》第 449 条的规定予以处罚。

4/ 委员会可惩处违反本条规定的任何人。

157. 年度报告

常设委员会或临时委员会应负责向劳动与社会事务部或有关当局提交其活动的年度报告。

第五章 罢工和停工

158. 一般原则

1/ 工人有权以本公告规定的方式罢工,以保护自己的利益。

2/ 雇主有权按照本公告规定的方式停工。

3/ 本条第(1)款和第(2)款的规定不适用于本公告第 137 条第(2)款所指企业的工人和雇主。

159. 需要满足的条件

在部分或全部发起罢工或停工之前,应采取以下措施:

1/ 发起罢工或停工的一方应提前通知另一方,说明其采取上述行动的原因;

2/ 双方应尽一切努力妥善解决劳动纠纷;

3/ 工人所举行的罢工,须有至少三分之二工会会员出席并经过半数支持;

4/ 应采取措施确保雇主和工人遵守企业的安全规定和事故预防程序。

160. 通知程序

1/ 根据本公告第159条第(1)款的规定,发起罢工或停工的一方必须向另一方以及劳动与社会事务部或有关当局发出通知。

2/ 本条第(1)款规定的通知应在采取行动前10天送达。

161. 禁止行为

1/ 在不影响本公告第160条第(1)款规定的情况下,如果在将纠纷提交委员会或法院后发起罢工或停工,并且在委员会作出任何指令或决定前30天或在法院作出决定前规定的期限内未结束,则罢工或停工是非法的。

2/ 拒绝执行或不适当地延迟执行全部或部分处理劳动纠纷的委员会或法院的指令或决定,或采取继续罢工或停工以抗议委员会或法院的指令或决定,均属违法;但是,如果罢工或停工是遵守该指令或决定的,则不构成违法。

3/ 禁止以暴力、武力威胁或任何非法行为进行罢工或停工。

第六章 费 用

162. 费用豁免

1/ 工人或工会、雇主或雇主协会依本公告第142条及第148条规定,向劳动关系委员会申请调解的案件,不得收取任何服务费用。

2/ 对于任何工人或工会提交给法院的劳动案件,不收取任何诉讼费用。

第十部分
时效期限和优先受偿权

第一章 时 效 期 限

163. 时效期限

1/ 除非本公告或其他相关法律规定了具体的时限,因雇佣关系产生的诉讼,从诉讼请求可执行之日起的一年后将失去时效。

2/ 由工人要求的恢复职务的申诉,从雇佣合同终止之日起的3个月后将失去时效。

3/ 由工人提起的关于工资、加班费、或其他报酬的索赔,从工资到期之日起的6个月后将不得提出。

4/ 在雇佣合同终止后6个月内如未提起诉讼,工人或雇主因雇佣合同终止而提出的任何付款要求均将被驳回。

5/ 有关法律应适用于本公告未涵盖的时效期限。

164. 时效期限的计算

1/ 除非本公告另有明确规定,否则时效期限应自权利产生之日起开始计算。

2/ 若时效期限的最后日期为非工作日,应顺延至下一个工作日。

165. 时效期限的中断

时效期限应被以下方式中断:

1/ 在作出最后决定前,负责裁定劳动纠纷的当局所采取的任何行动;

2/ 在作出最终书面决定之前,负责执行和实施本公告的主管当局所采取的任何行动;

3/ 其他部分关于索赔有效性的书面承认;但前提是以这种理由中断的时效期限次数不得超过 3 次。

166. 时效期限的放弃

任何一方均可放弃提出一段时效期间作为抗辩的权利;但在时效期限届满前放弃该权利无效。

167. 主管当局的自由裁量权

1/ 负责裁定劳动纠纷的机构确定迟延诉讼是由不可抗力造成的,可以在诉讼时效期满后受理;但是,应在不可抗力停止存在之日起 10 天内提起诉讼,否则不予受理。

2/ 在不影响本条第(1)款规定的一般性情况下,下列情况应视为不考虑时效期限的不可抗力:

a) 工人的疾病;

b) 为了完成工作任务而将工人调离居住地的;

c) 服兵役。

第二章 优先受偿权

168. 优先于其他债务

工人因雇佣关系提出的赔偿请求,应当优先于其他支付或者债务。

169. 赔偿支付的程序

1/ 如果企业被清算,执行人员、法律或法院授权执行清算的其他人员有义务在主管当局作出决定后 30 天内支付本公告第 168 条所述的索赔款项。

2/ 如果由于缺乏资产而未能在本条第(1)款规定的期限内支付索赔款项,则应在必要经费到账时尽快付款。

170. 家庭工人的留置权

如果企业被清算或停止经营,家庭工人可以对他们为该企业生产的货物行使留置权,且该留置权应与他们的索赔具有同等价值。该措施应被视为为执行本公告第 168 条规定的权利而采取的措施。

第十一部分
劳动法的执行

第一章 劳动管理

171. 劳动与社会事务部的权力

1/ 劳动与社会事务部可以发布执行本公告所必需的指令,特别是有关以下方面的指令:

a) 职业安全、健康和工作环境保护;

b) 工作条件标准;

c) 危险工种的确定;

d) 经与有关机构协商,确定对女工的健康和生殖系统特别有害或危险的工作类型;

e) 需要外国人工作许可的工作类型,及通常发放工作许可证的方式和私营职业介绍所在当地经营的条件;

f) 与其他有关机构协商,确定家庭工作合同的条件,需要提供学徒的职业类型以及与此有关的其他问题;

g) 职位空缺和求职者的登记程序;

h) 裁员程序;

i) 确定为支付工伤赔偿而安排保险范围所需的企业;

j) 常设咨询委员会的设立程序及其职权和责任;

k) 私营职业介绍所参与本地就业服务的条件;

l) 私营劳动监察服务提供者的认证要求程序;

m) 企业职业安全与卫生委员会的设立程序。

2/ 劳动与社会事务部应建立一个综合的劳动管理系统,以制定劳动法律和政策,协调、跟进和执行这些法律和政策,加强就业服务和劳动监察服务,并设立一个常设咨询委员会,该委员会由代表政府、雇主协会和工会的成员组成,负责就此提供咨询意见。

3/ 有关当局应建立一个由代表政府的成员组成的常设咨询委员会。雇主协会和工会将在研究和审查劳动法律和政策的执行情况以及就业服务和劳动监察服务的管理情况后,向其提供建议。

第一节 就业服务

172. 一般原则

就业服务应包括以下内容:

1/ 协助有能力并愿意工作的人获得工作;

2/ 协助雇主为其工作岗位招聘合适的工人;

3/ 确定在埃塞俄比亚雇佣外国国民的方式;

4/ 与有关部门和组织合作,编制培训计划;

5/ 进行与劳动力市场有关的研究;

6/ 与有关办事处合作,就如何改进国家一级的职业培训和如何向受益者分发培训以及如何适当执行就业政策进行研究。

173. 职业介绍所

职业介绍所应包括以下内容:

1/ 对求职者和职位空缺进行登记;

2/ 从登记的求职者中选择符合要求的求职者去竞争雇主通知的职位;

3/ 任何年满15周岁的求职者均可在提交必要文件后,由有关当局委托的机构进行登记。

174. 私营职业介绍所参与提供本地职业介绍服务的条件

为了促进提供全面的国家就业服务,私营职业介绍所可以按照政府发布的指令参与本地职业介绍服务。

175. 私营职业介绍所的许可证

1/ 任何人希望根据本公告从事私营职业介绍所的,均应从主管当局获得许可证。

2/ 有关当局应征收由部长理事会发布的法规规定的服务费,用于发放、更新、更换许可证。

176. 外籍人士的就业

1/ 任何外籍人士只有在持有劳动与社会事务部颁发的工作许可的情况下,才能在埃塞俄比亚从事任何类型的工作。

2/ 对于特定类型的工作,应给予三年期限的工作许可证,并每年续签一次;但是,劳动与社会事务部可以根据需要更改三年的期限。

3/ 如果劳动与社会事务部确定不需要外籍人士从事该工作的,则可以取消该工作许可证。

4/ 劳动与社会事务部可以依法对签发、续签或更换工作许可证收取服务费。

第二节 劳动监察机构

177. 劳动监察机构

劳动监察机构应当包括以下活动:

1/ 确保本公告的规定、根据本公告发布的法规和指令,以及其他与劳动关系有关的法律、登记的集体协议和负责裁定劳动纠纷的当局作出的决定和指令的执行;

2/ 开展研究、监督、教育和制定劳动标准,确保本公告和其他关于工作条件、职业安全、健康和工作环境的法律的规定得到执行;

3/ 编制职业病清单和伤残程度表;

4/ 对危险职业和事业进行分类;

5/ 进行有关工作条件的研究并汇编统计数据;

6/ 为工人制定培训计划,以防止工伤;

7/ 监督新企业的建立、现有企业的扩充与改造以及机器的安装,以确保工人的安全和健康;

8/ 采取行政措施以执行本公告以及根据本公告发布的法规和指令;

9/ 采取适当措施,要求负责裁定劳动纠纷的当局和法院执行本公告的规定,以及劳动监察机构在其合法活动中实施处罚;

10/ 向有意从事工作场所技术检查、咨询和培训的私人检查机构签发合格证书,并监督其工作表现。

178. 劳动监察员的权力和义务

1/ 劳动与社会事务部部长或有关当局应指派经授权的劳动监察员负责跟踪和监督监察服务。

2/ 在执行职责时,劳动监察员应持有由劳动与社会事务部或有关当局签发的带有公章的身份证。

3/ 劳动监察员有权在任何工作时间内进入其可能认为需要检查的任何工作场所,而无须事先通知,以便检查、测试或询问其是否遵守本公告第177条的规定,并应:

a) 单独或在证人在场的情况下讯问任何人;

b) 复制或提取任何纸张、文件或其他资料;

c) 在工作场所对任何物质进行取样并进行测试,以确保其不会对工人造成伤害;

d) 确保在适当的工作地点张贴相关的通知;

e）给任何工人拍照,并测量、绘制或测试建筑物、房间、汽车、工厂、机器或货物,并复制和登记文件,以确保工人的安全和健康。

4/ 如果根据本条第(3)款(c)项取样,应提前通知雇主,管理人或其代表有权到场。

179. 劳动监察应采取的措施

1/ 如果劳动监察员发现任何企业的场所、厂房、机器、设备、材料或工作方法对其工人的健康、安全或福利构成威胁的,则应指示雇主在规定的时间内采取必要的纠正措施。

2/ 如果雇主在收到依照本条第(1)款指示的规定时间内未能采取此类措施,则劳动监察员应发布指令,要求雇主:

a）为了防止对工人的健康、安全或福利造成威胁而必要现有条件的改变,必须在规定的时间内完成;

b）为防止对工人的安全或健康构成紧急的危险,必须立即采取任何措施。

3/ 如果劳动监察员对任何特定案件的技术或法律危险有疑问,应向劳动与社会事务部部长或有关当局报告,要求作出有关决定并据此下达指令。

180. 上诉

1/ 雇主对根据本公告第179条第(1)款及第(2)款发出的指令不服时,可于5个工作日内向主管法院提出上诉;但在上诉作出决定之前,劳动监察员为避免本公告第179条第(2)款(b)项所述的紧急的危险而发出的指令不得暂停执行。

2/ 法院对根据本条第(1)款提出的上诉裁决为最终裁决。如果在给定的时限内雇主没有上诉,则执行该决定。

181. 对劳动监察员的职能和责任的限制

1/ 劳动监察员应勤勉公正地履行职责,并考虑雇主和工人提出的任何合理建议。

2/ 劳动监察员在任何时间,无论在职或离职,都不得向任何人泄露其在根据本公告的规定完成其职责时可能获取的关于生产、商业的或其他工作过程的任何秘密。

3/ 除有关人员外,劳动监察员不得向任何人透露向其提出的关于法律条文缺陷或违反法律条文的投诉的来源,特别是,不得向任何雇主或其代表表示其视察是为了回应向劳动监察机构提出的投诉。

4/ 在任何情况下,劳动监察员均应将其对企业经营场所的视察通知该企业,除非其认为这种通知可能妨碍其职责的执行。

5/ 劳动监察员不得检查任何其拥有或与之有利害关系的企业。

6/ 劳动监察员应避免在劳动纠纷或集体谈判中充当调解人或仲裁人。

182. 禁止行为

下列行为应视为妨碍劳动监察员履行职责:

1/ 阻止劳动监察员进入工作场所或在场所内停留;

2/ 拒绝让劳动监察员检查与其任务有关的记录或文件;

3/ 隐瞒与工伤有关的日期及其发生的情况;

4/ 任何其他延迟或干扰劳动监察员行使职能的行为。

183. 私营监察机构

1/ 任何人可进行技术检查、咨询或培训,只须该人员经劳动与社会事务部或有关当局认证,可以从事需要特殊技能和技术资格的职业。

2/ 本条第(1)款规定的合格证书应由劳动与社会事务部或有关当局颁发。

3/ 为根据本条第(1)款颁发证书和其他相关问题而收取的服务费应由部长理事会条例规定。

第十二部分
行政措施和其他规定
第一章 行 政 措 施

184. 一般原则

在不违背刑事责任的情况下,依据第185条至第187条规定的行政措施均可以适用。

185. 对雇主的措施

1/ 雇主:

a) 使工人工作超出本公告规定的最长工作时间,或以任何方式违反有关工作时间的规定;

b) 违反本公告关于每周休息日、公共假日或休假的规定;或者

c) 违反本公告第19条的规定:考虑到其经济和组织地位以及过失发生的方式,如果是第一次违反,将被处以5 000比尔至10 000比尔的罚款;如果是第二次违反,处以10 000比尔至15 000比尔的罚款;如果是第三次违反,处以15 000比尔至30 000比尔的罚款;如果违规行为发生三次以上,则可能导致该企业被关闭。

2/ 雇主:

a) 未履行本公告第12条第(5)款规定的义务;

b) 未保存本公告或本公告项下发布的其他法律文书规定的记录,或未及时或未根据要求提交记录;

c) 违反本公告第14条第(1)款的规定;或者

d) 违反本公告第26条第(2)款的规定终止雇佣合同:考虑到其经济和组织地位以及过失发生的方式,如果是第一次违反,将被处以10 000比尔至20 000比尔的罚款;如果是第二次违反,将被处以20 000比尔至40 000比尔的罚款;如果是第三次违反,将被处以40 000比尔至60 000比尔的罚款;如果违规行为发生三次以上,则可能导致该企业被关闭。

186. 常用措施

1/ 任何雇主、雇主协会、雇主代表、工会或工会领袖:

a) 违反了根据本公告发布的有关工人安全的法规和指令,并实施了使工人的生命和健康面临严重危险或没有按照本公告的规定对女工或未成年工提供特殊保护的行为;

b) 违反本公告第117条的规定;

c) 违反本公告第161条的规定;

d) 不遵守劳动监察员根据本公告或其他法律规定发出的指令;

e) 故意向有关机构提交不准确的信息或申报,如果是第一次违反,处以5 000比尔至20 000比尔的罚款;如果是第二次违反,处以20 000比尔至40 000比尔的罚款;如果是第三次

违规,则处以最高 70 000 比尔的罚款;如果违规行为发生三次以上,则可能导致该企业被关闭。

2/ 考虑到企业的经济和组织地位或工会的一般设置以及违反行为的方式,违反本公告第 131 条第(2)款或第(4)款规定的任何雇主、工会、工会领袖或雇主代表,如果是第一次违反,则最高可处以 5 000 比尔至 20 000 比尔的罚款;如果第二次违反,则处以 20 000 比尔至 40 000 比尔的罚款;如果违规行为发生两次以上,则处以最高 70 000 比尔的罚款。

187. 针对私营职业介绍所的措施

1/ 未经本公告或根据本公告发布的法规和指令获得许可并在埃塞俄比亚从事职业介绍服务的任何人,应处以 5 年以上 10 年以下的有期徒刑并处以 100 000 比尔的罚款。

2/ 任何私营职业介绍所在其执照被吊销期间从事任何职业介绍活动的,应处以不少于 3 年以上 5 年以下有期徒刑,并处以 75 000 比尔的罚款。

3/ 除本条第(1)款和第(2)款规定的罪行外,任何违反根据本公告发布的法规或指令的人,应处以 2 年以下有期徒刑并处以最高为 75 000 比尔的罚款。

188. 提出诉讼的权力

劳动监察员有权对违反本公告规定和根据本公告发布的法规和指令的行为,向有管辖权的法院提起诉讼。

第二章 其他规定

189. 时效期限

本公告所涉及的任何种类的诉讼,必须在过失发生之日起一年内提起。

190. 暂行规定

尽管有本公告第 192 条的规定:

1/ 在不违反本公告的前提下,根据第 377/2003 号公告(经修订)发布的法规和指令应继续执行。

2/ 根据第 377/2003 号公告(经修订)缔结的集体协议应被视为已根据本公告缔结,并受本公告规定的约束。

3/ 根据第 377/2003 号公告(经修订)成立的工会和雇主协会,应视为已根据本公告成立。

4/ 根据第 377/2003 号公告(经修订)成立的劳动咨询委员会和劳动法庭委员会,应视为已根据本公告成立。

5/ 在本公告生效之前,任何劳动法庭尚未解决的劳动纠纷应按照先前的公告进行处理。

191. 残疾程度的确定

在根据本公告第 102 条第(1)款发布确定残疾程度的时间表之前,医疗委员会应继续定期进行残疾评估。

192. 废除法律

1/ 劳动公告第 377/2003 号公告、第 466/2005 号公告、第 494/2006 号公告和第 632/2009 号公告现予废除。

2/ 任何法律和惯例在与本公告不一致的情况下,对本公告规定的事项均不具有效力或作用。

193. 生效日期

本公告自其在《联邦政府公报》上刊登之日起生效。

2019 年 9 月 5 日在亚的斯亚贝巴签署

萨赫勒-沃克·祖德

埃塞俄比亚联邦民主共和国总统

第三编
税 收 法 规

第六部
联邦税收管理公告
(第 983/2016 号公告)

埃塞俄比亚联邦民主共和国联邦政府公报

第 22 年 103 号
2016 年 8 月 27 日,亚的斯亚贝巴

第 983/2016 号公告
联邦税收管理公告

鉴于有必要制定单独的、旨在规范国内税收管理的行政公告,增强税收管理系统的有效性、效率性和可衡量性;

鉴于引入预先税收裁定制度有助于解决由于税收征收管理部门内部对税收法律的不同解释而导致的纳税人案件长期搁置的问题;

鉴于有必要建立一个组织良好且能有效处理案件、审查纳税人对税收决定的申诉系统;

根据《埃塞俄比亚联邦民主共和国宪法》第55条第(1)款和第(11)款,现宣布如下:

第一部分
总　　则

1. 简称

本公告可称为《联邦税收管理第983/2016号公告》。

2. 定义

在税法(包括本公告)中,除非上下文另有规定,否则:

1/ "经修订的评估"是指管理局根据本公告第28条作出的经修订的评估;

2/ "可上诉决定"是指:

a) 反对决定;

b) 管理局根据税法作出的其他决定,但不包括:

(1) 税收决定;

(2) 管理局在作出税收决定期间作出的决定。

3/ "批准表格"具有本公告第79条的含义;

4/ "管理局"是指:

a) 埃塞俄比亚税务和海关总局;

b) 亚的斯亚贝巴税务局;和

c) 德雷达瓦税务局。

5/ "机构"是指在埃塞俄比亚或其他地方成立的公司、合伙企业、公共企业或公共金融机构,或其他个人机构;

6/ "委员会"是指根据本公告第86条设立的税务上诉委员会;

7/ "公司"是指根据《埃塞俄比亚商法典》成立的具有法人资格的商业组织,包括根据外国法律合并或成立的任何同等实体;

8/ 与公司有关的"控制成员"是指单独或与一个或多个相关人员一起直接或间接受益的持有以下权利的成员:

a) 公司会员权益附带的50%或以上的投票权；

b) 公司会员权益附带的50%或以上的股息权利；或者

c) 公司会员权益附带的50%或以上的资本权利。

9/"文件"包括：

a) 账簿、记录、登记册、银行对账单、收据、发票、凭证、合同或协议或进口报关单；

b) 持照税务代理人根据本公告第22条提供的证明或声明；或者

c) 电子数据存储设备上存储的任何信息或数据。

10/"预算税额"是指管理局根据本公告第26条作出的预算额；

11/"财政年度"是指埃塞俄比亚联邦民主共和国政府的预算年度；

12/"危险性评估"是指管理局根据本公告第27条进行的危险性评估；

13/"扣押令"是指管理局根据本公告第43条授权作出的扣押指令；

14/"国际协定"是指埃塞俄比亚联邦民主共和国政府与外国政府或国际组织之间的协定；

15/"国际组织"是指成员为主权国家或主权国家政府的组织；

16/"逾期纳税利息"是指根据（本公告）第37条征收的逾期纳税利息；

17/"持照税务代理人"是指根据本公告第96条或第97条获得许可的税务代理人；

18/"许可证颁发机构"是指根据任何法律授权颁发执照、许可证、证书、特许权或其他授权的任何机构；

19/"经理"是指：

a) 对于合伙企业，合伙企业的合伙人或总经理，或以该身份行事或拟以该身份行事的人；

b) 对于公司，为公司的首席执行官、董事、总经理，或其他类似人员，或以该身份行事或拟以该身份行事的人；

c) 对于任何其他机构，该机构的总经理或其他类似人员，或以该身份行事或拟以该身份行事的人。

20/"成员"，就机构而言，是指该机构中具有成员权益的人，包括公司的股东或合伙企业的合伙人；

21/"成员权益"，就机构而言，是指该机构的所有权权益，包括公司股份或合伙权益；

22/"部"或"部长"分别指财政和经济合作部或财政和经济合作部部长；

23/"合伙企业"是指根据《商法典》建立的合伙组织，包括根据外国法律成立的同等实体；

24/"罚款"是指违反本公告第15部分第2章规定或其他税法规定的税收行政处罚；

25/"罚款评估"是指管理局根据本公告第15部分第2章对处罚进行的评估；

26/"人员"是指个人、机构、政府、地方政府或国际组织；

27/"次要责任"指任何人根据本公告第16条第(4)款、第40条第(3)款(c)项、第41条第(12)款、第42条第(8)款、第43条第(10)款、第46条第(1)款、第47条第(1)款或第48条第(1)款承担的责任；

28/"自我评估"是指根据本公告第25条被视为自我评估纳税人所做的评估；

29/"自我评估申报"是指：

a）联邦所得税公告规定的纳税申报；

b）增值税公告规定的增值税申报表；

c）报关单，其中规定了与进口货物有关的增值税或消费税；

d）消费税公告中的消费税申报；

e）营业税公告规定的营业税申报表；

f）根据本公告第23条提出的预缴税款申报；或者

g）根据税法指定为自我评估申报的纳税申报。

30／"自我评估纳税人"是指需要提交自我评估申报的纳税人；

31／"税"是指根据税法征收的税款，包括以下内容：

a）预扣税；

b）根据联邦所得税公告预缴的税款和分期缴纳税款；

c）罚款；

d）逾期纳税利息；

e）根据联邦所得税公告应缴纳的任何其他税款。

32／"税收评估"是指自我评估、预计评估、危险评估、修订评估、罚款或利息评估或根据税法进行的任何其他评估；

33／"避税规定"是指以下各项的避税条款：

a）联邦所得税公告；和

b）增值税公告。

34／"税收决定"是指：

a）除自我评估外的税收评估；

b）对自我评估纳税人根据本公告第29条提出的申请的决定；

c）纳税人根据本公告第40条第（2）款应缴或将要缴纳的税额的确定；

d）从属责任或追回应付税款的费用确定；

e）逾期纳税利息的确定；

f）拒绝依第49条或第50条的规定申请退款的决定；

g）确定本公告第49条下的超额信用额度，本公告第50条下的退款额或根据本公告第50条要求偿还的退款额；

h）根据联邦所得税公告第92条第（3）款未缴的预扣税金额的确定。

35／"税收申报"是指：

a）根据联邦所得税公告要求提交的纳税申报；

b）根据联邦所得税公告要求提交的预扣税申报；

c）根据增值税公告要求提交的增值税纳税申报表；

d）海关入境规定的进口货物所应缴纳的增值税或消费税；

e）需要在消费税公告下提交的声明；

f）根据营业税公告要求提交的营业税申报表；

g）纳税人根据本公告要求提交的其他纳税申报表。

36／"税法"是指：

a) 本公告；

b) 联邦所得税公告；

c) 增值税公告；

d) 消费税公告；

e) 印花税公告；

f) 营业税公告；

g) 如果管理局负责税款、关税或征费的管理，与征收税款、关税或征费有关的任何其他法律(与海关有关的法规除外)；

h) 根据以上法律制定的任何法规或指令。

37/ "税务人员"是指：

a) 管理局局长；

b) 管理局的副秘书长；

c) 埃塞俄比亚税务和海关总局发布公告任命的负责税法的管理和执行的管理局官员或雇员；

d) 亚的斯亚贝巴和德雷达瓦市政府税务机关的官员或雇员；

e) 代表管理局履行职能时：

(1) 埃塞俄比亚联邦警察的成员；

(2) 埃塞俄比亚邮政服务部门的雇员或官员；

(3) 地方税务机关的雇员或官员。

38/ "纳税期间"，就某一税项而言，是指向管理局申报该税项的期间；

39/ "税收追回费用"是指：

a) 管理局在追缴本公告第30条第(3)款涉及的未缴税款所产生的费用；

b) 管理局在执行扣押程序中发生的本公告第41条第(9)款(a)项的费用；

40/ "税收代表"是指纳税人在埃塞俄比亚负责收支或付款的个人，包括以下人员：

a) 对于合伙企业而言，合伙企业合伙人或合伙企业的经理；

b) 对于公司而言，该公司的董事；

c) 对于无行为能力人而言，负责为其收取收益或代表其利益的法定代表。

d) 本公告第40条所指的与纳税人有关的接管人；

e) 对于任何纳税人而言，根据税法的规定，管理部门以书面形式通知其为纳税人的税收代表。

41/ "纳税人"是指负有纳税义务的个人，包括以下人员：

a) 就所得税而言，在一个纳税年度中没有应纳税所得额或享有免税优惠或承担在附表B项或C项下损失的个人；

b) 对于增值税，注册人或有义务注册增值税的人；

c) 对于营业税，营业额纳税人。

42/ "未缴税款"是指在到期日之前未缴纳的税款，或管理局根据本公告第32条将到期日延长，在到期日之前缴纳的税款；

43/ "预扣代理人"是指根据联邦所得税公告第十部分的规定，从付款中预扣税款的人；

44/ "预扣税"是指根据联邦所得税公告第10部分规定从付款中预扣的税款;

45/ 男性性别中的任何表达都包括女性。

3. 公允市场价值

1/ 为了贯彻税法的目的和遵守联邦所得税公告第79条的规定,商品、资产、服务或利益在特定时间和地点的公允市场价值是商品、资产、服务或利益在那个时间和地点的普通公开市场价值。

2/ 如果无法根据本条第(1)款确定商品、资产、服务或利益的公允市场价值,则公允市场价值是指任何类似商品、资产、服务或利益在那个时间和地点通常在公开市场上获得的对价,并根据类似商品、资产、服务或利益与实际商品、资产、服务或利益之间的差异进行调整。

3/ 本条第(2)款中,商品、资产、服务或利益在相同情形或其他情形下,与其他商品、资产、服务或利益在性质、质量、数量、功能、材料和声誉方面非常相似。

4/ 如果商品、资产、服务或利益的公允市场价值无法根据本条前面的子条款确定,则公允市场价值应为管理局确定的金额,该金额应遵循与普遍接受的价格一致的估价原则。

5/ 商品、资产、服务或利益的公允市场价值可以大于或小于商品、资产、服务或利益的实际价格。

6/ 管理局可以发布指令确定任何商品、资产、服务或利益的公允市场价值。

4. 关联人员

1/ 在税法和本条第(2)款的规定下,两个人之间的关系,一个人可以合理地被期望按照另一个人的指示、要求、建议或愿望行事,或者两个人都可以合理地被期望按照第三个人的指示、要求、建议或愿望行事,那么他们是关联人员。

2/ 仅仅因为一个人是另一个人的雇员或客户,或者两个人都是第三人的雇员或客户,两者不是关联人员。

3/ 在不违背本条第(1)款的一般性的前提下,以下为关联人员:

a) 个人及个人的亲属,除非管理局确信任何人均不得合理地期望按照他人的指示、要求、建议或愿望行事;

b) 一个机构和该机构的成员,该成员单独或与本条另一适用项所指的一个或多个关联人直接控制或通过一个或多个中间机构控制25%或更多的投票权、股利或资本时;

c) 一个人单独或与一个或多个关联人在本条的另一项规定适用下直接或通过一个或多个中间机构控制着两个机构25%或以上的投票权、股利或资本。

4/ 本条所称亲属是指:

a) 个人的配偶;

b) 个人或配偶的先辈、直系后代、兄弟、姐妹、叔叔、姑婶、侄子、侄女、继父、继母或养子女;

c) 个人或配偶的养子女的父母;

d) 本款(b)项所指的任何人的配偶。

5/ 本法所称个人的配偶是指:

a) 与个人合法结婚的人;

b) 与个人不定期地生活在一起的人。

6/ 在第一层血缘关系中,养子女被视为与其收养父母有亲属关系。

第二部分
税收法律的管理

5. 管理部门的职责

管理部门保障税法的执行。

6. 税务人员的职责和义务

1/ 税务人员应根据《埃塞俄比亚税收和海关当局设立公告》下的官员任命和《埃塞俄比亚税收和海关当局设立公告》第8条第(3)款下的权力或职责的任何委托,行使税法赋予官员的任何权力,或履行任何职责或职能。

2/ 税务人员应诚实公正行使权力,依照税法履行职责,礼貌和尊重地对待每一位纳税人。

3/ 在下列情形税务人员不得根据税法行使权力或履行职责:

a) 与税务人员有个人、家庭、业务、学业、雇佣或财务关系的;

b) 涉及利益冲突的。

4/ 税务人员或直接与税务事务有关的该部官员不得担任税务会计或顾问,不得接受任何准备税务申报或提供税务建议的人员的雇用。

7. 合作义务

所有联邦和州政府机关及其代理、机构、地方政府机关和协会及非政府组织都有义务与税务机关合作执行税法。

8. 税收信息的保密

1/ 任何税务人员应以其公职身份确保对收到的所有文件和信息保密。

2/ 本条第(1)款的规定不得阻止税务人员向以下人员披露文件或信息:

a) 另一位负责执行公务的税务人员;

b) 执法机构,就税法下的罪行指控某人或就税法下的相关罪行指控某人;

c) 在诉讼中确定某人的税务责任、罚款或逾期支付利息的责任,或在刑事案件中确定某人的税务责任、罚款或逾期支付利息的责任;

d) 在协议允许的范围内向与埃塞俄比亚订立协议的外国政府的主管当局提供交流信息;

e) 审计长因执行公务需要披露的;

f) 总检察长因履行公务需要披露的;

g) 地方税务局为履行公职而必须进行披露的;

h) 在税务局或统计部门为政府服务或进行研究的人员,披露信息对其履行公务是必要的,且披露信息未指明具体的人员;

i) 经该信息相关人员书面同意的其他人;

j) 法律规定的其他机关。

3/ 根据本条第(2)款收到信息的人员应该:

a) 维持资料的保密,但为达到准许披露资料的目的所需的最低限度除外;
b) 将反映该信息的所有文件退还管理局。

4/ 在本条中,"税务人员"包括:
a) 管理局顾问委员会的成员或前成员;
b) 管理局雇用或聘用的任何身份的人,包括承包商;
c) 管理局非在职成员、雇员或承包商。

第三部分
纳 税 人
第一章 登 记

9. 纳税人登记

1/ 在符合本条第(2)款和第(3)款的规定下,根据税法有责任纳税的人应向管理局申请登记,除非该人已经登记。

2/ 本条第(1)款不适用于:
a) 在埃塞俄比亚获得的唯一收入来源受联邦所得税公告第51条和第53条约束的非居民;
b) 唯一收入受联邦所得税公告第64条第2款约束的个人。

3/ 用人单位应当为在用人单位工作的职工申请登记,除非该职工已经登记。

4/ 用人单位没有为职工提出登记申请的,本条第(3)款不免除本条第(1)款规定的登记义务。

5/ 登记申请应:
a) 采取批准形式;
b) 连同该名人士的身份证明文件,包括该规例可能指明的生物识别标识;
c) 在法定申请注册的21天内或在管理局允许的更长期限内作出。

6/ 用人单位根据本条第(3)款向职工提出登记申请,该职工应提供本条第(5)款(b)项规定的生物识别标识。

7/ 除本条第(10)款另有规定外,依照本条第(1)款申请登记的义务,是除依照其他税法就某一特定税种申请登记的义务或选择外的另一种义务。

8/ 管理局应根据本条第(1)款规定为符合税法规定、享有纳税责任的登记申请人进行登记并以批准的形式颁发登记证书。

9/ 如果管理局拒绝对已提出登记申请的人进行登记,则管理局应在申请人提出登记申请后的14天内以书面形式将拒绝通知送达申请人。

10/ 根据本条第(1)款申请登记的,管理局应将登记时提供的资料用于税法规定或允许的该人员为某一特定税种进行的其他登记,而无须该人员另行提交任何登记表格。

11/ 尽管有本条第(10)款的规定,管理局仍可以要求申请人提供完成额外登记所必需的其他信息。

12/ 管理部门可以对未按照本条要求进行登记的人进行登记,并以批准的形式向该人颁发登记证书。

13/ 根据本条规定注册登记的,自注册证书上载明的日期起生效。

10. 变更通知

1/ 登记人应在以下内容发生更改后的30天内以书面形式通知管理局:

a) 登记人的姓名、实际地址、邮政地址、身体状况、主要活动或者其他活动;

b) 用于与管理部门交易的个人银行详细信息;

c) 登记人与管理部门通信的电子地址;

d) 管理部门发布的指令中指定的其他信息。

2/ 登记人根据本条第(1)款发出的变更通知,应被视为满足任何义务,即通知该登记人就另一税法项下的某一特定税务而发生的变更。

11. 注销登记

1/ 根据税法的规定不再需要登记的人应向管理局申请注销登记。

2/ 申请注销登记:

a) 以批准的形式;和

b) 就所有税法而言,在不再要求该人进行注册的30天内,或在管理部门允许的其他时间内。

3/ 根据本条第(1)款提出的申请,应视为满足该人根据其他税法为某一特定税务目的而申请注销登记的义务。

4/ 管理部门审查申请人已停止所有经营活动并不再满足税务目的而被要求注册的,应书面通知根据本条第(1)款提出注销登记的申请人。

5/ 根据本条第(4)款提出的注销登记通知应在收到申请后30天内送达申请人,管理部门可在注销登记通知送达后90天内对申请人的税务进行最后审计。

6/ 如果没有按照本条第(1)款的规定申请注销登记,管理局应书面通知该人或该人的税务代表,在以下情况下取消注销登记:确认已停止所有业务并且不再需要就所有税法进行登记的人,包括死亡的自然人、清算的公司或其他已经不存在的人。

7/ 根据本条第(4)款或第(6)款规定注销登记的,应包括依照其他税法为特定税种的注销登记。

8/ 注销登记自管理部门送达注销通知书中指明的日期起生效。

9/ 注销登记涉及注销另一税法规定的税务登记时,应当符合该另一税法规定的有关注销登记的要求。

第二章 纳税人识别号

12. 纳税人识别号

管理部门应当依照本章规定,向依照税法登记的纳税人颁发纳税人识别号("TIN"),纳税人应当按照税法的规定使用纳税人识别号。

13. TIN 的签发

1/ 管理部门应向根据本公告第9条为税法目的注册的纳税人签发 TIN。

2/ 出于所有税法的目的,应签发 TIN,纳税人有且只有一个 TIN。

3/ 管理局以书面通知向纳税人签发 TIN。

14. TIN 的使用

1/ 纳税人领取过 TIN 的,应当在为税法或者税法规定的其他目的申报、通知或者其他文件上载明,包括纳税人就预扣代理人对其支付的款项,向预扣代理人提供 TIN。

2/ 纳税人申请营业执照或者职业执照的,应当向许可机关提供纳税人的 TIN。

3/ 纳税人的 TIN 只有在自最初申请以来发生变化的情况下,才应在续签本条第(2)款所述的许可证时提供其 TIN。

4/ 颁发营业执照或者职业执照的机关,在纳税人没有提供其 TIN 的情况下,不得发给纳税人执照。

5/ 除本条第(6)款另有规定外,TIN 属于纳税人个人,其他人不得使用。

6/ 在下列情况下,持照税务代理人可以使用纳税人的 TIN:
a) 纳税人已书面同意持照税务代理人使用 TIN;和
b) 持照税务代理人仅在纳税人的税务事务中使用 TIN。

15. 取消 TIN

1/ 存在以下情况时,管理局应书面通知纳税人取消 TIN:
a) 根据本公告第 11 条,纳税人已注销登记;
b) 以非纳税人的真实身份向纳税人签发 TIN;
c) 先前已向纳税人签发了仍有效的 TIN。

2/ 管理局可以随时通过书面通知取消纳税人的 TIN,并向纳税人签发新的 TIN。

第三章 税 收 代 表

16. 税收代表的义务

1/ 纳税人的税收代表应负责履行税法规定的纳税人的任何义务,包括提交纳税申报表和缴纳税款。

2/ 纳税人有两个或两个以上税收代表的,则每个税收代表应对本条规定的任何义务承担连带责任,规定的义务可以由任何一方承担。

3/ 除税法另有规定外,依照本条第(4)款的规定,纳税人的税收代表依照本条第(1)款的规定应缴纳的税款,只能从税收代表处追缴,追缴的数额以纳税人税收代表持有或者控制的纳税人的货币、资产为限。

4/ 除本条第(5)款另有规定外,税收代表应以个人身份对应缴纳的税款负责,税款仍未缴纳时,税收代表应该:
a) 转让、收取或处置应收税款的已收或应计的任何款项;
b) 将属于纳税人的任何款项或资金进行处置或分拆,当税款可以合法地由该货币或基金支付时,这些款项或资金由税收代表持有,或在应缴税款后交给税收代表。

5/ 有下列情形之一的,税收代表对本条第(4)款规定的税款不承担个人责任:
a) 该款项由税收代表代表纳税人支付,其支付金额在法律上优先于纳税人应纳税额;或者
b) 在缴纳税款时,税收代表不知道也不能合理地期望知道纳税人的纳税义务。

6/ 本条的任何规定均不能免除纳税人履行根据税法规定的其税收代表未履行的纳税义务。

第四部分
文　　件

17. 记录保留义务

1/ 为遵守税法,纳税人应保存税法规定的文件(包括电子格式):

a) 阿姆哈拉语或英语;

b) 埃塞俄比亚;和

c) 确定纳税人在税法规定下的纳税义务。

2/ 除本条第(3)款或税法另有规定外,纳税人将本条第(1)款规定的文件保存为:

a)《商法典》规定的文件保存期限;或者

b) 自与纳税人相关的纳税申报表向管理局提交之日起的5年。

3/ 本条第(2)款规定的期间结束时,纳税人应保留根据公告或其他法律在该期间结束之前进行诉讼所必需的文件,直到诉讼程序和相关程序结束。

4/ 当本条第(1)款所指的文件不是阿姆哈拉语或英语时,管理局可通过书面通知,要求纳税人在通知的规定日期前由管理局批准的翻译人员翻译成阿姆哈拉语或英语,费用由纳税人承担。

5/ 尽管有本条第(1)款至第(4)款的规定,由部长发布的转让定价指令仍然适用。

18. 文件检查

根据税法要求保留文件的纳税人应在本公告第17条规定的期限内,在合理的时间将文件提供给管理局以备检查。

19. 收据

1/ 纳税人有设置账簿义务的,应当在印制发票前,向管理局登记发票种类和数量。

2/ 纳税人委托的印制收据的操作人员,应在印制收据前,确保已向管理局登记收据的种类和数量。

3/ 任何有义务维护账簿的纳税人均应开具收据。

4/ 管理局应发布实施本条的指示。

20. 销售登记机

1/ 部长会议应发布《销售登记机条例》。

2/ 该条例可对以下事项作出规定:

a) 纳税人必须使用销售登记机;

b) 纳税人使用销售登记机的条件;

c) 销售登记机出具的收据上包含的信息;

d) 销售登记机所需的功能;

e) 供应商申请认可销售登记机的程序及供应商的报告义务;

f) 对出售给纳税人的销售登记机进行登记。

3/ 本条规定：

a)"收银机"是指安装在电子可编程只读存储器芯片上的固件,并能记录商品或服务销售情况而不是普通的销售收据的机器；

b)"销售点机器"是指计算机化的收银机,具有记录和跟踪客户的订单以及借记卡和信用卡账户,管理库存以及执行类似功能的附加功能的机器；

c)"销售登记机"是指收银机和销售点机器。

第五部分
税收声明

21. 申报纳税

1/ 根据税法规定提交纳税申报表的纳税人,应以税法规定的批准格式和方式提交申报表。

2/ 除本条第(3)款另有规定外,管理局可通过书面通知要求纳税人在通知中规定的到期日之前提交：

a)就已提交的税务申报作出更完整的申报；或者

b)管理局在通知中指定的其他纳税声明。

3/ 本条第(2)款(a)项不适用于已提交的自我评估申报单。

4/ 管理局不受纳税人声明或纳税人提供的或代表纳税人提供的信息的约束,管理局可根据获得的任何可靠且可核实的信息来源确定纳税人的纳税责任。

5/ 在不违反本条第(6)款和本公告第82条的前提下,纳税人在其提交的纳税申报表上签字,纳税申报表应载明纳税人关于申报表及所附材料完整、准确的声明。

6/ 当纳税人为下列情形时,纳税人的税收代表或者持照税务代理人应当在纳税人的纳税申报表上签字,并作出本条第(5)款规定的声明：

a)非个人；

b)无行为能力的个人；或者

c)如果纳税人已向税收代表或者持照税务代理人提供书面签字的授权,则纳税人不再签字确认纳税申报声明。

7/ 当由纳税人的税收代表或者持照税务代理人签字确认纳税声明时,应认为纳税人知道该声明的内容,并应视为已经对本条第(5)款所述的完整性和准确性作了陈述。

22. 持照税务代理人纳税申报证明

1/ 持照税务代理人准备或协助准备纳税人的纳税申报表的,应向纳税人提供经批准的证明表格,证明持照税务代理人已审查纳税人的文件,该申报及相关文件在持照税务代理人所知范围内正确反映纳税申报涉及的数据和交易。

2/ 持照税务代理人拒绝提供本条第(1)款的证明,应向纳税人提供拒绝理由的书面陈述。

3/ 持照税务代理人编制或者协助编制纳税人纳税申报的,应当在申报书中载明是否向纳税人提供了本条第(1)款规定的证明或者本条第(2)款规定的声明。

4/ 持照税务代理人应在本公告第17条第(2)款规定的期限内,保留根据本条向纳税人提供的证明或声明的副本,并在需要时以书面通知的形式向管理局提交副本。

23. 预先纳税声明

1/ 纳税人停止从事任何活动的,应在停止从事该活动之日起 30 日内以书面形式通知管理局。

2/ 适用本条第(1)款的纳税人,应在停止活动之日起 60 天内,或在管理局书面通知纳税人的较短期限内:

a)就纳税人停止从事该活动的纳税期间以及未达到申报截止日期的任何前一个纳税期间,预先申报纳税;和

b)在提交申报单时支付预纳税申报单应缴的税款。

3/ 纳税人在纳税期间即将离开埃塞俄比亚,纳税人的离开不可能是暂时的,纳税人在离开前:

a)如果纳税人离境时尚未达到申报截止日期的纳税期间和以前的纳税期间,应当预先申报纳税;和

b)在提交申报单时支付根据预付税申报表应缴的税款,或管理局同意的其他应缴税款的安排。

4/ 在纳税期间,如果管理局有理由相信纳税人不会在纳税日前申报该纳税期间的税款,则管理局可以在纳税期间的任何时候通过书面通知要求:

a)纳税人或纳税人的税收代表在通知中指定的日期前提交该税收期的预先税收申报,该日期可在该纳税期间的纳税申报到期日前;和

b)在通知中指定的到期日之前缴纳根据预付税申报表应缴纳的任何税款。

5/ 如果纳税人需要缴纳一种以上的税,则分别适用本条。

6/ 本条所称"活动",是指根据税法产生应纳税所得额的业务或任何其他活动,但不包括产生应扣缴所得税作为最终税额的收入的活动。

24. 正式提交的纳税声明

纳税人申报纳税的,除证明有相反情况外,应当视为纳税人申报纳税或者经纳税人同意申报纳税。

第六部分
税 收 评 估

25. 自我评估

1/ 自评税纳税人如已就某课税年度以核准表格提出自评税申报,则本公告所述的纳税人在该课税年度内的应纳税额(包括无纳税额),即视为已就该课税年度内的应纳税额作出评估。

2/ 根据联邦所得税公告附表"B"或"C"规定,应缴纳所得税的自我评估纳税人以批准的形式提交了纳税期间的自我评估声明,并且纳税人在纳税期间有亏损,根据本公告的所有目的,应将该纳税人视为已对声明中所列损失金额进行了评估。

3/ 自我评估纳税人已依核定格式申报某一纳税年度的增值税纳税申报表,且该纳税年度

的进项税额超过该纳税年度的销项税额的,按本公告的所有规定,应将该纳税年度的超额进项税额视为已按该纳税年度申报的超额进项税额核定。

4/ 由纳税人填写并以电子方式提交的,具有批准格式的纳税申报单是自我评估申报表,须符合下列规定:

a) 表格包括管理局提供的预先填写的信息;

b) 应纳税额以电子方式计算,并在表格中填写相关信息。

26. 综合评估

1/ 纳税人未能按照税法规定在纳税期内提交纳税申报表的,管理局可根据已有证据,在任何时候,对下列事项作出评估(称为"综合评估"):

a) 在联邦所得税公告附表"B"或"C"项下发生损失的,为该纳税期间的损失金额;

b) 增值税公告项下的超额进项税,为该纳税期内的超额进项税额;

c) 在任何其他情况下,指该纳税期间的应纳税额(包括无纳税额)。

2/ 管理局应向根据本条第(1)款评估的纳税人送达评估报告,并书面通知纳税人,评估报告应载明下列事项:

a) 视情况而定的评估税额或结转的亏损或超额进项税额;

b) 就所评定的税款应缴纳的定额罚款(如有);

c) 就评定的税款应支付的滞纳金利息(如有);

d) 评估涉及的纳税期;

e) 缴税、罚款和利息的到期日是自通知送达之日起30天内;

f) 反对评估的方式,包括提出反对意见的期限。

3/ 本条第(2)款规定的估定税款通知书的送达,不得改变实施征税的税法所确定的估定税款的缴纳日期(称为"原缴纳日期"),逾期缴纳的罚款及其利息,仍按原缴纳日期缴纳。

4/ 本条仅适用于通过评估收取的税款。

5/ 本条的任何规定都不能免除纳税人提交与本条所送达的评估计税有关的纳税申报的义务。

6/ 在综合评估通知送达纳税人后,纳税人在纳税期间的税务申报不是自我评估申报。

7/ 管理局可随时进行评估。

8/ 管理局可发布实施本条的指示。

27. 危险评估

1/ 管理局可根据已有证据,在本公告第23条或第42条规定的情况下,对纳税人的应纳税额进行"危险评估"。

2/ 本条第(1)款仅在以下情况下适用:

a) 纳税人未在该纳税期间提交纳税申报表;和

b) 税收是通过评估收取的。

3/ 危险评估:

a) 可以在纳税人申报期限届满前申报;和

b) 应根据危险评估作出之日的现行法律进行。

4/ 管理局应向根据本条第(1)款评估的纳税人送达危险评估的书面通知,并具体说明以下内容：

a）评估的税额；

b）就所评定的税款应缴纳的罚款（如有）；

c）评估涉及的纳税期；

d）应缴税款和罚款的日期,该日期可以是应缴税款之前的一个日期；

e）反对评估的方式,包括对评估提出异议的期限。

5/ 管理局可以在危险评估通知中表明应立即缴纳的税款和罚款。

6/ 本条的任何规定均不得免除纳税人提交根据本条进行的危险性评估所涉及的纳税申报表的要求。

7/ 危险评估可以是根据本公告第28条修订的评估的主题,以便在所涉及的整个课税期间对纳税人进行危险评估。

8/ 将危险评估通知送达纳税人之后,纳税人在该期间提交的纳税申报不是自我评估申报。

28. 修订评估

1/ 按照本条规定,管理局可根据已有证据对税收评估（在本条中称为"原始评估"）进行变更、减免或增补,以确保：

a）如果根据联邦所得税公告附表"B"或"C"发生损失,则应根据纳税期间的正确损失额评估纳税人；

b）如果增值税公告规定的进项税额超过进项税额,则纳税人应按正确的进项税额纳税；

c）在任何其他情况下,纳税人应对纳税期应支付的正确税款（包括无纳税额）承担责任。

2/ 除税法另有规定外,管理局可根据本条第（1）款修订税收评估：

a）纳税人在任何时候发生欺诈、重大或故意疏忽的；或者

b）以下情况应在5年内修订：

（1）自我评估时,自我评估纳税人提交自我评估申报涉及的日期；

（2）就任何其他税项评税而言,管理局将评估通知送达纳税人的日期。

3/ 管理局在向纳税人送达根据本条第（1）款作出的修订评税通知书后,可在下列较后一种情况下进一步修订与修订评估有关的原始评估：

a）本条第（2）款（b）项规定的适用于原始评估的期限；或者

b）管理局在向纳税人送达已修订的评估通知1年后。

4/ 在本条第（3）款（b）项适用的任何情况下,管理局应仅限于在修订后的评估中对原评估所作的修改、减少或增加。

5/ 管理局应书面通知纳税人根据本条作出的修订评估,并具体说明以下内容：

a）与修订后的评估有关的原始评估以及做出修订评估的理由说明；

b）核定的税额或结转的损失或超额进项税额；

c）修订后的评估所定的罚款额（如有）；

d）就评定的税款应支付的滞纳金利息（如有）；

e）修订后的评估涉及的纳税期；

f) 根据修订后的评估应缴付的任何附加税、罚款和利息的到期日,为自通知送达之日起不少于 30 天的日期;

g) 反对修订后的评估的方式,包括对评估提出异议的时限。

6/ 如在修订评税项下须缴纳的附加税款额,任何有关该额外税项的迟缴罚款及迟缴利息,均须从与修订评税项有关的原评税项下的缴税到期日开始计算。

29. 申请对自我评估作出修订

1/ 已提交自我评估申报的纳税人可以向管理局申请,要求管理局对自我评估进行修订。

2/ 根据本条第(1)款提出的申请应:

a) 陈述纳税人认为需要作出的修订及作出修订的原因;

b) 在本公告第 28 条第 2 款(b)项(1)目规定的期限内提交给管理局。

3/ 根据本条第(1)款提出申请时,管理局应根据颁布的指令,在收到申请后的 120 天内作出修订自我评估或拒绝该申请的决定。

4/ 管理局决定修订自我评估的,则:

a) 修订后的评估应根据本公告第 28 条第(1)款做出;

b) 根据本公告第 28 条第(5)款,应将修订的评估通知送达纳税人。

5/ 管理局根据本条第(1)款拒绝修订申请的,应书面通知纳税人。

第七部分
征收和追缴税款和其他款项

第一章 缴纳税款及其他款项

30. 税收作为政府的债务

1/ 纳税人根据税法应缴纳的税款属于欠政府的债务,应向管理局缴纳。

2/ 纳税人应根据本公告第 82 条第(2)款的规定以电子方式缴纳税款,但经管理局以书面方式通知授权使用其他缴纳税款方式的除外。

3/ 纳税人未能在到期日前缴纳税款的,由纳税人承担管理局为追回未缴税款所产生的任何费用。

31. 次要债务和税收追回费用

1/ 管理局可向须承担次要债务或追缴税款费用的相关人员送达通知,并通知其须缴付的债款金额及缴付的到期日。

2/ 本公告的第七部分、八部分、九部分、十部分以及第 105 条中提及:

a) "税收",应包括次要债务和税收追回费用;

b) "未缴税款",应包括本款(a)项中规定的未在到期日支付的金额;

c) "纳税人",应包括对本款(a)项规定的金额负责的人。

3/ 个人支付的次要债务的金额,应当从与次要债务有关的纳税人的主要债务中抵免。

32. 延长纳税时间

1/ 纳税人可以书面形式向管理局申请延长缴纳税款的时间。

2/ 根据本条第(1)款提出申请的,管理局认为有正当理由的可发出以下指示:

a) 延长纳税人的纳税时间;或

b) 要求纳税人按管理局确定的分期付款方式缴纳税款。

3/ 管理局应当将对根据本条第(1)款的申请作出的决定书面通知纳税人。

4/ 根据本条第(2)款(b)项被允许分期缴纳税款的纳税人未按时缴付税款的,管理局可立即采取行动追讨拖欠税款的全部余额。

5/ 准予延期纳税或准予分期纳税,不免除从应缴税款之日起产生的逾期纳税利息的责任。

33. 税收优先权和扣押额

1/ 本条适用于以下税额:

a) 预扣税、增值税、营业税或消费税;和

b) 根据扣押令应支付的金额。

2/ 欠下、持有、收取或扣留本条适用的数额的人代表政府持有该数额,如果该人被清算或破产,则该数额:

a) 在清算或破产时,不构成清算或破产财产的一部分;和

b) 须在财产分配前先向管理局支付。

3/ 尽管有其他法律,但由个人享有的预扣税:

a) 不得就该人的任何债务或责任进行扣押;

b) 代扣代缴的税款或其他税款,应先行扣缴;和

c) 根据法院或法律的指令,纳税人从付款或金额中扣除其他款项之前应先扣除个人预扣税。

34. 纳税顺序

1/ 纳税人对与税务责任有关的罚款和滞纳金利息承担责任,其支付金额低于应缴税款、罚款和利息总额的,按下列顺序执行:

a) 首先,应纳税额;

b) 其次,滞纳金;

c) 然后,罚款。

2/ 纳税人在缴纳税款时有多项纳税义务,按纳税义务的产生顺序履行纳税义务。

35. 纳税担保

1/ 管理局认为有必要采取措施保障税收时,可要求纳税人以管理局认为适当的数额和方式提供担保:

a) 纳税人应缴或可能缴纳的税款;或

b) 纳税人根据税法要求退还税款的条件。

2/ 纳税担保可以通过现金或银行担保,并遵守管理局的其他合理要求。

3/ 纳税人在管理局送达以下通知时,有义务提供担保:

a) 担保的数额;

b) 提供担保的方式;和

c) 提供担保的到期日。

4/ 纳税人未按本条规定提供的保证金视为纳税人的未缴税款。

36. 保护

1/ 本条第（2）款的规定适用于以下人员：

a）根据联邦所得税公告从支付款项中扣缴税款并向管理局缴纳税款的扣缴义务人；

b）根据本公告第 16 条第（1）款向管理局缴纳税款的税收代表；

c）根据本公告第 40 条已向管理局付款的接管人；或者

d）根据扣押令已向管理局支付一定金额的人。

2/ 适用本条规定的人，不得因为按照税法代表纳税人向税务局缴纳税款而被起诉。

第二章　逾期纳税利息

37. 逾期纳税利息

1/ 除本条第（8）款规定外，纳税人未按本条第（2）款规定的期限缴纳税款的，从税款到期之日起至缴纳之日止，应按该期限内未缴纳的税款，以本条第（2）款规定的利率承担逾期纳税利息。

2/ 逾期纳税利率应是在本条第（1）款规定的期限开始前的第一个季度内在埃塞俄比亚实行的最高商业贷款利率的基础上提高 15%。

3/ 纳税人在本条第（1）款项下支付的逾期纳税利息，在发现与该利息有关的税款尚未支付时，应退还给纳税人。

4/ 根据本条规定应付逾期纳税利息，是在根据本公告第 105 条规定对未在到期日前缴纳税款的任何逾期纳税处罚之外的额外罚款。

5/ 逾期纳税利息应以单利按日计算。

6/ 管理局可通知逾期纳税人应付逾期纳税利息金额和付款到期日。

7/ 任何其他通知，包括税务局向纳税人发出的评税通知书，均可包括纳税人应付逾期纳税利息金额的通知。

8/ 在下列情况下，自通知之日至付款之日的期间内不产生逾期纳税利息：

a）管理局应以书面形式通知纳税人在税法（包括在税收评估中）规定中未履行的纳税义务；和

b）纳税人应在通知规定的时间内足额支付应纳税款的余额和截止到通知日期的逾期纳税利息。

9/ 个人因代扣代缴税款或者其应负的次要债务而逾期支付的利息，由该人自行承担，不得向他人追偿。

10/ 纳税人逾期支付利息的总额不得超过其应纳税额。

11/ 本条中"税款"不包括逾期纳税利息。

第三章　未缴税款的追回

38. 税收评估的执行

1/ 除本条第（2）款另有规定外，纳税人在本公告第 54 条允许的异议期内未对评估提出异议的，管理局对其核定的纳税评估在异议期满时为最终评估。

2/ 纳税人对税收评估提出异议的，下列情况中时间较晚的为最终评估：

a）如果纳税人未在本公告第 88 条规定的上诉期结束时向税务上诉委员会上诉税收评估的；

b）如果纳税人已在本公告第 57 条规定的联邦高等法院上诉期结束时，向税务上诉委员会上诉了税收评估的；

c）如果纳税人已在本公告第 58 条规定的联邦最高法院上诉期结束时，向联邦高等法院上诉税收评估的；或者

d）如果纳税人已在联邦最高法院作出最终裁决时向联邦最高法院上诉了该税收评估的。

3/ 根据本公告第 56 条第（2）款和第 57 条第（3）款，本条第（2）款的任何规定均不得阻止对争议税款的支付。

4/ 纳税人未支付根据本条第（1）款和第（2）款确定的最终评估应缴的税款，即为违约。

39. 优先求偿权

1/ 除本条第（2）款规定外，自纳税人依税法规定应纳税之日起，并在登记机关登记有担保债权前，登记机关对纳税人财产享有优先受偿权，直至纳税人缴纳税款为止。

2/ 在不违反本条第（7）款的情况下，本条第（1）款规定的优先担保债权应包括银行优先担保债权和与薪资有关的雇员优先担保债权，但不适用于本公告第 33 条第（1）款（a）项规定的税收。

3/ 当纳税人拖欠税款时，管理局可以书面通知纳税人，拟向登记机关申请将纳税人所拥有的任何资产的担保权益登记在案，以支付未缴税款及追回程序中产生的任何费用。

4/ 如果根据本条第（3）款收到通知的纳税人未能在通知送达后 30 天内缴纳通知中规定的税款，管理局可通过书面通知，指示登记机关在纳税人的利益范围内，将通知中规定的资产，为通知中规定的未缴税款提供担保。

5/ 当管理局根据本条第（4）款送达通知时，登记机关应免费将担保通知登记为抵押文书，或根据情况对通知中所述的资产收取费用，登记应在资产作为法定抵押权或抵押权存续期间进行，但须受任何在先抵押权或抵押权的约束，以获得未缴税款。

6/ 管理局在收到依本条第（5）款所担保的全部税款后，应立即通知登记机关撤销依本条第（4）款所作的指示，而登记机关应免费撤销担保通知书的登记。

7/ 根据本条第（2）款规定，银行对担保债权的优先权只适用于银行在发放任何贷款前，确认纳税人有管理局的完税证明的情形。

40. 接管人的职责

1/ 接管人应在被指定担任或拥有纳税人在埃塞俄比亚的资产后 14 天内以书面形式通知管理局。

2/ 管理局应确定纳税人的欠税额和资产受接管人控制的纳税人应缴纳的税额，并应在收到本条第（1）款通知后 30 天内以书面形式通知接管人。

3/ 在符合本条第（4）款的规定下，接管人：

a）在本条第（2）款规定的通知送达接管人或本条第（2）款规定的 30 天期限届满而未根据该条款规定送达通知之前，未经管理局事先批准，不得处置其在接管人控制下的纳税人的资产；

b）应从资产出售收益中拨出管理局根据本条第（2）款通知的金额，或管理局随后同意的

较小额度;和

c）对拥有资产的纳税人应缴纳的税款承担个人责任。

4/ 本条第(3)款任何规定均不妨碍接管人优先支付本条第(2)款通知的款项：

a）与根据本条第(2)款送达的通知中提及的税款具有法律优先权的债务；

b）接管人以接管人身份正当发生的费用,包括接管人的报酬。

5/ 如果两个或两个以上的人是纳税人的接管人,则本条规定的义务和责任连带适用于双方,但可由任何一方解除。

6/ 本条中,"接管人"是指纳税人或已故纳税人在埃塞俄比亚的资产满足以下任何一种情形的人：

a）公司的清算人；

b）法院或庭外任命的接管人；

c）破产管理人；

d）抵押权人；

e）遗产执行人。

41. 扣押财产

1/ 除本条第(2)款另有规定外,如果未在通知送达后30天内缴纳未缴税款,则管理局可向未按时缴纳税款的纳税人发出通知,说明管理局有意发出扣押令(简称"扣押令"),扣押纳税人的财产。

2/ 管理局发现纳税人缴纳税款有风险的,可立即签发扣押令。

3/ 纳税人未能在根据本条第(1)款或本条第(2)款送达的通知规定的期限内支付应付税款的,管理局可向纳税人以及拥有该纳税人财产的任何人发出扣押令。

4/ 扣押令可对纳税人的任何财产执行,但执行该指令时,纳税人的以下财产除外：

a）受债权人事先担保的债权；

b）在任何司法程序中都可能被扣押或执行的；或者

c）根据埃塞俄比亚法律不能被扣押的。

5/ 如果已对纳税人签发或将要签发扣押令,管理局可通过书面通知要求任何持有或控制载有与纳税人财产有关的证据或陈述文件的人,向管理局出示有关文件。

6/ 管理局可要求警务人员在执行扣押令期间在场,并应以确保财物安全的方式存放扣押的财物。

7/ 管理局根据本条扣押纳税人财产时,应向纳税人发出以下通知：

a）指明纳税人的扣押财产和未缴税款；

b）说明如果纳税人未按照通知规定的扣押期限缴纳税款的,管理局将处理该财产。

8/ 就本条第(7)款(b)项的而言,扣押期限为：

a）对于易腐货物,管理局根据货物状况认为的合理期限；

b）其他情况,为货物扣押后10天。

9/ 纳税人在扣押期结束前未缴清根据本条第(7)款送达的通知中指定的未付税款的,管理局可公开拍卖该财产,并按以下顺序使用收益：

a）首先,支付管理局确定的财产取得、保存和出售费用；

b) 其次,支付根据本条第(7)款送达的通知中指定的纳税人的未付税款;

c) 然后,支付纳税人的其他未缴税款;

d) 在不违反本条第(10)款的前提下,应将剩余的收益(如有)在出售财产后的45天内支付给纳税人。

10/ 经纳税人书面同意,可根据税法结转本条第(9)款(d)项提及的金额,以支付纳税人未来的任何纳税款项。

11/ 如果根据本条第(9)款公开拍卖出售财产的所得款项少于根据本条第(9)款确定的纳税人未缴税款与取得、保管和出售该财产的费用总额,管理局可根据本公告第七章的规定继续进行,以弥补差额。

12/ 未能或拒绝交出扣押令中的纳税人财产的个人应向政府承担未交出财产等额的价值,但不得超过纳税人未付的税款以及根据本条第(9)款(a)项确定的扣押费用。

13/ 根据本条发出扣押令的权力,只能由局长或由局长特别授权发出扣押令的税务官员行使。

14/ 根据本条扣押的财产应仅由管理局管理和核算,不得出于任何目的将该财产转移或转让给其他政府机构。

15/ 根据本条扣押财产的金额应与纳税人的应纳税额成比例。

42. 金融机构保留的资金和资产

1/ 管理局有合理理由认为纳税人的欠税行为处于危险之中并且迫切需要收取税费时,适用本条。

2/ 在适用本条的情况下,管理局可送达行政指令要求金融机构进行以下操作:

a) 冻结纳税人的账户;

b) 在金融机构持有的保管箱中冻结纳税人的现金、贵重物品、贵重金属或其他资产;和

c) 提供有关账户或保管箱内容的信息。

3/ 根据本条第(2)款向金融机构送达的指令,应指明该指令适用的纳税人的姓名、地址和 TIN。

4/ 根据本条第(2)款下达指令后,管理局可能会立即对纳税人当期和以前任何纳税年度应缴税款进行危险评估。

5/ 管理局应在指令通知送达金融机构后10天内,获得法院对该指令的授权。

6/ 如果在指令通知送达后10天内没有收到法院的指令授权,则该指令应失效。

7/ 根据本条第(2)款接受指令的金融机构,应自指令送达之日起至该指令根据其条款到期或根据第(6)款失效为止,均应遵守该指令。

8/ 如果金融机构在没有合理原因的情况下不遵守根据本条第(2)款向金融机构送达的指令,则应对该指令规定的金额承担个人责任。

43. 向第三方追缴未缴税费

1/ 纳税人未缴税款的,管理局可向纳税人有关的付款人发出行政指令(称为"扣押令"),要求付款人向管理局支付指令中指定的金额,但不超过未缴额。

2/ 扣押令要求付款人从支付给纳税人的工资、薪资或者其他类似报酬中定期扣除的,每次扣除的数额不得超过每次支付的工资、薪资或者其他报酬的三分之一(在缴纳所

得税后)。

3/ 仅在以下情况下,才可以在联名账户中向付款人送达扣押令:

a) 联名账户的所有持有人都有未付的税款;或者

b) 纳税人无须其他账户持有人的签名或授权,即可从账户(合伙账户除外)提取资金。

4/ 付款人应当在扣押令规定的日期以前支付扣押令规定的数额,但支付人对纳税人的款项应当到期或者代纳税人保管的日期之前支付。

5/ 声称无法遵守扣押令的付款人可以书面通知管理局,并在收到扣押令的 7 天内,说明付款人无法遵守该指令的原因。

6/ 付款人根据本条第(5)款向管理局送达通知时,管理局应书面通知:

a) 接受通知并取消或修改扣押令;或者

b) 拒绝该通知。

7/ 当纳税人已支付全部或部分应缴税款或已作出使管理局满意的支付税款的安排时,管理局应通过书面通知付款人,撤销或修改扣押令。

8/ 管理局应将根据本条送达给付款人的指令或通知的副本送达纳税人。

9/ 管理局应将付款人根据本条所付的任何款项抵充纳税人所欠的税款。

10/ 付款人在无合理原因的情况下未能遵守扣押令的,应对通知中规定的金额承担个人责任。

11/ 本条不适用于根据埃塞俄比亚法律不能作为扣押对象的任何数额。

12/ 本条所称付款人:

a) 欠或随后可能欠纳税人的钱;

b) 为纳税人持有或随后可能为纳税人持有金钱;

c) 代他人持有货币以支付给纳税人;

d) 从其他人那里获得向纳税人付款的授权。

44. 离境禁止令

1/ 管理局有理由认为纳税人可以离开埃塞俄比亚而不满足以下情形时,可限制纳税人的出境:

a) 已缴纳个人应缴或将要缴纳的税款;或者

b) 已缴纳由一个机构支付或将由该机构支付的税款,该机构中该人士为经理或公司中的控股成员。

2/ 在适用本条的情况下,管理局可以发布指令(称为"离境禁止令"),禁止相关人离开埃塞俄比亚,直到:

a) 个人、机构或公司全额缴纳应纳税额或应纳税款,将由个人、机构或公司支付;或者

b) 管理局认可本款(a)项缴纳税款的安排。

3/ 离境禁止令应规定以下内容:

a) 适用该指令人员的姓名、地址和 TIN;和

b) 个人、机构或公司应缴纳或将要缴纳的税额。

4/ 根据本条第(2)款发出的离境禁止令自发出之日起 10 日后失效,有管辖权的法院经管理局申请,可将该指令的有效期延长至法院决定的期间。

5/ 管理局应向离境禁止令中指定的人送达离境禁止令的副本,但未收到该指令的副本不影响根据本条提起诉讼的效力。

6/ 接到关于某人的离境禁止令后,国家情报和安全局局长应采取必要措施遵守该指令,包括扣押纳税人的护照、身份证件或任何其他授权纳税人离开埃塞俄比亚的文件。

7/ 个人、机构或公司缴纳了离境禁止令中规定的税款或作出了管理局同意的缴税安排,管理局应签发离境证明并向国家情报和安全局官员出示该证明,确保纳税人在满足其他移民要求的前提下离开埃塞俄比亚。

8/ 对于政府、税务、海关、国家情报和安全服务、警察或其他官员根据本条所做的任何合法行为,不得提起或维持任何刑事或民事诉讼。

9/ 离境禁止令只能由税务局长或税务局长特别授权的税务官签发。

45. 暂停营业

1/ 纳税人经常不符合下列规定的,适用本条:

a) 按照税法的规定保存文件;或者

b) 按时缴纳税款。

2/ 适用本条规定的,管理局可书面通知纳税人,拟在不超过 14 天的临时期限内关闭纳税人的部分或全部营业场所,纳税人在 7 天内缴纳应缴税款或按税法规定保存文件的除外。

3/ 如纳税人未遵守本条第(2)款规定的通知,或未能保留所需文件,管理局可以发布指令(称为"关闭令")以关闭纳税人部分或全部营业场所,但期限不得超过 14 天。

4/ 管理局执行关闭令时可进入关闭令中规定的任何处所,并可要求执行关闭令时有警察在场。

5/ 管理局应在关闭令涉及的处所的正面张贴以下字样的告示:

"因违反联邦税收管理公告第 45 条的规定暂时关闭。"

6/ 在下列情况下,管理局应重新开放纳税人的处所:

(a) 税务局长或其授权官员确信纳税人已采取足够的措施以确保将来妥善保存文件;

(b) 纳税人缴纳应缴税款。

7/ 关闭令只能由税务局长或税务局长特别授权的税务官发布。

46. 税收责任转移

1/ 纳税人(称为"转让人")承担与其经营业务相关的未缴纳税款义务,且纳税人已将该业务的全部或部分资产转让给关联人员(简称"受让人"),受让人应对转让人与业务有关的未付税款义务(简称"转让责任")承担个人责任。

2/ 本条第(1)款不妨碍管理局从转让人处追回全部或部分已转让的债务。

47. 机构应缴税款

1/ 如果一个机构在到期日之前未缴纳税款,未缴纳税款时的机构管理者或者在未缴纳税款前 6 个月内是该机构的管理者,对于未缴纳的税款应当承担连带责任。

2/ 本条第(1)款不适用于以下人员:

a) 没有经过管理者的认可或者该管理者不具有相关知识而导致该机构未缴纳税款;和

b) 在考虑到人的本性和所有情况下,该管理者采取了有效措施仍然未能阻止该机构未缴纳税款。

48. 欺诈或逃税的税收责任

1/ 一位注册审计师、注册会计师或公共审计师,他们:

a) 辅助、教唆、劝告或者促成纳税人进行欺诈,导致税收短缺或者逃税;

b) 在知情的情况下参与或与纳税人所从事的导致税收差额或逃税的欺诈行为有牵连,应与纳税人共同承担因欺诈或逃税所导致的税收差额或逃税的连带责任。

2/ 如果有根据本条第(1)款应承担责任的注册审计师、注册会计师或公共审计师,则管理局应将该行为报告给:

a) 注册会计师协会、埃塞俄比亚会计和审计委员会或有权对该人进行许可的其他机构,并要求理事会撤销该人的执业许可证;或者

b) 负责颁发营业执照的执照颁发机构。

3/ 在本条中的"税收差额"的具体规定见本公告第109条。

第八部分
抵免、退款、免除税务责任

49. 税收抵免

1/ 代扣代缴税款或预付税款的纳税人在一个纳税年度里其被允许的税收抵免总额超过所得税负债时,管理局应当按照以下顺序计算超额:

a) 首先,支付纳税人根据联邦所得税公告所欠的任何税款(预扣税除外);

b) 然后支付纳税人根据任何其他税法所欠的税款;

c) 在符合本条第(2)款规定的情况下,并经纳税人以书面通知提出申请后,在纳税人提交税收抵免当年的纳税申报单之日起90日内,将余款(如有)退还给纳税人。

2/ 经纳税人书面同意,可根据任何税法结转本条第(1)款(c)项所指的金额,以支付纳税人未来的任何应纳税额。

3/ 如果管理局未按照本条第(1)款(c)项的规定向纳税人支付退款,则该纳税人应享有从90日结束到实际退款期间的利息。

4/ 本条第(3)款规定的利率应是本条第(3)款规定的期限开始前一个季度在埃塞俄比亚实行的最高商业贷款利率。

50. 退还多缴的税款

1/ 在不违反本条第(2)款的情况下,如果纳税人根据税法(本公告第49条所规定的除外)多缴了税款,则纳税人可以审批表的形式向管理局提出申请,在缴纳税款之日起3年内退还多缴的税款。

2/ 本条仅在退税不要求管理局进行修订评估时适用。

3/ 管理局应将纳税人根据本条第(1)款提出的申请所作的决定以书面形式通知纳税人。

4/ 当纳税人根据本条第(1)款提出申请并且管理局确信纳税人根据税法已多缴税款时,管理局应按以下顺序适用于多付金额:

a) 首先,支付纳税人根据税法所欠的任何其他税款(预扣税除外);

b) 其次,支付纳税人根据任何其他税法所欠的税款;

c）然后,根据本条第(5)款的规定,在确定纳税人有权获得退款后的45天内将剩余的余额(如有)退还给纳税人。

5/ 经纳税人书面同意,可将本条第(4)款(c)项所述的金额结转以支付纳税人未来的任何应纳税款。

6/ 如果管理局错误地将本条规定的税款退还给纳税人,则纳税人应按照管理局的通知要求,在通知书规定的日期之前偿还错误退还的款额。

7/ 因纳税人申报退还错误而被错误支付的,应当按照本公告第37条第(2)款规定的从错误支付之日起至退还之日止的期间支付逾期纳税利息。

8/ 为了实现本公告的目的,纳税人根据本条第(7)款要求偿还的退款金额应被视为纳税人应纳税额。

51. 遇到严重困难时的减免

1/ 如果部长确信:

a）纳税人全部缴纳税款,因自然原因、随之而来的灾害、灾难,或者非因纳税人的疏忽或过失造成的个人困难,将会给纳税人造成严重困难;

b）由于纳税人死亡,其所欠全部税款的缴纳将给纳税人的家属带来严重困难的。

2/ 根据本条第(3)款的规定,如果适用本条,部长可以免除纳税人或已故纳税人遗产执行人全部或部分应缴纳的税款以及就应缴纳的税款应付的任何逾期利息。

3/ 根据本条第(1)款给予纳税人的减免应在部长会议发布的条例所规定的范围内。

4/ 如果部长基于欺诈或误导性信息而决定免除纳税人或已故纳税人遗产执行人税收的决定,则应恢复免除的纳税义务,并且本公告的适用应视为纳税人从未免除纳税义务。

5/ 部长应将根据本条规定免除的每笔税款和利息及其原因记录予以公开,并每半年向审计长报告一次。

第九部分
税 收 纠 纷

52. 声明的原因

当管理局拒绝根据税法提出申请的人时,拒绝通知应包括拒绝理由的说明。

53. 税收终结和上诉决定

1/ 除根据本部分进行的法律程序外:

a）税收或上诉决定应是最终决定性的,不得以任何理由在委员会或法院或任何其他程序中提出争议;

b）出示纳税评估通知书或税务处理决定书,或出示由管理局认证为纳税评估通知书或税务处理决定书的副本文件,应是作出适当评估或决定的最终证据,并且评估或决定的金额和详情是正确的;

c）在进行自我评估的情况下,出示自我评估申报的原件或由管理局证明为该申报的副本的文件应为申报内容的最终证据。

2/ 当管理局以电子方式向纳税人送达纳税评估通知书或纳务处理决定书时,本条第(1)

款（b）项所指的评估或决定通知书的副本包括一份经管理局认证的文件，该文件用于鉴定评估和决定，并指明评估或决定的电子传输的详细信息。

3／当纳税人以电子方式提交自我评估申报时，本条第（1）款（c）项中提及的申报副本包括由管理局认证的文件，该申报用于鉴定申报并指明申报的电子传输详细信息。

4／在本条中，"决定"是指本公告第2条（34）款中"税收决定"定义的（b）项，（c）项，（d）项，（f）项，（g）项或（h）项所指的决定。

54. 反对税收决定的通知

1／对税收决定不满意的纳税人可以在送达该决定通知后的21天内以书面形式向管理局提交反对该决定的通知。

2／当被反对的税收决定是一个修正评估时，纳税人对修正评估提出异议的权利应限于对原始评估所作的变更、减少和增加。

3／只有在满足以下条件时，纳税人根据本条第（1）款提交的异议通知才应被视为有效通知：

a）异议通知准确地说明了纳税人对税收决定提出异议的理由、纳税人认为必须作出的修正该决定的修改方案以及作出这些修改的理由；

b）纳税人就税收评估提出异议时，已缴纳了该纳税评估项下纳税人未在该异议中提出异议部分的应纳税额；和

c）纳税人在争议税款全部缴付后，仍愿意支付争议的评估税款。

4／当管理局认为纳税人提出的异议通知尚未有效提交时，管理局应立即将书面通知送达纳税人，并说明以下内容：

a）反对意见未得到有效提出的原因；和

b）异议将失效，除非随后提出有效异议：

（1）自异议相关的税收决定通知书送达之日起21天；或者

（2）自本款规定的通知送达之日起10天。

5／当根据本条第（4）款将异议视为已失效时，管理局应向纳税人发出书面通知。

6／纳税人可以在本条第（1）款的异议期限结束之前，以书面形式向管理局申请延长提交异议通知的期限。

7／当根据本条第（6）款提出申请时，管理局可允许自第（1）款中的异议期限结束之日起将时间延长最多10天。适用该条文需要满足以下条件：

a）由于没有在埃塞俄比亚、疾病或其他合理原因，在本条第（1）款或第（4）款规定的期限内，纳税人无法提出异议通知；和

b）纳税人提交异议通知没有不合理的延迟。

55. 做出异议决定

1／管理局应在其内部设立审查部门作为常设机构，以对根据本公告第54条有效提出的异议进行独立审查，并拟对异议作出的决定向管理局提出建议。

2／管理局应发布指令，规定审查异议的程序（包括听证会），以及向管理局提出建议的依据和作出决定程序。

3／如果审查部门对税收评估提出异议，认为应增加所评估的税收数额，则审查部门应建

议管理局将税收评估移交给税务人员复议。

4/ 在考虑了审查部门的建议后,管理局应作出决定,允许全部或部分异议,或不允许异议,该决定被称为"异议决定"。

5/ 管理局应书面通知纳税人异议决定,并采取一切必要的措施使该决定生效,如在对税收评估提出异议的情况下作出修正评估。

6/ 异议决定通知书应载对重要事实的调查结果陈述、决定的理由以及向委员会提出上诉的权利。

7/ 如果管理局在纳税人提出异议通知之日起的180天内没有作出异议决定,则纳税人可以在180天期限结束后的30天内向税务上诉委员会提出上诉。

56. 向税务上诉委员会提出上诉

1/ 不满意上诉决定的纳税人可根据本公告第88条向税务上诉委员会提出上诉通知。

2/ 向税务上诉委员会提出的有关对税收评估的异议的通知书,只有在纳税人已根据税收评估向管理局缴付了争议税的50%的情况下,才视为有效提交。

3/ 本条第(2)款对"争议税"的提及不应包括就争议税应支付的罚款和逾期纳税利息。

4/ 税务上诉委员会可发出指令,规定根据本条第(1)款申请延长提交上诉通知书的时间。

57. 向联邦高等法院上诉

1/ 对税务上诉委员会的决定不满的诉讼当事人可在收到决定通知后的30天内向联邦高等法院提出上诉通知。

2/ 联邦高等法院可应诉讼当事人向税务上诉委员会提出的书面申请,延长根据本条第(1)款提交上诉通知的时间。

3/ 纳税人就反对税收评估向联邦高等法院提出的上诉通知,只有在纳税人已缴付争议税的75%的情况下,才视为有效提交。

4/ 向联邦高等法院提出上诉仅应仅针对法律问题,并且上诉通知应说明将在上诉中提出的法律问题。

5/ 联邦高等法院应审理上诉,并可以:

a) 决定确认税务上诉委员会的决定;

b) 决定撤销税务上诉委员会的决定:

(1) 作出决定以取代税务上诉委员会的决定;或者

(2) 按照法院的指示将决定退回税务上诉委员会或管理局进行复议;或者

c) 决定驳回上诉;或者

d) 作出法院认为适当的其他决定。

6/ 本条第(3)款所称"争议税"是指由税务上诉委员会确定应缴纳的、由纳税人在上诉通知书中提出异议的税款,但不包括与争议税有关的罚款和逾期纳税利息。

58. 向联邦最高法院上诉

1/ 对联邦高等法院的决定不满的诉讼当事人,可在收到该决定通知后的30天内,向联邦最高法院提出上诉通知。

2/ 联邦最高法院可应诉讼当事人向联邦高等法院提出的书面申请,延长根据本条第(1)

款提出上诉通知的时间。

59. 举证责任

在根据本部分进行的有关税收决定的任何程序中,应由纳税人承担证明该税收决定不正确的责任。

60. 执行委员会或法院的决定

1/ 管理局应在接到税务上诉委员会、联邦高等法院或联邦最高法院的决定通知后的 30 天内采取行动,包括向纳税人提供修正评估通知,这是实施该决定所必需的。

2/ 本公告第 28 条规定的修改纳税评估的期限,不适用于为执行税务上诉委员会或法院的决定而作出的修改。

第十部分
信息收集和执行

61. 完税清单

1/ 纳税人可以以批准的形式向管理局申请完税证明。

2/ 如果纳税人认为纳税人已经履行了根据税务机关发出的指令所确定的税法纳税义务,则管理局应在纳税人根据本条第(1)款提出申请后的 14 天内,管理局向其颁发完税清单证明。

3/ 如果根据本条第(1)款提出申请的纳税人未在前一个或多个年份进行税收登记,则管理局应在纳税人提交纳税申报单,表明纳税人已在管理局注册后的 14 天内向纳税人签发纳税证明书。

4/ 除非纳税人出示完税证明,否则联邦或州政府的任何部、市、部门或办公室,或其他政府机构不得向纳税人签发或续签任何许可证,或允许纳税人参加公开招标。

5/ 如果管理局拒绝向纳税人签发完税证明,则管理局应在纳税人根据本条第(1)款提出申请后的 14 天内向纳税人提供该决定的通知。

62. 公司组织章程的备案

1/ 机构应在机构注册之日起 30 天内向管理局提交组织章程大纲、组织章程细则、章程、合伙协议或其他成立或注册文件的副本。

2/ 机构应在对本条第(1)款所指文件作出任何更改后 30 天内,以书面形式通知管理局。

63. 公共审计师

1/ 审计师应在向客户提供报告之日起 3 个月内向管理局提交其客户的审计报告。

2/ 如果审计师未遵守本条第(1)款的规定,管理局应将未通过的情况通知埃塞俄比亚会计和审计委员会或埃塞俄比亚注册会计师协会,并可要求委员会或协会撤销审计师的执照。

3/ 在本条中,"审计师"是指《财务报告公告》所定义的注册审计师和公共审计师。

64. 与非居民的服务合同通知

1/ 与非居民订立埃塞俄比亚来源服务合同的人,应在合同签订之日或合同开始履行之日起 30 日之内,以批准的形式通知管理局。

2/ 在本条中,"埃塞俄比亚来源服务合同"是指以履行服务为主要目的的合同(雇用合同除外），无论是否提供商品，这些服务给埃塞俄比亚带来了收入来源。

65. 取得信息或证据的通知

1/ 为了执行任何税法，管理局可以书面通知要求任何人是否应承担税负责任：

a）在通知规定的时间内提供与通知规定的该人或其他任何人有关的信息；

b）在通知指定的时间到通知指定的地点提供有关通知中指定的该人或其他任何人的税务的证据；

c）在通知规定的时间之前，出示由该人保管或由该人控制的与通知所指定的其他任何人的税务有关的所有文件。

2/ 当根据本条第(1)款发出的通知要求出示文件时，只要在通知中以合理的确定性描述文件即可。

3/ 下列情况下，本条仍具有效力：

a）与在提供信息或出示任何文件（包括电子格式）方面的特权或公共利益有关的任何法律；或者

b）任何合同保密义务。

66. 进入和搜索的权力

1/ 为了执行任何税法，管理局：

a）在任何时候都可以完全免费地获得以下资料，无须另行通知：

（1）任何处所、地方、物品或财产；

（2）任何文件；

（3）任何数据存储设备；

b）可以摘录或复制根据本款(a)项获得访问权的任何文件，包括电子格式的文件；

c）可以扣押管理局认为提供对确定纳税人的纳税义务可能具有重大意义的证据的任何文件，并可以保留确定纳税人的纳税义务所必需的或针对税法规定的任何程序的文件；

d）如果没有提供存储在数据存储设备上的信息的硬拷贝或在数据存储媒体上的副本，则可以在需要复制所需信息时扣押和保留该设备。

2/ 本条第(1)款的权力只能由局长或局长特别授权行使此权力的税务人员行使。

3/ 如果应所有人或合法占用人的要求，税务人员无法出示总干事的书面授权，允许其根据第(1)款行使权力，则税务人员不得进入或留在任何处所或场所。

4/ 根据本条第(1)款行使权力所涉及的处所或场所的所有人或合法占用人，应向管理局提供所有合理的设施和协助，包括：

（a）不论是在数据存储设备上还是在其他地方，以口头或书面方式回答与该处所或该处所的任何文件有关的问题；或者

（b）提供对解密信息的访问权限，该解密信息是解密根据本条要求访问的数据所必需的。

5/ 根据本条第(1)款扣押了文件或数据存储设备的人，可在正常办公时间内，按照管理局规定的条款和条件，自费检查并复印文件，包括在数据存储设备上的电子文件副本。

6/ 局长或局长授权的税务人员应签字确认根据本条移走和保留的任何文件或数据存储设备。

7/ 下列情况下，本条仍具有效力：

a）任何有关特权（包括法律职业特权）的法律或有关进入处所或场所的公共利益的法律，或有关出示任何财产或文件（包括电子格式）的法律；或者

b）任何保密的合同义务。

67. 行政互助协议的执行

1/ 部长可以代表政府与外国政府签订、修改或终止行政互助协议。

2/ 如果在埃塞俄比亚具有法律效力的行政互助协议的条款与税法之间有任何冲突，则以行政互助协议为准。

3/ 如果在埃塞俄比亚具有法律效力的税收条约或行政互助协议规定了情报交换或相互协助以追回税款或提供程序，则管理局应使用本公告或任何其他法律赋予的权力履行埃塞俄比亚根据条约或协定承担的义务：

a）"税"，包括与信息交换或相互协助有关的外国税；

b）"未缴税款"包括本款（a）项中规定的在到期日之前尚未支付的款项；

c）"纳税人"包括应承担本款（a）项规定的金额的人；

d）"税法"包括根据本款（a）项规定征收外国税的法律。

4/ 在本条中：

a）"国际协议"是指埃塞俄比亚联邦民主共和国政府与一个或多个外国政府之间的协议；

b）"行政互助协议"是指与税收事项有关的行政互助的税收信息交换协议或其他国际协议；

c）"税收协定"是指与避免双重征税和防止逃税有关的国际协定。

第十一部分
事 前 裁 定

第一章 公 开 裁 定

68. 具有约束力的公开裁定

1/ 本部可以根据本公告第69条作出公开裁定，其中规定了本部适用税法的解释。

2/ 根据本公告第69条作出的公开裁定，将对本部和管理局具有约束力，直至被撤销。

3/ 公开裁定对纳税人不具有约束力。

69. 作出公开裁定

1/ 本部应通过在本部的官方网站上发布公告的方式作出公开裁定。

2/ 公开裁定应声明该裁定为公开裁定，并应有标题，标明裁定的标的和识别号。

3/ 公开裁定自公开裁定规定之日起生效，未规定日期的自该裁定在本部的官方网站上发布之日起生效。

4/ 公开裁定阐明本部在裁定规定的情况下对适用税法的意见，而不是本部就本公告或任何其他法律的目的作出的决定。

70. 撤销公开裁定

1/ 本部可以通过在本部的官方网站上发布撤销通知来全部或部分撤销公开裁定，撤销自以下日期中的较晚日期起生效：

a）撤销通知中指定的日期；或者

b) 撤销裁定的通知在本部的官方网站上公布的日期。

2/ 当法案通过或本部作出另一项与现有公开裁定不一致的公开裁定时,自实施不一致的法案或公开裁定之日起,在存在不一致的范围内,原有公开裁定应被视为撤销。

3/ 已全部或部分撤销的公开裁定:

a) 应继续适用于在公开裁定被撤销前开始的交易;

b) 在公开裁定被撤销后开始的交易不适用。

第二章 私人裁定

71. 具有约束力的私人裁定

1/ 纳税人可以向本部申请私人裁定,阐明本部关于将税法适用于由纳税人进行或拟进行的交易的立场。

2/ 根据本条提出的申请应采用书面形式,并:

a) 包括与申请有关的交易的全部信息,以及与交易有关的所有文件;

b) 明确提出需要裁定的问题;

c) 提供一份完整的说明,列出纳税人对于该交易适用相关税法的意见。

3/ 在不违反本公告第 72 条的前提下,本部应在收到根据本条提出的申请之日起 60 天内,向纳税人发布关于该问题的私人裁定。

4/ 如果纳税人已完全和真实地披露了与作出私人裁定有关的交易的所有方面,并且该交易已按照纳税人对私人裁定的申请书中的描述在所有重大方面进行,则私人裁定对本部和管理局具有约束力。

5/ 私人裁定对纳税人不具有约束力。

6/ 当私人裁定与作出私人裁定时有效的公开裁定不一致时,在不一致的范围内,私人裁定优先适用。

72. 拒绝私人裁定申请

1/ 如果符合以下任何条件,则本部可以拒绝纳税人的私人裁定申请:

a) 管理局或本部(视情况而定)已在以下方面对该申请主题的问题作出决定:

(1) 纳税人税收评估通知书已送达;

(2) 根据本公告第 69 条作出的公开裁定已生效;

(3) 根据本公告第 71 条发布的私人裁定已生效。

b) 申请涉及与纳税人有关的税务审计问题、纳税人提出的异议或纳税人根据本公告第 29 条提出的自我评估的修订申请;

c) 申请无正当理由或无充分事由的;

d) 与该申请有关的交易尚未进行,并且有合理的理由相信该交易将不会进行;

e) 纳税人未向本部提供足够的信息据以作出私人裁定;

f) 本部认为,考虑到符合该申请所需的资源以及本部认为相关的其他事项,遵守该申请是不合理的;

g) 裁定的作出涉及避税条款的适用问题。

2/ 本部应向纳税人送达拒绝根据本条作出私人裁决的书面通知。

73. 作出私人裁定

1/ 本部应通过向纳税人提供私人裁定的书面通知作出私人裁定,该裁定应在裁定中指定的期间内持续有效,或在指定的日期前已根据本公告第74条的规定撤销。

2/ 本部可以根据对未来事件或其他适当情况的假设作出私人裁定。

3/ 私人裁定应声明其为私人裁定,列出所裁决的问题,并包含以下内容:

a)纳税人;

b)与私人裁定有关的税法;

c)该裁定适用的纳税期限;

d)该裁定所涉及的交易;

e)裁定所依据的任何假设。

4/ 私人裁定阐明了本部对裁定申请中提出问题的意见,而不是本部就本公告或任何其他法律的目的作出的决定。

74. 撤销私人裁定

1/ 本部可以基于合理的理由,通过向纳税人发出书面通知全部或部分撤销私人裁定,撤销应自撤销通知中指定的日期起生效。

2/ 立法通过,或者本部作出的公开裁定与现有的私人裁定不一致的,自不一致的立法或公开裁定适用之日起,在不一致的范围内,私人裁定将被视为撤销。

3/ 已撤销的私人裁定:

a)应继续适用于在撤销裁定之前开始的纳税人交易;和

b)裁定撤销后开始的纳税人交易,在裁定撤销的范围内,不得适用。

75. 公布私人裁定

1/ 本部应在其官方网站上发布根据本公告第73条作出的私人裁定,但裁定所涉及的纳税人的身份以及裁定中提及的任何机密商业信息不得在出版物中注明。

2/ 除本条第(3)款另有规定外,纳税人可以依据本条第(1)款的规定,就本裁定所列事实、本裁定所涉纳税期间以及有关税法的适用问题,向本部和管理局作出具有约束力的声明。

3/ 根据本公告第74条撤销私人裁定后,本部应立即在本部的官方网站上发布撤销通知,声明该裁定自本公告第74条确定的日期起不再具有约束力。

第三章 本部的其他建议

76. 管理局提供的其他建议

本部提供的任何出版物或其他建议(口头或书面建议)对本部或管理局均不具有约束力,但根据本部分具有约束力的公共裁定或私人裁定除外。

第十二部分
通讯、表格和通知

77. 工作语言

阿姆哈拉语应是税法的联邦语言;管理局可拒绝承认任何非阿姆哈拉语的通信或文件。

78. 表格和通知

1/ 管理局批准或发布的表格、通知、税收声明、报表、表格和其他文件,可以是管理局为有效管理税法而确定的格式,除非税法要求,否则无须在管理局的官方网站上发布此类文件。

2/ 管理局应将本条第(1)款所指的文件在管理局的办公室和其他任何地点公开提供,或以邮寄、电子方式或通过管理局确定的其他方式提供给公众。

79. 批准表格

1/ 纳税申报表、申请书、通知书、声明或其他文件,在下列情况下应视为由纳税人以批准的格式提交:

a) 采用管理局批准的文件格式;

b) 包含表格要求的信息(包括任何所附文件);和

c) 按表格要求签名。

2/ 如果该纳税人提交的纳税申报、申请、通知、声明或其他文件不符合格式要求,管理局应立即以书面形式通知纳税人。

3/ 如果所提交的文件实质上包含批准表格要求的文件信息,则管理局可决定接受未按批准表格形式提交的文件。

80. 向管理局提交文件的方式

1/ 管理局根据本公告第82条第(2)款要求纳税人以电子方式向管理局提交纳税申报、申请、通知、声明或其他文件,除非经管理局书面通知授权根据本条第(2)款提交文件。

2/ 当本条第(1)款不适用于纳税人时,纳税人应根据税法以亲自交付或普通邮递的方式向管理局提交纳税申报、申请、通知、声明或其他文件。

81. 送达通知书

1/ 管理局根据税法向纳税人发出、送达或给出的通知或其他文件,应通过以下方式书面通知:

a) 亲自将其交付给纳税人或纳税人的税收代表或持照税务代理人。如果找不到任何人接收,则将通知贴在纳税人在埃塞俄比亚的营业场所或住所的门上或其他可用部分上;

b) 用挂号信将其送达到纳税人在埃塞俄比亚的经常或最后营业地点或住所;

c) 根据本公告第82条第(3)款以电子方式将其送达给纳税人。

2/ 如果本条第(1)款规定的任何一种送达方式均无效,则可以在任何可以刊登法院公告的报纸上以公开的形式解除公告,并向纳税人收取公告费用。

3/ 在完全遵守或部分遵守了通知书或文件之后,不得质疑根据税法提供的通知书或其他文件的有效性。

82. 电子税收系统的适用

1/ 尽管本公告有其他条款的规定,但管理局可以授权通过计算机系统或移动电子设备以电子方式进行以下操作:

a) 根据税法提交注册申请或TIN申请;

b) 根据税法提交纳税申报表或其他文件;

c）根据税法缴纳的税款或其他款项；
d）根据税法支付退款；
e）管理局提供的任何文件；
f）税法规定或允许的其他行为或事情。

2/ 在符合本条第（4）款的规定下，管理局可以指示纳税人使用计算机系统或移动电子设备以电子方式执行本条（1）款中提及的任何事情。

3/ 在符合本条第（4）款的规定下，管理局可以通过使用计算机系统或移动电子设备以电子方式处理本条第（1）款中提及的任何事宜。

4/ 如果管理局确信纳税人没有能力以电子方式接收或进行通信或付款，则本条第（2）款和第（3）款不适用于该纳税人。

5/ 纳税人根据本条提交纳税申报表并以电子方式纳税，除非得到管理局的其他授权，否则纳税人应继续这样做。

83. 提交文件或缴纳税款的截止日期

如果以下行为的截止日期：

1/ 提交纳税申报、申请、通知、声明或其他文件；

2/ 缴税；

3/ 根据税法从事的其他任何行为。

在埃塞俄比亚的周六、周日或公共假日，截止日期则应为下一个工作日。

84. 不影响通知书有效性的瑕疵

1/ 本条适用于以下情形：

a）根据税法已将税收评估通知书或任何其他文件送达纳税人；

b）该通知实质上与该通知所依据的税法相符，或与之目的和意义相符；

c）根据共同的意图和理解，被评估、拟被评估或受通知影响的纳税人在通知中被指定。

2/ 适用本条时：

a）只要提供了适当的税收评估通知书或其他文件通知，该通知书就不会因未遵守该通知书所依据的税法规定而受到影响；

b）不应将税收评估或其他文件的通知因形式不规范而被撤销或视为无效或可撤销；

c）税收评估或其他文件的通知不因其中的错误、瑕疵或遗漏而受到影响。

3/ 税收评估不得因以下原因而作废：

a）税收评估中关于被评估纳税人名称、收入或其他金额的描述或应纳税金的错误；

b）税收评估与已妥为送达的税收评估通知书有任何差异；

前提是该错误或差异不太可能欺骗或误导被评估的纳税人。

85. 错误更正

管理局根据税法向纳税人提供的税收评估通知书或其他文件中包含文书、算术或其他任何不涉及法律解释或案件事实争议的错误时，为了纠正错误，管理局可以在送达税收评估通知书或其他文件通知送达之日起的 5 年内尽快修改税收评估书或其他文件。

第十三部分
税务上诉委员会

86. 成立税务上诉委员会
1/ 特此设立税务上诉委员会,以听取针对可上诉决定的上诉。
2/ 委员会主席由总理任命。
3/ 委员会应对总理负责。

87. 任命委员会委员
1/ 总理应考虑到委员会的需要,任命总理认为必要人数的委员会委员。
2/ 在不违反本条第(3)款的前提下,如果个人满足以下任何一项条件,则可以被任命为委员会委员:
 a) 该个人是在税务或商业事务方面具有丰富经验的律师;
 b) 该个人是注册会计师协会的成员,在税务上具有丰富经验;
 c) 该个人曾担任税务人员,在税务上具有丰富的技术和行政经验;
 d) 该个人具有与委员会职能有关的特殊知识、经验或技能。
3/ 以下人员不得被任命为委员会委员:
 a) 在职税务人员或停止担任税务人员未满两年的个人;
 b) 根据与避税或逃税有关的税法被处罚或被定罪的个人;
 c) 根据《腐败犯罪公告》或任何其他法律被判犯有腐败罪的个人;
 d) 未解除破产的个人。
4/ 委员会委员:
 a) 可以被任命为全职或兼职委员;
 b) 任期三年,可以连任;
 c) 应按总理确定的条款和条件就职,包括与报酬和出勤费有关的条款和条件。
5/ 在下列情况下,委员会委员的个人任命应终止:
 a) 该人被雇用或聘为税务人员;
 b) 个人根据与避税或逃税有关的税法,应承担处罚或被定罪的责任;
 c) 根据《腐败犯罪公告》或任何其他法律,该人被判犯有腐败罪;
 d) 个人成为未解除破产的人;
 e) 个人以书面形式向总理提出辞职;
 f) 个人的任期届满,而且没有再次被任命为委员会委员;或者
 g) 个人因无法履行职务或经证实有不当行为而被总理以书面通知的形式免职。
6/ 委员会委员在正当履行本部分规定的职责时的任何作为或不作为,概不承担任何诉讼责任。

88. 上诉通知书
1/ 任何人可对可上诉的决定,以批准的表格形式向委员会提交上诉通知书,并在送达有关决定通知书后30天内提出。

2/ 上诉通知书应包括对上诉理由的陈述。

3/ 如果有充分理由，委员会可以提出书面申请，延长根据本条第(1)款提交上诉通知书的时间。

4/ 委员会可发布指令，指定处理延期提交上诉通知书的程序。

5/ 在本条中，"批准的形式"是指委员会主席批准的有关上诉通知的形式。

89. 有权向委员会提交文件

1/ 管理局应在收到上诉通知书副本后30天内，或在委员会可能允许的其他时间内，向委员会提交：

a) 与上诉通知书有关的上诉决定通知书；

b) 如果本款(a)项所指的通知中没有列出作出决定的理由，则应说明作出该决定的理由；

c) 与委员会审查该决定有关的任何其他文件。

2/ 如果委员会对根据本条第(1)款(b)项提交的陈述不满，委员会可通过书面通知要求管理局在通知指定的时间内提交进一步的理由说明。

3/ 如果委员会认为其他文件可能与上诉有关，则委员会可通过书面通知要求管理局在通知规定的时间内向委员会提交文件。

4/ 管理局应将根据本条向委员会提交的任何陈述或文件的副本提供给上诉人。

90. 委员会诉讼程序

1/ 委员会主席应担任委员会其中一个小组的成员。委员会主席应考虑上诉提出的问题，在主席认为适当的情况下，指派一名或多名成员参加上诉听证。

2/ 总理可发布指示，指导委员会进行诉讼。

3/ 委员会成员在任何程序中有重大利益、金钱利益或其他利益，而且该利益可能与履行其职能的正常工作相抵触时，应将该利益汇报给委员会主席，委员会主席应进行记录，且该成员应不参加诉讼。

4/ 委员会主席可将权力下放给地区税务上诉委员会，以听取根据本公告第88条提出的任何上诉。

91. 委员会的决定

1/ 委员会应听取并确定本条第(5)款或第(7)款规定的上诉并作出决定。

2/ 委员会应在上诉通知提出后的120日之内作出上诉决定。

3/ 考虑到案件的复杂性和司法利益，委员会主席可书面通知上诉当事方，将决定上诉的期限延长至不超过60天。

4/ 委员会未能遵守本条第(2)款或第(3)款，不影响委员会就上诉作出的决定的有效性。

5/ 如果上诉涉及税收评估，则委员会可以作出以下决定：

a) 确认、减少或以其他方式修改税收评估；或者

b) 按照委员会的指示，将税收评估退回管理局重新审议。

6/ 如果委员会在考虑与税收评估有关的上诉时认为应增加所评估的税收金额，则委员会应根据第(5)款(b)项将税收评估退回管理局重新审议。

7/ 如果上诉涉及任何其他可上诉决定，则委员会可作出确认、更改或撤销该决定的决定，或根据委员会的指示将决定退回管理局重新审议。

8/ 委员会应在作出决定后的 7 日内将上诉决定的副本送达上诉各方。

9/ 委员会的决定应包括作出决定的理由和对重大事实问题的调查结果,并提及这些调查结果所依据的证据或其他材料。

10/ 委员会关于上诉的决定一经作出便生效,或者由委员会在决定通知中指定的其他日期生效。

11/ 如果委员会的决定有利于纳税人,则管理局应在收到根据本条第(8)款作出的决定的通知之日起 30 日内实施执行该决定所需的步骤,包括送达经修订的评估通知。

92. 委员会的行政事项

1/ 委员会主席应负责管理委员会的行政事务。

2/ 委员会应设有书记官和主席确定的其他工作人员。

3/ 委员会书记官应有权执行本条第(1)款规定的协助主席的一切必要或方便的事情,并可以代表主席就委员会的行政事务行事。

93. 财政

1/ 委员会的预算由政府分配。

2/ 委员会应保留完整且准确的账簿。

3/ 委员会的账簿和其他财务文件应由审计长或审计长指定的审计员审计。

94. 委员会的年度报告

1/ 委员会主席应为每个财政年度编写委员会事务报告。

2/ 根据本条第(1)款提交的财政年度报告应在财政年度结束后的 3 个月内提交总理。

第十四部分
税收代理许可

95. 申请税务代理人执照

1/ 希望提供税务代理服务的个人,合伙企业或公司可以以批准的形式向管理局申请税务代理许可。

2/ 在本部分中,"税务代理服务"是指:

a) 代表纳税人准备纳税申报表;

b) 代表纳税人准备异议通知书;

c) 就适用税法向纳税人提供咨询;

d) 代表纳税人与管理局交涉;

e) 代表纳税人与管理局进行任何其他业务的交易。

96. 税务代理人的执照

1/ 管理局在确认申请人为提供税务代理服务的合适人选后,应根据本公告第 95 条向个人申请人签发税务代理人执照。

2/ 管理局应在满足以下条件的情况下,根据本公告第 95 条的规定,向作为合伙企业的申请人签发税务代理人执照:

a) 合伙企业的合伙人或雇员为提供税务代理服务的合适人选;和

b）合伙企业中的各合伙人都具有良好的品格且为人正直。

3/ 管理局应在满足以下条件的情况下，根据本公告第95条向属于公司的申请人签发税务代理人执照：

a）公司的雇员是提供税务代理服务的合适人选；和

b）公司的每位董事，经理和其他执行官都具有良好的品格并且正直。

4/ 该规定可为确定一个人何时适合及适宜提供税务代理人服务提供指引。

5/ 管理局应根据本公告第95条的规定，以书面形式将申请决定通知申请人。

6/ 签发给税务代理人的执照自签发之日起生效，有效期为3年，并可根据本公告第97条进行续期。

7/ 管理局可以随时以其确定的方式发布获得税务代理人许可的名单。

8/ 税务代理人执照是专业执照，只有取得了营业执照后，税务代理人才能从事税务代理业务。

97. 税务代理人执照的续期

1/ 税务代理人可以向管理局提供该税务代理人执照续期申请。

2/ 根据本条第(1)款提出的申请应为：

a）以批准的形式；和

b）在税务代理人执照期满之日起21日内或在管理局允许的延后日期内向管理局提交。

3/ 如果税务代理人继续满足第96条的许可条件，则管理局应根据本条第(1)款对提出申请的税务代理人执照进行续期。

4/ 税务代理人的续期自续期之日起3年内有效，并可根据本条继续续期。

5/ 管理局应根据本条第(1)款向申请人提供书面通知，说明申请的决定。

98. 提供税务代理服务的限制

1/ 除本条第(2)款规定的持照税务代理人以外的任何人都不得提供有偿税务代理服务。

2/ 除第95条第(2)款(a)项"税务代理人服务"定义规定的服务外，本条第(1)款不适用于执业律师在其职业的一般过程中提供的税务代理服务。

99. 取消税务代理人执照

1/ 持照税务代理人应在停止从事税务代理人业务之前7日内书面通知管理局。

2/ 当税务代理人不想继续成为持照税务代理人时，可以书面形式向管理局申请取消税务代理人的执照。

3/ 存在下列情况之一的，管理局应取消税务代理人的执照：

a）由税务代理人准备和提交的税务申报存在严重虚假信息，除非税务代理人让管理局确信这不是由于税务代理人的任何故意或疏忽行为造成的；

b）税务代理人不再满足作为税务代理人的许可条件，或管理局认为该税务代理人有职业不当行为；

c）税务代理人已停止作为税务代理人开展业务，包括在公司或合伙企业的情况下，该公司或合伙企业不复存在；

d）税务代理人已根据本条第(2)款申请注销税务代理人执照；

e）税务代理人的执照已过期，并且该代理人尚未根据本公告第97条提出执照续期申请。

4/ 管理局应以书面形式通知注销税务代理人执照的决定。

5/ 税务代理人执照的注销应自下列日期中较早的日期起生效：

a) 税务代理人停止从事税务代理人业务之日；或者

b) 在向税务代理送达注销通知后60天。

6/ 尽管有税法的规定，但如果管理局认为某持照税务代理人有职业不当行为，管理局应将其不当行为报告给：

a) 注册会计师协会、埃塞俄比亚会计和审计委员会或有权授权该人担任会计师、审计师或律师的其他机构（视情况而定）；和

b) 负责颁发营业执照的发证机构。

第十五部分
行政、刑事处罚和奖励

第一章　一　般　规　定

100. 行政和刑事责任的一般规定

1/ 如果一项作为或不作为同时引起行政和刑事责任，则不应仅因其负有行政责任就免除行为人的刑事责任。

2/ 受到行政处罚评估或被刑事起诉的纳税人不应免除应缴税款的责任。

第二章　行　政　处　罚

101. 有关登记及取消登记的处罚

1/ 除本公告规定的其他行政处罚外，未按本公告规定申请登记的，对申请人处以应缴税款25%的罚款，从申请登记之日起至提交登记申请之日止或到管理局自行申请登记之日止付清。

2/ 如果纳税人没有本条第(1)款所述的应纳税额，则纳税人应自当日起每月或从应纳税之日起至实际登记之日止，每月缴纳1 000比尔的罚款。

3/ 如果根据本条第(1)款规定的处罚金额少于根据本条第(2)款规定的处罚，则应适用本条第(2)款的处罚。

4/ 无正当理由未按本公告规定申请注销登记的，自被要求注销登记之日起至其提交注销登记申请之日或被当局自行撤销登记之日止，或不足一个月的，将被处以每个月1 000比尔以下的罚款。

102. 未能保存文件的处罚

1/ 除本条第(2)款另有规定的以外，纳税人未按税法规定保存相关文件的，则应对纳税人处以其未保存单据的纳税期间根据税法应纳税额的20%的罚款。

2/ 如果纳税人在本条第(1)款所称未纳税期间内没有纳税的，处以罚款：

a) 纳税人未能保存纳税单据的，每个纳税年度处以20 000比尔罚款；或者

b) 纳税人未能保存其他任何税收目的单据的，处以每个纳税期间2 000比尔罚款。

3/ 依照本条第(1)款规定的处罚金额少于根据本条第(2)款规定的处罚时，应适用本条

第(2)款中的罚款。

4/ 在不影响本条第(1)款,第(2)款和第(3)款的情况下,负责签发营业执照的发证机关应在管理局通知下,撤销未保存单证超过2年的纳税人的营业执照。

5/ "A"类纳税人未在第17条第(2)款指定的期间内保留文件,应处以50 000比尔的罚款。

6/ "B"类纳税人未在联邦所得税公告第33条第(4)款规定的期限内保留文件,应处以20 000比尔的罚款。

103. 关于TIN的处罚

1/ 纳税人未在税收发票,税收借方或贷方通知单,税收申报单或税法要求的任何其他文件上注明其TIN的,每项失误将被处以3 000比尔的罚款。

2/ 除本公告第14条第(6)款适用外,如果纳税人有下列行为,则应处以10 000比尔的罚款:

a) 提供其TIN供其他人使用;

b) 使用他人的TIN。

3/ 如果纳税人或他人因本条第(2)款(a)项或(b)项所述的行为而获得的金钱利益超过10 000比尔,则罚款应与纳税人获得的金钱利益相同。

104. 逾期提交的处罚

1/ 任何人如未能在到期日之前提交纳税申报表,则应对与失误相关的每个纳税期或不足该纳税期的部分,追缴迟缴的未缴税款的5%的罚款,但追缴的罚款不得超过未缴税款的25%。

2/ 根据本条第(1)款,规定纳税人未提交第一个纳税期或其一部分的纳税申报表所承担的罚款,不得超过50 000比尔。

3/ 就本条而言,未缴税款是指应在税单中填报的税额与到期日已缴税款之间的差额。

4/ 在任何情况下,处罚不得低于以下最低额:

a) 10 000比尔;

b) 应在税单中填报的税额的100%。

5/ 虽有本条规定,但纳税人在纳税期间不缴纳税款的,对未提交纳税申报的每一个纳税期间,应当处以10 000比尔的罚款。

105. 逾期付款的处罚

1/ 纳税人未在到期日之前缴纳税款的,应承担以下滞纳金:

a) 到期日后一个月或不足一个月的期限内仍未缴纳的未缴税款的5%;

b) 每个月或其后一个月,在税款仍未缴纳情况下,额外缴纳未缴税款的2%。

2/ 根据本条核定的罚款金额不得超过其应纳税额。

3/ 纳税人已缴纳的滞纳金,如发现不应缴纳的,依照本公告第50条第(4)款的规定退还纳税人。

4/ 本条不适用于本公告第106条关于未缴税款的规定。

106. 预扣税处罚

1/ 根据联邦所得税公告的要求,未预扣税或已预扣税的人未向管理局缴纳税款,应就应预扣或实际预扣但未移交给管理局的税款处以 10% 的罚款。

2/ 当本条第(1)款适用于某机构时,除了该款规定的处罚外,该机构的经理,总会计师或该机构负责确保预扣税付款的人员,应处以每笔 2 000 比尔的罚款。

3/ 当适用联邦所得税公告第 92 条时,供应商和购买者均应分别承担 20 000 比尔的罚款。

4/ 根据联邦所得税公告第 92 条,为避免预扣税,拒绝向根据该条负有预扣税义务的人提供货物或服务者应承担 10 000 比尔的罚款。

107. 增值税处罚

1/ 未按《增值税公告》规定申请登记的人,从被要求登记之日起至提交登记申请之日或经管理局自行登记之日止,每个月或不足一个月的罚款为 2 000 比尔。

2/ 除本条第(1)款规定的罚款外,该条所适用的人还应付对该人自被要求申请登记之日起至被要求提交登记申请之日或被管理局自行申请登记之日止的应缴纳增值税所得额 100% 的罚款。

3/ 依照本条第(2)款的规定处罚,不得免除该人在该条规定的期间内所进行的应税交易中应缴纳的增值税责任,但应纳增值税额应扣除该人在这些交易中支付的所有营业税。

4/ 故意开具不正确的纳税发票,导致应税交易中应纳税额减少或者应纳税交易中可抵扣的增值税增加的人,处以 50 000 比尔的罚款。

108. 未能开具税务发票

纳税人未按规定开具税务发票的,对于每笔未开具税务发票的交易应缴纳 50 000 比尔的罚款。

109. 少报税款的处罚

1/ 纳税人申报的应纳税税额少于其应缴纳的正确税额(差额称为"税收短缺"),应处以不足税额 10% 的罚款。

2/ 对于本条第二次适用于纳税人的情况,应将本条第(1)款规定的罚款提高至 30%。

3/ 对于本条第三次或以后适用于纳税人的情况,应将本条第(1)款规定的罚款提高至 40%。

4/ 纳税人提交自我评估申报前,本部未对其申报作出裁定的,纳税人对该税法的适用采取合理的争议立场,造成税收差额的,不受本条规定的处罚。

110. 避税处罚

税务局在评定纳税人时如发现已采用了避税条款,纳税人应承担一项避税处罚,应为适用反避税条款应免征税款两倍的避税罚款。

111. 不遵守电子税收制度的处罚

1/ 当管理局根据税法要求纳税人提交纳税申报表或以电子方式缴税而纳税人未履行时,管理局应以书面形式通知纳税人,以让其提供未履行的原因。

2/ 纳税人在本条第(1)款项下的通知送达之日起 14 日内,未提交纳税申报或者未以电子方式缴纳税款的,且未向管理局提供足以使其满意的理由时,应承担相当于 50 000 比尔的罚款。

112. 税务代理人的处罚

如果持照税务代理人未能满足以下条件,则应处以 10 000 比尔的罚款:

1/ 根据本公告第 22 条的要求向其客户提供证书或声明;

2/ 在本公告第 22 条第(4)款规定的期限内提供给客户的证书和声明;

3/ 根据本公告第 99 条第(1)款的要求通知管理局,税务代理人已停止从事税务代理人业务。

113. 与销售登记机有关的罚款

1/ 使用销售登记机的任何人,如有以下行为应受到处罚:

a) 如果被发现使用未经税务机关认可或注册的销售登记机或销售软件的,应处 50 000 比尔罚款;

b) 在无收据或发票的情况下进行交易,或使用非销售登记机生成的其他收据,应处 50 000 比尔罚款,机器正在维修或任何其他正当理由除外;

c) 如果造成对财政记录的破坏或改变,或试图造成对财政记录的破坏或改变的,应处以 100 000 比尔罚款;

d) 用于阻止税务人员检查销售登记机的审核系统,或未由服务中心进行年度机器检查的,应处以 25 000 比尔罚款;

e) 没有与授权服务中心签订有效的服务合同就使用正在运行的销售登记机,或者未连接终端就使用销售登记机,或者未保留除销售登记机以外的检查手册,或用于开具退款收据而未在退款书中正确记录退货或客户要求退款的内容的,应处以 25 000 比尔罚款;

f) 未通知税务部门和机器服务中心由于盗窃或无法弥补的损坏而在导致销售登记机停止使用 3 天内或由于其他原因未在 4 小时内报告机器故障的,应处以 10 000 比尔罚款;

g) 没有通知税务局正在使用销售登记机的正确营业地点,应处以 50 000 比尔罚款;

h) 未能在终止营业的情况下提前 3 天通知税务局更改名称或地址或未通知税务部门和服务中心的,应处以 25 000 比尔罚款;

i) 没有在安装机器的地方张贴包含以下任意一项或全部信息的明显告示的,应处以 10 000 比尔罚款:

(1) 销售登记机的用户名称,商号,营业地点,纳税人身份证号码,认可证号和许可证号;

(2) 出具文字说明"在发生机器故障的情况下,销售人员必须出具经税务部门授权的手工收据";

(3) 文字显示为"如果未开具收据,请勿付款"。

j) 由未经税务局认可的人员更改或改进销售机器软件的,应处以 30 000 比尔罚款。

2/ 经认可并被允许提供销售登记机或软件的任何人,如有以下行为应承担以下罚款:

a) 未能将营业地址的变更通知税务局的,应处以 100 000 比尔罚款;

b) 出售未经税务局认可的销售登记机,应处以 500 000 比尔罚款;

c) 未能从税务局获得每台销售登记机的机器注册码,或者未在机器的可见部分上粘贴机器码标签的,应处以 50 000 比尔罚款;

d) 没有预先通知税务局对使用中的销售登记机进行任何更改,或者未插入或添加不正确的信息,或者未从指导销售使用的手册中删除正确的信息的,应处以 100 000 比尔罚款;

e) 无法更换因盗窃或持续不可弥补的损坏导致销售登记机的丢失,未能在服务中心要求的 3 天内提前通知税务部门的,应处以 50 000 比尔罚款;

f) 未保留与已签字确认协议的服务中心有关的信息,或者未将与服务中心终止的合同或新订立的协议通知税务局的,应处以 50 000 比尔罚款。

3/ 任何销售注册处机器服务中心如有以下行为,应承担以下罚款:

a) 未在更改销售登记机的财务记录后 2 天内向税务局报告的,应处以 20 000 比尔罚款;

b) 未能对合同规定的销售登记机进行年度技术检查的,应处以 20 000 比尔罚款;

c) 安排未经供应商认证且未在税务局注册的人员,每安排一人应处以 50 000 比尔罚款。

114. 其他处罚

1/ 未按本公告第 10 条的规定通知任何变更的纳税人,应处以 20 000 比尔的罚款。

2/ 未按照本公告第 62 条的规定向管理局提交组织章程大纲,组织章程细则,章程,合伙协议或其他组建或注册文件或对该文件的任何修改,管理局对于未归档的文件每个月或不足一月的,处以 10 000 比尔的罚款。

3/ 未按照本公告第 63 条的规定向管理局提交审计报告的公共审计员,应就该未归档的文件每个月或不足一月的处以 10 000 比尔罚款。

4/ 本条第(3)款规定的罚款是埃塞俄比亚会计和审计委员会针对公共审计员执照采取的任何措施之外的补充。

5/ 任何人如果未按照本公告第 64 条的规定通知管理局的,应处以每天 1 000 比尔的罚款。

6/ 如果纳税人未按照联邦所得税公告第 79 条的规定提供与相关人员的交易详细信息的,则应处以 100 000 比尔的罚款。

7/ 任何有义务提供信息的人未按管理局要求提供信息的,负有提供信息的人或组织负责人,应处以 5 000 比尔的罚款。

115. 行政处罚评估

1/ 管理部门应当向被判处行政处罚的人提供经评估的处罚通知。

2/ 如果同一行为或不作为可能涉及一项以上税收的行政处罚,则应在对每种税收分别进行评估之后,将这些罚款汇总。

3/ 负有行政处罚责任的人可以以书面形式向管理局申请豁免应缴罚款,并且该申请应包括要求减免的理由。

4/ 根据本条第(3)款的要求,管理局可自行或根据其动议,全部或部分免除根据管理部门发布的指令对任何人施加的行政罚款。

5/ 管理局应保留每项被豁免行政处罚的公开记录,并每季度向本部报告一次。

第三章 税 收 犯 罪

116. 税收犯罪案件的程序

1/ 税收犯罪违反埃塞俄比亚刑法,应根据埃塞俄比亚《刑事诉讼法》被起诉和被提出上诉。

2/ 违反本章税法的犯罪行为,应被解释为违反该税法的单独犯罪行为,并根据有关规定对每项犯罪行为处以规定的罚款。

117. 有关 TIN 的犯罪

1/ 个人:

a）获取或试图获取多个 TIN；
b）允许其他人使用自己的 TIN；
c）使用他人的 TIN；
如有以上行为，处以 20 000 比尔的罚款和 1 至 3 年有期徒刑。

2/ 本条第(1)款(a)项分别适用于获取或试图获取的每个 TIN。

3/ 本条第(1)款(b)项和(c)项不适用于在本公告第 14 条第(6)款规定的情况下使用 TIN。

118. 虚假或误导性陈述和欺诈性文件

1/ 意图欺骗管理局或不计后果的人：
a）向管理局作出虚假或误导性陈述；或者
b）在没有充分理由的情况下，遗漏本应包含在可能会误导管理部门声明中的任何细节；
c）向管理局提供欺诈性文件的，处以 50 000 至 100 000 比尔的罚款，并处以 3 至 15 年有期徒刑。

2/ 在本条第(1)款中提及某人向管理部门所作的陈述时，应包括该人向另一人所作的陈述，而该人在知悉或合理预期该人会将陈述转交给管理部门。

3/ 凡有偷税意图，以代理人身份，以身故、住址不明、无法定能力出具委托书、无营业利益、不存在的人的名义取得营业执照从事经营活动的，除依照本条第(1)款的规定承担企业的税务责任外，还应依照本条第(1)款的规定予以处罚。

119. 欺诈或非法开具发票

1/ 个人：
a）制备、生产、销售或分发欺诈性发票；或者
b）使用欺诈性发票以减少其应纳税额或要求退款；
处以 100 000 比尔的罚款，并处以 7 至 10 年有期徒刑。

2/ 如果某人根据本条第(1)款从欺诈性发票中获得的金钱利益大于 100 000 比尔，则第(1)款中的制裁应等同于获得的金钱利益，并处以 10 至 15 年有期徒刑。

3/ 拥有，出售，租赁或以其他方式提供用于制造、准备或打印欺诈性发票的机器、设备或软件的人，应处以 200 000 比尔的罚款，并处以 10 至 15 年有期徒刑。

4/ 根据本条第(3)款对犯罪定罪的，不得损害没收的机器、设备或软件以及犯罪所得。

5/ 任何人拥有、保留、协助或安排销售，或委托使用虚假发票的，应判处 3 至 5 年的有期徒刑。

120. 与发票有关的一般罪行

1/ 任何负有开具发票义务的纳税人，在没有税务发票条件下而进行交易的，应处以 25 000 至 50 000 比尔的罚款，并处以 3 至 5 年有期徒刑。

2/ 如果某人通过在同一笔发票的复印件中输入不同的价格来拉低销售价格，则应处以 100 000 比尔的罚款，并处以 5 至 7 年的有期徒刑。

3/ 如果销售的实际价格大于 100 000 比尔，则根据本条第(2)款的规定，应处以发票上所指定的最高价格的罚款，并处以 7 至 10 年有期徒刑。

4/ 提供或接受无交易发票的，处以 100 000 比尔至 200 000 比尔的罚款，并处以 7 至 10 年的有期徒刑。

5/ 如果适用本条第(4)款的发票金额超过 200 000 比尔,根据本条第(1)款的规定,应处以与发票上所列金额相等的罚款,并处以 10 至 15 年有期徒刑。

6/ 未经管理局授权印制税收发票的任何人,应处以 300 000 至 500 000 比尔的罚款,并处以 2 至 5 年的有期徒刑。

7/ 第二次根据本条第(6)款被定罪的人,应没收其印刷机和/或其业务,并吊销其营业执照。

121. 要求非法退款或超额信贷

1/ 纳税人以伪造收据或采用任何其他类似方法进行欺诈,要求管理局退款或税收抵免的,应处以 50 000 比尔的罚款,并处以 5 至 7 年有期徒刑。

2/ 对本条第(1)款所述的犯罪定罪,不能免除纳税人根据第 50 条退还税款的义务。

122. 增值税犯罪

1/ 未注册增值税发票而提供税收发票的人,应处以 200 000 比尔的罚款,并处以 7 至 10 年有期徒刑。

2/ 注册人:

a) 拒绝提供增值税公告所要求的借方票据或税收抵免票据;或者

b) 提供除增值税公告所允许以外的借方票据或税收抵免票据;

一经定罪,可处以 10 000 比尔的罚款,并处以 1 年有期徒刑。

123. 印花税犯罪

1/ 个人:

a) 执行或签字确认(作为证人除外)须缴纳印花税的文件,但未缴纳印花税;

b) 伪装或隐藏文件的真实性质,意图不支付印花税或支付较低的印花税;

处以 25 000 至 50 000 比尔的罚款,并处以 3 至 5 年有期徒刑。

2/ 个人:

a 被授权出售邮票或加盖邮票的纸张违反了印花税公告或法规;或者

b) 未经授权出售或提供要出售的邮票或加盖邮票的纸张;

处以 5 000 至 25 000 比尔的罚款,并处以 3 至 5 年有期徒刑。

124. 与追税有关的犯罪

1/ 委托纳税人的财产受托人未按照任何税法履行其义务的,应处以 5 000 比尔的罚款,并处以 1 年的有期徒刑。

2/ 个人根据第 41 条收到扣押令后:

a) 出售、交换或以其他方式处置作为订单标的的财产;

b) 隐藏、破坏、毁损或损坏作为订单标的的财产;或者

c) 销毁、隐藏、移除、损坏、更改、取消或删除与订单标的财产有关的任何文件;

处以 2 至 3 年的有期徒刑。

3/ 在不违反本条第(5)款的情况下,未向管理局支付扣押令中规定的金额的人,应被处以 2 至 3 年有期徒刑。

4/ 根据本公告第 43 条第(5)款,通知管理局的人,被视为遵守了向其送达的扣押令,直至其收到根据本公告第 43 条第(6)款主管当局发出的撤销或修订扣押令的通知书,或拒绝根据

本公告第 43 条第(5)款发出的通知。

5/ 对犯有本条第(3)款所指的罪行的定罪的,并不免除根据扣押令要求支付款项的责任。

6/ 违反离境禁止令而离开或企图离开埃塞俄比亚的,应处以 2 至 3 年有期徒刑。

7/ 金融机构如不遵守本公告第 42 条发布的指令,应处以同等于管理局因不履行而未征收的税款的罚款。

8/ 如果根据本条第(7)款所述的罪行是在金融机构管理人知悉的情况下或由于其疏忽造成的,则该管理人应被处以 2 至 3 年的有期徒刑。

9/ 任何人未经管理局许可,打开或拆除根据第 45 条作出关闭令涉及处所的告示的,应处以 2 至 3 年的有期徒刑。

125. 逃税

1/ 凡意图逃税,隐瞒其收入或未在到期日前提交纳税申报表或缴纳税款的,将处以 100 000 至 200 000 比尔的罚款,并处以 3 至 5 年的有期徒刑。

2/ 负有从付款中预扣税款义务的预扣代理人,未在到期日之前向管理局缴纳预扣税款,并意图逃税的,应处以 3 至 5 年的有期徒刑。

126. 妨碍税收管理法

1/ 任何人根据税法妨碍或试图妨碍税务人员履行职责的,应处以 1 至 3 年的有期徒刑。

2/ 任何人妨碍或企图妨碍税法执行的,应处以不低于 10 000 比尔的罚款,并处以 3 至 5 年的有期徒刑。

3/ 在本条中,以下行为和其他类似行为构成妨碍:

a) 拒绝遵守管理局检查文件的要求,或拒绝提供与纳税人的税务有关的报告或信息,包括拒绝遵守根据本公告第 65 条送达纳税人的通知;

b) 不遵守根据本公告第 65 条送达纳税人的通知,要求纳税人出席并提供证据;

c) 阻止总干事或授权官员行使本公告第 66 条规定的访问权;

d) 拒绝提供第 66 条第(4)款规定的合理协助或便利;

e) 在管理局的办公室滋事或妨碍管理局的雇员履行其工作职责。

127. 未经授权的税收

根据税法未获授权收税或企图收税的人,应处以 50 000 至 75 000 比尔的罚款,并处以 5 至 7 年的有期徒刑。

128. 协助或教唆税收犯罪

协助、教唆、协助、煽动或串谋实施税法规定的犯罪的,税法中被称为"主要犯罪",应处以与主要犯罪相同的制裁。

129. 与税务上诉委员会有关的犯罪

1/ 个人:

a) 委员会成员行使其作为成员的权力或职能时侮辱委员会成员;

b) 未经授权中断委员会的程序;

c) 在委员会所在地或附近制造干扰或参与制造干扰,意图破坏委员会的程序;

d) 以任何方式妨碍委员会的职能;

处以 500 至 3 000 比尔的罚款或处以 6 个月至 2 年有期徒刑。

2/ 个人:

a) 在无合理辩解的情况下,拒绝或不遵从到委员会出席的传票,或不出示任何文件或不向委员会提供任何资料;

b) 在无合理辩解的情况下,拒绝宣誓或不向委员会证实事实真相;

c) 在无合理辩解的情况下,拒绝或未能回答委员会在提起诉讼期间向该人提出的任何问题;

处以 300 至 3 000 比尔的罚款,并处以 6 个月至 2 年有期徒刑。

3/ 任何人故意向委员会提供虚假或误导性证据的,应处以不低于 50 000 比尔的罚款,并处以 3 至 5 年的有期徒刑。

130. 税务代理人的犯罪

违反本公告第 98 条规定未取得税务代理人执照而提供税务代理服务的,应处以 1 年至 3 年有期徒刑。

131. 与销售登记机有关的罪行

1/ 任何人有义务使用销售登记机,如有下列情形即属违法:

a) 如果被发现使用未经管理局认可或注册的销售登记机,则应处以 3 年以上 7 年以下有期徒刑;

b) 如果他(除销售登记机正在维修或其他正当理由以外)进行了无收据或发票的交易,或使用了非销售登记机产生的任何其他收据,应处以 2 年以上 5 年以下有期徒刑;

c) 如果对销售登记机的财务记录造成损坏或变更,或试图对财务记录造成损坏或变更,应处以 3 年以上 5 年以下有期徒刑。

2/ 任何经认可并注册为供应销售登记机的人,如有下列情形均属犯罪:

a) 出售未经税务局认可的软件或销售登记机,则将处以 3 年以上 5 年以下有期徒刑;

b) 未能提前通知管理局使用中的销售登记机的任何更改,或者如果在指导销售登记机使用的手册中插入了不正确的信息或遗漏了正确的信息,则应处以 3 年以上 5 年以下有期徒刑。

3/ 任何人未经许可提供销售登记机或软件、分发销售登记机或软件,应处以 5 至 7 年有期徒刑。

4/ 任何未通过供应商认证和/或未经管理局注册而安排了服务人员的销售登记机服务中心,将被处以 50 000 比尔的罚款或不超过一年的有期徒刑。

5/ 销售登记机服务中心的任何人员,在不知情的情况下,擅自拆卸或组装销售登记机,或故意拆除销售登记机上的印章,或更改据报没有任何故障的销售登记机的零件,或有任何类似的行为,均属违法,一经定罪,处以不超过 10 000 比尔的罚款,并处以 1 年以上 3 年以下有期徒刑。

6/ 任何违反使用销售登记机规则和程序的税务人员:

a) 在没有服务人员在场的情况下拆卸或组装销售登记机或批准其使用;或更改机器注册代码;或者

b) 故意或过失地未在 24 小时内向管理局报告用户、服务中心或其人员或销售登记机的供应商所犯的罪行;

一经定罪,将处以不超过5 000比尔的罚款,并处以1年以上3年以下的有期徒刑。
132. 机构犯罪
1/ 如果触犯税法犯罪的人是机构,则在犯罪发生时担任该机构经理的每个人都应被视为犯了同一罪行。

2/ 本条第(1)款不适用于以下情况的人:

a) 犯罪行为是在未经当事人同意或不知情的情况下发生的;和

b) 当事人已经进行了尽职调查和警告,以确保处于类似职位的谨慎人士也应采取类似的措施。

133. 公布名称
1/ 管理局可随时在其网站上及通过其他大众媒体公布因税法定罪,而最终由法院裁定犯有罪行的人员名单。

2/ 根据本条第(1)款发布的清单应具体说明以下事项:

a) 被定罪者的姓名、照片和地址;

b) 管理局认为适当的犯罪细节;

c) 发生违法行为的纳税期;

d) 因犯罪而被定罪的人未缴纳的税款金额;

e) 对被定罪者的罚款金额(如有)。

第四章 奖 励

134. 提供可核实的逃税信息的奖励
1/ 任何人士提供可核实及客观的逃税信息,包括隐瞒、少报、欺诈或其他不适当的手段,管理局据此发出的指令,给予该人士在管理局征收税款时所逃税额的20%作为奖励。

2/ 在下列情况下,任何人无权根据本条第(1)款获得报酬:

a) 参与逃税;

b) 报告逃税是个人职责的一部分。

3/ 管理局应根据指令提供本条规定的奖励细节。

135. 杰出表现奖
1/ 管理局对有杰出表现的税务人员和模范履行纳税义务的纳税人,应当给予奖励。

2/ 部长应根据本条规定提供奖励的细节。

第十六部分
其 他 规 定

136. 颁布法规和指令的权力
1/ 部长会议可发布适当执行本公告所必需的规章。

2/ 部长可根据本条第(1)款发布必需的指令,及适当执行本公告和条例。

137. 过渡性规定
1/ 本公告适用于因作为或不作为而在公告生效前作出的税务决定。

2/ 尽管本公告第(1)款有以下规定：

a) 在本公告生效之前应缴纳的未缴税款的行政处罚,应根据本公告生效之前的现行税法进行评估。

b) 本公告生效之时,在税务上诉委员会中未决的任何案件,均应根据本公告之前的现行税法进行裁定,视为未公告未颁布。

c) 现有税务投诉审查委员会和税务上诉委员会应继续运作,直至根据本公告成立新的税务投诉审查部门和联邦税务上诉委员会。

d) 如果申请和上诉的期限在本公告开始之前已经届满,本公告中的任何内容都不能解释为由于本公告规定了较长的期限,就能够根据本公告进行申请和上诉。

3/ 就本公告而言,如果在本公告开始时未成立注册会计师协会,则本公告中对该协会的任何规定均应视为对埃塞俄比亚会计和审计委员会的规定,直至该协会成立为止。

4/ 部长会议关于强制使用销售登记机第139/2007号条例应继续适用于本公告的第20条,直至由部长会议发布的新条例取代。

138. 不适用的法律

根据本公告第137条的规定,与本公告不符的任何法律均不适用于本公告规定的事项。

139. 生效日期

1/ 本公告自其在联邦政府公报上颁布之日起生效。

2/ 除了本条第(1)款规定外,本公告第十一部分和第十四部分的规定自部长通过在广泛发行的报纸上公布之日起生效。

3/ 尽管有本条第(1)款的规定,本公告第十四部分的规定应自管理局通过在广泛发行的报纸上公布之日起生效。

2016年8月20日在亚的斯亚贝巴签署

穆拉图·特肖梅(博士)

埃塞俄比亚联邦民主共和国总统

第七部
部长理事会联邦税收管理条例
（部长理事会第 407/2017 号条例）

埃塞俄比亚联邦民主共和国联邦政府公报

第 23 年 79 号
2017 年 8 月 9 日，亚的斯亚贝巴

部长理事会第 407/2017 号条例
部长理事会税收管理条例

本条例由部长理事会根据《埃塞俄比亚联邦民主共和国第 916/2015 号公告》第 5 条行政机关职权定义和《联邦税收管理第 983/2016 号公告》第 136 条规定发布。

第一部分
总　　则

1. 简称

本条例可以称为"部长理事会联邦税收管理第 407/2017 号条例"。

2. 定义

除非上下文另有规定,在本条例中:

1)《公告》是指《联邦税收管理第 983/2016 号公告》;

2)"已废止公告"是指《所得税第 286/2002 号公告(经修订)》《采矿所得税第 53/1993 号公告》及其所有修正案,以及《石油经营所得税第 96/1986 号公告》及其所有修正案;

3) 本条例中所用术语的含义,视情况而定,应当与《公告》或者《联邦所得税第 979/2016 号公告》中的含义相同。

第二部分
税 法 管 理

3. 提供机密信息

在不损害《公告》第 8 条第(2)款的前提下,管理局只有在向总干事或者其代表提出书面请求并且经授权提供该文件或者信息时,才应当提供机密文件或者信息。

第三部分
注　　册

4. 身份证明文件

1/ 个人注册申请应当附有下列身份证明文件:

a) 个人现居地身份证或载有个人资料的埃塞俄比亚或外国现行护照页的核证副本;或者

b) 个人现行埃塞俄比亚驾驶执照的认证副本;或者

c) 载有个人信息并附有个人照片的个人现行外国驾驶执照页面的认证副本;或者

d) 个人出生证明的认证副本。

2/ 尽管有本条第(1)款的规定,管理局仍可以要求申请人提供其认为必要的其他证据;

3/ 成立公司的注册申请必须附有公司成立证书或者注册证书;

4/ 合伙企业的注册申请必须附有合伙企业契约;

5/ 任何其他机构的注册申请必须附加注册证书或者其他形成或者创建的文件。

5. 生物识别信息

1/ 为了个人的注册目的,管理局可以要求个人提交生物识别信息,以便:

a) 确保正确识别个人身份;或者

b) 防止身份盗用或者欺诈。

2/ 在本条中,与个人有关的"生物识别信息"是指用以验证个人身份的生物学数据,并且可以包括下列内容:

a) 面部识别;

b) 指纹识别;

c) 声音识别;

d) 虹膜或者视网膜识别。

第四部分
税 务 代 表

6. 非居民税务代表

1/ 根据《联邦所得税公告》第4条第(4)款,非居民通过在埃塞俄比亚设立常驻机构的人员(称为"代理人")的活动在埃塞俄比亚开展业务,该代理人就《公告》而言,应为非居民的税务代表;

2/ 根据本条第(1)款,代理人作为非居民税务代表的待遇应与根据《公告》第2条第(40)款被视为非居民税务代表的任何其他人相同。

第五部分
困 难 情 形

7. 减免税收债务的限额

局长根据《公告》第51条可免除的税收债务和逾期付款利息的最高额为10 000 000(壹仟万)比尔。

第六部分
通 知 和 纳 税

8. 提交申报表和缴税的方式

除《公告》或本条例另有规定外,任何人应当向管理局提交纳税申报表或者其他文件,并以下列方式纳税:

1/ 在《公告》第 82 条第(2)款适用的情况下,按照管理局依据该条的指示以电子方式支付或者付款;或者

2/ 在任何其他情况下,可以亲自交付或者邮寄到管理局的办公室。

第七部分
税务上诉委员会

第一章　委员会在听证会中的权力

9. 委员会的权力

1/ 委员会可以:

a) 宣誓或者肯定地接受证据;

b) 在不违反本条例第 11 条第(2)款的情况下,在已经收到听证合理通知的一方缺席的情况下进行;或者

c) 偶尔暂停听证会。

2/ 委员会主席可以传唤某人出席委员会听证会以作证;

3/ 被传唤在委员会前出庭作证的人有权按照委员会的指示,依据联邦高级法院允许的证人费率获得酬金。

第二章　委员会的决定

10. 中止、驳回或者恢复上诉申请

1/ 上诉人可以随时通过向委员会书记官提交书面通知,中止或者撤回对委员会的上诉,委员会应当驳回上诉;

2/ 如果申请人未能亲自或者未委托代表出席委员会听证会,委员会可以驳回上诉;

3/ 如果申请人未能遵守委员会正在审议中的上诉的指示,主席可以代表委员会驳回上诉;

4/ 如果委员会依据本条第(2)款或第(3)款驳回上诉,上诉人可以自收到驳回上诉的通知之日起 30 天内,向委员会申请恢复上诉;

5/ 如果已经依据第(4)款提出了申请,委员会可以在主席的任何指示下恢复上诉。

11. 当事人协议

如果在上诉过程中的任何阶段,当事人就委员会关于上诉的决定或者与部分上诉的有关决定的条款达成书面协议:

1/ 如果协议与委员会的决定条款有关,委员会可以根据协议条款作出决定;

2/ 如果达成的协议涉及部分上诉决定,委员会可以实施协议的条款。

12. 发回管理局的决定

1/ 依据《公告》第 91 条的规定,如果委员会将上诉决定发回给管理局进行复议,管理局可以考虑委员会的指示:

a) 确认上诉的决定;

b) 变更上诉的决定;或者

c) 撤销上诉的决定并做出新的决定,包括在《公告》第 91 条第(6)款适用时增加税收评估。

2/ 当管理局依据本条第(1)款变更或者撤销上诉决定时,经变更的决定或者新的决定应当被视为向委员会提起上诉的标的,上诉人可以继续进行上诉或者撤回上诉。

13. 决定更正

1/ 委员会如认为某一决定的案文或某一决定理由的书面陈述有错误,可改变该决定的案文或理由的书面陈述;

2/ 依据本条第(1)款修改的文本应当被视为委员会的决定;

3/ 就本条目的而言,文本中决定或者理由说明的错误包括:

a) 印刷或者文书错误;或者

b) 决定与理由说明之间的任何不一致。

第三章 委员会的管理

14. 听证地点

委员会听证会应当在委员会主席指定的地点举行。因此,委员会应当通知当事人听证地点。

15. 费用

对于当事人在诉讼中产生的费用,委员会可以作出其认为公平合理的指令。

16. 向委员会提交文件

要求提交给委员会的任何文件应当提交给委员会书记官处。

17. 文件送达地址

上诉人应当将其上诉地址书面通知书记官,以送达与上诉有关的任何文件。

第八部分
税务代理许可

18. 提供税务代理服务的合适人选

1/ 在不违反本条第(2)款和第(3)款的前提下,个人是提供税务代理服务的合适人选,如果个人有:

a) 至少具有税务、会计、商业、法律、经济学、管理或其他类似学科的第一学位的资格;和

b) 过去 5 年在埃塞俄比亚至少有 2 年全职经验:

(1) 在持牌税务代理人的监督下提供税务代理服务;或者

(2) 担任税务官员。

2/ 如果个人在其他司法管辖区具有与本条第(1)款(b)项(1)目相同的经验,管理局可以认为其满足本条第(1)款(b)项(1)目的规定;

3/ 下列人员不被视为提供税务代理服务的合适人选:

a) 无法偿还债务或者被司法宣布破产的个人;

b) 被专业机构认定有犯罪行为的个人;

c) 被裁定犯有与不诚实有关的刑事罪并且尚未复职的个人；

d) 包括依据已废止公告而具有不令人满意税务遵从记录的个人。

第九部分
其他部分

19. 过渡条款

1/ 依据已废止公告设立的税务上诉委员会（简称"前委员会"）成员的任命应在《公告》下设立的税务上诉委员会（称为"新委员会"）开始运作时终止；

2/ 依据《公告》第 87 条,适用本条第(1)款的人有资格被任命为新委员会的成员；

3/《公告》第 87 条第(3)款(b)项中提到的"税法"应当包括已废止公告；

4/ 如果向前委员会提出上诉,且上诉在前委员会停止运作之前尚未完成,则上诉应当由新委员会遵守新委员会主席的指示作出决定。

20. 发出指令的权力

部长可以发布指令以正确实施本条例。

21. 生效日期

本条例自其在《联邦政府公报》上颁布之日起生效。

2017 年 8 月 9 日在亚的斯亚贝巴签署

海尔马里亚姆·德萨莱尼

埃塞俄比亚联邦民主共和国总理

第八部
部长理事会联邦所得税条例
(部长理事会第 410/2017 号条例)

埃塞俄比亚联邦民主共和国联邦政府公报

第 23 年 82 号
2017 年 8 月 24 日,亚的斯亚贝巴

部长理事会第 410/2017 号条例
部长理事会联邦所得税条例

本条例由部长理事会依据《埃塞俄比亚联邦民主共和国第 916/2015 号公告》第 5 条"行政机关权力和责任定义"和《联邦所得税第 976/2016 号公告》第 99 条颁布。

第一部分
一 般 原 则

1. 简称

本条例可以称为《部长理事会联邦所得税第 410/2017 号条例》。

2. 定义

除非上下文另有规定,在本条例中:

1/《公告》是指《联邦所得税第 979/2016 号公告》;

2/ "已废止公告"是指《所得税第 286/2002 号公告(经修订)》《采矿所得税第 53/1993 号公告(经修订)》和《石油经营所得税第 296/1986 号公告(经修订)》;

3/ 所用术语和短语的含义应当与《公告》或者《联邦税收管理第 983/2016 号公告》(视具体情况而定)相同。

第二部分
《公告》术语的适用

3. 利息

储蓄信贷协会作为存款回报或会员对协会的贡献所支付的金额,无论如何,均应视为为《公告》目的而支出的利息。

4. 常设机构

1/ 在确定某人是否超过《公告》第 4 条第(2)款(c)项规定的 183 天期限时,应当考虑该人或有关人员的关联项目;

2/ 当某人经营建筑工地或者进行《公告》第 4 条第(3)款所述的项目或者活动时,有关人员进行的任何相关活动应当加上该类人员经营建筑工地或者进行项目或者活动的期间,以确定是否超过 183 天期限。

5. 居民个人

1/ 在不违反本条第(2)款的情况下,为《公告》第 5 条第(2)款(c)项的目的,计算个人在埃塞俄比亚停留的天数:

a) 个人在埃塞俄比亚停留的一天的一部分(包括到达埃塞俄比亚的日期和离开埃塞俄比

亚的日期)应当计为停留一整天;

b) 个人全部或者部分停留在埃塞俄比亚的下列日期应当计为停留一整天:

(1) 公共假期;

(2) 请假一天,包括病假;

(3) 个人在埃塞俄比亚的活动因罢工、停工、供应延迟、不利的天气条件或者季节性因素而中断的一天;

(4) 个人在埃塞俄比亚进行任何活动之前,期间或之后在埃塞俄比亚度假的天数。

2/ 个人仅因为在埃塞俄比亚境外两个不同地方之间过境而在埃塞俄比亚境内的一天或一天的一部分,不算作在埃塞俄比亚停留的一天。

6. 股份与债券

1/《公告》第59条第(7)款(c)项中提及的"股份和债券"包括股份或债券中的任何权益,例如,就股份而言,获得股份的权利或者收购股权。

2/ 处置居民公司发行的股份或者债券所产生的收益应当为埃塞俄比亚人的收入来源。

第三部分
附表"A"收入

第一节
附加福利

7. 第三部分定义的第一节

1/ 在本部分中:

a) "雇员股份计划"是指雇主公司或者关联公司可以将股份分配给雇主公司雇员的协议或安排;

b) "管家人员"是指管家、厨师、司机、园丁或者其他家庭助理;

c) "市场贷款利率",就一个月而言,是指:

(1) 对于商业银行,本月埃塞俄比亚国家银行向埃塞俄比亚商业银行发放的贷款和再贴现贷款的贷款利率;或者

(2) 对于任何其他人,本月在埃塞俄比亚商业银行贷款最低利率;

d) "关联公司",就公司而言,是指与上述公司有关联关系的另一个公司;

e) "偏远地区"是指距离城市中心30公里,人口为20 000人的位置;

f) "服务"包括财产的使用和任何设施的提供;

g) "车辆"是指设计用来承载小于1吨且少于9名乘客的机动车辆。

2/ 在本节中:

a) 所称"雇主"包括相关雇主和根据与雇主或者相关雇主的安排行事的第三方;

b) 所称"雇员"包括相关雇员。

8. 附加福利

1/ 就《公告》第12条第(1)款(b)项而言,在不违反本条的前提下,雇主为雇员提供的下列福利是附加福利:

a) 债务免除；

b) 家政人员；

c) 住房；

d) 贴息贷款；

e) 餐点或者茶点；

f) 私人支出；

g) 财产或者服务；

h) 雇员股份计划；

i) 车辆；

j) 其他附加福利。

2/ 如果雇员获得了福利，雇员在获得福利时所发生的支出是在获得就业收入时发生，则福利不是附加福利。

3/ 在确定一项福利是否是一项附加福利以及附加福利的价值时，应当不考虑该福利转移的任何限制以及该福利不能以其他方式转换为现金的事实。

4/ 就《公告》或者本条例而言，下列利益不被视为附加利益：

a) 根据《公告》附表"E"的免税收益；

b) 在考虑到雇主提供类似福利的频率之后，福利的价值很小，以致依据部长发布的指示，其是不合理的或者行政上不可行的；

c) 由雇主或者代表雇主在食堂、自助餐厅或者饭厅提供的餐点或茶点津贴，完全是为了雇员的利益，并且所有非临时雇员均以同等条件享有；

d) 在下列情况向偏远地区的非管理人员提供住宿或者住房：

（1）雇员通常的工作地点在偏远地区；和

（2）雇主有必要向偏远地区的雇员提供住宿或者住房，因为雇主的业务性质使得雇员很可能频繁地从一个居住地搬到另一个居住地或者偏远地区没有足够的合适的住房；

e) 雇主提供移动电话供雇员使用；

f) 雇主支付雇员拨打的移动电话的费用，包括用雇主提供的移动电话；

g) 雇主为雇员参加大学、学院或者其他提供成人教育课程的机构支付学费；

h) 为雇员的利益提供保障服务；

i) 旅馆、饭店和其他类似机构为其雇员提供餐饮服务；

j) 提供制服和相关工作材料。

9. 债务免除附加福利

1/ 雇主免除雇员支付或偿还欠雇主的款项的责任属债务豁免附带福利。

2/ 债务免除附加福利的价值应当为免除的数额。

10. 家政人员附加福利

家政人员附加福利的价值，应是当月家政人员因向雇员提供服务而获得的雇佣收入总额，减去雇员为该等服务支付的任何款项。

11. 住房或者住宿附加福利

1/ 当雇主拥有住所或者住房时，雇主向雇员提供为期一个月的住房附加福利的价值应当为当月住宿或者住房的公平市场租金,减去雇员为住宿或住房所支付的任何款项。

2/ 当雇主租用住所或者住房时,雇主向雇员提供为期一个月的住房附加福利的价值应当为雇主在当月所支付的该住所或住房的租金,减去雇员为住宿或者住房所支付的任何款项。

12. 贴息贷款附加福利

1/ 如果贷款利率低于市场贷款利率,雇主向雇员提供的贷款为贴息贷款附加福利。

2/ 一个月的贴息贷款附加福利的价值应当为雇员当月为该贷款所支付的利息(如果有),以及该雇员如果以当月市场借贷利率而为贷款支付的利息之间的差额。

13. 餐点或者茶点附加福利

餐点或者茶点附加福利的价值应当为用人单位提供餐点的总费用,减去雇员工为餐费或者茶点所支付的任何费用。

14. 车辆附加福利

1/ 雇主向雇员提供全部或者部分供其私人使用的车辆,即是车辆附加福利。

2/ 在不违反本条第(3)款和第(4)款的情况下,一个月的车辆附加福利的价值应当为依据下列公式计算得出的数额:

$$\frac{A \times 5\%}{12}$$

其中:"A"是雇主取得车辆的成本,或者如果车辆是由雇主租赁的,则"A"是指在租赁开始时车辆的公平市场价值。但是如果是免税进口的车辆,其附加福利的价值应当包括关税以及本应在车辆上支付的税款。

3/ 依据本条第(2)款计算的车辆附加福利的价值,应当减去下列各项:

a) 雇员为使用车辆或者维护和运行费用而支付的任何款项;

b) 雇员在从事工作中使用车辆(如果有)的比例;

c) 没有将车辆提供给员工私人使用的月份(如果有)的比例。

4/ 如雇主持有车辆超过5年,则本条第(2)款的公式中"A"部分的价值应为根据本条第(2)款所确定金额的50%。

5/ 在本文中提到的"提供给员工供私人使用的车辆"包括提供给员工供私人使用的车辆,即使员工在任何时候并没有实际将车辆用于私人用途。

15. 私人支出附加福利

1/ 在不违反本条第(3)款的情况下,雇主支付的支出是私人支出附加福利,只要该项支出能给雇员带来私人利益。

2/ 私人支出附加福利的价值应当为依据本条第(1)款被视为私人支出附加福利的支出数额。

3/ 本条不适用于雇主依据本条例第18条以外的其他条款附加福利支出。

16. 财产或者服务附加福利

1/ 雇主向雇员转让财产或者提供服务即为财产或者服务附加福利。

2/ 除本条第(3)款另有规定下,财产或者服务附加福利的价值应当为:

a) 如果雇主在正常业务过程中向客户提供财产或者服务,则为该财产或者服务的正常售价的75%;或者

b）在任何其他情况下，雇主获得财产或者服务的成本。

3/ 依据本条第（2）款确定的财产附加福利的价值应当减去雇员为财产或者服务支付的任何款项。

4/ 就本条第（2）款（a）项而言，如果财产或者服务附加福利是作为航空公司运营人的雇主提供的免费或者补贴的航空旅行，则正常售价为雇主提供的航班的标准经济票价。

17. 雇员股份计划权益

1/ 根据雇员股份计划向雇员配发的股份，包括因行使选择权或购股权而分配的股份，即雇员股份计划附加福利。

2/ 根据雇员股份计划授予雇员的购股权或者选择权的价值，不应当被视为附加福利或者以其他方式计入就业收入：

a）如果雇员行使权利或者选择权，则适用本条；或者

b）如果员工处分权利或者选择权，《公告》第59条应当适用权利或者选择权属于"B"类应税资产的处分。

3/ 依据本条第（4）款，雇员股份计划附加福利的价值应当为配股当日的股票公允市场价值减去雇员对股份的出资。

4/ 如果依据雇员持股计划分配给雇员的股份受到股权转让限制，雇员将被视为在下列较早时间获得雇员股份计划福利：

a）雇员能够自由转让股份的时间；或者

b）雇员处分股份的时间。

5/ 当本条第（4）款适用时，股份的公平市场价值在根据本条第（4）款确定雇员股份计划收益时确定。

6/ 在本条中，"雇员出资"，就雇员股份计划分配给雇员的股份而言，是指雇员给予的对价（如有）总和：

a）股份；和

b）授予获得股份的任何权利或者选择权。

18. 其他附加福利

1/ 雇主向本部分其他条款未涵盖的雇员提供的福利是其他附加福利。

2/ 其他附加福利的价值是在提供福利时确定的福利的公平市场价值，减去雇员为该福利而支付的任何款项。

19. 附加福利的税收责任限制

1/ 尽管有本节的规定，附加福利的应纳税总额应当在任何情况下不得超过雇员工资收入的10%；

2/ 就本条而言，"工资"不包括其他与就业有关的福利。

第二节
境外人员就业收入

20. 境外人员就业收入

1/《公告》第93条第（1）款应适用于非居民雇主雇用的居民雇员，但非居民雇主的埃塞俄比亚常设机构雇员除外。

2/ 居民雇员取得境外人员就业收入一个日历月,缴纳外国所得税的,准予其扣减下列金额中较低者的税额:

a) 已付的外国所得税;或者

b) 境外人员就业所得应缴纳的就业所得税,按适用于常驻员工的就业所得税平均税率计算,适用于该员工当月的外籍就业所得。

3/《公告》第45条第(3)款、第(4)款和第(5)款应当适用于本条所允许的税收抵免,依据是对"企业所得税"指的是"就业所得税",而"税收年度"指的是"日历月"。

4/ 在本条中:

a) "受雇人每月平均所得税率",就一个日历月的居民雇员而言,是指受雇人在扣除任何课税前,该月应缴的受雇人所得税额占受雇人该月受雇总收入的百分比;

b) "境外人员就业收入"是指依据公告附表"A"应纳税的境外人员就业收入;

c) "境外人员所得税"是指由外国政府或者外国政府的政治分支机构征收的所得税,包括预扣税,但不包括罚款、额外税款或者与此有关的应支付利息;

d) "居民雇员"是指拥有埃塞俄比亚国籍的雇员。

第四部分
附表"B"收入

21. 超过一年的租金收入

对于公告第15条第(5)款所适用的出租人或次出租人而言,其收到的租金收入超过一年的,其收到的租金收入总额应被视为在收到租金收入的纳税年度内取得的,但应纳税额应按租金收入在该纳税年度内的比例分摊计算。

22. 企业资产租赁

来自企业租赁的收入,包括属于企业正常运营一部分的货物、设备和建筑物,应当依据公告附表"C"纳税。

23. 租赁建筑物、家具和设备的折旧

就公告第15条第7款(c)项的目的而言,租赁建筑物、家具和设备折旧的纳税年度的扣除额应当依据公告第25条和本条例第五部分第二节的规定确定,其依据如下:

1/ 租赁建筑物是一种折旧资产,是对不动产的结构性改进;和

2/ 建筑物租赁的任何家具和设备均为折旧资产。

24. 租金收入损失

1/ 纳税义务人记载的纳税年度租金收入总额,超过纳税年度公告第15条第(7)款(c)项规定的扣减额,超过的部分视为当年租金损失。

2/ 公告第26条和本条例第42条应当适用于有租金损失的纳税人,其依据是,这些条款中提及的"损失"是指"租金损失"。

25. 境外人员租金收入

1/ 纳税义务人在缴纳境外人员所得税的纳税年度有境外人员租金收入的,可以抵免下列税款中的较低者:

a）已缴纳的境外人员所得税；或者

b）通过将适用于纳税人的平均租金所得税的平均税率适用于该纳税年度纳税人的境外人员净租金收入，计算得出的针对纳税人的境外人员租金收入的应付租金所得税。

2/《公告》第45条第（3）款、第（4）款和第（5）款应当适用于本条所允许的税收抵免，其依据是"企业所得税"是指"租金所得税"。

3/ 在本条中：

a）对埃塞俄比亚一个纳税年度的居民而言，"租金所得税的平均税率"，是指该居民在扣除任何税收抵免之前，该年应缴的租金所得税占该居民当年应纳税的租金收入的百分比；

b）"境外人员所得税"是指外国政府或者外国政府的政治分支机构征收的所得税，包括预扣税，但不包括就该税应缴的罚款、附加税或者利息；

c）"外国租金收入"是指依据附表"B"应缴纳的外国收入；和

d）"净外国租金收入"，是指该纳税年度外国出租收入总额扣除《公告》第15条第（7）款规定的与该收入来源有关款项后的余额。

26. 租赁新建筑物的通知

就《公告》第17条第（1）款而言，新建筑物竣工或租赁的通知期限应当在该建筑物竣工或租赁之日起一个月内发出。

第五部分
附表"C"收入

第一节
扣 除 额

27. 代表费用

就《公告》第27条第（1）款（i）项而言，"代表支出"是指员工为促进和提升业务而接待企业外部客人所发生的接待支出。

28. 支付给国外贷款人的利息扣除额

《公告》第23条第（2）款（a）项（2）目所述的国外贷款人所支付的利息，只有在借款人向管理局提供埃塞俄比亚国家银行向国外贷款人提供的贷款授权书副本的情况下，才可以扣除。

29. 雇员医疗费用

雇主为其雇员支付的医疗费用，包括依据雇员的健康保险计划支付的保险费，应当依据《公告》第22条第1款（a）项扣除。

30. 从事餐饮服务的机构提供的餐饮服务

1/ 旅馆、餐馆或者其他类似机构为其雇员提供餐饮服务所发生的支出，应当依据《公告》第22条第（1）款（a）项扣除。

2/ 依据本条第（1）款允许的扣除限额应当由部长发布的指令确定。

31. 业务推广费用

依照《公告》第22条第（1）款（a）项，本地或国外业务推广费用的扣除限额应当由部长发布的指令确定。

32. 承租人自费维护、修理或者改善企业资产

承租人根据与出租人订立的合同条款,自愿为维护、修理或者改善租赁的商业资产而发生的费用,应当从承租人的营业收入中扣除。

33. 慈善捐赠

1/ 根据《公告》第24条第(1)款扣除的慈善捐款应当适用于纳税人管理自己的慈善活动所发生的费用。

2/ 就《公告》第24条第(1)款(b)项而言,政府呼吁是指联邦政府或者地区州的呼吁,其中包括亚的斯亚贝巴和德雷迪瓦市政府的呼吁。

3/ 为了本条第(1)款的目的,"慈善捐赠"是指为支持教育、健康、环境保护或者以人道主义援助形式提供的捐款,而不是为纳税人自己的雇员提供的捐赠。

34. 资本货物租赁协议中允许扣除的业务资产

1/ 根据资本货物租赁协议持有的业务资产所支付的租赁付款为可从业务总收入中扣除的业务支出。

2/ 根据本条第(1)款实现扣除的人无权对资产进行折旧。

35. 总公司费用

在埃塞俄比亚经营业务的常设机构向其母非居民机构支付的款项,应扣除母非居民机构为常设机构的利益而支付的实际费用,但这种费用是在取得、保障或维持业务收入时发生的。

第二节
折旧扣除

36. 折旧资产和企业无形资产的折旧扣除

1/ 在不违反本条第(2)款的情况下,纳税人可以依据本条例第37条规定的直线法或者本条例第38条规定的价值递减法确定依据《公告》第25条第(1)款允许的折旧扣除额:

a) 纳税人在按照财务报告标准编制的财务账目中使用了相同的折旧方法;和

b) 纳税人对纳税人拥有的所有折旧资产使用相同的折旧方法。

2/ 下列资产应当采用直线法进行折旧:

a) 无形业务;

b) 不动产的结构性改进。

3/ 为了计算与不动产结构改进有关的折旧扣除,结构改进的成本不应当包括该改进地所处土地的成本。

4/ 如果转让人已将资产或者无形资产的成本全额折旧,则纳税人从关联人("转让人")获得的折旧资产或者无形资产的成本不得扣除折旧。

37. 直线折旧

1/ 在不违反《公告》第25条第(3)款和第(4)款的前提下,纳税人在纳税年度内按照直线法对应折旧资产或者无形业务的折旧扣除,应当依据本条例第39条规定的折旧比率对资产成本进行计算。

2/ 除《公告》第25条第(4)款外,纳税人就本纳税年度和以前各税年度可折旧的资产或者无形资产可享受的或者将享受的扣除总额,不得超过本纳税年度扣除总额。

38. 价值递减折旧扣除

1/ 在不违反《公告》第 25 条第(3)款和第(4)款的前提下,纳税人在纳税年度按照递减价值法可就应折旧资产折旧扣除额,应当应用本条例第 39 条规定的汇率与资产在年初的账面净值计算。

2/ 如果《公告》第 25 条第(4)款适用于某纳税年度的折旧资产,则该资产的账面净值应以该资产在该纳税年度仅用于取得营业收入为基础计算。

3/ 如果纳税人的折旧资产余额不超过 8 000 比尔,应当在余额对应的纳税年度中全额扣除。

39. 折旧扣除率

1/ 适用于可折旧资产的折旧率按下列类别列于下表:

折 旧 资 产	直线率
计算机、软件和数据储存设备	20%
温室大棚	10%
对温室以外不动产的结构改进	5%
任何其他折旧资产	15%
用于采矿和石油开发业务的可折旧资产	25%

2/ 适用于企业无形资产的折旧率应当为:

a) 初步支出为 25%;

b) 对于使用寿命超过 10 年的无形资产,但本段第(a)项所述的无形资产除外,折旧率为 10%;或者

c) 对于其他无形资产,将其无形资产的使用寿命除以 100%。

3/ 在本条中,"预备支出"是指纳税人在开始营业之前发生的依《公告》第 25 条第(7)款(a)项中关于"无形资产"定义中第(4)段所指的支出。

40. 部分用作商业资产建筑物允许的折旧

部分用作商业资产的建筑物的折旧只能按照与用作商业资产的财产的比例进行。

41. 维修和改进

1/ 在不违反本条第(2)款的前提下,应当允许纳税人在纳税年度内扣除当年对折旧资产进行修理或改进的费用。

2/ 根据本条第(1)款允许的扣除额不得超过纳税年度末资产净账面价值的 20%。

3/ 如果年内对可折旧资产的修理或者改进成本超过资产账面净值的 20%,则修理或者改进的全部费用应当计入资产的账面净值。

第三节
亏 损 结 转

42. 亏损结转

1/ 如果纳税人依据《公告》第 26、38 或者 46 条结转的亏损超过一个纳税年度,应当首先扣除最早年度的亏损。

2/ 只有在对纳税人的损失证明书进行了审计并为管理局所接受的情况下,才可以结转亏损。

3/ 尽管有本条第(2)款的规定,纳税人仍可以结转亏损,如果:

a) 纳税人已向管理局提交了账簿,表明损失已经由外部审计师审计;和

b) 在下一个纳税年度纳税人申报纳税前,管理局未审核纳税人的账簿。

4/ 本条第(3)款的任何规定均不能阻止管理局随后对损失进行审计,并依据《联邦税收管理公告》第 28 条的规定向纳税人提供关于损失的修订评估通知。

43. 亏损向后结转

就《公告》第 32 条而言,在履行长期合同中遭受的损失可以向后结转,直到将损失全数扣除为止。

第四节
外汇兑换损益

44. 外汇兑换损益

1/ 纳税人获得的外币汇兑收益应当计入营业收入。

2/ 在不违反本条第(3)款的前提下,如果纳税人在一个纳税年度发生了外汇兑换损失,该损失应当抵减纳税人在该年度中获得的外币汇兑收益,但须符合下列条件:

a) 可以将未使用的亏损金额无限期结转,以抵销外币汇兑收益,直至完全抵销;

b) 纳税人已证明损失金额,使管理局满意。

3/ 本条第(2)款不适用于金融机构发生的外币汇兑损失,除非该金融机构证明损失金额足以使管理局满意,则该损失金额可以扣除。

4/ 纳税人在实现损益时获得外币汇兑收益或者发生外币汇兑损失。

5/ 在确定纳税人是否已就外币交易取得外币汇兑收益或招致外币汇兑损失时,必须考虑纳税人或相关人士就该交易订立的套期保值合同下纳税人的地位。

6/ 在本条中:

a) "债务义务"是指向他人付款的义务,包括应付账款以及本票、汇票和债券下的义务;

b) "外币汇兑收益"是指归因于外币交易的货币汇率波动引起的收益;

c) "外币汇兑损失"是指与外币交易有关的货币汇率波动引起的损失;

d) "外币交易"是指为开展业务以取得业务收入而进行的以下任何交易:

(1) 外币交易;

(2) 发行或者取得外币债务;或者

(3) 以外币计价的其他交易;

e) "套期保值合同"是指为了消除或减少因货币汇率波动对另一合同当事人可能产生的不利财务后果风险而签订的合同。

第五节
银行和保险公司

45. 银行损失准备金

银行应被允许在一个纳税年度中扣除其当年损失准备金的 80%,前提是储备金的数额是根据埃塞俄比亚国家银行规定的审慎要求计算的,并且符合财务报告标准。

46. 普通保险公司未到期风险准备金

1/ 在不违反本条第(2)款规定的前提下,经营普通保险业务的保险公司,其未到期风险准

备金余额,在当年年底按照财务报告标准计算的,准予在一个纳税年度内扣除。

2/ 如果保险公司是通过埃塞俄比亚常设机构经营业务的非居民公司,则本条第(1)款允许的扣除额应当限于公司在埃塞俄比亚未到期风险准备金的余额。

3/ 在一个纳税年度,经营普通保险业务的保险公司的营业收入应当包括该公司依据本条第(1)款或第(2)款(视情况而定)在上一个纳税年度中扣除的未到期风险准备金金额。

4/ 在本条中,"普通保险"是指除《商法典》所定义的人寿保险以外的所有保险。

47. 人寿保险业务应税所得额

1/ 从事人寿保险业务的保险公司,每一纳税年度的应纳所得税额根据以下公式计算:

$$(A+B+C+D)-(E+F+G+H)$$

其中:

"A"是指公司在本年度获得的人寿保险保费,但不包括当年退还给保单持有人的保费;

"B"是指公司在本年度与人寿保险业务相关的投资收益;

"C"是指在该年度内已取消的人寿保险准备金的金额;

"D"是指公司在本年度内取得的与人寿保险业务有关的任何其他收入;

"E"是指公司在本年度从事人寿保险业务的承保费用,包括支付的佣金、再保险费、风险分析费用、政府的保单费用以及运营费用;

"F"是指人寿保单准备金的增加额,包括本年度发行的新人寿保单的初始准备金;

"G"是指寿险保单项下所支付的索赔金额,超过了本年度所支付的寿险保单的预留金额和从预留金额中赚取的收入之和;和

"H"是指公司在本年度内与人寿保险业务相关的任何其他可扣除开支。

2/ 如果公司从事人寿保险业务以及包括普通保险业务在内的其他业务,则该公司从人寿保险业务中获得的应纳税所得额应与纳税人其他业务的应纳税所得额分开计算。

3/ 在本条中,"人寿保险"具有《商法典》赋予该术语的含义。

第六节
微 型 企 业

48. 微型企业记账的义务

就《公告》第82条而言,微型企业应当被视为个人,并应根据此类企业的年营业额履行记账义务。

第七节
"C"类纳税人

49. "C"类纳税人的推定营业税

1/ "C"类纳税人应缴纳的推定营业税应当按照本条例所附附表计算。

2/ 纳税人的年度应纳税所得额,应当按照纳税义务人年度总收入所在的收入范围内的最高年度营业额进行评估。

3/ 部长应当修改附表,依据附表,至少每3年对"C"类纳税人应缴税款进行评估。

4/ 纳税人为车辆所有人,驾驶其从事运输服务业务所使用的车辆的,在计算该车辆所有人应缴纳的税款时,应当计算该车辆所有人应当缴纳的就业所得税。

第六部分
附表"C"收入

50. 资产临时租赁收益

就《公告》第 58 条而言,"资产临时租赁所得"是指不从事动产或者不动产租赁业务的人取得的收入总额。

51. 常设机构的返还利润

1/ 根据《公告》第 62 条的规定,非居民机构通过埃塞俄比亚的常设机构经营业务的返还利润应根据该机构的纳税年度征收。

2/ 一个纳税年度的机构返还利润应根据下列公式计算:

$$A+(B-C)-D$$

其中:

"A"是指纳税年度开始时常设机构的资产总成本(扣除负债);

"B"是指根据财务报告准则计算的常设机构在该纳税年度的净利润;

"C"是指常设机构该纳税年度就应纳税所得额应缴纳的企业所得税;和

"D"是指纳税年度结束时该常设机构的资产总成本(扣除负债);

3/ 在计算一个纳税年度的常设机构返还利润时,该常设机构在纳税年度结束时的资产总成本应当为下一个纳税年度开始时的资产总成本。

52. 业务利润调整对派息的影响

机关申报的营业利润低于主管机关根据税务稽核结果调整后的营业利润的,不影响根据机关申报的营业利润向股东分配股利的纳税。

53. 以捐赠方式处置投资资产应缴纳的资本收益税

1/ 就《公告》第 59 条而言,通过捐赠处置的资本资产,其应缴纳税款应当按资产的原始成本与捐赠方式处置时的资产成本之间的差额计算应纳税额。

2/ 接受捐赠者应当对通过捐赠处置的资本资产缴纳税款。

第七部分
免 税 收 入

54. 免税收入

1/ 下列收入项目免征所得税:

a) 从事出口业务的投资者为转让知识而聘用的外籍专业人员,按部长发布的指示支付不超过 5 年的就业收入;

b) 为同一雇主工作的非熟练雇员在任何 12 个月内连续或间歇地工作不超过 30 天所获得的雇佣收入;但临时雇员在 12 个月内间歇性地为同一雇主工作超过 30 天,其受雇人员的应缴税款,只可按该雇员上一次受雇的收入计算;

c）就本条（b）款中的豁免而言，"非熟练雇员"是指未接受过职业培训的雇员、未使用需要特殊技能的机械或设备，且在一个日历年内被雇主雇用的时间总计不超过 30 天的雇员。

2/ 根据《公告》第 65 条第（1）款（a）项（1）目，雇主为支付雇员医疗费用而支付金额的豁免，应当包括雇主根据雇员医疗保险计划代表雇员支付的保险费。

第八部分
资　　产

55. 资产处置与收购

就折旧和资本利得税而言，当可登记资产以出售、交换或赠与的方式转让时，在被授权行使公证员职能的实体登记出售、交换或赠与时，转让人被视为已处置该资产，受让人被视为已取得该资产。

56. 成本

1/ 公告中规定的"A"类应税资产的成本应根据部长发布的指令确定的通货膨胀进行调整。

2/ 如果纳税人收购资产是以下金额的衍生：

a）在公告规定的纳税义务人的收入中，资产的成本为该资产所包含的费用加上纳税义务人为该资产所支付的任何费用；或者

b）免税收入，资产成本是免税额加上纳税人为该资产支付的任何金额。

57. 股权转让

如果非居民转让的股份与埃塞俄比亚的资产直接或间接相关，则该股份应视为已在埃塞俄比亚转让。

第九部分
行政和程序规则

58. "B"类纳税人保管的账簿

1/ 管理局应当通过指令确定要求"B"类纳税人连同其简化账簿一并提交的文件。

2/ "B"类纳税人只要符合财务报告标准规定的要求，便可以自愿按权责发生制记账。

59. "C"类纳税人应保留的账簿和文件

1/ 就《公告》第 82 条第（3）款而言，"C"类纳税人可保留"B"类纳税人必须维持的账簿。持有账簿的"C"类纳税人的税款应当按照管理局可接受的账簿进行评估。

2/ 尽管有本条第（1）款的规定，雇用工人的"C"类纳税人应当保留显示支付给雇员的任何就业收入金额和从该收入中扣缴的任何税款的文件。

60. 按"C"类纳税人缴纳税款

1/《公告》第 49 条所称"C类"纳税人，按照以上缴为基础的标准推定营业税或者以指标为基础的推定营业税方法纳税。

2/ 从事运输服务业务的"C"类纳税人应当在缴纳就业收入预扣税的同时缴纳营业税。

61. 预扣税的不适用

为了《公告》第 92 条的目的,部长应当通过指令具体说明:

1/ 不适用预扣税的服务类型;

2/ 不适用预扣税义务的人员。

62. 国内支付的预扣税

1/ 依据《公告》第 92 条的规定,预扣缴税款的扣缴义务人应当向依据本条款扣缴税款的收款人出具一份连续编号的正式收据。

2/ 如果预扣代理人是政府机构,则本条第(1)款所指的收据应当由该部认证。

3/《联邦税收管理公告》第 19 条适用于本条第(1)款提及的由政府机构以外的扣缴义务人开具的收据。

63. 向扣缴义务人提供商业许可证的要求

除《公告》第 92 条第(4)款规定的税号(TIN)要求外,还应要求纳税人提交其营业执照。

64. 扣缴义务人的责任

1/ 扣缴义务人未向税务机关申报代扣代缴税款,但向税务机关提供主要纳税义务人已缴纳税款的证据的,不适用《公告》第 97 条第(3)款。

2/ 本条第(1)款的规定不排除根据《税收管理公告》第 106 条第(1)款规定的罚款。

65. 账簿的延迟提交

1/ 账簿不得因迟交而被拒绝;

2/ 本条第(1)款的规定应当:

a) 不适用于因未提交纳税申报表而被评估的税款;

b) 不排除根据《税收管理公告》第 102 条规定的罚款。

66. 停业后所得收入

依《公告》第 74 条的目的,税务机关应当对停止营业后取得收入的纳税人的纳税程序发布指示。

第十部分
其 他 规 定

67. 合并折旧资产

1/ 在《公告》开始时在折旧池中有正余额的纳税人应当继续根据已废止公告对折旧池中的余额进行折旧。

2/ 如果本条第(1)款适用的纳税人将折旧资产处置为折旧池,处置的对价应当减少折旧池的折旧基数。

3/ 如果由于处置本条第(1)款所述的可折旧资产,折旧池的折旧基数为负数:

a) 负数计入营业收入;和

b) 该资产池被视为已结清,且该池中剩余的任何资产均被视为已完全折旧。

4/ 纳税人在《公告》生效之日或者之后购得折旧资产的,应当按照本条例第 38 条的规定对资产进行折旧,资产成本不得添加到本条第(1)款所指的折旧池中。

68. 业务亏损结转

1/ 根据已废止公告,有营业亏损但未根据已废止公告完全扣除的纳税人,应当继续根据已废止公告扣除;

2/ 根据已废止公告所发生的任何损失,不得因《公告》第 26 条第(4)款的目的而予以考虑。

69. 指令豁免

部长在《公告》生效之前发布的指令中规定的豁免将一直有效,直到以下日期中的较早者出现:

1/ 指令根据其条款失效的日期;或者

2/ 部长废除该指令的日期。

70. 已废止和不适用的法律

1/《所得税第 78/2002 号条例(经修订)》被本条例废止;

2/ 被废止的条例在本条例施行前的纳税年度继续适用。

71. 生效日期

本条例适用于自 2016 年 7 月 8 日起产生的收入。

2017 年 8 月 24 日在亚的斯亚贝巴签署

海尔马里亚姆·德萨莱尼

埃塞俄比亚联邦民主共和国总理

税表(略)

第四编
工业园区法规

第九部
工业园区公告
（第 886/2015 号公告）

埃塞俄比亚联邦民主共和国联邦政府公报

第 21 年 39 号
2015 年 4 月 9 日，亚的斯亚贝巴

第886/2015号公告
工业园区公告

鉴于,有必要通过在战略要地建立工业园区来加速国家的经济转型和发展,以促进和吸引国内外的生产性直接投资,从而提升工业水平并创造就业机会;

认识到,促进出口、保护环境和人类福祉、节约用地以及建立和扩大规划中的城市中心的必要性;

认识到,在建立、发展、运营、管理和调整工业园区方面,立法至关重要;

因此,现根据《埃塞俄比亚联邦民主共和国宪法》第55条第(1)款的规定,兹宣布如下:

第一部分
总　　则

1. 简称

本公告可以称为《工业园区公告第886/2015号》。

2. 定义

在本公告中,除非上下文另有规定,否则:

1/ "工业园区"是指由相关机构指定的具有明显边界的地区,以发展综合、互补、多元或选定的工业功能,在有计划地实施基础设施和道路、电力、水等各项服务的基础上,一站式运作,并制定特别激励计划,以期实现有计划、系统地发展工业、减轻污染对环境和人的影响以及城市中心的发展,包括经济特区、科技园区、出口加工区、农产品加工区、自由贸易区等投资理事会指定的区域;

2/ "资产"是指由公营、公私合营或私营实体拥有的与工业园区有关的任何动产或不动产以及无形财产的权益;

3/ "土地"是指指定用于工业园区的任何土地;

4/ "已开发土地"是指配备有例如道路、水、电、通信、交通运输和液体污水排放设施,减少空气污染的设施以及其他重要基础设施的土地;

5/ "租赁"是指一种土地使用权制度,通过该制度可以按一定期限的合同获得对工业园区土地的使用权;

6/ "开始发展"是指:

a) 对于工业园区开发商而言,兴建道路、水、电、通信、交通运输和液体污水处理设施等基础设施的基础工程,以及建筑物的地基工程;

b) 对于工业园区企业而言,至少在工业园区土地上建造或安装钢筋混凝土柱,以便在工业园区土地上建造允许的建筑或建筑物;

7/ "转租"是指工业园区开发商或工业园区经营者将已开发的工业园区土地通过划拨或

租赁的方式转让给工业园区企业；

8/"投资"是指园区内的经营者和工业园区企业按照签发的许可证或者订立的协议，由工业园区开发商、工业园区经营者或工业园区企业（视情况而定）以现金或实物或两者兼有的资本支出，以建立新的或扩大或升级的工业园区；

9/"公司"是指根据《部长理事会第326/2014号条例》设立的工业园区开发公司；

10/"工业园区开发商"，是指任何盈利的公营、公私合营或私营开发商，包括根据《投资公告》和《投资条例》《工业园区开发商许可》和《工业园区开发商协议》中规定的从事设计、建造或开发工业园区的公司；

11/"工业园区经营者"是指根据《投资公告》和《投资条例》《工业园区经营者许可》和《工业园区经营者协议》经营、维护或促进工业园区的任何获利企业，包括公司；

12/"工业园区企业"是指由埃塞俄比亚人、外国人或共同拥有的公营、私营或公私合营企业，根据《投资公告》和《投资条例》《工业园区企业许可证》和《工业园区企业协议》，通过转租或租用或建造工业园区内的工厂，从事以营利为目的的生产活动或提供服务；

13/《投资公告》和《投资条例》是指《第769/2012号投资公告（经修订）》以及《为国内投资者保留的投资鼓励措施和投资领域部长理事会第270/2012号条例（经修订）》；

14/"协议"是指在以下情况下缔结的协议：

a）委员会和工业园区开发商在工业园区内设计、建造、开发或提供其他服务；

b）工业园区开发商和工业园区经营者在工业园区内运营、维护、推广或提供其他专业支持服务；

c）工业园区开发商或工业园区经营者、工业园区企业；

15/"工业园区居民"是指由委员会授予工业园居住证明书，以便在工业园居民区居住的自然人；

16/"政府"是指埃塞俄比亚联邦民主共和国政府或地方政府；

17/"地区"是指《埃塞俄比亚联邦民主共和国宪法》第47条第（1）款所指的任何州，包括亚的斯亚贝巴和迪里达瓦市政府；

18/"理事会""委员会"是指根据《埃塞俄比亚投资理事会或埃塞俄比亚投资委员会设立部长理事会第313/2014号条例》设立的理事会或委员会；

19/"主管当局"是指对工业园区的特定领域或地理区域具有监管权和职责的任何联邦、地区或城市管理政府机关；

20/"投资许可证"是指由工业园区开发商委员会、工业园区经营者或工业园区企业颁发的，以投资者身份从事工业园区开发相关活动的许可证；

21/"关税区域"是指适用埃塞俄比亚与该国工业园区有关的常规海关法律的地区；

22/"工业园区海关管制区"是指属于工业园区的一部分，海关有权监管，但被视为不属于关税区域的地区；

23/"适用法律"是指工业园区内任何补充或根据本公告和《工业园区条例》解释的适用的公告、条例或指示；

24/《条例》是指部长理事会发布的执行本公告的条例；

25/"三方模式"是指劳动和社会事务部、工业园区开发商的雇主、工业园区经营者或工业园区企业的雇员以及雇员代表通过建设性协商解决劳资问题；

26/ "基本公用设施"，是指与工业园区有关的公用设施，例如水、电、通信、天然气和《条例》中规定的其他类似公用设施；

27/ "人"是指任何自然人或法人；

28/ 任何男性性别的表达都适用于女性。

3. 适用范围

本公告的规定应在埃塞俄比亚境内统一适用于联邦工业园区的活动或与其有关的活动，以及在联邦工业园区内进行任何活动的任何人。

4. 目标

本公告具有以下目标：

1/ 规范工业园区的设计、开发和运营；

2/ 为国家技术和工业基础设施的发展做出贡献；

3/ 鼓励私营部门参与制造业和相关投资；

4/ 增强国家经济发展的竞争力；

5/ 创造充足的就业机会，实现经济的可持续发展。

第二部分
工业园区开发商和工业园区经营者的权利和义务

5. 工业园区开发商的权利

任何工业园区开发商均有权：

1/ 设计、建造、发展、开发工业园区并提供服务；

2/ 转租已开发的工业园区用地；

3/ 按照生产、办公、居住和其他服务规定的比例，将其在工业园区内的不动产、建筑物和房间出租或出售给工业园区企业；

4/ 签订工业园区土地开发、经营和推广转租协议；

5/ 按照工业园区发展协议经营、维护和促进工业园区；

6/ 按照规定雇用埃塞俄比亚公民和外国人；

7/ 参与金融市场，以按照本公告和其他适用法律发布的《条例》中规定的方式获得贷款、资金担保和其他金融资源；

8/ 根据与公用设施供应商达成的委托协议，为从事工业园区内的工业园区企业提供服务，收取费用；具体办法由《条例》规定；

9/ 享受免税和关税减免以及根据适用法律给予的其他奖励。

6. 工业园区开发商的义务

任何工业园区开发商都有义务：

1/ 根据许可证和工业园区开发商或工业园区协议的要求，在工业园区、现场基础设施、办公空间和其他设施中建造不动产，供委员会一站式使用以及供税务和海关总署使用；

2/ 为国内培训机构参与工业园区开发设计工作提供必要的条件；

3/ 在工业园区开发协议规定的期限内开始开发;

4/ 完成工业园区分阶段开发的履行要求以及许可证规定的资本和债务融资的财务义务和时间安排;

5/ 出示证明其财务来源的可信赖文件;

6/ 不得以任何方式将未开发的工业园区土地转让给第三方;

7/ 遵守本公告、《条例》、环境保护法规和其他适用法律以及许可中规定的其他义务;

8/ 通过专门培训传授所需的知识和技能,由埃塞俄比亚国民代替外籍人员或专业人员。

7. 工业园区经营者的权利

工业园区内的任何工业园区经营者均有权:

1/ 转让正在转租的已开发工业园区土地和出租或转租不动产,提供公用设施及其他服务,代表工业园区开发商,提供基本服务和其他收费服务;

2/ 根据工业园区经营者的协议运营、管理、维护和促进工业园区发展;

3/ 根据该条例雇用埃塞俄比亚人和外国人;

4/ 使用本公告、《条例》和其他相关法律规定的其他权利。

8. 工业园区经营者的义务

工业园区内的任何工业园区经营者都有义务:

1/ 遵守本公告、《条例》和许可条款;

2/ 根据工业园区许可证,运营、维护和促进工业园区发展,并使其资产和效益处于运营状态;

3/ 保持现成的办公空间和设施,用于一站式商店和海关服务;

4/ 禁止以任何方式将未开发的工业园区土地转让给第三方,但公司将工业土地转让给其他工业园区开发商的除外;

5/ 将国内制造企业与工业园区企业联系起来,以发展其技术能力并从国际市场中受益;

6/ 遵守本公告、《条例》、适用法律、许可说明或协议中规定的社会和环境以及其他任何义务;

7/ 通过专门培训转移所需的知识和技能,由埃塞俄比亚国民代替外籍人员或专业人员。

第三部分
工业园区企业与投资

9. 工业园区企业的权利

任何工业园区企业均有权:

1/ 可以获取工业园区许可证,以便在工业园区内进行投资活动。《条例》中应当规定提交许可证申请的方式、要求和作出决定;

2/ 在获得本条第(1)款所指的许可后,获得适用法律规定的税收、关税和其他激励措施;

3/ 根据许可证的条款和条件自由开展投资活动,但禁止危害公共秩序、道德、安全和保障以及人类和动物健康及植物生命的活动;具体细节由《条例》规定;

4/ 根据本公告和其他适用法律规定的海关处理,以转租方式取得土地,拥有、出售自有建筑物、租赁其他不动产、出口到国外、进口到任何工业园区、在工业园区海关控制区出售货物和服务。

10. 工业园区企业的义务

任何工业园区企业都有义务：

1/ 在工业园区企业许可和协议规定的期限内开始开发；

2/ 进行许可证中规定的投资活动；

3/ 允许进行技术和职业教育与培训的创业培训、协作培训和高等教育的培训；

4/ 遵守本公告和《条例》中规定的义务，尤其是其中所载的环境、社会和雇员义务以及其他适用法律中的义务；

5/ 通过专门培训转移所需的知识和技能，由埃塞俄比亚国民代替外籍人员或专业人员。

11. 理事会处罚投机活动的行政措施

1/ 如果工业园区开发商或工业园区运营商未经理事会行政机关的事先批准，违反各自工业园许可证、协议、本公告和《条例》的规定，以租赁或转租的方式转让其获得的土地，应按照理事会发布的指令进行处罚。

2/ 本条第（1）款的规定不影响工业园区企业与工业园区开发商或工业园区运营商就工业园区开发区内已开发土地达成的转租协议。

3/ 为了执行本规定，理事会应跟踪所有工业园区土地的年度公平市场租赁价格。

12. 商业登记与合规

1/ 任何潜在的工业园区开发商、工业园区经营者或工业园区企业均应就其成立和注册向委员会提交以下文件：

a）由潜在的工业园区相关投资者的所有者或代理商正式签字确认的申请表；

b）公证的组织章程大纲和章程；

c）如果是分支机构，则应提供证明母公司在原籍国的注册和法人资格的文件。

2/ 根据本条第（1）款注册的工业园区开发商、工业园区经营者或工业园区企业，应具有法人资格。

3/《条例》中规定了与工业园区商业登记及相关运营批准以及许可、报告、检查、破产和清算相关的细节。

第四部分
工业园区工作许可证和居住证

13. 工业园区外籍人员入境、工作许可和居留权

1/ 任何工业园区开发商、工业园区经营者或工业园区企业均可聘请外籍人员担任其最高的管理、监督、培训或其他技术职务。

2/ 外籍人员及其家属的入境、工作许可和居留证应通过委员会作为一站式服务机构或移民和国籍事务部以及劳工和社会事务部的协调职能而加快执行；其方式应在《条例》中规定。

14. 工业园区居住证

1/ 任何自然人，无论是埃塞俄比亚人还是外国人，都可以成为工业园区居民，但须满足

《条例》规定的要求。

2/ 法规中应规定工业园区居住证和工作证的分类和签发。

15. 工业园区居民权利

工业园区居民应有权：

1/ 在居留证所指定的期限内居住；

2/ 在工业园区停留期间内，进口不含关税和其他费用的个人物品，其细节应在《条例》中规定；

3/ 建立社区委员会，以便在设施和服务方面更好地了解工业园区开发商和工业园区经营者；

4/ 将其个人财物转移给其他工业园区居民；其详情应在《条例》中作出规定；

5/ 享有《条例》中规定的其他权利。

16. 工业园区居民义务

工业园区居民有义务：

1/ 除非本公告另有规定，否则需为任何进口货物支付所有适用的关税和其他适当费用；

2/ 根据相关法律缴纳个人所得税和其他税款；

3/ 尊重其他法律规定的义务。

17. 工业园区居民投机管理办法

如果工业园区居民违反工业园区居住证、本公告或《条例》的规定将其工业园区不动产转让给第三方，委员会可采取以下行政措施：

1/ 撤销工业园区居住证；

2/ 归还工业园区开发商或工业园区运营商在其居住期间给予的资产；

3/ 向工业园区居民征收此类资产的租金，期限最长为 30 天。

18. 撤销工业园区居民证

1/ 委员会可在提供 90 天的事先通知和正当程序的前提下，尤其是在行政听证会之后，基于以下原因撤销工业园区居民证：

a）如果工业园区居民未能满足本公告、《条例》、操作规则和程序、工业园区居民证书或任何其他相关法律的要求；

b）通过错误陈述或通过提供虚假信息或声明获得的工业园区居民证；

2/ 吊销工业园区居民证，终止居民享有任何权利；已终止的不动产应视情况归还给工业园区开发商或工业园区经营者。

3/ 已被撤销工业园区居民证或离开园区的居民可在缴纳关税和税款后变卖其个人财物。

4/ 委员会还可以按照《条例》的规定采取进一步的行政措施。

第五部分
保障和保护国民待遇

19. 国民待遇

在不影响该国其他相关法律关于外国投资者的规定的前提下，任何外国投资者单独或与埃塞俄比亚人共同均可作为工业园区开发商、工业园区经营者或工业园区企业加入。

20. 担保与保护

1/ 除非出于公共目的要求,否则不得征用工业园区投资,并应及时支付适当的赔偿。

2/ 如果投资者是外国投资者,则应以国际金融市场上任何可兑换货币支付赔偿。

3/ 任何非法征收的工业园区开发企业、工业园区经营者或者工业园区企业有权收回其资产或者投资,并按照规定计算合理的利率,征用时间为自征用时起至归还时止。

4/ 征收方式和构成非法征收、补偿、返还的,适用有关法律的规定。

21. 适用的外汇规则

任何遵守国家法律的工业园区开发商或工业园区经营者或工业园区企业应:

1/ 有权向国外银行和国内金融机构借款;

2/ 允许其股票、债券和其他证券在国外证券市场上市;

3/ 有权根据《第769/2012号投资公告》第26条第(1)款第(a)至(g)项的规定,以汇款当日的现行汇率,以可兑换外币进行汇款;汇款详情应在《条例》中规定。

第六部分
土地使用和环境保护

22. 收购工业园区动产和不动产

1/ 工业园区开发商可以通过租赁系统拥有工业园区土地,并可以通过转租转让已开发的工业园区土地。

2/ 经理事会批准,工业园区经营者可拥有并管理他通过与工业园区开发商协议获得的工业园区土地。

3/ 经委员会批准并签发投资许可证后,工业园区企业可以拥有其通过与工业园区开发商或工业园区运营商协议获得的工业园区内的土地。

4/ 工业园区用地不受土地权属、城乡用地和招标投标制度的限制。

5/ 关于工业园区土地现场登记、土地租赁、转租、场地开发、建设、安全和公用事业供应的细节,应在条例中规定。

6/ 工业园区开发企业、工业园区经营者、工业园区企业有权将其开发的土地和其他与土地开发投资相适应的不动产、动产抵押,向金融机构贷款,具体办法由条例规定。

7/ 未经理事会书面许可,工业园区开发商或工业园区经营者不得向第三方转让已租赁和已开发的工业园土地,除非转让给工业园区企业。

23. 建筑规范

尽管有其他法律法规的规定,但有关工业园区土地开发、基础设施以及工业园区建筑物和构筑物的建造的规范或标准,仍应在《条例》中予以规定,以确保对工业园区的项目进行适当的设计、规划、建设、管理、土地开发以及相关项目的监督管理和质量控制。

24. 环境条例

1/ 联邦和地区环境法规应在工业园区内适用。

2/ 环境与森林部应在工业园区内设立办事处,负责工业园区内环境规范、标准、保障措施、管理和缓解计划的实施、监督、保护和执行。

3/ 有关工业园区的环境义务的细节应在《条例》中规定。

25. 工业园区设计与改造

1/ 工业园区应由理事会指定。

2/ 理事会在指定工业园区时应考虑：

a) 拟建项目的性质；

b) 拟建的工业园区的面积和周长；

c) 清理障碍，接近工业投入和基础设施，有助于成为人口中心以及项目的性质包括接近医疗和娱乐中心；

d) 与总体规划、土地使用等的兼容性。

3/《条例》中应规定指定程序的细节；

4/ 对工业园区的任何修改和撤销均应由理事会决定。

26. 工业园区开发商选拔要求

工业园区开发商的选拔应当按照《条例》进行。

27. 一站式商店

1/ 任何工业园区主管部门提供的服务均应通过高效、简化的一站式商店提供。

2/ 委员会应在工业园区内提供一站式服务，使其他主管机构参与进来并协调其日常职能。

3/ 主管当局应在一站式服务机构履行其特定职能的过程中保持其职责。

4/ 与一站式服务有关的细节应在《条例》中规定。

28. 劳工事务

1/《第 377/2003 号劳工公告（经修订）》适用于任何工业园区；

2/ 在不影响本条第（1）款的前提下，劳务合同可以由雇主和雇员在考虑到工业园区的独特特征之间进行谈判；

3/ 劳动和社会事务部应根据三方形式与工业部协商，制定有关劳动问题的规则和程序，其细节应在《条例》中规定；

4/ 工业部应在必要时与有关政府部门和工业园区开发商（运营商）合作组织技术和职业培训计划；

5/ 工业部应主要通过集群和其他做法，促进一般的技术转让和技能发展，特别是国内制造业部门的能力建设。

第七部分
监管机构和申诉程序

29. 监管机构

1/ 理事会应指定并监理工业园区的管理和监督。

2/ 理事会须就任何工业园区发展商、工业园区营办商或工业园区企业就委员会决定提出的投诉作出裁决。

3/ 理事会应在《条例》中规定其行使其监管任务的方式。

4/ 工业部应确保并监督工业园区企业应协助提供扩展服务、技术、投入、营销和制造方法等。

5/ 委员会除了行使《第 769/2012 号投资公告（经修订）》规定的职责外,还应向工业园区开发商、工业园区经营者或工业园区企业颁发许可证;与工业园区开发商和工业园区运营商签订协议。

6/ 本条规定的理事会和委员会的详细职能应在《条例》中规定。

30. 处罚、暂停及撤销许可证

1/ 理事会应:

a) 如果工业园区开发商或工业园区经营者违反了许可证、本公告的条例或指令中规定的条件或任何其他相关法律,理事会应当对其作出处罚,以便其在条例规定的期限内采取整改措施;

b) 如果工业园区开发商或工业园区经营者未按照本条(a)项规定采取整改措施,则应按照规定的期限暂停工业园区开发商或工业园区经营者,直至采取整改措施为止。

2/ 如果工业园区开发商或工业园区经营者未根据本条第(1)款(b)项采取整改措施,并且出现以下原因之一,委员会可撤销许可证:

a) 宣布破产;

b) 前提是基于虚假信息或虚假陈述给予许可;

c) 未能根据协议开发土地或管理工业园区(视情况而定);

d) 通知适当的机构终止其活动。

3/ 许可证一经撤销,该许可证持有人所拥有的土地须归还出租该土地的实体。

4/ 吊销许可证将终止工业园区开发或工业园区运营协议。

5/ 委员会可以:

a) 向工业园区企业发出惩戒,园区企业违反许可证、实施本公告或者其他相关法律的规定或指令的,应在规定的期限内采取整改措施;

b) 如果未按照本条(a)项规定采取整改措施,则按照规定的期限停工,直至采取整改措施。

6/ 如果工业园区企业未能根据本条第(5)款(b)项采取整改措施,并且出现以下原因之一,委员会则可以撤销许可证:

a) 宣布破产;

b) 证明许可是基于虚假信息或虚假陈述提供的;

c) 没有按照协议开发土地;

d) 自愿通知适当的机关其活动的终止。

7/ 根据本条的撤销条款将剥夺许可证持有人的权利,使其不享有本公告规定的权利。

31. 投诉渠道

1/ 任何工业园区开发商、工业园区经营者、工业园区企业或工业园区居民有权就主管机关采取的措施向本委员会提出投诉。

2/ 任何此类投诉均可在采取有关措施之日起 30 天内向委员会提出。

3/ 委员会应在30天内就提交的投诉作出决定。

4/ 如果对委员会的决定在30天内提出申述,理事会应受理,并须在30天内作出裁决。

5/ 不服理事会决定的一方可以在收到该决定后30天内向具有管辖权的法院提出上诉。

6/ 关于投诉和提出决定的方式应在条例中规定细节。

第八部分
其他规定

32. 颁布法规和指令的权力

1/ 部长理事会可发布适用于工业园区的一系列激励措施条例和其他必要条例。

2/ 理事会可以发布执行本公告和根据本条第(1)款发布的条例所必需的指令。

33. 临时规定

1/ 任何现有的工业园区或信息技术园区,只要符合指定标准并受本公告管辖,就应在本公告生效时假定为工业园区。

2/ 前提:

a) 政府与工业园区、工业园区开发商或工业园区经营者签订了协议;

b) 政府对工业园区、工业园区开发商、工业园区经营者或工业园区企业的激励措施应继续适用。

3/ 依据本公告和《条例》,任何先前就工业开发区或工业园区的开发和运营而提出的申请,均须视为在委员会面前待决。

4/ 工业园区发展公司应假定是根据本公告成立的。

34. 不适用的法律

与本公告不符的公告、条例、指示或惯例,对于本公告中规定的事项,均不具有效力。

35. 生效日期

本公告自其在《联邦政府公报》上颁布之日起生效。

2015年4月9日在亚的斯亚贝巴签署

穆拉图·特肖姆(博士)

埃塞俄比亚联邦民主共和国总统

GROUP ONE
INVESTMENT LAWS AND REGULATIONS

TITLE ONE
A PROCLAMATION ON INVESTMENT
(Proclamation No. 769/2012)

FEDERAL NEGARIT GAZETA
OF THE FEDERAL DEMOCRATIC REPUBLIC OF ETHIOPIA

18th Year No. 63
ADDIS ABABA 17th September, 2012

PROCLAMATION No. 769/2012
A PROCLAMATION ON INVESTMENT

WHEREAS, the encouragement and expansion of investment, especially in the manufacturing sector, has become necessary so as to strengthen the domestic production capacity and thereby accelerate the economic development of the country and improve the living standards of its peoples;

WHEREAS, it has become necessary to further increase the inflow of capital and speed up the transfer of technology into the country;

WHEREAS, it has become necessary to enhance and promote the equitable distribution of investments among regions and benefit the society by ensuring competitiveness among investments made by investors;

WHEREAS, it has become essential to put in place a system of supervision to ensure that permits and incentives granted to investors are used for the intended purposes;

WHEREAS, the system of administration of investment needs to be transparent and efficient;

WHEREAS, it has been considered that the establishment of industrial development zones helps, by creating enabling and competitive condition, to interrelate manufacturing sectors based on value creation as well as to attract and expand investment;

WHEREAS, to these ends, it has become necessary to revise the existing law on investment;

NOW, THEREFORE, in accordance with Article 55(1) of the Constitution of the Federal Democratic Republic of Ethiopia, it is hereby proclaimed as follows:

PART ONE
GENERAL

1. Short Title

This Proclamation may be cited as the "Investment Proclamation No. 769/2012".

2. Definitions

In this Proclamation, unless the context otherwise requires:

1/ "investment" means expenditure of capital in cash or in kind or in both by an investor to establish a new enterprise or to expand or upgrade one that already exists;

2/ "enterprise" means an undertaking established for the purpose of profit making;

3/ "capital" means local or foreign currency, negotiable instruments, machinery or equipment, buildings, working capital, property rights, patent rights, or other business assets;

4/ "investor" means a domestic or a foreign investor having invested in Ethiopia;

5/ "domestic investor" means an Ethiopian national or a foreign national treated as a domestic investor as per the relevant law, and includes the government, public enterprises as well as cooperative societies established as per the relevant law;

6/ "foreign investor" means a foreigner or an enterprise wholly owned by foreign nationals, having invested foreign capital in Ethiopia or a foreigner or an Ethiopian incorporated enterprise owned by foreign nationals jointly investing with a domestic investor, and includes an Ethiopian permanently residing abroad and preferring treatment as a foreign investor;

7/ "foreign capital" means capital obtained from foreign sources, and includes the re-invested profits and dividends of a foreign investor;

8/ "expansion" or "upgrading" includes increasing in volume, by at least 50% the attainable production or service rendering capacity of an existing enterprise or increasing in variety, by at least 100%, by introducing a new production or service rendering line of an existing enterprise or increment by both;

9/ "public enterprise" means an enterprise, wholly or partially owned by the federal or regional government;

10/ "transfer of technology" means the transfer of systematic knowledge for the manufacture of a product, for the application or improvement of a process or for the rendering of a service, including management and technical know-how as well as marketing technologies, but may not extend to transactions involving the mere sale or lease of goods;

11/ "export-oriented non-equity based foreign enterprise collaboration" means a 100% export-oriented contractual agreement between a domestic investor and foreign enterprise in which the foreign enterprise provides, among others, all or some of the following:

a) guaranteed external market access;

b) production know-how of products for export market;

c) export marketing know-how;

d) export business management know-how;

e) strategies for the supply of raw materials and intermediate inputs needed for export products;

12/ "government" means the federal government or a regional government;

13/ "region" means any state specified under Article 47(1) of the Constitution of the Federal Democratic Republic of Ethiopia and includes the Addis Ababa and Dire Dawa city administrations;

14/ "Agency" means the Ethiopian Investment Agency to be established by regulation of the Council of Ministers;

15/ "Investment Board" means the highest governing body of the Agency;

16/ "appropriate investment organ" means the Agency or the executive organ of a region empowered to issue investment permits;

17/ "industrial development zone" means an area with distinct boundary designated by the appropriate organ to develop identical, similar and interrelated industries together or to develop multi-faceted industries based on a plan fulfilling infrastructures such as road, electric power and water and having incentive schemes with purposes containing industrial development, mitigating the impacts of environmental pollution and administering the development of urbans with plan and system;

18/ any expression in the masculine gender includes the feminine.

3. Scope of Application

The provisions of this Proclamation may not be applicable to investments in the prospecting, exploration and development of minerals and petroleum resources.

4. Jurisdiction

1/ The administration of the following investments shall be under the jurisdiction of the Agency:

a) wholly foreign owned investment;

b) joint investment made by domestic and foreign investors;

c) investment made by a foreign national, not Ethiopian by origin, treated as a domestic investor pursuant to Article 2(5) of this Proclamation;

d) investment made, in areas eligible for incentives, by a domestic investor who is required to obtain a business license from the concerned federal organ.

2/ Notwithstanding the provisions of Sub-Article (1) of this Article, the issuance, renewal, replacement and cancellation of investment permits for air transport services and for generation or transmission or distribution of electrical energy shall be carried out by the Ethiopian Civil Aviation Authority and the Ethiopian Electricity Agency respectively, representing the Agency.

3/ The Ethiopian Civil Aviation Authority and the Ethiopian Electricity Agency shall:

a) carry out functions delegated to them under Sub-Article (2) of this Article in accordance with this Proclamation, and regulations and directives issued hereunder;

b) forward to the Agency information regarding the services they have rendered by way of delegation.

4/ Investments other than those referred to in Sub-Article (1) and (2) of this Article shall fall under the jurisdiction of regional investment organs.

PART TWO
INVESTMENT OBJECTIVES AND AREAS OF INVESTMENT

5. Investment Objectives

The investment objectives of the Federal Democratic Republic of Ethiopia are designed to improve the living standards of the peoples of Ethiopia through the realization of sustainable economic and social development, the particulars of which are the following:

1/ to accelerate the country's economic development;

2/ to exploit and develop the immense natural resources of the country;

3/ to develop the domestic market through the growth of production, productivity and services;

4/ to increase foreign exchange earnings by encouraging expansion in volume, variety and quality of the country's export products and services as well as to save foreign exchange through production of import substituting products locally;

5/ to encourage balanced development and integrated economic activity among the regions and to strengthen the inter-sectoral linkages of the economy;

6/ to enhance the role of the private sector in the acceleration of the country's economic development;

7/ to enable foreign investment play its role in the country's economic development;

8/ to create ample employment opportunities for Ethiopians and to advance the transfer of technology required for the development of the country.

6. Areas of Investment Reserved for the Government or Joint Investment with the Government

1/ The following areas of investment shall exclusively be reserved for the government:

a) transmission and distribution of electrical energy through the integrated national grid system;

b) postal services with the exception of courier services;

c) air transport services using aircraft with a seating capacity of more than fifty passengers.

2/ Investors shall be allowed to invest in the following areas only jointly with the government:

a) manufacturing of weapons and ammunition;

b) telecom services.

3/ The Council of Ministers may, whenever it deems necessary, determine, by issuing regulation, that areas of investment exclusively reserved for the government or for joint investment with the government be opened to private investors.

7. Areas of Investment Reserved for Domestic Investors

Areas of investment exclusively reserved for domestic investors shall be specified by regulation to be issued by the Council of Ministers.

8. Areas of Investment Allowed for Foreign Investors

Areas of investment open for foreign investors shall be determined by regulation to be issued by the Council of Ministers.

9. Investments to be Undertaken Jointly with the Government

The Privatization and Public Enterprises Supervising Agency shall receive investment proposals submitted by any private investor intending to invest jointly with the government; it shall submit same to the Ministry of Industry for decision and, upon approval, designate a public enterprise to invest as partner in the joint investment.

PART THREE
FORMS OF INVESTMENT AND CAPITAL REQUIREMENT FOR FOREIGN INVESTORS

10. Forms of Investment

1/ Investments may be carried out in one of the following forms:

a) sole proprietorship;

b) business organization incorporated in Ethiopia or abroad;

c) public enterprise established in accordance with the relevant law;

d) cooperative society formed in accordance with the relevant law.

2/ Any investment made in the forms prescribed under Sub-Article (1) of this Article shall be registered in accordance with the Commercial Code or other applicable law.

11. Minimum Capital Requirements for Foreign Investors

1/ Any foreign investor, to be allowed to invest pursuant to this Proclamation, shall be required to allocate a minimum capital of USD 200,000 for a single investment project.

2/ Notwithstanding the provision of Sub-Article (1) of this Article, the minimum capital required of a foreign investor investing jointly with a domestic investor shall be USD 150,000.

3/ The minimum capital required of a foreign investor investing in architectural or engineering works or related technical consultancy services, technical testing and analysis or in publishing work shall be:

a) USD 100,000 if the investment is made wholly on his own;

b) USD 50,000 if the investment is made jointly with a domestic investor.

4/ A foreign investor re-investing his profits or dividends generated from his existing enterprise may not be required to allocate a minimum capital.

5/ Any foreign investor having brought investment capital into the country shall have registered same by the Agency and obtain a certificate of registration. The Agency shall send a copy of the certificate to the National Bank of Ethiopia.

PART FOUR
INVESTMENT PERMIT

12. Requirement of Investment Permit

1/ The following investors shall be required to obtain investment permits:

a) foreign investors;

b) domestic and foreign investors investing in partnership;

c) foreign nationals, not Ethiopian by origin, treated as a domestic investors pursuant to Article 2(5) of this Proclamation;

d) domestic investors investing in areas eligible for incentives and who are seeking to be beneficiaries of such incentives.

2/ Notwithstanding the provision of Sub-Article (1) of this Article, domestic investors, excluding foreign nationals who are not of Ethiopian origin, shall have the right to invest, without having an investment permit, in conformity with the relevant laws of the country:

a) in areas not eligible for incentives; or

b) waiving their right of entitlement in those areas eligible for incentives.

3/ Notwithstanding the provision of Sub-Article (1) of this Article, a foreign investor intending to buy an existing enterprise in order to operate it as it stands or to buy shares of an existing enterprise shall obtain prior approval from the Ministry of Trade.

4/ The Ministry of Trade shall, upon receipt of a request made in accordance with Sub-Article (3) of this Article, ascertain, in both cases of transfer, that the enterprise is engaged in areas allowed for foreign investors, the minimum capital requirement provided for in this Proclamation and other requirements laid down in the Commercial Registration and Business Licensing Proclamation are fulfilled.

5/ The Ministry of Trade shall, after examining the request in accordance with Sub-Article (4) of this Article:

a) replace the business license or register the share transfer, upon receipt of the appropriate fee, where the application is found acceptable; or

b) notify to the investor its decision and the reason thereof in writing, where the application is found unacceptable.

13. Application for Investment Permit by a Domestic Investor

An application for investment permit by a domestic investor shall be made in a form designed for such purpose and submitted to the appropriate investment organ together with the following documents in one copy:

1/ where the application is signed by an agent, a photocopy of his power of attorney;

2/ where the investment is to be made by an individual person, a photocopy of his identity card or a photocopy of the identity card evidencing his domestic investor status and his recent two passport size photographs;

3/ where the investment is to be made by a business organization, a photocopy of its memorandum and articles of associations or where the business organization is to be newly established, in addition, it shall submit a photocopy of the shareholders identity cards or a photocopy of identity cards evidencing their domestic investor status;

4/ where the investment is to be made by a public enterprise, a photocopy of the regulation under which it is established or a photocopy of its memorandum and articles of associations;

5/ where the investment is to be made by a cooperative society, a photocopy of its articles of association.

14. Application for Investment Permit by a Foreign Investor

1/ Application for investment permit by a foreign investor shall be made in a form designed for such purpose and submitted to the Agency together with the following documents in one copy:

a) where the application is signed by an agent, a photocopy of his power of attorney;

b) where the investment is to be made by an individual person, a photocopy of the relevant pages of a valid passport showing his identity and his recent two passport size photographs;

c) where the investment is to be made by an Ethiopian permanently residing abroad, preferring treatment as a foreign investor, a photocopy of a document evidencing that he is residing abroad;

d) where the investment is to be made by a business organization incorporated in Ethiopia:

(1) a photocopy of its memorandum and articles of associations or where it is to be newly established, in addition, it shall submit a photocopy of the relevant pages of a valid passport of each shareholder showing his identity and recent two passport size photographs of the general

manager;

(2) where there is a foreign national treated as a domestic investor in the business organization, a photocopy of the identity card evidencing the domestic investor status;

(3) where there is a juridical person or a branch of a foreign juridical person in the business organization, a photocopy of its memorandum of association and articles of association or similar documents of the parent company, commercial registration certificate and a photocopy of the minutes of resolution passed by the authorized organ of the parent company authorizing the juridical person or the branch to invest in Ethiopia.

e) where the investment is to be made by an Ethiopian branch of a foreign business organization incorporated abroad:

(1) a photocopy of its memorandum and articles of associations or a similar document of the parent company;

(2) a photocopy of a document attesting the appointment of the branch manager and his two recent passport size photographs, a photocopy of the relevant pages of a valid passport or identity card of the branch agent and a photocopy of commercial registration certificate of the business organization;

(3) a photocopy of the minutes of resolution of the authorized organ of the parent company authorizing the establishment of a branch company in Ethiopia.

f) where it is a joint investment by domestic and foreign investors, in addition to the documents provided under Sub-Article (1)(d) of this Article, a photocopy of the identity card or a photocopy of the identity card evidencing the domestic investor status of the domestic investor, as the case may be;

g) a document evidencing the financial position or, identity or profile of the investor, as deemed appropriate by the Agency.

2/ All documents under Sub-Article (1) of this Article whose sources are outside of Ethiopia shall be authenticated by a foreign and domestic notary.

3/ Where the permit is requested by a person whose permit was cancelled due to deliance of project, the Agency shall ascertain that the causes of the deliance and cancellation are rectified.

15. Application for Investment Permit for Expansion or Upgrading

An application for investment permit to expand or upgrade an existing enterprise shall be made in a form designed for such purpose and submitted to the Agency together with the following documents in one copy:

1/ where the application is signed by an agent, a photocopy of his power of attorney;

2/ where the investment is made by a sole proprietor, a photocopy of the relevant pages of his valid passport or an identity card of his domestic investor status or a photocopy of his identity card and his two recent passport size photographs, as the case may be;

3/ where the investment is made by a business organization, a photocopy of the company's memorandum and articles of associations and two recent passport size photographs of the general manager;

4/ a photocopy of a valid business license of the existing enterprise; and

5/ a photocopy of project feasibility study.

16. Issuance of Investment Permit

1/ Upon receipt of an application made in accordance with Article 13, Article 14 or Article 15 of this Proclamation, the appropriate investment organ shall, after examining the intended investment activity in light of this Proclamation, and regulations and directives issued hereunder:

a) issue investment permit upon receipt of the appropriate fee, where the application is found acceptable; or

b) notify the investor of its decision and the reason thereof in writing, where the application is found unacceptable.

2/ The appropriate investment organ shall, after issuing the investment permit, notify the concerned institutions so that the latter could conduct the necessary follow up.

3/ A holder of an investment permit may not be required to obtain a business license until the commencement of production or rendering of service upon completion of his project.

4/ An investment permit may not be transferred to another person without prior written approval of the appropriate investment organ.

5/ Where an investment permit is transferred to another person or where any change is made in its content, it shall be submitted to the appropriate investment organ for approval.

6/ No investor may, at any time, be allowed to invest by holding both a domestic and a foreign investment permit.

17. Renewal of Investment Permit

1/ An investment permit shall be renewed every year until the investor commences the marketing of his products or services.

2/ An application for renewal of an investment permit shall be submitted and renewed with in one month after the end of a period of one year for which the permit remains valid.

3/ The appropriate investment organ shall renew the investment permit, where satisfied, as to the existence of sufficient cause for the delay in the commencement or completion of his project implementation.

4/ Notwithstanding the provision of Sub-Article (1) of this Article, any investor who has not commenced implementing his project within two years since the issuance of the investment permit, shall have his permit cancelled without any precondition.

18. Transfer of an Investment Project Under Implementation Phase

1/ Any investor wishing to transfer his project, which is under implementation phase and for which a business license is not yet issued, to another investor shall submit his request, by filling an application form designed for this purpose, to an appropriate investment organ and get the approval of same.

2/ The investor shall submit, together with his application specified in Sub-Article (1) of this Article, the following documents:

a) a photocopy of renewed investment permit;

b) a photocopy of the sales agreement authenticated by a notary;

c) a photocopy of land lease agreement transferred to the buyer as the case may be.

19. Suspension or Revocation of Investment Permit

1/ Where an investor violates the provisions of this Proclamation or regulations or directives issued to implement this Proclamation, the appropriate investment organ may suspend the investment permit until the investor takes due corrective measures.

2/ The appropriate investment organ may revoke an investment permit where it ascertains that:

a) the investor obtained the permit fraudulently or by submitting false information or statements;

b) incentives granted are misused or illegally transferred to another person;

c) the investor has failed, without good cause, to renew the permit in accordance with Article 17 of this Proclamation;

d) the investor fails to submit progress report of his project for two consecutive periods; or

e) the project can not commence operation with in the period and the Agency believes the project will not be operational.

3/ The appropriate investment organ shall notify the concerned institutions as to the measures of revocation taken in accordance with this Article. Upon revocation of an investment permit, the investor shall immediately lose entitlements to all benefits.

4/ An investor whose investment permit is revoked shall return, within one month as of the day of revocation, all the benefits granted to him to the Ethiopian Revenue and Customs Authority and other appropriate organs.

5/ An investment permit may not be suspended or revoked by any organ other than the appropriate investment organ having issued same.

6/ An investor whose investment permit is revoked may not be issued with a new investment permit before the lapse of one year from the date of revocation.

20. Duty to Report and Cooperate

Any investor with investment permit shall:

1/ submit progress reports on the implementation of his project to the appropriate investment organ at the end of every three months; and

2/ provide information concerning his investment activities whenever required by the appropriate investment organ.

PART FIVE

REGISTRATION OF TECHNOLOGY TRANSFER AND COLLABORATION AGREEMENTS WITH DOMESTIC INVESTERS

21. Technology Transfer Agreement

1/ Where any investor concludes a technology transfer agreement related to his investment, he shall submit same to the Agency for registration.

2/ An application for registration of a technology transfer agreement submitted in accordance with this Article shall fulfill the following:

a) a completed application form signed by the recipient of the technology;

b) a photocopy of the authenticated agreement between the recipient and provider of the technology;

c) a photocopy of a valid business license or investment permit of the recipient of the technology; and

d) a certificate of registration or business license of the provider of the technology.

3/ The Agency shall, upon receipt of a complete application for registration in accordance with Sub-Article (2) of this Article, issue a certificate of registration to the investor.

4/ A technology transfer agreement which is not registered with the Agency in accordance with this Article shall have no legal effect.

5/ The Agency shall notify the relevant federal executive organs the registration of technology transfer agreement made in accordance with this Article.

22. Export-Oriented Non-Equity Based Foreign Enterprise Collaboration Agreement

1/ Any domestic investor concluding a collaboration agreement with export-oriented non-equity based foreign enterprise shall register same with the Agency.

2/ An application for registration of a collaboration agreement made in accordance with this Article shall fulfill the following:

a) a completed application form signed by the domestic investor;

b) a photocopy of the authenticated collaboration agreement between the domestic investor and the foreign enterprise;

c) a photocopy of a valid business license or an investment permit of the domestic investor; and

d) a business registration certificate or a business license of the foreign enterprise.

3/ The Agency shall, upon receipt of a complete registration application in accordance with Sub-Article (2) of this Article, issue the certificate of registration to the investor.

4/ A collaboration agreement not registered with the Agency in accordance with this Article shall have no legal effect.

5/ The Agency shall notify the relevant federal executive organs the registration of the collaboration agreement made in accordance with this Article.

PART SIX
INVESTMENT INCENTIVES, GUARANTEES AND PROTECTION

23. Investment Incentives

1/ Areas of investment specified by regulation to be issued by the Council of Ministers pursuant to the investment objectives stated under Article 5 of this Proclamation shall be eligible for investment incentives.

2/ The regulation to be issued pursuant to Sub-Article (1) of this Article shall determine the type and extent of the entitlement to incentives.

24. Ownership of Immovable Property

1/ Notwithstanding the provisions from Article 390 to Article 393 of the Civil Code a foreign investor or a foreign national treated as domestic investor shall have the right to own a dwelling house and other immovable property requisite for his investment.

2/ The provisions of Sub-Article (1) of this Article shall also include those who have invested prior to the issuance of this Proclamation.

25. Investment Guarantees and Protection

1/ No investment may be expropriated or nationalized except for public interest and then, only in conformity with the requirements of the law.

2/ Adequate compensation, corresponding to the prevailing market value, shall be paid in advance in case of expropriation or nationalization of an investment for public interest.

3/ For the purpose of this Article the word "nationalization" shall be used interchangeably with the word "expropriation" and results in the payment of appropriate or adequate compensation.

26. Remittance of Funds

1/ Any foreign investor shall have the right, in respect of his approved investment, to make the following remittances out of Ethiopia in convertible foreign currency at the prevailing rate of exchange on the date of remittance:

a) profits and dividends accruing from the investment;

b) principal and interest payments on external loans;

c) payments related to a technology transfer agreement registered in accordance with Article 21 of this Proclamation;

d) payments related to a collaboration agreement registered in accordance with Article 22 of this Proclamation;

e) proceeds from the transfer of shares or of partial ownership of the enterprise to a domestic investor;

f) proceeds from the sale or liquidation of the enterprise; and

g) compensation paid to an investor pursuant to Article 25(2) of this Proclamation.

2/ Notwithstanding the provision of Sub-Article (1) of this Article, a local partner in a joint investment may not be allowed to remit funds out of Ethiopia.

3/ Expatriates employed in an enterprise may remit, in convertible foreign currency, salaries and other payments accruing from their employment in accordance with the foreign exchange laws of the country.

PART SEVEN
INVESTMENT ADMINISTRATION

27. Investment Administration Organs

The organs of investment administration comprise the Agency and regional investment organs to be defined by the laws of the respective regions.

28. Powers and Duties of the Agency

The Agency shall:

1/ serve as a nucleus for matters of investment and promote, coordinate and enhance activities thereon;

2/ initiate policy and implementation measures needed to create a conducive and competitive investment climate and follow up the implementation of same upon approval;

3/ negotiate bilateral investment promotion and protection treaties with other countries where potential investment is likely to flow into the country and sign same upon approval by the Council of Ministers;

4/ prepare and distribute pamphlets, brochures, films and other materials, and organize such activities as exhibitions, workshops and seminars locally or abroad as may be appropriate, participate in similar activities and conduct trainings with a view to encourage and promote investment and build the image of the country;

5/ realize liaison and coordination between investors, public offices, regional governments and other relevant organs, with a view to enhancing investment;

6/ collect, compile, analyze, update and disseminate any investment related information;

7/ prepare and promote concrete investment opportunity profiles, provide upon request, match-making service of possible joint investment partners;

8/ issue, renew and cancel investment permits within its jurisdiction and register investment capital brought into the country by foreign investors;

9/ register technology transfer agreements related to investments;

10/ register export-oriented non-equity-based collaboration agreements made between a domestic investor and a foreign enterprise;

11/ monitor the implementation of investment projects for which it has issued permits, ensure that the terms of the investment permit are complied with and incentives granted to investors are used for the intended purposes;

12/ provide advisory service, information and technical support to investors and assist in the provision of information to ensure the existence of supply chains among investment projects;

13/ carry out post-investment support and monitoring services in collaboration with organs established for such purpose;

14/ provide advisory service and technical support which help strengthen regional investment organs; organize joint consultation forums;

15/ raise the awareness of investors on the contents of this Proclamation and regulations and directives issued hereunder;

16/ cause investment bottlenecks to be resolved in collaboration with appropriate government organs.

29. Powers and Duties of the Investment Board

The Investment Board shall:

1/ supervise and follow up the implementation of this Proclamation and the activities of the Agency;

2/ decide on policy issues arising in connection with the implementation of this Proclamation;

3/ recommend, as necessary, amendments to this Proclamation and regulations issued hereunder;

4/ issue directives necessary for the implementation of this Proclamation and regulations issued hereunder;

5/ decide on appeals submitted to it by investors against decisions of the Director General of the Agency;

6/ where necessary, forward recommendations, for approval by the Council of Ministers, to grant new or additional incentives other than what is provided for under existing regulation;

7/ where necessary, forward recommendations, for approval by the Council of Ministers, investment areas exclusively reserved for domestic investors to be open for foreign investors.

30. One-Stop Shop Service

1/ The Agency shall, in accordance with the relevant laws, provide one-stop shop services referred to in this Article for investors it has issued with investment permits engaging in areas of manufacturing in accordance with Article 4 of this Proclamation.

2/ The Agency shall provide the following services representing the competent federal or regional executive organs, as appropriate:

a) permitting exemption incentives from the payment of customs duty;

b) issuance of construction permit;

c) notarization of memorandum and articles of associations and amendments thereto;

d) effecting commercial registration, and renewal, amendment, replacement or cancelation of same;

e) effecting registration of trade or firm name, and amendment, replacement or cancelation of same;

f) issuance of work permits to expatriate employees, and renewal, replacement, suspension or cancelation of same;

g) issuance of business license;

h) grading of construction contractors;

i) issuance of tax identification number (TIN).

3/ Amendments, renewal, replacement and cancelation pertaining to the services referred to in paragraphs (c) to (f) of Sub-Article (2) of this Article shall only be made by the Agency until the investor is issued with a business license.

4/ The Agency shall provide the following services on behalf of investors:

a) execution of investors' requests for land required for their investment projects;

b) execution of investors' requests for loan;

c) execution of foreign investors' requests for residence permits;

d) execution of investors' requests for approval of environmental impact assessment studies conducted on their investment projects; and

e) execution of investors' requests to acquire water, electrical power and telecom services.

5/ For the implementation of Sub-Article (4) of this Article the appropriate federal executive organs shall establish investment desks that expedite and facilitate investors' requests submitted by the Agency. The regional executive organs may accept this practice and establish investment desks.

6/ Without prejudice to the provision of Sub-Article (5) of this Article, the appropriate federal or regional executive organs shall take measures necessary to help the Agency properly discharge its duties specified under Sub-Article (4) of this Article.

7/ Upon receipt of an application in accordance with Sub-Article (2) of this Article, the Agency shall, after examining the request in light of the relevant laws:

a) issue the necessary documents, upon receipt of the appropriate fee and causing the investor to enter an undertaking to observe the relevant laws of the country, where the application is found acceptable; or

b) notify the investor of its decision and the reason thereof in writing, where the application is found unacceptable.

8/ The Agency shall, after rendering the services provided for in Sub-Article (2) of this Article, notify the concerned federal and regional executive organs for the necessary follow up.

9/ Without prejudice to the requirements to be fulfilled in accordance with the relevant laws, an investor submitting his request to the Agency to be issued with a business license shall furnish his project feasibility study.

10/ Regional investment organs may give, to investors they have issued with investment permits, the one-stop shop services provided for in this Article, in accordance with the relevant federal and regional laws.

31. Investment Related Information

1/ The appropriate federal and regional executive organs shall transfer complete and updated information regarding land required for investment projects, investment capital brought into the country as well as other necessary investment related information to the Agency and regional investment organs in order to help them facilitate the proper discharge of their powers and duties under this Proclamation.

2/ Each regional investment organ shall transmit to the Agency information compiled with respect to the resource potential and investment opportunities of the region as well as periodic reports on investment activities therein.

3/ The appropriate investment organ shall compile, analyze and distribute, as necessary, the information it acquired pursuant to Sub-Article (2) of this Article.

4/ Any federal or regional executive organ shall have the duty to provide information relating to investment whenever so required by the appropriate investment organ.

32. Lodging of Complaints

1/ Any investor shall have the right to lodge complaints related to his investment with the appropriate investment organ.

2/ An investor who has a grievance against the decision of the appropriate investment organ may, within 30 days from receipt of the decision, appeal to the Investment Board or to the concerned regional organ, as may be appropriate.

PART EIGHT
INDUSTRIAL DEVELOPMENT ZONES

33. Establishment of Industrial Development Zones

1/ In order for the industrial sector to have a leading role in the economy of the country the federal government shall establish industrial development zones in regions.

2/ Without prejudice to the provision of Article 6 of this Proclamation industrial zone development shall be undertaken by the federal government or, where deemed necessary, by joint investment of the government and private sector.

34. Administration of Industrial Development Zones

1/ The organ responsible for administering and supervising industrial development zones shall be determined by regulation to be issued by the Council of Ministers.

2/ The organ to be designated by the Council of Ministers in accordance with Sub-Article (1) of this Article shall, in conformity with the procedures provided under this Proclamation and regulation issued hereunder, and the approved plans and agreements of the country, submit recommendations to the Council of Ministers for reduction or expansion of industrial development zone.

3/ Where the recommendation specified under Sub-Article (2) of this Article is approved a leasehold land within or adjacent to industrial development zones may be possessed by negotiation or decision for the purpose of:

a) incorporating the land with existing industrial development zone;

b) getting passage to enter in to industrial development zones; or

c) maintaining natural resources, heritages and places required by laws to be preserved.

35. Regulations Related to Industrial Development Zones

1/ An organ to engage in the federal government development activities of industrial development zone shall be established by regulation of the Council of Ministers.

2/ Matters concerning designation, allocation standard, boundary delimitation of industrial development zones, the rights and duties of investors engaged in, the services expected from the government and supervision theron, completion of construction activities and supervision thereon, incentives other than those under this Proclamation and the implementation of this Part of the Proclamation, shall be determined by the Council of Ministers regulation.

3/ Unless otherwise it is to be governed by this special Part and regulations based on the provisions of this special Part of this Proclamation, the provision of this Proclamation and regulations issued hereunder shall be applicable to industrial development zones.

PART NINE
MISCELLANEOUS PROVISIONS

36. Loans and Utilization of Foreign Currency

1/ An investor who acquires an external loan shall have such loan registered with the National Bank of Ethiopia in accordance with the directive of the Bank.

2/ For the purpose of his investment activities, any foreign investor shall be allowed to open and operate foreign currency accounts in authorized local banks in accordance with directive of the National Bank of Ethiopia.

37. Employment of Expatriates

1/ Any investor may employ duly qualified expatriate experts required for the operation of his business.

2/ An investor who employs expatriates pursuant to Sub-Article (1) of this Article, shall be responsible for replacing, within a limited period, such expatriate personnel by Ethiopians by arranging the necessary training thereof.

3/ Notwithstanding the provisions of Sub-Article (1) and (2) of this Article, a foreign investor shall, without any restriction, have the right to employ expatriate employees on top management positions for his enterprise.

38. Duty to Observe Other Laws and Protection of Environment

Any investor shall have the obligation to observe the laws of the country in carrying out his investment activities. In particular, he shall give due regard to environmental protection.

39. Power to Issue Regulation

The Council of Ministers may issue regulations necessary for the implementation of this Proclamation.

40. Repealed and Inapplicable Laws

1/ The Investment Proclamation No. 280/2002 (as amended) is hereby repealed.

2/ No law or customary practice shall, in so far as it is inconsistent with this Proclamation, have effect with respect to matters provided for in this Proclamation.

41. Effective Date

This Proclamation shall enter into force on the date of publication in the Federal Negarit Gazeta.

Done at Addis Ababa, this 17th day of September, 2012.

GIRMA WOLDEGIORGIS
PRESIDENT OF THE FEDERAL
DEMOCRATIC REPUBLIC OF ETHIOPIA

TITLE TWO
A PROCLAMATION TO AMEND THE INVESTMENT PROCLAMATION
(Proclamation No. 849/2014)

FEDERAL NEGARIT GAZETTE
OF THE FEDERAL DEMOCRATIC REPUBUC OF ETHIOPIA

20th Year No. 52
ADDIS ABABA 22nd July, 2014

PROCLAMATION No. 849/2014
A PROCLAMATION TO AMEND THE INVESTMENT PROCLAMATION

WHEREAS it has become necessary to amend the Investment Proclamation No. 769/2012;

NOW, THEREFORE, in accordance with Article 55(1) of the Constitution of the Federal Democratic Republic of Ethiopia, it is hereby proclaimed as follows:

1. Short Title

This Proclamation may be cited as the "Investment (Amendment) Proclamation No. 849/2014".

2. Amendment

The Investment Proclamation No. 769/2012 is hereby amended as follows:

1/ Sub-Articles (14), (15) and (17) of Article 2 of the Proclamation are deleted and replaced by the following new Sub-Articles (14), (15) and (17):

"14/ 'Commission' means the Ethiopian Investment Commission to be established by regulation of the Council of Ministers;

15/ 'Investment Board' means the Ethiopian Investment Board to be established by regulation of the Council of Ministers;

17/ 'industrial development zone' means an area with distinct boundary designated by the appropriate organ to develop identical, similar or interrelated industries together or to develop multifaceted industries, based on a planned fulfillment of infrastructures and various services such as road, electric power and water, and having special incentive schemes, with a broad view to achieving, planned and systematic, development of industries, mitigation of the impacts of environmental pollution and development of urban centers, and includes special economic zones, industrial parks, technology parks, export processing zones, free trade zones and the likes designated by the Investment Board;"

2/ any reference to the "Agency" appearing anywhere in the Proclamation is deleted and replaced by the "Commission";

3/ Article 27 of the Proclamation is deleted and replaced by the following new Article 27:

"27. Investment Administration Organs

The organs of investment administration shall comprise the Investment Board, the Commission and regional investment organs to be defined by the laws of the respective regions."

4/ Sub-Articles (5), (6) and (7) of Article 29 of the Proclamation are deleted and replaced by the following new Sub-Articles (5), (6) and (7):

"5/ decide on appeals submitted to it by investors against decisions of the Commission;

6/ where necessary, authorize the granting of new or additional incentives other than what is provided for under the existing regulations;

7/ where necessary, and without prejudice to the provisions of Article 6 of this Proclamation, authorize the opening of investment areas for foreign investors, otherwise exclusively reserved for domestic investors."

5/ Sub-Article (2) of Article 33 of the Proclamation is deleted and replaced by the following new Sub-Article (2):

"2/ Without prejudice to the provisions of Article 6 of this Proclamation, industrial zone development shall be undertaken by the federal government or, where deemed necessary, by joint investment of the government and a private investor or by private investors."

6/ Sub-Articles (1) and (2) of Article 34 of the Proclamation are deleted and replaced by the following new Sub-Articles (1) and (2):

"1/ The Investment Board shall oversee the administration and supervision of industrial development zones.

2/ The Investment Board shall, in conformity with the procedure; provided for under this Proclamation and regulations issued hereunder and the approved investment plans and agreements of the country, decide the reduction or expansion of the boundaries of industrial development zones."

7/ The phrase "Where the recommendation specified under Sub-Article (2) of this Article is approved a leasehold land within or adjacent to industrial development zones may be possessed by negotiation or decision for the purpose of:" appearing at the beginning of Sub-Article (3) of Article 34 of the Proclamation is deleted and replaced by the new phrase "Where the reduction or expansion of the boundary of an industrial zone is decided pursuant to Sub-Article (2) of this Article, a leasehold land within or adjacent to industrial development zones may be possessed by negotiation or decision for the purpose of:"

8/ Sub-Articles (2) and (3) of Article 35 of the Proclamation are deleted and replaced by the following new Sub-Articles (2) and (3):

"2/ Measures concerning designation, allocation standard and boundary delimitation of industrial development zones, the rights and duties of investors engaged therein, the services expected from the government and supervision thereon, execution of construction activities and supervision thereon, incentives other than those granted under this Proclamation and the implementation of the provisions of this Part, shall be determined by directives of the Investment Board.

3/ Without prejudice to exceptions made by the provisions of this Part and directives of the Investment Board issued pursuant to Sub-Article (2) of this Article, other provisions of this Proclamation and regulations issued hereunder shall be applicable to industrial development zones."

3. Effective Date

This Proclamation shall enter into force on the date of publication in the Federal Negarit Gazette.

Done at Addis Ababa, this 22nd day of July, 2014
MULATU TESHOME (DR.)
PRESIDENT OF THE FEDERAL
DEMOCRATIC REPUBLIC OF ETHIOPIA

TITLE THREE
COUNCIL OF MINISTERS REGULATION ON INVESTMENT INCENTIVES AND INVESTMENT AREAS RESERVED FOR DOMESTIC INVESTORS
(Proclamation No. 270/2012)

FEDERAL NEGARIT GAZETTE

OF THE FEDERAL DEMOCRATIC REPUBUC OF ETHIOPIA

19th Year No. 4
ADDIS ABABA 29th November, 2012

COUNCIL OF MINISTERS REGULATION No. 270/2012 COUNCIL OF MINISTERS REGULATION ON INVESTMENT INCENTIVES AND INVESTMENT AREAS RESERVED FOR DOMESTIC INVESTORS

This Regulation is issued by the Council of Ministers pursuant to Article 5 of the Definition of Powers and Duties of the Executive Organs of the Federal Democratic Republic of Ethiopia Proclamation No. 691/2010 and Article 39 of the Investment Proclamation No. 769/2012.

PART ONE
GENERAL

1. Short Title

This Regulation may be cited as the "Investment Incentives and Investment Areas Reserved for Domestic Investors Council of Ministers Regulation No. 270/2012".

2. Definitions

In this Regulation unless the context otherwise requires:

1/ "Proclamation" means the Investment Proclamation No. 769/2012;

2/ the definitions provided for in Article 2 of the Proclamation shall also apply to this Regulation;

3/ "Agency" means the Ethiopian Investment Agency re-established under the Council of Ministers Regulation No. 269/2012;

4/ "Board" means the Investment Board referred to in Article 6(1) of the Council of Ministers Regulation No. 269/2012;

5/ "capital goods" means machinery, equipment and their accessories needed to produce goods or render services and include workshop and laboratory machinery and equipment necessary for same;

6/ "construction material" includes basic inputs necessary for the construction of investment projects;

7/ "customs duty" includes indirect taxes levied on imported goods;

8/ "income tax" means tax levied on profits from business and categorized as the revenue of the federal government, regional governments or as their joint revenue.

3. Investment Areas Reserved for Domestic Investors

1/ The following areas of investment are exclusively reserved for Ethiopian nationals:

a) banking, insurance and micro-credit and saving services;

b) packaging, forwarding and shipping agency services;

c) broadcasting service;

d) mass media services;

e) attorney and legal consultancy services;

f) preparation of indigenous traditional medicines;

g) advertisement, promotion and translation works;

h) air transport services using aircraft with a seating capacity up to 50 passengers.

2/ For the purpose of Sub-Article (1) of this Article, a business organization may have Ethiopian nationality, provided that its total capital is owned by Ethiopian nationals.

4. Investment Areas Allowed for Foreign Investors

1/ A foreign investor shall be allowed to invest in areas of investment specified in the Schedule attached hereto, except those areas provided for in number 1.3.3, 1.4.2, 1.7, 1.11.3, 1.11.4, 5.3, 6.2, 8.2, 9.2, 9.3 and 12 of the Schedule.

2/ Notwithstanding the provisions of Sub-Article (1) of this Article, the Board may allow foreign investors to invest in areas other than those specified in the Schedule, except those areas provided for in Article 6 (1) and (2) of the Proclamation and Article 3(1) of this Regulation.

3/ A foreign investor who invests pursuant to subarticle (1) or (2) of this Article may acquire a private commercial road transport vehicle necessary for his business operations.

PART TWO
INVESTMENT INCENTIVES

SECTION ONE   EXEMPTION FROM INCOME TAX

5. Income Tax Exemption for New Enterprise

1/ Any investor who invests to establish a new enterprise shall be entitled to income tax exemption as provided for in the Schedule attached hereto.

2/ Any investor who invests to establish a new enterprise in:

a) the State of Gambela Peoples;

b) the State of Benshangul/Gumuz;

c) the State of Afar (except in areas within 15 kilo meters right and left of the Awash River);

d) the State of Somali;

e) Guji and Borena Zones of the State of Oromia; or

f) South Omo Zone, Segen (Derashe, Amaro, Konso and Buiji) Area Peoples Zone, Bench-Maji Zone, Sheka Zone. Dawro Zone, Kaffa Zone or Konta and Basketo Special Woredas of the State of Southern Nations, Nationalities and Peoples;

shall be entitled to an income tax deduction of 30% for three consecutive years after the expiry of the income tax exemption period specified in the Schedule attached hereto.

6. Income Tax Exemption for Expansion or Upgrading of Existing Enterprise

Any investor expanding or upgrading his existing enterprise pursuant to Article 2(8) of the Proclamation shall, with respect to the additional income generated by the expansion or upgrading, be entitled to income tax exemption as provided for in the Schedule attached hereto.

7. Additional Income Tax Exemption for Investors Exporting Products or Services

Any investor who exports or supplies to an exporter as production or service input, at least 60% of his products or services shall be entitled to income tax exemption for two years in addition to the exemption provided for in the Schedule attached hereto.

8. Condition for Reducing Incentive

Notwithstanding the provisions of Article 5, 6 and 7 of this Regulation, the income tax exemption to be granted to an investor who engages in an area of manufacturing industry or information and communication technology development, without constructing his own production or service rendering building, shall be one year lesser than what is provided for in the Schedule attached hereto.

9. Duty to Submit Information

An investor shall be entitled to the exemptions specified in Article 5, 6 and 7 of this Regulation provided that he submits all the required information to the relevant tax authority.

10. Commencement of Period of Income Tax Exemption

1/ The period of exemption from income tax shall begin from the commencement date of production or provision of service by the investor.

2/ For the implementation of Sub-Article (1) of this Article, the appropriate investment organ shall notify the relevant tax collecting authority the commencement date of production or provision of service by the investor.

11. Declaration of Income During Income Tax Exemption Period

An investor who is entitled to income tax exemption shall declare, every year, the income he has obtained during the exemption period to the appropriate tax collecting authority

12. Loss Carry Forward

1/ An investor who has inclined loss within the period of income tax exemption shall be allowed to carry forward such loss for half of the income tax exemption period after the expiry of such period.

2/ Notwithstanding the provisions of Sub-Article (1) of this Article, for the purpose of calculating the period of loss carry forward, a half-year period shall be considered as a full income tax period.

3/ Notwithstanding the provisions of Sub-Article (1) and (2) of this Article, an investor who has incurred loss during the income tax exemption period may not be allowed to carry forward such loss for more than five income tax period.

SECTION TWO   EXEMPTION FROM CUSTOMS DUTY

13. Exemption of Capital Goods and Construction Materials from Customs Duty

1/ Any investor engaged in one of the areas of investment specified in the Schedule attached hereto, except those specified under numbers 7, 11, 14 and 15 of the Schedule, may import duty-free capital goods and construction materials necessary for the establishment of a new enterprise or the expansion or upgrading of an existing enterprise.

2. For the implementation of Sub-Article (1) of this Article, the investor shall submit, in

advance, the list of capital goods and construction materials to be imported duty-free and get approval of same from the appropriate investment organ.

3/ If an investor entitled to a duty-free incentive buys capital goods or construction materials from local manufacturing industries, he shall be refunded with the customs duty paid for the raw materials or components used as inputs for the production of such goods.

4/ An investor eligible to a duty-free incentive pursuant to this Article, shall be allowed to import spare parts the value of which is not greater than 15% of the total value of the capital goods within five years from the date of commissioning of his project.

14. Exemption of Motor Vehicles from Customs Duties

The total or partial exemptions of motor vehicles from customs duties shall be determined by directive to be issued by the Board based on the types and nature of investment projects.

15. Transfer of Duty-Free Imported Goods

1/ Capital goods or construction materials or motor vehicles imported free of customs duty may be transferred to persons with similar duty-free privileges.

2/ Notwithstanding the provision of Sub-Article (1) of this Article, the capital goods or construction materials or motor vehicles imported free of customs duty may be transferred, upon effecting payment of the appropriate customs duty, to persons having no similar duty-free privileges.

3/ The investor may re-export the duty-free imported capital goods or construction materials or motor vehicles.

4/ Any investor who contravenes the provisions of this Article shall be punishable in accordance with the relevant provisions of the Customs Proclamation.

PART THREE
MISCELLANEOUS PROVISIONS

16. Repealed and Inapplicable Laws

1/ The Investment Incentives and Investment Areas Reserved for Domestic Investors Council of Ministers Regulation No. 84/2003 (as amended) is hereby repealed.

2/ No regulation, directive or customary practice shall, in so far as it is inconsistent with this Regulation, be applicable with respect to matters provided for in this Regulation.

17. Transitory Provisions

1/ Notwithstanding the provision of Article 16 of this Regulation, incentives granted pursuant to the Investment Incentives and Investment Areas Reserved for Domestic Investors Council of Ministers Regulation No. 84/2003 (as amended) and the directives issued there under shall continue to be effective.

2/ Where an investor eligible for incentives granted pursuant to the Investment Incentives and Investment Areas Reserved for Domestic Investors Council of Ministers Regulation No. 84/2003 (as amended) and directives issued there under has not yet exercised his right, opts instead to be a beneficiary of incentives provided for in this Regulation, he may notify the appropriate investment organ and be entitled thereto.

18. Effective Date

This Regulation shall come into force on the date of publication in the Federal Negarit Gazette.

Done at Addis Ababa, this 29th day of November, 2012.

HAILEMARIAM DESSALEGN
PRIME MINISTER OF THE FEDERAL
DEMOCRATIC REPUBLIC OF ETHIOPIA

SCHEDULE INVESTMENT AREAS AND INCOME TAX EXEMPTIONS

No.	Investment Areas	In Addis Ababa and Special Zone of Oromia surrounding Addis Ababa	In Other Areas
1	Manufacturing		
	1.1 Food Industry		
	1.1.1 Processing of meat and meat products 1.1.2 Processing of fish and fish products 1.1.3 Processing of fruit and/or vegetables 1.1.4 Manufacture of edible oil 1.1.5 Processing of milk and/or manufacture of dairy products 1.1.6 Manufacture of starches and starch products 1.1.7 Processing of pulses, oil seeds or cereals, excluding flour production 1.1.8 Manufacture of other food products	Exemption from income tax for 3 years	Exemption from income tax for 5 years
	1.1.9 Manufacture of sugar	Exemption from income tax for 5 years	Exemption from income tax for 6 years
	1.1.10 Manufacture of chocolate, candy, biscuits and other sweets (excluding ice crème and cakes)	Exemption from income tax for 1 year	Exemption from income tax for 2 years
	1.1.11 Manufacture of macaroni, pasta and/or similar products	Exemption from income tax for 3 years	Exemption from income tax for 5 years
	1.1.12 Manufacture of baby food, roasted and ground coffee, soluble coffee, tea, yeast, vinegar, mayonnaise, artificial honey, iodized salt or similar food products 1.1.13 Processing of animal feeds	Exemption from income tax for 2 years	Exemption from income tax for 4 years
	1.2 Beverage Industry		
	1.2.1 Manufacture of alcoholic beverages	Exemption from income tax for 1 year	Exemption from income tax for 2 years

续 表

No.	Investment Areas		In Addis Ababa and Special Zone of Oromia surrounding Addis Ababa	In Other Areas
1	1.2.2	Manufacture of wine	Exemption from income tax for 3 years	Exemption from income tax for 4 years
	1.2.3	Manufacture of beer and/or beer malt	Exemption from income tax for 2 years	Exemption from income tax for 3 years
	1.2.4	Manufacture of soft drink, mineral water or other bottled water	Exemption from income tax for 1 year	Exemption from income tax for 2 years
	1.3	**Textile and Textile Products Industry**		
	1.3.1	Preparation and spinning of cotton, wool, silk and similar textile fibers	Exemption from income tax for 4 years	Exemption from income tax for 5 years
	1.3.2	Weaving, finishing and printing of textiles	Exemption from income tax for 5 years	Exemption from income tax for 6 years
	1.3.3	Finishing of fabrics, yarn, warp and weft, apparel and other textile products by bleaching, dyeing, shrinking, sanforizing, mercerizing or dressing	Exemption from income tax for 3 years	Exemption from income tax for 4 years
	1.3.4	Other textile finishing activities	Exemption from income tax for 2 years	Exemption from income tax for 3 years
	1.3.5 1.3.6 1.3.7	Manufacture of knitted and crocheted fabrics Manufacture of made-up textile articles, except apparel Manufacture of carpets	Exemption from income tax for 4 years	Exemption from income tax for 5 years
	1.3.8 1.3.9	Manufacture of wearing apparel (including sport wears) Manufacture of accessories for textile products	Exemption from income tax for 5 years	Exemption from income tax for 6 years
	1.4	**Leather and Leather Products Industry**		
	1.4.1	Tanning of hides and skins up to finished level	Exemption from income tax for 5 years	Exemption from income tax for 6 years
	1.4.2	Tanning of hides and skins below finished level	Not eligible for income tax exemption	Not eligible for income tax exemption
	1.4.3 1.4.4 1.4.5	Manufacture of leather products (luggage, hand bags, leather balls and similar products) Manufacture of leather shoe Manufacture of accessories for leather products	Exemption from income tax for 5 years	Exemption from income tax for 6 years

续 表

No.	Investment Areas	In Addis Ababa and Special Zone of Oromia surrounding Addis Ababa	In Other Areas
1	**1.5 Wood Products Industry** Manufacture of wood products (excluding saw milling timber making and assembling of semifinished wood products)	Exemption from income tax for 2 years	Exemption from income tax for 3 years
	1.6 Paper and Paper Products Industry		
	1.6.1 Manufacture of pulp 1.6.2 Manufacture of paper	Exemption from income tax for 5 years	Exemption from income tax for 6 years
	1.6.3 Manufacture of paper packages	Exemption from income tax for 3 years	Exemption from income tax for 4 years
	1.6.4 Manufacture of other paper products	Exemption from income tax for 1 year	Exemption from income tax for 2 years
	1.7 Printing Industry	Not eligible for income tax exemption	Not eligible for income tax exemption
	1.8 Chemical and Chemical Products Industry		
	1.8.1 Manufacture of basic chemicals (including ethanol) 1.8.2 Manufacture of fertilizers and/or nitrogen compounds	Exemption from income tax for 5 years	Exemption from income tax for 6 years
	1.8.3 Manufacture of plastics and/or synthetic rubber in primary forms 1.8.4 Manufacture of pesticides, herbicides or fungicides	Exemption from income tax for 3 years	Exemption from income tax for 5 years
	1.8.5 Manufacture of paints, varnishes or similar coatings; printing, writing and painting inks and mastics 1.8.6 Manufacture of soap and detergents, cleaning and polishing preparations, perfumes and toilet preparations	Exemption from income tax for 2 years	Exemption from income tax for 4 years
	1.8.7 Manufacture of man-made fibers	Exemption from income tax for 5 years	Exemption from income tax for 6 years
	1.8.8 Manufacture of other chemical products (propellant powders, explosives, photographic films and similar products)	Exemption from income tax for 2 years	Exemption from income tax for 3 years
	1.9 Basic Pharmaceutical Products and Pharmaceutical Preparations Industry		
	1.9.1 Manufacture of inputs of basic pharmaceutical products and pharmaceutical preparations	Exemption from income tax for 5 years	Exemption from income tax for 6 years

No.	Investment Areas		In Addis Ababa and Special Zone of Oromia surrounding Addis Ababa	In Other Areas
1	1.9.2	Manufacture or formulation of pharmaceuticals	Exemption from income tax for 4 years	Exemption from income tax for 5 years
	1.10	**Rubber and Plastics Products Industry**		
	1.10.1	Manufacture of rubber products	Exemption from income tax for 3 years	Exemption from income tax for 5 years
	1.10.2	Manufacture of plastic products used as inputs for construction of buildings, vehicles or other industrial products; plastic pipes or tubes and fittings used for irrigation and drinking water supply as well as for sewerage system	Exemption from income tax for 4 years	Exemption from income tax for 5 years
	1.10.3	Manufacture of other plastic products excluding plastic shopping bags	Exemption from income tax for 1 year	Exemption from income tax for 2 years
	1.11	**Other Non-Metallic Mineral Products Industry**		
	1.11.1 1.11.2	Manufacture of glass and/or glass products Manufacture of ceramic products	Exemption from income tax for 4 years	Exemption from income tax for 5 years
	1.11.3	Manufacture of cement	Not eligible for income tax exemption	Exemption from income tax for 4 years
	1.11.4	Manufacture of clay and cement products	Not eligible for income tax exemption	Not eligible for income tax exemption
	1.11.5	Cutting, shaping and finishing of marble and limestone (excluding quarrying)	Exemption from income tax for 1 year	Exemption from income tax for 2 years
	1.11.6	Manufacture of lime, gypsum and/or similar coatings	Not eligible for income tax exemption	Exemption from income tax for 2 years
	1.11.7	Manufacture of millstone, glass paper or sound-absorbing or heat-insulating materials	Exemption from income tax for 1 year	Exemption from income tax for 2 years
	1.12	**Basic Metals Industry (Excluding mining of the mineral)**		
	1.12.1	Manufacture of basic iron and steel	Exemption from income tax for 5 years	Exemption from income tax for 6 years
	1.12.2	Manufacture of basic precious and other nonferrous metals	Exemption from income tax for 3 years	Exemption from income tax for 4 years
	1.12.3	Casting of iron and steel	Exemption from income tax for 4 years	Exemption from income tax for 5 years
	1.13	**Fabricated Metal Products Industry (Excluding Machinery and Equipment)**		

续　表

No.	Investment Areas		In Addis Ababa and Special Zone of Oromia surrounding Addis Ababa	In Other Areas
1	1.13.1	Manufacture of structural metal products, tanks, reservoirs and containers or steam generators	Exemption from income tax for 3 years	Exemption from income tax for 4 years
	1.13.2	Except corrugated metal sheets for roofing and nails, manufacture of other fabricated metal products (hand tools, articles and similar products)	Exemption from income tax for 1 year	Exemption from income tax for 2 years
	1.14	**Computer, Electronic and Optical Products Industry**		
	1.14.1	Manufacture of electronic components and boards	Exemption from income tax for 4 years	Exemption from income tax for 5 years
	1.14.2 1.14.3 1.14.4	Manufacture of computers and peripheral equipment Manufacture of communication equipment Manufacture of consumer electronic (television, DVD, radio and similar equipments)	Exemption from income tax for 3 years	Exemption from income tax for 4 years
	1.14.5 1.14.6	Manufacture of measuring, testing, navigating, control equipment or watches and clocks Manufacture of medical equipment (irradiation, electro-medical or electrotherapeutic equipment)	Exemption from income tax for 3 years	Exemption from income tax for 4 years
	1.14.7 1.14.8	Manufacture of optical instruments or photographic equipment Manufacture of magnetic and optical media	Exemption from income tax for 2 years	Exemption from income tax for 3 years
	1.15	**Electrical Products Industry**		
	1.15.1	Manufacture of electric motors, generators, transformers or electricity distribution or control apparatus	Exemption from income tax for 4 years	Exemption from income tax for 5 years
	1.15.2 1.15.3 1.15.4 1.15.5 1.15.6	Manufacture of accumulators or batteries Manufacture of electrical wires or cables (including fiber optics) and related products Manufacture of electric lighting equipment Manufacture of domestic electrical appliances Manufacture of other electrical equipment	Exemption from income tax for 2 years	Exemption from income tax for 4 years
	1.16	**Machinery/Equipment Industry**		

No.	Investment Areas		In Addis Ababa and Special Zone of Oromia surrounding Addis Ababa	In Other Areas
1	1.16.1	Manufacture of general-purpose machinery (motor, lifting and handling equipments, pumps and similar)	Exemption from income tax for 5 years	Exemption from income tax for 6 years
	1.16.2	Manufacture of special-purpose (for agriculture, food processing; beverage, textile and mining production and similar activities) machinery		
	1.17	**Vehicles, Trailers and Semi-Trailers Industry**		
	1.17.1	Manufacture of motor vehicles	Exemption from income tax for 2 years	Exemption from income tax for 3 years
	1.17.2	Manufacture of bodies/components for motor vehicles, trailers and/or semi-trailers	Exemption from income tax for 3 years	Exemption from income tax for 4 years
	1.17.3	Manufacture of parts and accessories for motor vehicles		
	1.17.4	Manufacture of railway locomotives and rolling stock	Exemption from income tax for 5 years	Exemption from income tax for 6 years
	1.17.5	Manufacture of other transport equipment (boats, bicycles, motor bicycles and similar equipments)	Exemption from income tax for 2 years	Exemption from income tax for 3 years
	1.18	**Manufacture of office and household furniture (excluding those made of ceramic)**	Exemption from income tax for 1 year	Exemption from income tax for 2 years
	1.19	**Manufacturing of other equipment (jewellery and related articles, musical instruments, sports equipment, games and toys and similar products)**		
	1.20	**Integrated Manufacturing, with Agriculture**	Exemption from income tax for 4 years	Exemption from income tax for 5 years
2	Agriculture			
	2.1 Crop Production			
	2.1.1	Annual Crop Production		
	2.1.1.1	Growing of cereals, leguminous crops and/or oil seeds and rice	Not eligible for income tax exemption	Exemption from income tax for 3 years
	2.1.1.2	Growing of vegetables and/or herbs	Exemption from income tax for 3 years	Exemption from income tax for 4 years
	2.1.1.3	Growing of fiber crops	Not eligible for income tax exemption	Exemption from income tax for 5 years

续 表

No.	Investment Areas	In Addis Ababa and Special Zone of Oromia surrounding Addis Ababa	In Other Areas
2	2.1.1.4 Growing of other annual crops (animal feed, medicinal crops, aromatic, spices and similar crops)	Exemption from income tax for 2 years	Exemption from income tax for 3 years
	2.1.1.5 Production of certified seed	Exemption from income tax for 3 years	Exemption from income tax for 4 years
	2.1.2 Growing of Medium-Term Crops		
	2.1.2.1 Growing of flowers 2.1.2.2 Growing of medium-term fruits (strawberry, blueberry and similar crops)	Exemption from income tax for 3 years	Exemption from income tax for 4 years
	2.1.2.3 Growing of medium-term spices, aromatic and/or medicinal crops (hulu, curmuma, black pepper and similar crops)	Not eligible for income tax exemption	Exemption from income tax for 4 years
	2.1.3 Perennial Crops Production		
	2.1.3.1 Growing of perennial fruits (mango, avocado, banana, orange, papaya, grapes, passion fruits and similar crops) 2.1.3.2 Growing of beverage crops (coffee, tea and similar crops)	Not eligible for income tax exemption	Exemption from income tax for 5 years
	2.1.3.3 Growing of other perennial crops (rubber tree, palm, jatropha, and similar crops)	Not eligible for income tax exemption	Exemption from income tax for 6 years
	2.2 Animal Production		
	2.2.1 Farming of domestic animals and production of milk, eggs, raw wool and similar products	Exemption from income tax for 3 years	Exemption from income tax for 4 years
	2.2.2 Farming of wild animals and production of milk, eggs and similar products	Not eligible for income tax exemption	Exemption from income tax for 3 years
	2.2.3 Farming of bees/production of honey	Exemption from income tax for 2 years	Exemption from income tax for 4 years
	2.2.4 Production of silk 2.2.5 Fish farming in artificial ponds (aquaculture)	Exemption from income tax for 3 years	Exemption from income tax for 4 years
	2.3 Mixed (crop and animal) farming	Exemption from income tax for 3 years	Exemption from income tax for 4 years
	2.4 Forestry	Exemption from income tax for 8 years	Exemption from income tax for 9 years

续表

No.	Investment Areas	In Addis Ababa and Special Zone of Oromia surrounding Addis Ababa	In Other Areas
3	Information and Communication Technology Development in areas to be determined by directive to be issued by the Ministry of Communication and Information Technology	Exemption from income tax for 4 years	Exemption from income tax for 5 years
4	Electricity generation, transmission and distribution	Exemption from income tax for 4 years	Exemption from income tax for 5 years
5	**Hotel and Tourism**		
	5.1 Star-designated hotel (including resort hotel), motel, lodge and restaurant	Not eligible for income tax exemption	Not eligible for income tax exemption
	5.2 Grade 1 tour operation	Not eligible for income tax exemption	Not eligible for income tax exemption
	5.3 Tour operation below grade 1	Not eligible for income tax exemption	Not eligible for income tax exemption
6	**Construction Contracting**		
	6.1 Grade 1 construction contracting (including water well and mineral exploration drilling) 6.2 Construction contracting below grade 1 (including water well and mineral exploration drilling)	Not eligible for income tax exemption	Not eligible for income tax exemption
7	**Real Estate Development**	Not eligible for income tax exemption	Not eligible for income tax exemption
8	**Education and Training**		
	8.1 Provision of secondary and higher education by constructing own building 8.2 Provision of kindergarten, elementary and junior secondary education by constructing own building 8.3 Provision of technical and vocational (including sports) training service	Not eligible for income tax exemption	Not eligible for income tax exemption
9	**Health Services**		
	9.1 Provision of hospital service by constructing own building 9.2 Provision of diagnostic center service by constructing own building 9.3 Provision of clinical service by constructing own building	Not eligible for income tax exemption	Not eligible for income tax exemption

续 表

No.	Investment Areas	In Addis Ababa and Special Zone of Oromia surrounding Addis Ababa	In Other Areas
10	**Architectural and Engineering Works, Technical Testing and Analysis** 10.1　Architectural and engineering works and related technical consultancy services 10.2　Technical testing and analysis	Not eligible for income tax exemption	Not eligible for income tax exemption
11	Publishing	Not eligible for income tax exemption	Not eligible for income tax exemption
12	Capital Goods Leasing, Excluding Leasing of Motor Vehicles	Not eligible for income tax exemption	Not eligible for income tax exemption
13	**Import Trade** Importation of LPG and bitumen	Not eligible for income tax exemption	Not eligible for income tax exemption
14	**Export Trade** Export trade excluding exporting of raw coffee, 'chat', oil seeds, pulses, precious minerals and hides and skins bought from the market; natural forestry products and live sheep, goat, camel, cattle and equines not raised by the investor	Not eligible for income tax exemption	Not eligible for income tax exemption
15	**Wholesale Trade** Supply of petroleum and its by-products as well as wholesale of own products	Not eligible for income tax exemption	Not eligible for income tax exemption

TITLE FOUR
COUNCIL OF MINISTERS REGULATION TO AMEND THE INVESTMENT INCENTIVES AND INVESTMENT AREAS RESERVED FOR DOMESTIC INVESTORS REGULATION No. 270/2012 (Council of Ministers Regulation No. 312/2014)

FEDERAL NEGARIT GAZETTE

OF THE FEDERAL DEMOCRATIC REPUBUC OF ETHIOPIA

20th Year No. 62
ADDIS ABABA 13th August, 2014

COUNCIL OF MINISTER REGULATION NO. 312/2014
COUNCIL OF MINISTERS REGULATION TO AMEND THE INVESTMENT INCENTIVES AND INVESTMENT AREAS RESERVED FOR DOMESTIC INVESTORS REGULATION No. 270/2012

This Regulation is issued by the Council of Ministers pursuant to Article 5 of the Definition of Powers and Duties of the Executive Organs of the Federal Democratic Republic of Ethiopia Proclamation No. 691/2010 and Article 39 of the Investment Proclamation No. 769/2012.

1. Short Title

This Regulation may be cited as the "Investment Incentives and Investment Areas Reserved for Domestic Investors Council of Ministers (Amendment) Regulation No. 312/2014".

2. Amendment

The Investment Incentives and Investment Areas Reserved for Domestic Investors Council of Ministers Regulations No. 270/2012 is hereby amended as follows:

1/ The following new Sub-Article (9) is added under Article 2 of the Regulation:

"9/ 'existing enterprise' means an enterprise engaged in production or rendering services having a business license or any other appropriate license."

2/ The following new Item No. 1.21 is added after Item No. 1.20 of the Schedule attached to the Regulation:

1.21 Industrial development zone (including private industrial development zone investment, the establishment of which is agreed with the government prior to the issuance of the Proclamation)	Exemption from income tax for 10 years	Exemption from income tax for 15 years

3/ The existing provision of Article 7 of the Regulation is renumbered as Sub-Article (1) and the following new Sub-Articles (2) and (3) are added:

"2/ An investor who has invested within an industrial development zone shall be entitled, in addition to what is provided for in Sub-Article (1) of this Article and the Schedule attached hereto, to 2 years income tax exemption if the investment is made in an industrial zone located in Addis Ababa or Special Zone of Oromia surrounding Addis Ababa or to 4 years income tax exemption if the investment is made in an industrial zone located in other areas, provided that he exports 80% or above of the product from his manufacturing industry or supplies as production input to an investor who exports his products.

3/ An investor who has invested or is to invest within private industrial development zone, the establishment of which is agreed with the Government prior to the issuance of the Proclamation, shall be entitled to the incentive provided for in Sub-Article (2) of this Article upon fulfilling the preconditions stipulated therein."

4/ Article 8 of the Regulation is deleted and Articles 9 to 18 are renumbered as Articles 8 to 17, respectively.

5/ The following new Sub-Article (5) is added under Article 12 of the Regulation (as renumbered pursuant to Sub-Article (3) of this Article):

"5/ Without prejudice to the provisions of Sub-Article (1) of this Article, any investor engaged in:

a) manufacturing industry or agriculture who has invested at least 200,000 United States Dollars or equivalent Ethiopian Birr at the prevailing rate of exchange and has created permanent employment opportunity for at least 50 Ethiopian nationals shall be entitled to import, at any time, duty-free capital goods necessary for his existing enterprise;

b) another area of investment eligible for customs duty exemption and has invested at least 200,000 United States Dollars or equivalent Ethiopian Birr at the prevailing rate of exchange and has created permanent employment opportunity for at least 50 permanent employees shall be allowed to import duty-free capital goods necessary for the existing enterprise up to 5 years from the date of acquiring a business license or other appropriate license."

3. Effective Date

This Regulation shall enter into force on the date of publication in the Federal Negarit Gazette.

Done at Addis Ababa, this 13th day of August, 2014.

HAILEMARIAM DESSALEGN
PRIME MINISTER OF THE FEDERAL
DEMOCRATIC REPUBLIC OF
ETHIOPIA

GROUP TWO
LABOR LAWS AND REGULATIONS

TITLE FIVE
LABOUR PROCLAMATION
(Proclamation No. 1156/2019)

FEDERAL NEGARIT GAZETTE

OF THE FEDERAL DEMOCRATIC REPUBUC OF ETHIOPIA

25th Year No. 89
ADDIS ABABA 5th September, 2019

Proclamation No. 1156/2019
LABOUR PROCLAMATION

WHEREAS, it is essential to ensure worker-employer relations are governed by basic principles of rights and obligations with a view to enabling workers and employers to secure durable industrial peace; sustainable productivity and competitiveness through cooperative engagement towards the all-round development of our country;

WHEREAS, it has been found necessary to lay down a working system that guarantees the rights of workers and employers to freely establish their respective associations and to engage, through their duly authorized representatives, in social dialogue and collective bargaining, as well as to draw up procedures for the expeditious settlement of labour disputes, which arise between them;

WHEREAS, there is a need to create favorable environment for investment and achievement of national economic goals without scarifying fundamental workplace rights by laying down well considered labour administration; and determine the duties and responsibilities of governmental organs entrusted with the power to monitor labour conditions; occupational health and safety; and environmental protection together with bilateral and tripartite social dialogue mechanisms; political, economic and social policies of the Country;

WHEREAS, it has been found necessary to reformulate the existing labour law with a view to attaining the aforementioned objectives and in accordance with the and in conformity with the international conventions and other legal commitments to which Ethiopia is a party;

NOW, THEREFORE, in accordance with Article 55 (1) and (3) of the Constitution of the Federal Democratic Republic of Ethiopia, it is hereby proclaimed as follows:

PART ONE
GENERAL

1. Short Title

This Proclamation may be cited as the "Labour Proclamation No. 1156/2019".

2. Definitions

In this Proclamation unless the context provides otherwise:

1/ "Employer" means a person or an undertaking who employs one or more natural persons in accordance with Article 4 of this Proclamation.

2/ "Undertaking" means any entity established under a united management for the purpose of carrying on any commercial, industrial, agricultural, construction or any other lawful activity.

Any branch carrying on the activities of an undertaking which is designated separately and which enjoys operational or organizational autonomy shall be deemed to be a separate undertaking.

3/ "Worker" means a person who has an employment relationship with an employer in accordance with Article 4 this Proclamation.

4/ "Ministry" or "Minister" means the Ministry or Minister of Labour and Social Affairs respectively.

5/ "Appropriate authority" means, a Regional state organ vested with the power of implementing labour laws.

6/ "Work rules" means internal rules which govern, subject to the provisions of this Proclamation and other relevant laws, working hours, rest period, payment of wages and methods of measuring work done, maintenance of safety and prevention of accidents, disciplinary measures and their enforcement as well as other conditions of work.

7/ "Condition of work" means the entire field of labour relations between workers and employers including hours of work, wage, leave, payments due to dismissal, workers health and safety, compensation to victims of employment injury, dismissal because of redundancy, grievance procedure and any other similar matters.

8/ "Regional state" means any State referred to in Article 47(1) of the Constitution of Federal Democratic Republic of Ethiopia, and includes the Addis Ababa and Dire Dawa city administrations.

9/ "Social dialogue" means a process of information exchange, dialogue or negotiation of bilateral or tripartite nature between employer and employees or involving the Government on economic and social issues of mutual interests towards arriving at common understanding.

10/ "Managerial employee" means an employee who, by laws or delegation of the employer, is vested with powers to lay down and execute management policies, and depending on the type of activities of the undertaking, with or without the aforementioned powers an employee who is vested with the power to hire, transfer, suspend, layoff, dismiss or assign employees, and includes a legal service head who recommend measures to be taken by the employer regarding such managerial issues, using his independent judgment, in the interest of the employer.

11/ "Sexual harassment" means to persuade or convince another through utterances, signs or any other manner, to submit for sexual favor without his/her consent.

12/ "Sexual violence" means sexual harassment accompanied by force or an attempt thereof.

13/ "private employment agency" (herein after "Agency") means any legally licensed person, to provide one or two of the following local Employment services without charging directly or indirectly any fee from the worker:

a) Local employment exchange service without being a party to an employment relation; or

b) Deploying of employees under its authority to the service of a service user enterprise, by entering into contract of employments with such employees; or combines both services.

14/ "License" means a certificate to be issued by a competent organ certifying that the entity is qualified to engage in private employment exchange service.

15/ "Discrimination" any distinction, exclusion or preference made on the basis of nation, race, color, sex, religion, political opinion, national extraction, social origin, HIV/AIDS status, disablement and others which has the effect of nullifying or impairing equality of opportunity or treatment in employment or occupation.

16/ "emplyment of private service" means an employment of a non profite careening, cleaning guardianship, gardening, driving and other related services for the employer and his family consumption.

17/ "commercial traveler and Representatives" shall have the meaning prescribed under commercial code.

18/ "Person" means any natural or juridical person.

19/ Provisions of this Proclamation set out in the masculine gender shall also apply to the feminine gender.

3. Scope of Application

1/ Without prejudice to Sub-Article (2) of this Article, this Proclamation shall be applicable to employment relations based on a contract of employment that exist between a worker and an employer including recruitment process.

2/ This Proclamation shall not, however, be applicable to the following employment relations:

a) contracts for the purpose of upbringing, treatment, care or rehabilitation;

b) contracts for the purpose of educating or training other than apprentice;

c) where the employee is a managerial employee;

d) contracts of personal service;

e) contracts relating to persons such as members of the Armed Force, members of the Police Force, employees of state administration, judges of courts of law, prosecutors and others whose employment relationship is governed by special laws;

f) Contracts relating to a person who performs an act, for consideration, at his own business or professional responsibility.

3/ Notwithstanding the provision of Sub-Article(1) of this Article:

a) unless the Council of Ministers by regulation decides, or an international agreement to which Ethiopia is a signatory provides otherwise, employment relations between Ethiopian nationals and foreign diplomatic missions or international organizations operating with in the territory of Ethiopia shall be governed by this Proclamation;

b) the Council of Ministers may by Regulation determine the inapplicability of this Proclamation to employment relations established by religious or charitable organizations;

e) the Council of Ministers shall issue Regulation governing conditions of work applicable to personal services.

PART TWO
EMPLOYMENT RELATIONS

CHAPTER ONE   CONTRACT OF EMPLOYMENT

SECTION ONE   FORMATION OF CONTRACT OF EMPLOYMENT

4. Element of a Contract of Employment

1/ A contract of employment shall be deemed formed where a natural person agrees directly or indirectly to perform work for and under the authority of an employer for a definite or indefinite period or piece of work in consideration for wage;

2/ A contract of employment shall be stipulated clearly and in such manner that the parties are left with no uncertainty as to their respective right and obligation under the terms thereof;

3/ A contract of employment shall specify the type of employment and place of work, the rate of wages, method of calculation thereof, manner and interval of payment and duration of the contract;

4/ A contract of employment shall not be concluded for the performance of unlawful or immoral acts;

5/ The contract of employment shall not laydown less favorable conditions forth employee than those provided for by laws, collective agreement or work rules.

5. Form

Unless otherwise provided by laws, a contract of employment shall not be subject to any special form.

6. Contract of Employment made in Writing

Subject to the provisions of the relevant law, a written contract of employment shall specify the following:

1/ The name and address of the employer;

2/ The name, age, addresses and work card number, if any, of the worker;

3/ the agreement of the contracting parties made in accordance with Article 4(3) of this Proclamation; and

4/ The signature of the contracting parties.

7. Contract of Employment not made in Writing

1/ Where a contract of employment is not made in writing, the employer shall, with in 15 days from the conclusion of the contract give the worker a written and signed letter containing the elements specified under Article 6 of this Proclamation.

2/ if the letter referred to in Sub-Article(1) of this Article is not wholly or partly objected by the worker within 15 days from the date of receipt, it shall be deemed a contract of employment concluded between the worker and the employer.

8. Failure to Comply Condition

Failure to comply with the requirements of the provisions of Article 6 or 7 of this Proclamation shall not deprive the worker of his right sunder this Proclamation.

SECTION TWO DURATION OF CONTRACT OF EMPLOYMENT

9. Contract of Employment for an Indefinite Period

Any contract of employment shall be deemed to have been concluded for an indefinite period except for those provided for under Article 10 here under.

10. Contract of Employment for Definite Period or Piecework

1/ A contract of employment may be concluded for a definite period or for piece work in the case of:

a) The performance of specified piece work for which the employee is employed;

b) the replacement of a worker who is temporarily absent due to leave or sickness or other causes;

c) The performance of work in the event of abnormal pressure of work;

d) The performance of urgent work to prevent damage or disaster to life or property, to repair defects or breakdowns in works, materials, buildings or plants of an undertaking;

e) An irregular work which relates to permanent part of the work of an employer but performed on irregular intervals;

f) Seasonal works which relate to the permanent part of the works of an employer but performed only for a specified period of the year but which are regularly repeated in the course of the years;

g) An occasional work which does not form part of the permanent activity of the employer but which is done intermittently;

h) The temporary placement of a worker who has suddenly and permanently vacated from a post having a contract of an indefinite period;

i) The temporary placement of a worker to fill a vacant position in the period between the preparation of an organizational structure and its implementation.

2/ A contract of employment under Sub-Article (1) (h) or (i) of this Article shall not exceed 45 working days and shall be done only once.

11. Probation Period

1/ A worker may be employed for a probation period for the purpose of testing his suitability to a job position in which he is anticipated to hold.

2/ A worker re-employed by the same employer for the same job shall not be subject to probation.

3/ When the parties agree to have a probation period, the agreement shall be made in writing; in such a case, the probation period shall not exceed 60 working days beginning from the first date of employment.

4/ Unless the law or work rules or collective agreement provides otherwise, the probationary worker shall have the same right and obligation that a worker who has completed his probation period possesses.

5/ If the worker, during his probation, proves to be unfit for the post, the employer can terminate the contract of employment without notice and without being obliged for severance payment or compensation.

6/ A worker on probation may terminate his contract of employment without notice as well.

7/ If a worker continues to work after the expiry of the probation period, a contract of employment for the intended period or type of work shall be deemed to have been concluded from the beginning of the probation period.

SECTION THREE OBLIGATIONS OF THE PARTIES

12. Obligations of an Employer

An employer shall in addition to special stipulations in the contract of employment have the following obligations:

1/ a) to provide work to the worker in accordance with the contract of employment; and

b) unless otherwise stipulated in the contract of employment, to provide the worker with implements and materials necessary for the performance of the work;

2/ To pay the worker wages and other benefits in accordance with this Proclamation or the collective agreement;

3/ To deduct union dues from the worker's regular wage, where the worker requests in writing of such deduction, and transfer the cash into the trade union's bank account;

4/ To respect the worker's human dignity;

5/ To take all the necessary occupational safety and health measures and to abide by the standards and directives to be given by the appropriate authorities in respect of these measures;

6/ To cover the cost of medical examination of the worker whenever such medical examination is required by laws or the appropriate authority;

7/ To keep a register containing the relevant particulars specified in Article 6 hereof, weekly rest days, public holidays and utilized leave of the worker, health conditions of the employee except for HIV/AIDS, and employment injury record and other particulars required by the Ministry or appropriate authority;

8/ Up on termination of a contract of employment or whenever the worker so requests, to provide the worker, free of charge, with a certificate stating the type of work he performed, the length of service and the wage she was earning;

9/ To observe the provisions of this Proclamation, collective agreement, work rules, directives and orders issued in accordance with law;

10/ To record and keep in formation as required by this Proclamation, and any other information necessary for the appropriate organ to carry out its powers and duties, and submit same within a reasonable time when requested by the competent authority;

11/ Under take registration of information on workplace location and work related data as per the form prepared by the Ministry; and

12/ Whenever an enterprise has a work rules it should arrange awareness raising program for the concerned workers.

13. Obligations of Workers

Every worker shall have the following obligations:

1/ To personally perform the work specified in his contract of employment;

2/ To follow instructions given by the employer based on the terms of the contract and work rules;

3/ To handle with due care all equipment and tools entrusted to him for work;

4/ To report for duty always in fit mental and physical conditions;

5/ To give all proper aid when an accident occurs or an imminent danger threatens life or property in a workplace without endangering his safety and health;

6/ To inform immediately the employer any act which endangers himself or co-workers or which prejudice the interests of the Undertaking;

7/ To comply with the provisions of this Proclamation, collective agreement, work rules and directives issued in accordance with the law.

14. Prohibited Acts

1/ It shall be unlawful for an employer where any of the following acts are committed by the employer or a managerial employee to:

a) Restrain the worker in any manner from exercising his rights or take any retaliatory action against him because he exercises his right;

b) Discriminate against female workers, in matters of remuneration, on the ground of their sex orientation;

c) Terminate a contract of employment contrary to the provisions of this Proclamation;

d) Coerce or in any manner compel any worker to join or not to join a trade union; or to continue or cease membership of a trade union; or to require a worker to quit membership from one union and require him to join another union; or to require him to cast his vote to a certain candidate or not to a candidate in elections for trade union offices;

e) Compel any worker to execute any task which is hazardous to his life;

f) Discriminate between workers on the basis of Nation, sex. religion, political outlook, HIV/AIDS disablement or disablement or any other grounds;

g) Unduly delay a collective bargaining by withholding relevant information for the negotiation or perform any other act contrary to good faith;

h) Commit sexual harassment or sexual assault at workplace;

i) Physically abuse anyone in a work place;

j) Coerce a worker in any manner to work or discharge an obligation.

2/ It shall be unlawful for a worker to:

a) Intentionally commit in the workplace any act which endangers life or property;

b) Take away property from the work place without the express authorization of the employer;

c) Making use of falsified document or an attempt thereof;

d) To use drugs prohibited by laws or use alcoholic beverges and have impared physical and mental status at the work place;

e) Except for HIV/AIDS test, refuse to submit himself for medical examination when required by laws or by the employer for good cause;

f) Refuse to observe safety and accident prevention rules and to take the necessary safety precautions;

g) Conduct meeting during working hours in disregard to the time assigned by the collective agreement or without obtaining the permission of the employer;

h) Commit sexual harassment or sexual violence at workplace:

i) Physically abuse anyone in a work place.

SECTION FOUR   MODIFICATION OF CONTRACT OF EMPLOYMENT

15. Conditions of Modification

conditions of a contract of employment which are not determined by this Proclamation may be modified by:

1/ Collective agreement;

2/ Work rules issued in accordance with this Proclamation; or

3/ Written agreement of the parties.

16. Amalgamation, Division or Transfer of Ownership

without prejudice to Article 15 of this Proclamation, amalgamation, division or transfer of owner ship of an under taking shall not have the effect of modifying a contract of employment.

SECTION FIVE TEMPORARY SUSPENSION OF RIGHTS AND OBLIGATIONS ARISING FROM CONTRACT OF EMPLOYMENT

17. General

1/ Rights and obligations arising from a contract of employment may be temporarily suspended in the manner provided for by this Section.

2/ Temporary suspension of rights and obligations arising from a contract or employment shall not imply termination or interruption or the contract: provided, however, that the contract of employment shall interrupt the obligation of:

a) The worker to perform the work;

b) The employer to pay wages, other benefits and allowances unless otherwise provided for by this Proclamation or by a collective agreement.

18. Grounds for Suspension

the following shall be valid grounds for the suspension in accordance with Article 17 of this proclamation:

1/ leave without pay granted by the employer upon request by the worker;

2/ leave of absence for the purpose of holding office in trade unions or other social services;

3/ detention for a period not exceeding 30 days; provided, however, that the employer is notified within 10 days or is supposed to know of the detention;

4/ national call;

5/ full or partial suspension, due to force majeure, of the activities of the employer for a period of not less than 10 consecutive days;

6/ financial problems, not attributable to the fault of the employer, that requires the suspension of the activities of the employer for not less than 10 consecutive days.

19. Duty to Inform

in order to suspend rights and obligations arising from contract of employment are suspended in accordance with Article 18 (5) or (6) above the employer shall inform the Ministry or the competent authority in writing with in three working days of the occurrence of the ground for suspension.

20. Decisions of the Ministry or the Appropriate Authority

1/ the Ministry or the appropriate Authority shall determine the existence of a good cause for suspension with in three working days upon receipt of the written notice pursuant to Article 19 above. Where the Ministry or the appropriate authority does not notify its decision within three days, the organization shall be deemed allowed to suspend.

2/ where the Ministry or the appropriate authority finds that there is no good cause for suspension it shall order the resumption of the work and payment for the days on which workers were suspended.

3/ the party who is aggrieved by the decision in accordance with Sub-Articles (1) or (2) of this Article may, within five working days, appeal to the competent labour court.

21. Effect of Confirmation or Authorization of Suspension

1/ where the Ministry or the appropriate authority confirms or proves the existence of good causes for suspension, it shall fix the duration of the suspension; provided, however, that duration of the suspension shall not exceed 90 days.

2/ where the competent authority or the appropriate authority is convinced that the employer cannot resume its activities with in the period set under Sub-Article (1) of this Article, the contract of employment shall be put to an end and worker shall be entitled to the benefits specified under Articles 39 and 44 of this Proclamation.

22. Effects of Expiry of the Period of Suspension

the worker shall report for work on the working day following the date of expiry of suspension; and the employer shall reinstate the worker, who so reports for work, in a relevant position to his profession without adversely affecting his job position and wage.

CHAPTER TWO   TERMINATION OF EMPLOYMET RELATIONS

23. General

1/ a contract of employment shall only be terminated upon initiation by the employer or worker and in accordance with the provisions of the law or a collective agreement or by the agreement of the parties.

2/ the amalgamation, division or transfer of ownership of an undertaking shall not have the effect of terminating a contract of employment.

SECTION ONE   TERMINATION OF CONTRACT OF EMPLOYMENT BY THE OPERATIONS OF THE LAW OR BY AGREEMENT

24. Termination of contract of Employment by the Operations of the Law

a contract of employment shall terminate on the following grounds:

1/ on the completion of the work where the contract of employment is for a specified work;

2/ up on the death of the worker;

3/ up on the retirement of the worker in accordance with the relevant law;

4/ when the undertaking ceases operation permanently due to bankruptcy or for any other cause;

5/ when the worker is unable to work due to partial or total permanent in capacity.

25. Termination of Contract of Employment by Agreement

1/ the parties may terminate their contract of employment by agreement; provided, however, that waiver by the worker of any of his right under the law shall have no legal effect.

2/ termination of employment by agreement shall be effective and binding on the worker only where it is made in writing.

SECTION TWO TERMINATION OF CONTRACT OF EMPLOYMENT UPON THE INITIATION OF THE PARTIES

SUB-SECTION ONE TERMINATION OF CONTRACT OF EMPLOYEMENT BY THE EMPLOYER

26. General

1/ A contract of employment may only be terminated where there are grounds attributed to the worker's conduct or with objective circumstances a rising from his ability to do his work or the organizational or operational requirements of the undertaking.

2/ The following shall not be deemed to constitute legitimate grounds for the termination of a contract of employment:

a) Member ship of the worker in a trade union or his participation in its lawful activities;

b) Seeking or holding office as workers' representative;

c) Submission of grievance by the worker against the employer or his participation in judicial or other proceedings;

d) The worker's Nation, Sex, Religion, Political outlook, Marital status, Race, Color; Family responsibility; Pregnancy; Disablement or Social status.

27. Termination of Contract of Employment without Prior Notice

1/ Unless otherwise determined by a collective agreement, a contract of employment shall be terminated without prior notice only on the following grounds:

a) Unless the reason for being late is justified by the collective agreement, work rule or contract of employment, being late for duty eight times in six months period while being warned in writing of such a problem;

b) Absence from duty for a total five days in six months period while being warned in writing of such a problem; and where the absence cannot be classified in any of the leaves provided under the Proclamation;

c) Deceitful or fraudulent conduct in carrying out his duties;

d) Misappropriation of the property or fund of the employer with intent to procure for himself or to a third person unlawful enrichment;

e) Performance result of a worker, despite his potential, is persistently below the qualities and quantities stipulated in the collective agreement or determined by the agreement of the parties;

f) Being responsible for brawls or quarrels at work, having regard to the gravity of the case;

g) Conviction for an offence where such conviction renders him incompatible for the post which he holds;

h) Being responsible for causing damage intentionally or through gross negligence to any property of the employer or to another property which is directly connected with the work of the Undertaking;

i) Commission of any of the prohibited acts under Article 14 (2) of this Proclamation;

j) Absence from work due to a court sentence passed against the worker for more than thirty days;

k) Commission of other violations stipulated in a collective agreement as grounds for terminating contract of employment without notice.

2/ Where an employer terminates a contract of employment in accordance with this Article, he shall give written statement specifying the reasons for and the date of termination.

3/ The right of an employer to terminate contract of employment in accordance with this Article, shall lapse after thirty working days from the date the employer knew the existence of a ground for the termination.

4/ The grounds for suspension of a worker from duty before terminating the contract of employment of the worker in accordance with this Article may be determined by collective agreement, provided, however, that the duration of such suspension shall not exceed 30 working days.

28. Termination of contract of Employment with Prior Notice

1/ The following grounds relating to the loss of capacity of, and situations affecting, the worker shall constitute good cause for terminating a contract of employment with prior notice:

a) The worker's manifest loss of capacity to perform the work to which he has been assigned; and his lack of skill to continue his work as a result of his refusal or inability to make use of an opportunity of training arranged by the employer to upgrade his skill or after having been trained, his inability to acquire the necessary skill;

b) The worker is, for reasons of health or disability, permanently unable to carry out his obligation under the contract of employment;

c) The worker's unwillingness to move to a locality where the undertaking relocates;

d) The post of the worker is cancelled for good cause and the worker cannot be transferred to another job position.

2/ Any loss of capacity of work referred to in Sub-Article (1) (a) of this Article shall, unless otherwise provided by a collective agreement, be verified by a periodical job performance evaluation.

3/ The following grounds attributable to the organizational or operational requirements of an undertaking shall constitute good causes for the termination of a contract of employment with prior notice:

a) Any event which entails direct and permanent cessation of the worker's activities in part or in whole resulting in the necessity of a terminating a contract of employment;

b) Without prejudice to the provisions of Article 18 (5) and (6) demand fall for the products or services of the employer resulting in the reduction of the volume of the work or profit of the undertaking and thereby requiring termination of a contract of employment;

c) A decision to alter work methods or introduce new technology with a view to raise productivity resulting in termination of a contract of employment.

4/ Where the cancellation of a job position affects a workforce in accordance with Article 29 (1) of this Proclamation, the termination shall be undertaken in compliance with the requirements laid down in accordance with Article 29(3).

29. Reduction of Workforce

1/ In this Proclamation "reduction of workforce" means termination of workforce of an undertaking for any of the reasons presided for by Article 28 (3) of this Proclamation affecting a number of workers representing at least ten percent of the number of workers employed or, in the case where the number of workers employed in an undertaking is between twenty and fifty, termination of at least five employees over a continuous period of not less than ten days.

2/ The expression "number of workers" referred to in Sub-Article (1) of this Article means the average number of the workers employed by an employer concerned within the twelve months preceding the date when the employer took measures of reduction of workers.

3/ Whenever a reduction of workforce takes place in accordance with Article 28(3) of this Proclamation, the employer shall conduct consultation with a Trade Union or workers' representatives in order to retain workers having skills and higher rate of productivity in their posts. In case of comparable skill and rate of productivity, the workers to be affected first by the reduction shall be in the following order:

a) Those having the shortest length of service in the Undertaking;

b) Those having fewer dependents;

c) The redduction shall affected first workers except those that are listed under (d) up to (e) of this Sub-Article;

d) Those employees with disability;

e) Those who sustained employment injury in the Undertaking;

f) Workers' representatives; and

g) Expectant mothers and mothers within four months post-natal.

30. Exceptions

1/ The procedure laid down in this Proclamation shall not apply to the reduction of workers due to normal decrease in the volume of a construction work as a result of its successive completion unless the reduction affects workers employed for parts of the work before the work for which they are employed is completed.

2/ For the purpose of Sub-Article (1) of this Article, "construction work" includes the construction, renovation, upgrading, maintenance and repair of a buildings, roads, rail-way lines, dams and bridges, installation of machinery and similar works.

SUB-SECTION TWO TERMINATION OF CONTRACT OF EMPLOYEMENT BY THE WORKER

31. Termination of Contract of Employment with Prior Notice

Without prejudice to Article 32 of this Proclamation, any worker who has completed his probation period may, by giving thirty days prior notice to the employer, terminate his contract of employment.

32. Termination of Contract of Employment without prior notice

1/ The following shall be good causes to terminate a contract of employment without prior notice:

a) Where the employer has committed any act contrary to human dignity and morals or other acts punishable under the Criminal Law against the worker;

b) Where the workers have been a victim of sexual harassment or sexual violence by the employer or a managerial employee;

c) In the case of imminent danger threatening the worker's safety or health, where the employer, having been made aware of such danger, failed to act within the time limit in accordance with the early warning given by the competent authority or appropriate trade union or the worker himself to avert the danger;

d) Where the employer has repeatedly failed to fulfill his basic obligations towards the worker as prescribed under this Proclamation, collective agreement, work rules or other relevant laws.

2/ Where a worker terminates his contract of employment for reasons referred to under Sub-Article (1) of this Article, he shall inform the employer in writing the reasons for termination and the date on which the termination is to take effect.

33. Period of Limitation

A worker's right to terminate his contract of employment in accordance with Article 32 (1) of this Proclamation shall expire after fifteen working days from the date on which the act occurred or ceased to exist.

CHAPTER THREE COMMON PROVISIONS WITH RESPECT TO TERMINATION OF CONTRACT OF EMPLOYMENT

SECTION ONE NOTICE TO TERMINATE A CONTRACT OF EMPLOYMENT

34. Procedure for Giving Notice

1/ Notice of termination required under the provisions of this Proclamation shall be in writing. The notice shall specify the reasons for the termination of the contract and the date on which the termination shall take effect.

2/ Notice of termination by the employer shall be delivered to the worker in person. Where it is not possible to find the worker or he refuses to receive the notice, it shall be affixed on the notice board in the work place of the worker for 10 consecutive days.

3/ Notice of termination by the worker shall he handed over to the employer or its representative or delivered to its registry office.

4/ Notice of termination issued to a worker by an employer during the time in which the contract of employment is suspended as per Article 17 of this Proclamation shall be null and void.

35. Period of Notice

1/ The period of notice given by the employer shall be as follows:

a) One month, in the case of a worker who has completed his probation and has a period of service not exceeding one year;

b) Two months, in the case of a worker who has a period of service above one year and not exceeding nine years;

c) Three months, in the case of a worker who has a period of service of more than nine years;

d) Two months, in the case of a worker who has completed his probation and whose contract of employment is to be terminated due to reduction of work force.

2/ Notwithstanding the provisions of Sub-Article (1) of this Article, the period of notice for a contract of employment for a definite period or piece work shall be as agreed upon by the parties to the contract.

3/ The period of notice fixed in this Proclamation shall run from the first working day following the date on which notice is dully given.

4/ The obligations of the parties arising from the contract of employment shall remain intact during the period of notice.

SECTION TWO   PAYMENT OF WAGES AND OTHER PAYMENTS ON TERMINATION OF CONTRACT OF EMPLOYMENT

36. Period of Payment

Where a contract of employment is terminated, wages and other payments connected with the termination due to the worker shall be paid within seven working days from the date of termination; provided, however, that the time of payment may be extended where the worker delays, because of his own fault, to return property or any sum of money which he received from or is due to the employer.

37. Amount in Dispute

In the event of a dispute as to the amount claimed by the worker, the employer shall pay the worker the admitted amount within the time limit specified under Article 36 of this Proclamation.

38. Effects of Delay

Where an employer fails to pay the sum due to the worker within the time limit specified under Article 36 of this Proclamation, the labour division of a competent court may order a penalty payment of up to three months' the work's wage except where the delay is due to causes beyond the control of the employer.

SECTION THREE   SEVERANCE PAY AND COMPENSATION

39. General

1/ A worker who has completed his probation period and who is not eligible for pension shall have the right to receive severance pay from the employer where:

a) His contract of employment is terminated because of permanent cessation of operation of the Undertaking due to bankruptcy or for any other cause;

b) His contract of employment is terminated by the initiation of the employer in violation of the law;

c) He is reduced as per the conditions prescribed under this Proclamation;

d) Where the worker resigned due to sexual harassment or sexual violence by the employer or managerial employee; or where such act was committed by a coworker and the incident was reported to the employer but the latter failed to take appropriate measure in due time;

e) He has terminated his contract of employment because of the employer's maltreatment affecting his human dignity or morale or constituting a criminal offence under the Criminal Code;

f) He has resigned due to failure of the employer to take measures despite being informed of a threat to his safety or health;

g) His contract of employment is terminated because of his partial or total disability as certified by medical board;

h) Where he has given service to the employer for a minimum of five years' service and his contract of employment is terminated because of sickness or death or his contract of employment is terminated on his own initiative provided that he has no contractual obligation relating to training to render service to the employer;

i) His contract of employment is terminated on his own initiative because of HIV/AIDS.

2/ Where a worker dies before receiving severance pay, it shall be paid to his dependents' referred to in Article 110(2) of this Proclamation.

3/ The allocation of severance pay to dependents of the deceased shall be effected in the same manner as in Article 110 of this Proclamation.

40. Amount of Severance Pay

1/ The severance pay referred to in Article 39 of this Proclamation shall:

2/ Be thirty times the average daily wages of the last week of service for the first year of service; and for the service of less than one year, be calculated in proportion to the period of service.

3/ In the case of a worker who has served for more than a year, payment shall be increased by one-third of the amount referred to in Sub-Article (1) of this Article for every additional year of service; provided, however, that the total amount shall not exceed twelve months' wage of the worker.

4/ Where a contract of employment is terminated in accordance with Article 24(4) and 29 of this Proclamation, the worker shall be paid, in addition to payments under Sub-Article (1) and (2) of this Article, an amount equal to the worker's average daily wage of the last week of service multiplied by 60.

41. Compensation for Termination of Contract of Employment without Notice

1) A worker who terminates his contract of employment in accordance with Article 32(1) of this Proclamation shall be entitled, in addition to the severance pay referred to in Article 40 of this Proclamation, to a payment of compensation which shall be thirty times his daily wages of the last week of service. This provision shall apply to a worker covered by the relevant pension law.

2) However, where the termination is based on Article 32 (1)(b) the worker shall, in addition to severance pay, be entitled to compensation of his daily wage multiplied by ninety. This provision shall also apply to a worker covered by the relevant pension law.

SECTION FOUR CONSEQUENCES OF UNLAWFUL TERMINATION OF CONTRACT OF EMPLOYMENT

42. General

Where an employer or a worker fails to comply with the requirements laid down in this Proclamation or other relevant law regarding termination of a contract of employment, the termination shall be unlawful.

43. Reinstatement or Compensation of a Worker in the Case of unlawful termination

1/ Where a contract of employment is terminated because of those grounds mentioned under Article 26 (2) of this Proclamation, the employer shall be obliged to reinstate the worker; provided, however, that the worker shall be compensated if he wishes to quit his employment.

2/ Without prejudice to Sub- Article (1) of this Article, where a contract of employment is terminated contrary to the provisions of Articles 24, 25, 27, 28 and 29 of this Proclamation, the labour dispute settlement tribunal may order the reinstatement of the worker or the payment of compensation.

3/ Notwithstanding Sub-Article (2) of this Article, the labour tribunal may affirm the termination of the worker upon payment of compensation even if the worker requests for re-instatement where the tribunal is of the view that the maintenance of the particular worker and employer relations, by its nature or due to the controversy of the parties concerned, is likely to give rise to serious difficulties. Similarly, where a worker who, after obtaining judgment of reinstatement declines to be re-instated, the tribunal may order the termination of the worker upon payment of compensation for the inconvenience he sustained having regard to the nature of the work and other circumstances of the case.

4/ The compensation to be paid under Sub-Article (1), (2) or (3) of this Article to a worker who is not reinstated shall, in addition to the severance pay referred to in Article 40 of this Proclamation, be:

a) In the case of a contract of employment for an indefinite period, 180 times the average daily wages and a sum equal to his wage for the appropriate notice period in accordance with Article 44 of this Proclamation;

b) In the case of a contract of employment for a definite period or for piecework, a sum equal to the wages which he would have obtained if the contract of employment has continued up to its date of expiry or completion of the work; provided, however, that such compensation shall not exceed 180 times his averaged daily wage. The provisions of Sub-Article (4) of this Article shall also be applicable to a worker covered by the relevant pension law.

5/ Where the First Instance Court orders the reinstatement of the worker in accordance with Sub-Article (1) or (2) of this Article, the court shall order back-pay of wage for a period not exceeding 6 months. Where the decision of reinstatement is confirmed by the appellate Court, it shall order back pay of wage for a period not exceeding one year.

44. Exceptions

Notwithstanding the provisions of Article 43, non-compliance by the employer with the notice requirements specified under Article 35 shall only result in the payment by the employer, wages in lieu of the notice period.

45. Liability of the Worker to Pay Compensation

1/ A worker who terminates his contract of employment in disregard of the provisions of Article 31 or 35(2) of this Proclamation shall be liable to pay compensation to the employer.

2/ However, the compensation payable by the worker in accordance with Sub-Article (1) of this Article shall not exceed 30 days' wages of the worker and be payable from the remaining payment due to the worker.

CHAPTER FOUR   SPECIAL CONTRACTS

SECTION ONE   HOME WORK CONTRACT

46. Formation of Contract

1/ There shall be a home work contract when a natural person habitually performs work, for an employer, in his own home or any other place freely chosen by him in return for wages without any direct supervision or direction by the employer.

2/ In agreement for the sale of raw materials or tools by an employer to a home worker and there sale of the products to the employer or any other similar arrangements made between the employer and the home worker shall be deemed a home work contract.

3/ The contract concluded between a home worker and an employer shall be deemed to be made for a definite period or piece-work.

4/ The Minister may, in consultation with the concerned organs, prescribed by directive the provisions of this proclamation that shall apply to home workers and manner of their application.

47. Keeping of Records

An employer who employs a worker on the basis of a home work contract shall keep a register containing the following and other relevant particulars:

1/ Full name, age, marital status and address of the worker;

2/ The address where the work is to be carried out;

3/ The type, price, quality and quantity of material supplied by the employer to the worker;

4/ The type of work, quality and quantity ordered;

5/ The time and place of delivery of the product or material;

6/ Amount and manner of payment.

SECTION TWO   CONTRACT OF APPRENTICESHIP

48. Formation of Contract

1/ There shall be a contract of apprenticeship where an employer agrees to give a person complete and systematic training in a given occupation related to the function of his under taking in accordance with the skills of the trade and the person in return agrees to obey the instruction given to carry out the training and works related there to.

2/ The contract of apprenticeship shall be concluded with the person whose age is not less than fifteen years.

3/ The contract of apprenticeship and its modifications shall be valid only where it is made in writing and approved by the Ministry or the appropriate organ.

49. Contents of the Contract

A contract of apprenticeship shall specify at least the following:

1/ The nature and duration of the training of apprenticeship;

2/ The stipend to be paid during the training;

3/ The conditions of work.

50. Obligations of the Parties

1/ The apprentice shall diligently follow the training and endeavor to complete it successfully.

2/ The employer shall not assign the apprentice on an occupation which is not related and does not contribute to his training.

51. Termination of a Contract

1/ A contract of apprenticeship shall terminate on the following grounds:

a) At the expiry of the period fixed for the apprenticeship;

b) Up on giving notice by either of the contracting parties;

c) When the apprentice terminates the contract without notice.

2/ The employer may terminate the contract of apprenticeship by giving notice in accordance with Sub-Article (1)(b) of this Article, where:

a) He is no longer able to discharge his obligation on account of change of work or other cause beyond his control; or

b) The apprentice violates the disciplinary rule of the undertaking; or

c) The apprentice is permanently incapable of continuing his training or completing his training within the specified time limit.

3/ The apprentice may terminate the contract of apprenticeship by giving notice of termination in accordance with Sub-Article (1)(b) of this Article, where:

a) The employer fails to observe his obligations under the contract or this Proclamation; or

b) The apprentice has good cause relating to his health or family or other similar grounds.

4/ The apprentice may terminate the contract of apprenticeship without giving notice in accordance with Sub-Article (1)(c) of this Article, where:

a) He proves, by appropriate medical certificate, that he cannot discharge his obligations without seriously endangering his health; or

b) The employer unilaterally changes the terms of the contract.

5/ The provisions of this Proclamation regarding severance pay compensation and reinstatement shall not be applicable to contracts of apprenticeship.

52. Certificate

The employer shall, up on the termination of the contract of apprenticeship, give the apprentice a certificate which specifies the occupation he has been trained in, the duration of the training and other similar particulars.

PART THREE
WAGES

CHAPTER ONE   DETERMINATION OF WAGES

53. General

1/ "Wages" means the regular payment to which a worker is entitled in return for the performance of the work that he performs under a contract of employment.

2/ For the purposes of this Proclamation, the following payments shall not be considered as wages:

a) Over-time pay;

b) Amount received by way of per-diems, hardship allowances, transport allowance, relocation expenses, and similar allowance payable to the worker on the occasion of travel or change of his residence;

c) Bonus;

d) Commission;

e) Other incentives paid for additional work results;

f) Service charge received from customers.

54. Conditions of Payments for Idle Time

1/ Unless otherwise provided for in this Proclamation or the relevant law, wages shall be paid only for work performed.

2/ Not with standing Sub-Article (1) of this Article, a worker shall be entitled to payment of his wage if, while being ready to work, he is unable to work due to an interruption in the supply of tools or raw materials or due to other causes not attributable to him.

CHAPTER TWO   MODE AND EXECUTION OF PAYMENT

55. General

1/ Wages shall be paid in cash, provided, however, that where the employer and workers agree, it may be paid in kind. Wages paid in kind may not exceed the market value in the area of the payment in kind and in no case may exceed 30% of the wages paid in cash.

2/ A Regulation of the Council of Ministers shall determine the powers and responsibilities of a Wage Board which shall comprise representatives of the Government, employees and trade unions together with other stakeholders that will periodically revise minimum wages based on studies which take into account the country's economic development, labour market and other considerations.

56. Execution of Payments

1/ Unless agreed otherwise, wages shall be paid on working days and at the place of work.

2/ In case where the day of payment mentioned in Sub-Article (1) of this Article falls on weekly rest day or a public holiday, the day of payment shall fall on the preceding working day.

57. Payment in Person

Unless otherwise provided by laws or collective agreement or work rules, wages shall be paid directly to the worker or to a person authorized by him.

58. Time of Payment

Wages shall be paid at such intervals as a provided for by laws or collective agreement or work rule or contract of employment.

59. Deduction from Wages

1/ The employer shall not deduct from, attach or set off the wages of the worker except where it is provided otherwise by laws or collective agreement or work rules or in accordance with a court order or a written agreement of the worker concerned.

2/ Unless the worker expresses his consent in writing, the amount that may be deducted at any one time from the worker's wage shall in no case exceed one-third of his monthly wage.

60. Keeping Record of Payment

1/ The employer shall keep a register of payment specifying the gross pay and method of calculation of the wage, other remunerations, the amount and type of deduction the net pay and other relevant particulars on which the signature of the worker is a fixed unless there is a special arrangement.

2/ The employer shall have the obligation to make the register accessible and to explain the entries thereof, to the worker upon the latter's request.

3/ The fact that a worker has received without protest the amount indicated on the register shall not constitute waiver of his right to any part of his wages that was due.

PART FOUR
HOURS OF WORK, WEEKLY REST AND PUBLIC HOLIDAYS

CHAPTER ONE   HOURS OF WORK

SECTION ONE   NORMAL HOURS OF WORK

61. Maximum Daily or weekly Hours of Work

1/ In this proclamation, "normal hours of work" means the time during which a worker actually performs work or avails himself for work in accordance with law, collective agreement or work rules.

2/ Normal hours of work shall not exceed 8 hours a day or 48 hours a week.

62. Reduction of Normal Hours of Work

1/ The Ministry may issue Directive reducing normal hours of work for economic sectors, industries or occupations where there are special conditions of work.

2/ Reductions of normal hours of work under this Proclamation shall not entail reduction in the wages of a worker.

63. Arrangement of Weekly Hours of Work

Hours of work shall spread equally over the working days of a week, provided, however, where the nature of the work so requires, hours of work in any one of the working days may be shortened and the difference be distributed over the remaining days of the week without extending the daily limits of eight hours by more than two hours.

64. Averaging of Normal Hours of Work

Where the circumstances in which the work has to be carried out are such that normal hours of work cannot be distributed evenly over the individual week, normal hours of work may be calculated as an average over a period longer than one week, provided, however that the average number of hours over a period shall not exceed eight hours per day or forty-eight hours per week.

65. Exclusion

Unless otherwise provided in a collective agreement or employment contract, the provisions of this Proclamation governing working hours shall not be applicable to commercial travelers or commercial representatives.

SECTION TWO OVERTIME WORK

66. General

1/ Work done in excess of the normal daily hours of work fixed in accordance with the provisions of this Proclamation shall be deemed to be overtime.

2/ Work done within the limits referred to in Articles 61, 63 and 64 of this Proclamation shall not be deemed to be overtime.

3/ Overtime shall be worked only in cases expressly provided for under Article 67 and on the express instructions of the employer.

4/ The instructions given under Sub-Article (3) of this Article and the actual overtime worked by each worker shall be recorded by the employer.

67. Circumstances in which Overtime Work is Permissible

1/ A worker may not be compelled to work overtime, however, overtime may be worked whenever the employer cannot be expected to resort to other measures and only where there is:

a) Accident, actual or eminent;

b) Force-majeure;

c) Urgent work;

d) Substitution of absent workers assigned on work that runs continuously without interruption.

2/ Notwithstanding the provisions of Sub-Article (1) of this Article, overtime work shall not exceed four hours in a day and twelve hours in a week.

68. Overtime Payment

1/ In addition to his normal wage, a worker who works over-time shall be entitled at least on the following rate of payments:

a) In the case of work done between 6:00 a.m. in the morning and 10:00 p.m. in the evening, at the rate of 1.5 multiplied by the ordinary hourly rate;

b) In the case of night time work between 10 p.m. in the evening and 6 a.m. in the morning, at the rate of 1.75 (one and three fourth) multiplied by the ordinary hourly rate;

c) In the case of work done on weekly rest day, at the rate of 2 multiplied by the ordinary hourly rate;

d) In the case of work done on a public holiday, at the rate of 2.5 multiplied by the ordinary hourly rate.

2/ Payment for over-time work shall be effected on the day fixed for payment of wage and together with wage.

CHAPTER TWO WEEKLY REST

69. General

1/ A worker shall be entitled to a weekly rest period covering not less than twenty-four non-interrupted hours in the course of each period of seven days.

2/ Unless otherwise determined by a collective agreement or work rule, the weekly rest day shall, whenever possible:

a) Fall on a Sunday;

b) Be granted simultaneously to all of the workers of the undertaking.

3/ The weekly rest period shall be calculated as to include the period from 6 a.m. to the next 6 a.m.

4/ Notwithstanding the provisions of Sub-Article (1) of this Article, where the nature of his task did not enable the worker to make use of his weekly rest day, the employer shall grant 4 working days of rest in a month.

70. Special Weekly Rest Day

1/ Where the nature of the work or the service provided by the employer is such that the weekly rest cannot fall on Sunday, another day may be made a weekly rest instead.

2/ The provisions of Sub-Article (1) of this Article shall be applicable to the following and other similar activities:

a) Work that has to supply the necessities of life to meet the health, recreational or cultural requirements of the general public;

b) Essential public services as stipulated under Article 137(2) of this Proclamation.

c) Work which, because of its nature or for technical reasons, if interrupted or postponed could cause difficulties or damages.

71. Works Done on Weekly Rest Days

1/ A worker may be required to work on any weekly rest day only where it is necessary to avoid serious interference with the ordinary working of the under taking in the case of:

a) Accident, actual or threatened;

b) Force majeure;

c) Urgent work to be done.

2/ Without prejudice to the provisions of Article 68 (1)(c) of this Proclamation, a worker who, by virtue of the provisions of this Chapter, works on a weekly rest day, shall be entitled to a compensatory rest period. However, he shall be compensated in the form of cash if his contract of employment is terminated before he utilized the compensatory rest period.

72. Application

The provision soft of this chapter shall not apply to commercial travelers or commercial representatives.

CHAPTER THREE   PUBLIC HOLIDAYS

73. General

Public holidays observed under the relevant law shall be paid Public Holidays.

74. Non-Reduction of Wages for Public Holidays

1/ A worker who is paid on a monthly basis shall incur no reduction of his wages on account of having not worked on a Public Holiday.

2/ The payment of wages on a Public Holiday to a worker other than workers mentioned under Sub-Article (1) of this Article shall be determined by his contract of employment or collective agreement.

75. Payment for Working on Public Holidays

1) A worker shall be paid his hourly wages multiplied by two for each hour of work on a public holiday.

2) Where a public holiday coincides with another public holiday or falls on a rest day designated by laws, a worker shall be entitled to only one public holiday payment for working on such a day.

PART FIVE
LEAVE

CHAPTER ONE   ANNUAL LEAVE

76. General

1/ An agreement by a worker to waive in any manner his right to annual leave shall be null and void.

2/ Unless otherwise provided in this Proclamation, it is prohibited to pay wages in lieu of the annual leave.

77. Amount of Annual Leave

1/ A worker pursuant to this Article shall be entitled to uninterrupted annual leave with pay. Such leave shall in no case be less than:

a) Sixteen (16) working days for the first year of service;

b) Sixteen (16) working days plus one working day for every additional two years' service.

2/ The wage a worker receives during his annual leave shall be equal to what he would have received if he had continued to work.

3/ For purpose of determining the qualifying period of service required for the entitlement of an annual leave, 26 days of service in an undertaking shall be deemed to be equivalent to one month of employment.

4/ A worker whose contract of employment is terminated pursuant to this Proclamation shall be entitled to his pay for the leave he has not taken.

5/ Where the length of service of a worker is below one year, the worker shall be entitled to an annual leave proportional to the length of his service.

78. Granting of Leave

1/ A worker shall be granted his first annual leave after one year of service and his next and sub sequent annual leave in the course of each calendar year.

2/ An employer shall grant a worker his leave in accordance with a leave schedule in the course of the calendar year in which it becomes due.

3/ The leave schedule referred to in Sub-Article (2) of this Article shall be drowned up by the employer with due regard as far as possible to:

a) the interest of the worker; and

b) the need for maintaining the normal operation of the undertaking.

79. Dividing and Postponing Annual Leave

1/ Notwithstanding the provisions of Article 77(1) of this Proclamation, if a worker requests and the employer agrees, his leave may be granted in two parts.

2/ Annual leave may be postponed when the worker requests and the employer agrees.

3/ An employer may, for reasons dictated by operational requirements of the undertaking, postpone the leave of a worker.

4/ Any leave postponed in accordance with Sub-Articles (2) and (3) of this Article shall not be postponed for more than two years.

5/ Where a worker on annual leave falls sick and required medical treatment as inpatient, his annual leave shall be suspended and his sick leave pursuant to Articles 85 and 86 of this Proclamation shall commence.

80. Recalling of Worker on Leave

1/ A worker on annual leave may be recalled only where unforeseen circumstances required his presence at his job duties.

2/ A worker who is recalled from leave shall be entitled to a payment covering the remainder of his leave excluding the time lost for the trip.

3/ The employer shall cover the transport expenses and per-diem incurred by the worker as a direct consequence of his being recalled.

CHAPTER TWO
SPECIAL LEAVES

81. Leave for family events

1/ A worker shall been titled to leave with pay for three working days where;

a) He concludes marriage; or

b) His spouse, descendants, ascendants, brother, sister, uncle, aunt relative whether by consanguinity or affinity dies entitled 3 working days leave with pay.

2/ A male employee shall be entitled to three consecutive days paternity leave with full pay.

3/ A worker shall be entitled to leave without pay for up to five consecutive days in the case of exceptional and serious events. However, such leave may be granted only twice in a budget year.

82. Union Leave

Trade union leaders shall be entitled to leave with pay for the purpose of presenting cases in labour disputes, negotiating collective agreements, attending union meetings, participating in seminars or training courses. The manner of granting such leave may be determined by collective agreement.

83. Leave for special purpose

1/ A worker who appears at hearings before bodies competent to hear labour disputes or to enforce labour laws shall be granted leave with pay only for the time utilized for the said purpose.

2/ A worker shall be granted leave with pay for the purpose of exercising his voting rights or discharging his obligation as a witness before judicial or quasi-judicial organs.

3/ The manner in which educational or training leave is to be granted and the form and extent of the financial assistance to be provided may be determined in a collective agreement or work rules.

84. Notification

A worker wishing to take leave in accordance with the provisions of this Chapter shall notify the employer in advance and present the necessary supporting evidence whenever the employer requests him.

CHAPTER THREE SICK LEAVE

85. Duration of Leave

1/ Where a worker, after having completed his probation, is rendered incapable of working due to sickness other than employment injury, he shall be entitled to a sick leave.

2/ The leave referred to in Sub-Article (1) of this Article shall, in no case, be more than six months counted consecutively or separately in the course of any twelve months' period starting from the first day of his sickness.

3/ Where a worker absents himself from work due to sickness, he shall, except where the employer is in a position to be aware of the sickness or it is impractical, notify the employer on the day following his absence.

4/ Without prejudice to stipulations in collective agreement or work rules, a worker shall be entitled to sick leave up on presenting a valid medical certificate issued by a duly recognized medical facility.

86. Payment

The period of sick leave provided for in Article 85 shall be granted to a worker in the following manner:

1/ For the first one month, with payment of 100% of his wages;

2/ For the next two months, with payment of 50% of his wages;

3/ For the next three months, without pay.

PART SIX
WORKING CONDITIONS OF WOMEN AND YOUNG WORKERS

CHAPTER ONE WORKING CONDITIONS OF WOMEN

87. General

1/ Women shall not be discriminated against in all respects on the basis of their sex.

2/ Without prejudice to the generality of Sub-Article (1) of this Article, priority shall be given to women if they get equal result with men when competing for employment, promotion or any other benefit.

3/ It is prohibited to assign women on works that may be listed by the Ministry to be particularly dangerous to women or hazardous to their health.

4/ No pregnant woman shall be assigned to night work between 10 p.m. and 6 a.m. or be assigned on overtime work.

5/ She shall be transferred to another place of work if her job is hazardous to her health or to the fetus as ascertained by a Physician.

6/ An employer shall not terminate the contract of employment of women during her pregnancy and until four months after her confinement.

7/ Notwithstanding the provisions of Sub-Article (6) of this Article, contract of employment may be terminated for reasons stipulated under Article 27 (b-k) and Article 29 (3) but not related pregnancy and delivery.

88. Maternity Leave

1/ An employer shall grant leave to a pregnant worker with pay for medical examination connected with her pregnancy provided, however, that she may be required to present a medical certificate of her examination.

2/ A pregnant worker shall, upon the recommendation of a physician, be entitled to a leave with pay.

3/ A pregnant worker shall be granted a period of 30 consecutive days of leave with pay of pre-natal leave and a period of 90 consecutive days of leave post- natal.

4/ Where a pregnant worker does not deliver within the 30 working days of her pre-natal leave, she is entitled to an additional leave until her confinement in accordance with Sub-Article (2) of this Article. However, if birth takes place before the expiry of the pre-natal leave, the 90 working days of post-natal leave shall commence.

5/ on any pregnant worker certified her giving up pregnancy by physician shall not be implemented Article 86 provision of leave without pay.

CHAPTER TWO   WORKING CONDITIONS OF YOUNG WORKERS

89. General

1/ For the purpose of this Proclamation, "young worker" means a natural person who has attained the age of 15 but is below the age of 18 years.

2/ It is prohibited to employ a person less than 15 years of age.

3/ It is prohibited to assign young workers on work, which on account of its nature or due to the condition in which it is carried out endangers their lives or health.

4/ The Ministry may prescribe the list of activities prohibited for young workers which shall include in particular:

a) Work in the transport of passengers and goods by road, railway, air and internal water ways, dock sides and ware houses involving heavy weight lifting, pulling or pushing or any other related type of labour;

b) Work connected with electric power generation plants, transformers or transmission lines;

c) Underground work such as mines and quarries;

d) Work in sewers and tunnel excavation.

5/ The provision of Sub-Article (4) of this Article shall not apply to work performed by young workers in fulfillment of course requirements in vocational schools that are approved and inspected by the Competent Authority.

90. Limits of Hours of Work

Normal hours of work for young workers shall not exceeds seven hours a day.

91. Night and Over time Work

It is prohibited to assign young workers on:

1/ Night work between 10 p.m. and 6 a.m.;

2/ Overtime work;

3/ Work done on weekly rest days; or

4/ Work done on Public Holidays.

PART SEVEN
OCCUPATIONAL SAFETY AND HEALTH AND WORKING ENVIRONMENT

CHAPTER ONE   PREVENTIVE MEASURES

92. Obligations of an Employer

An employer shall take the necessary measure to safe guard adequately the health and safety of workers; it shall in particular:

1/ Comply with the occupational health and safety requirements provided for in this Proclamation.

2/ Take appropriate steps to ensure that workers are properly instructed and notified concerning the hazards of their respective occupations; and assign safety officer; and establish an occupational health and safety committee.

3/ Provide workers with protective equipment, clothing and other materials and instruct them of their use.

4/ Register employment accidents and occupational diseases and report same to the labour inspection service.

5/ Arrange, according to the nature of the work, at his own expense for the medical examination of newly employed workers and for those workers engaged in hazardous work, as may be necessary with the exception of HIV/AIDS Unless and otherwise the country has obligation of international treaty to do so.

6/ Ensure that the work place and premises of the undertaking do not pose threats to the health and safety of workers.

7/ Take appropriate precautions to ensure that all the processes of work in the undertaking shall not be a source or cause of physical, chemical, biological, ergonomic and psychological hazards to the health and safety of the workers.

8/ Implement the instructions given by the Competent Authority in accordance with this Proclamation;

93. Obligations of Worker

Any worker shall:

1/ Co-operate in the formulation of work rules to safeguard the workers' health and safety, and implement same;

2/ Inform forthwith to the employer any defect related to the appliances used and incidents of injury to health and safety of workers that he is aware of in the undertaking;

3/ Report to the employer any situation which he may have reason to believe could present a hazard and which he cannot prevent on his own, and any incident of injury to health which arises in the course of or in connection with work;

4/ Make proper use of all safety devices and other appliances furnished for the protection of his health and safety or for the protection of the health and safety of others;

5/ Observe all health and safety instructions issued by the employer or by the Competent Authority.

94. Prohibited Acts

Now worker shall:

1/ Interfere with, remove, displace, damage or destroy any safety devices or other appliances furnished for his protection or the protection of others; or

2/ Obstruct any method or process adopted with a view to minimizing occupational hazard.

CHAPTER TWO   OCCUPATIONAL INJURIES

SECTION ONE   LIABILITY

95. General

1/ For the purpose of this Proclamation, "occupational injury" means an employment accident or occupational disease.

2/ Subject to the provisions of the relevant pension law, the provisions of this Chapter shall apply where an employment injury is sustained by a worker during or in connection with the performance of his work.

96. Liability Irrespective of Fault

1/ The employer shall be liable, irrespective of fault, for employment injuries sustained by his worker and such liability shall be determined in accordance with, the provisions of this Chapter.

2/ The employer shall not be liable for any injury intentionally caused by the worker upon himself. In particular, any injury resulting from the following acts shall be deemed to be intentionally caused by the worker:

a) Non-observance of express safety instructions given by the employer or the provisions of accident prevention rules; or

b) Reporting to work in a state of intoxication caused by taking alcoholic beverage or drug that prevents him from properly regulating his body or understanding.

3/ The provisions of Sub-Article (1) of this Article shall not affect the right of a worker to claim damages in accordance with the relevant law where an occupational injury is a result of fault on the part of the employer.

97. Occupational Accident

For the purpose of this Proclamation "occupational accident" means any organic injury or functional disorder sustained by a worker as a result of any cause extraneous to the injured worker or any effort he makes during or in connection with the performance of his work sand includes:

1/ Any injury sustained by a worker while carrying out his employer's order, even away from the work place or outside his normal hours of work;

2/ Any injury sustained by a worker before or after his work or during any interruption of work provided that he is present in the workplace or the premises of the undertaking by reason of his duties;

3/ Any injury sustained by a worker while he is travelling to or from a place of work in a transport service provided by the under taking which is available for the common use of its workers or in a vehicle hired and expressly destined by the under taking for the same purpose;

4/ Any injury sustained by a worker as a result of an action of the employer or a third party during the performance of his work.

98. Occupational Disease

1/ For the purpose of this Proclamation an "occupational disease" means any disorder:

a) The type of work performed by the worker; or

b) pathological condition whether caused by physical, chemical or biological agents which arise as consequence of the surroundings in which the worker is obliged to work during a certain period prior to the date when the diseases become evident.

2/ Occupational disease shall not include endemic or epidemic diseases which are prevalent and being contracted in the area where the work is done, except in the case of workers exclusively engaged in combating such diseases by reason of their occupation.

3/ The Ministry shall, in consultation with the concerned authority, issue directives which contain schedules listing diseases to be of occupational origin. The said schedule shall be revised at least every five years.

4/ The occurrence of any of the diseases listed in the relevant schedule to any worker having been engaged in anyone of the corresponding types of work specified therein, shall by itself, constitute sufficient proof of the occupational nature of the disease.

5/ Notwithstanding Sub-Article (4) of this Article, any proof shall be admitted to establish the occupational origin of a disease not listed in the relevant schedule and of diseases listed when they manifest themselves under conditions different from those establishing a presumption of their occupational nature.

6/ In the absence of proof to the contrary, any disease which occurs frequently only to persons employed in certain occupations shall be presumed to be of an occupational origin where the worker suffering from such a disease was engaged in such occupation and the existence of the disease is ascertained by a medical practitioner.

7/ The date on which an occupational disease became evident, which is. the first date on which the worker became incapacitated or the date of the first medical diagnosis of the disease or the date of the injured worker's death, shall be considered as the date on which an occupational disease contracted.

8/ Where a worker after being cured from an occupational disease listed in the relevant schedule, re-contracts the disease as a result of his being engaged in anyone of the corresponding work specified in the said list, it shall be presumed that he has contracted afresh occupational disease.

SECTION TWO DEGREE OF DISABLEMENT

99. General

1/ "Occupational disablement" means any employment injury as a consequence of which there is a decrease or loss of capacity to work.

2/ Disablement shall have the following effects:

a) Temporary disablement;

b) Permanent partial disablement;

c) permanent total disablement; and

d) Death.

100. Temporary Disablement

Temporary disablement results from the reduction, for a limited period of time, of the worker's capacity for work partially or totally.

101. Permanent Partial or Total Disablement

1/ "Permanent partial disablement" means incurable employment injury decreasing the injured worker's capacity.

2/ "Permanent total disablement" means incurable employment injury which presents the injured worker from engaging in any kind of gainful work.

3/ Injuries which, although not resulting in incapacity for work, cause serious mutilation or disfigurement of the injured person shall, for the purpose of compensation and other benefits, be considered as permanent partial disablement.

102. Assessment of Disablement

1/ The degree of permanent total or partial disablement shall be fixed in accordance with the assessment table of disablement prescribed by directives issued by the Ministry.

2/ The degree of disablement shall be assessed by a medical board in accordance with the assessment table provided for in Sub-Article (1) of this Article. The Board shall, as far as it is possible, determine the extent of the degree of disablement within twelve months from the date of injury.

3/ Assessment of disablement may be reviewed in accordance with Sub-Articles (1) and (2) of this Article where the worker's condition deteriorates or improves or is wrongly diagnosed:

a) On the initiation of the relevant authority; or

b) Up on the request of the concerned worker or employer the issue may be revised pursuant to Sub-Articles (1) and (2) of this Article.

4/ Where the result of the review so warrants, the rights of the worker to a disablement benefit shall be recognized or withdrawn or that the rate payable shall be increased or reduced, as the case may be.

5/ Where a worker who has suffered an employment injury sustains additional employment injury, his disablement shall be reassessed in light of his new circumstances.

CHAPTER THREE   BENEFITS IN THE CASE OF EMPLOYMENT INJURIES

SECTION ONE   GENERAL

103. Payment and Responsibility to Pay

Injury benefits shall be paid in accordance with the *provisions of* this Chapter.

104. Special Obligation

1/ An employer shall have to discharge the following obligations:

a) To provide the injured with first aid in time;

b) To take the injured by an appropriate means of transport to the nearest medical facility;

c) To notify the occurrence of occupational injury to the relevant organ.

2/ The employer shall have the obligation to cover the funeral expenses specified under Article 110 (1) (b) of this Proclamation.

SECTION TWO   MEDICAL SERVICES

105. Types of medical services

Where a worker sustains employment injury, the employer shall cover the following medical service expenses:

1/ General and specialized medical and surgical care;

2/ Hospital and pharmaceutical care;

3/ Any necessary prosthetic or orthopedic appliances.

106. Duration of medical services

Medical services Provide for injury shall be withdrawn in accordance with the decision of a Medical Board.

SECTION THREE   VARIOUS KINDS OF CASH BENEFITS

107. General

1/ A work who has sustained employment injury shall been titled to:

a) Periodical payment while he is temporarily disabled;

b) Disablement pension or gratuity or compensation where he sustains permanent disablement;

c) Dependents' pension or gratuity or compensation to his dependent where he dies.

2/ Periodical payment may be withheld where a worker who has claimed or is receiving same:

a) Refuses or ignores to submit himself to medical examination or in any way intentionally obstructs or unnecessarily delays such examination;

b) be haves in a manner calculated to delay his recovery; or

c) Violates the directives issued by the competent appropriate organ for the behavior of injured workers.

3/ As soon as the circumstances that occasioned the suspension ceases, the periodical payment shall recommence; provided, however, that there shall be no entitlement to back pay for the period of suspension.

108. Periodical Payment

1/ The employer shall pay the periodical payment referred to in Article 107 (1) (a) of this Proclamation for a period not exceeding one year.

2/ The periodical payments referred to in Sub-Article (1) of this Article shall be at the rate of full wage of the worker's previous average yearly wages during the first three months following the date of injury, not less than 75% of the worker previous average yearly wages during the next three months and not less than 50% of his previous average yearly wages for the remaining six months.

3/ Periodical payments shall cease whichever of the following takes place first:

a) When the worker is medically certified to be no longer disabled;

b) On the day the worker becomes entitled to disablement pension or gratuity;

c) Twelve months from the date the worker ceased to work.

109. Disablement Payments

1/ Unless otherwise provided by a Collective Agreement, disablement benefits payable to workers of an undertaking Covered by this Proclamation shall be in accordance with the applicable pension scheme or insurance scheme.

Where the undertaking doesn't arrange an insurance scheme, the relevant pension scheme shall be applied.

2/ Notwithstanding the provisions of Sub-Article (1) of this Article, the disablement benefit covered by an insurance scheme shall in no case be less than the amount prescribed under Sub-Article (4) of this Article.

3/ An employer shall pay a lump sum of disablement benefit to workers who are not covered by pension law.

4/ The amount of the disablement benefit to be paid by the employer shall be:

a) where the injury sustained by the worker is permanent total disablement, a sum equal to five times his annual wages;

b) where the injury sustained by the worker is below permanent total disablement a sum proportionate to the degree of disablement shall be calculated on the basis of the compensation provided for by Sub-Article 4 (a).

5/ Where an apprentive sustaine disablement his disablement benefit shall be calculated by reference to the wages which he would probably have been receiving as a qualified worker after the completion of his apprenticeship.

110. Dependents' Benefits

1/ Where a worker or an apprentice dies as a result of an employment injury, the following benefits shall be payable to depends:

a) Dependents' compensation in accordance with the provisions of Sub-Articles (2) and (3) of this Article; and

b) Unless the amount stipulated by the provisions of a collective agreement or work rules is higher, payment for funeral expenses shall be in no case less than two month wages of the worker.

2/ The following shall be considered as dependents:

a) The widow or widower;

b) Children of the deceased who are under 18 years old; and

c) Any parent who was being supported by the deceased.

3/ The amount of the dependents' benefit for workers not covered by the pension scheme, shall be a sum equal to five times the annual salary of the deceased and shall be paid by the employer in lump sum in accordance with the following proportion:

a) 50% for the widow or widower;

b) 10% each for the deceased's children who are below the age of 18 years old;

c) 10% each for the deceased's parents who were being supported by him.

4/ If the total of dependents' benefit calculated in accordance with Sub-Article (3) of this Article is in excess of 100% of the total amount to be apportioned, the amount of compensation for each dependent shall, without affecting the share of the widow or widower, be proportionately reduced to 100%. If the total amount of dependents' compensation is less than 100% of the total amount to be apportioned, the amount of compensation of each dependent shall be proportionately increased to make it 100%.

111. Burden of Proof

The benefits referred to in Article 110 of this Proclamation shall not be payable where the worker dies after twelve months from the date of the injury unless it is proved that the injury was the main cause of his death.

112. Benefits not Taxable

1/ The benefits payable in accordance with the provisions of this Section shall be exempted from income tax.

2/ The benefits payable under the provisions of this Section shall not be assigned, attached or deducted by way of set off.

PART EIGHT
COLLECTIVE RELATIONS

CHAPTER ONE   TRADE UNIONS AND EMPLOYERS' ASSOCIATIONS

113. The Right to Form associations

1/ Workers and employers shall have the right to establish and organize Trade Unions or employers' associations, respectively, and actively participate there in:

2/ In this Proclamation:

a) "Trade Union" means an association formed by workers;

b) "Employers' Association" means an association established by employers;

c) "Federation" means an organization established by more than one trade union or employers' association;

d) "Confederation" means an organization established by more than one trade union federations or employer's federations.

114. Formation of Associations

1/ A trade union may be established in an under taking where the number of workers is ten or more; provided, however, that the number of members of the union shall not be less than ten.

2/ Workers who work in different undertakings but in similar activities which have less than ten workers may form a general trade union, provided, however, that the number of the members of the union shall not be less than ten.

3/ Trade unions may jointly form trade union federation and federations may jointly form trade union confederations as well.

4/ Employers' associations may jointly form employers' federation and employer's federations may jointly form employers' confederation as well.

5/ No trade union or employers' association may form a confederation without forming trade union or employers' federations.

6/ Any federation or confederation of trade unions or employers' associations may join international organizations of trade unions or employers.

7/ No worker may belong to more than one trade union at any given time for the same employment. Where this provision is not observed, the latest member ship shall prevail; and where the formalities of membership were simultaneous, all of them shall be without effect.

8/ Notwithstanding Sub-Article (4) of this Article, any employer may join an established employers' federation.

115. Function of Associations

Associations shall have the following functions:

1/ to observe the conditions of work and fulfill the obligations set forth in this Proclamation; protect the rights and interests of their members, in particular, represent members in collective bargaining and labour disputes before the competent organ when so requested or authorized by their members; provided, however, that:

a) where there exist more than one trade union at a given undertaking, the trade union which will be the exclusive bargaining agent and undertake consultation with authorities, is the one which secures 50% plus and more than one membership of all employees of the undertaking;

b) the organization which secured the majority membership of the workers shall be recognized by the Ministry or the appropriate Authority;

c) if an organization subsequently failed to secure the majority membership of workers, the other organization that secure majority shall be recognized instead.

2/ to ensure that laws, regulations, directives and declarations are known to and be complied with and implemented by members;

3/ to initiate laws and regulations pertaining to labour relations and to participate actively during their formulation and amendments;

4/ to discharge other tasks provided for in the bylaws of their respective organizations.

116. Function of Federations and Confederations

In addition to those matters mentioned under Article 115 of this Proclamation, federations and confederations shall have the following functions:

1/ To strengthen the unity and spirit of cooperation among their member unions;

2/ To participate in the determination or improvement of the conditions of work at the trade or sectorial level;

3/ To encourage members to enhance their participation in the development of the country's economy;

4/ To represent their members in any forums; and

5/ To discharge other tasks as assigned to them in their bylaws.

117. Prohibited Act

It shall be unlawful to an employers' or workers' organization to unduly delay collective bargaining contrary to good faith.

118. By Laws of Association

Trade unions and employers' associations shall freely formulate their own by laws. The constitutions may include, among other things, the following:

1/ Name of the association;

2/ Address of the Head Office of the association;

3/ Objective of the association;

4/ Date of establishment of the association;

5/ Emblem of the association;

6/ Requirements for assumption of leadership positions of the association;

7/ Union due so fits members;

8/ Financial and property administration of the association;

9/ Meeting and election procedures of the association;

10/ Disciplinary procedures;

11/ The conditions for dissolution the association; and

12/ Status of the property in case of the dissolution of the association.

119. Registration of Associations

1/ Every association shall be registered by the Ministry or the appropriate Authority in accordance with this Proclamation.

2/ Every organization shall, upon application for registration, submit to the Ministry or the appropriate Authority the following documents:

a) by laws of the association;

b) Document containing the names, address and signatures of its members and leadership;

c) In the case of a general union, the names of undertakings where members are working;

d) Where the association is a federation or a confederation, the names, address and signatures of their leaderships and the member trade unions or employers' associations;

e) Name and emblem of the association.

3/ The Ministry or the appropriate Authority shall, after examining the documents and ascertaining that they are duly completed, issue a certificate of registration within fifteen working days of receiving the application. Where the Ministry or the appropriate organ does not notify its decision within the prescribed period, the association shall be deemed registered. In such cases, a certificate of registration shall be issued to the association.

4/ An organization which is not registered in accordance with the provisions of this Article may not perform functions set forth in this Proclamation.

5/ The first registration of a trade union shall be exempt from stamp duty.

6/ A trade union or employers association registered by the Ministry or competent Authority in accordance with this Proclamation shall have legal personality and have the capacity to undertake, in particular, the following:

a) To enter into contract;

b) To sue and be sued;

c) To own, use and transfer property;

d) To represent members at any level; and

e) To undertake any lawful act necessary for the attainment of its objectives.

120. Refusal to Register

The Ministry or the appropriate Authority may refuse to register an association due to any one of the following grounds:

1/ Where the association does not fulfill the requirements laid down in this Proclamation, Regulation sand Directives issued in accordance with this Proclamation;

2/ Where the objectives and the by laws of the association are illegal;

3/ Where the name of the association is similar with another organization established prior to it or so closely similar as to confuse its members and the general public in any manner; or

4/ Where one or more of its elected leaders have been restricted from certain civil rights by court and the association is not willing to replace them.

121. Cancellation of Registration

1/ The Ministry or the appropriate Authority may file before the competent court to cancel the certificate of registration of an association, on anyone of the following grounds:

a) Where the certificate of registration was obtained by fraud or mistake or deceit;

b) Where any of the objectives or the by laws of the association is found to be illegal under this Proclamation and the association is not willing to strike out the illegal provisions or conditions; or

c) Where the association is found to have engaged in activities which are prohibited under this Proclamation or performed acts which are contrary to its objectives and constitution; and it is not willing to cease or correct or eliminate them.

2/ The Ministry or the appropriate Authority may, upon request by an association, ensure that the association is dissolved in such manner as it thinks appropriate.

122. Notice to Cancel Registration of Association

1/ The Ministry or the appropriate Authority shall, before filing for the cancellation of the registration of an association in accordance with Article 121 (1) of this Proclamation, give to the concerned association one month prior notice specifying the grounds for the cancellation in order to provide it an opportunity to contend. The Ministry or the appropriate Authority my not rely on any ground other than those enumerated in Article 121(1) of this Proclamation.

2/ Where the period of notice provided for in sub-Article (1) of this Article has expired and the association does not oppose the notice or the reply is unacceptable by the Ministry or competent Authority, it may file to the competent court for the cancellation of registration.

3/ Without prejudice to Sub-Article (2) of this Article, the Ministry or the appropriate Authority may in the meantime suspend the association from engaging in acts prohibited by this Proclamation or contrary to its objectives and by laws as provided for under Sub-Article 1(c) of Article 121 of this Proclamation.

123. Appeal

Where the Ministry or the appropriate Authority refuses registration of the association, the organization may appeal to the Competent Court within 15 working days from the date of receipt of the decision in writing. The Ministry or the appropriate Authority shall be given the opportunity to defend its decision before the Court.

124. Consequence of Cancellation of Registration or Dissolution on Request of Association

An association shall be deemed dissolved as of the date of cancellation of its registration by the decision of a court or dissolution by the Ministry or the appropriate authority up on request by the Association.

CHAPETER TWO   COLLECTIVE AGREEMENT

SECTION ONE   GENERAL

125. Definition

1/ "Collective agreement" means an agreement on conditions of work concluded in writing between representatives of one or more trade unions and one or more employers or representatives or agents of employers associations.

2/ "Collective bargaining" means a negotiation process between employers and workers organizations or their representatives concerning conditions of work in order to reach at collective agreement or the renewal or modifications there of.

126. Bargaining

1/ Any trade union shall have the right to bargain with one or more employers or their association in matters provided for in Article 129 of this Proclamation;

2/ Any Employer or employers' associations shall have the right to bargain with their workers organized in a trade union.

127. Representation

1/ The following shall have the right to represent workers in collective bargaining:

a) Where there is a trade union, the leaders of the trade union or members who are authorized in accordance to the by laws of the union to negotiate and sign collective agreement;

b) Where there is a general trade union, the leaders of the general trade union who are authorized in accordance with the by laws of the union to negotiate and sign collective agreement.

2/ Persons delegated by the concerned employer or employers or employers' association shall have the right to represent them in collective bargaining.

128. Advisors

Any party to a collective bargaining may be assisted by advisors who provide expert advice during the negotiation process.

129. Subject Matter of a Collective Agreement

Matters concerning employment relations and conditions of work as well as relations of employers and their associations with trade unions may be determined by a collective agreement.

130. Contents of the Collective Agreement

Without prejudice to the generality of Article 129 of this Proclamation, the following may, among other things, be determined by collective agreement:

1/ Matters specified by the provisions of this Proclamation or other laws to be regulated by collective agreement;

2/ the conditions for maintenance of occupational safety and health and the manner of improving social services;

3/ workers' participation, particularly, in matters pertaining to promotion, wages, transfer, reduction and discipline;

4/ conditions of work, on work rules and grievance procedures;

5/ apportionment of working hours and interval break times;

6/ parties covered by the collective agreement and its duration of validity;

7/ On the establishment and working system of bipartite social dialogue.

8/ On the establishment of daycare.

131. Procedure for Collective Bargaining

1/ A party desiring to initiate a collective bargaining may request the other party in writing. It shall also prepare and submit draft proposal necessary for the negotiation.

2/ The requested party shall within 10 working days of receiving the request, appear for collective bargaining.

3/ The parties shall before commencing collective bargaining draw up the rules of procedure for bargaining.

4/ Each party shall have the duty to bargain in good faith.

5/ Issues on which the parties could not reach agreement by negotiations in good faith may be submitted to the competent Labour Tribunal.

6/ Parties to a collective agreement shall commence renegotiation, at least three months before its period of expiry, to amend or replace it. However if the renegotiation is not finalized within three months subsequent to the date of its expiry, the provisions of the collective agreement pertaining to wages and other benefits, unless their validity is extended by a written agreement of the negotiating parties, shall cease to be operative.

132. Registration of Collective Agreement

1/ Upon signing a collective agreement, the parties shall send sufficient copies of same to the Ministry or the appropriate authority for registration.

2/ Unless there exists a valid reason to deny registration, the Ministry or the appropriate Authority shall register the collective agreement within 15 working days from the date of receipt of copies thereof.

133. Accession of Collective Agreement

A collective agreement which has already been signed and registered by third parties may be acceded to by other negotiating parties.

SECTION TWO   CONDITIONS OF VALIDITY OF COLLECTIVE AGREEMENT

134. Duration of Validity of Collective Agreement

1/ Any provision of a collective agreement which provides for conditions of work and benefits which are less favorable than those provided for under this Proclamation or other laws shall have no effect.

2/ Unless otherwise provided there in, a collective agreement shall produce legal effect as of the date of signing by the parties.

3/ Unless expressly stipulated otherwise in a collective agreements, no party may challenge the collective agreement within three years from the date of its validity; provided, however; that;

a) Up on the occurrence of a major economic change, a challenge to the collective agreement may be initiated to the Ministry or the appropriate Authority by either party before the expiry of the fixed time;

b) The Ministry or the appropriate Authority shall, up on receipt of a challenge to a collective agreement in accordance with Sub-Article 3(a) of this Article, assign a conciliator with a view to enabling the parties settle the issue by agreement. If the parties fail to settle the issue amicably, Article 144 of this Proclamation shall apply;

c) the parties may at any time change or modify their collective agreement; provided, however, that without prejudice to the special conditions set forth in paragraphs (a) and (b) of this Sub-Article, a party may not be obliged to bargain a collective agreement to change or modify it before its date of validity expires.

SECTION THREE   SCOPE OF APPLICATION OF A COLLECTIVE AGREEMENT

135. Scope of Application

1/ The provisions of a Collective Agreement shall be applicable to all parties covered by it.

2/ Where the collective agreement is more favorable to the workers in similar matters than those provided for by laws, the provision of the collective agreement shall prevail. However, where the law is more favorable to the workers than the collective agreement, the law shall be given effect.

136. Exception

1/ Where a trade union which is a party to a collective agreement is dissolved, the collective agreement shall remain valid between the employer and the workers.

2/ In the case of amalgamation of two or more undertakings, unless provided otherwise by the parties:

a) Where each of the undertakings had the irrespective collective agreement, the collective agreement concluded by the undertaking which had more workers shall be applicable to the amalgamated undertaking;

b) Where each of the undertakings had their respective collective agreement and the numbers of their workers were equal, the collective agreement which, in general, is more favorable to the workers shall be applicable to the amalgamated undertaking;

c) Where only one of the undertakings had a collective agreement, it shall be applicable to the amalgamated under taking.

3/ Where an undertaking is acquired by another or is divided, the provisions of Sub-Article (2) of this Article shall, as the case may be, be applicable.

PART NINE
LABOUR DISPUTE

CHAPTER ONE   GENERAL

137. Definitions

In this Proclamation:

1/ "Conciliation" means the activity conducted by a person or persons appointed by the parties or appointed by the competent Authority at the request of the parties for the purpose of bringing the parties together and seeking an amicable resolution of a labour dispute which their own efforts alone could not resolve;

2/ "Essential public service undertakings" means those services which shall be rendered without interruption to the general public and are the following undertakings:

a) air transport services;

b) electric power supply;

c) water supply and city cleaning and sanitation services;

d) urban light rail transport service;

e) Hospitals, Clinics, dispensaries and pharmacies;

f) fire brigade services; and

g) telecommunication services;

3/ "Labour dispute" means any dispute between a worker and an employer or trade union and employers' association in respect of the application of law, collective agreement, work rules, employment contract and also any disagreement arising during collective bargaining or in connection with collective agreement.

4/ "Lock-out" means an industrial measure applied by employer through the closing of the place of work with a view to persuading workers to accept certain labour conditions in connection with a labour dispute or to influence the outcome of the dispute;

5/ "Strike" means the slow-down of work by any number of workers in reducing their normal out-put on their normal rate of work or the temporary cessation of work by any number of workers acting in concert in order to persuade their employer to accept certain labour conditions in connection with a labour dispute or to influence the outcome of the dispute.

CHAPTER TWO LABOUR COURTS

138. Establishment of Labour Divisions

1/ Labour divisions shall be established Courts, at Federal and Regional level.

2/ The Ministry or the appropriate authority shall submit proposals for the decision of the appropriate authority on the number of labour divisions to be established in accordance with Sub-Article (1) of this Article.

139. Labour Division First Instance Court

1/ The labour division of a Federal and Regional First Instance Court shall have jurisdiction to settle and determine the following and other similar individual labour disputes;

a) disciplinary measures including dismissal;

b) claims related to the termination of employment contracts;

c) claims related to hours of work; remuneration, leaves and rest day;

d) claims related to the issuance of certificate of service and clearance;

e) claims pertaining to employment injury, transfer, promotion, training and other similar issues;

f) Unless otherwise provided in this Proclamation, suits pertaining to violations provisions of this Proclamation.

2/ The labour division of a Regional First Instance Court shall render its decisions within 60 days from the date on which the suit is filed.

3/ The party who is aggrieved with the decision of the First Instance Court may, within 30 days from the date on which the decision was delivered, lodge an appeal to the labour division of the Federal or Regional appellate court.

140. The Labour Division of Appellate court

1/ The labour division of Appellate the Frist Instance Court shall have jurisdiction to hear and decide on the following matters:

a) appeals submitted from the labour division of the First Instance Court in accordance with Article 139 of this Proclamation;

b) objections on question of jurisdiction;

c) appeals submitted against the refusal of the registration of an organization by the Ministry or appropriate Authority in accordance with Article 123 of this Proclamation;

d) appeals submitted by an employer who is affected by the order of labour inspector in accordance with Article 180(1) of this Proclamation;

e) appeals submitted against the decision of the Ministry or appropriate Authority in accordance with Article 20 (3) Article of this Proclamation;

f) Request submitted by Ministry or appropriate Authority for the cancellation of the registration of an organization in accordance with Article 122 (2) of this Proclamation;

g) Apples against the decision of the Board on question of law in accordance with Article 155 of this proclamation.

2/ The decision of the appellate court on appeal submitted under Sub-Article (1) of this Article shall be final.

3/ The labour division of the Federal or Regional Appellate Court shall render its decision within 60 days from the date of the appeal lodged in accordance to Sub-Article (1) of this Article.

CHAPTER THREE ALTERNATIVE DISPUTE SETTLEMENT MECHANISM PERTAINING TO LABOUR ISSUES

141. Social Dialogue

Employers and workers or their respective associations may introduce social dialogue in order to prevent and resolve labour disputes amicably.

142. Assigning of Conciliator

1/ When a dispute in respect of matters specified under Article 143 is brought to the attention of the Ministry or the appropriate Authority by either of the parties to the dispute it shall assign a conciliator with a view to amicable settlement of the case.

2/ The Ministry or the Appropriate Authority may assign conciliators at the Federal, Regional and, when necessary, at the Woreda levels.

143. Duty and Responsibility of Conciliator

1/ A conciliator appointed by the Ministry or the appropriate Authority shall endeavor to bring about a negotiated settlement on the following and other similar collective labour disputes:

a) issues of wages and other benefits which are not determined by work rules or collective agreements;

b) establishment of new conditions of work;

c) the conclusion, amendment, duration and invalidation of collective agreement;

d) the interpretation of any provisions of this Proclamation, collective agreements or work rules;

e) procedure of employment and promotion of workers;

f) issues affecting workers in general and the very existence of the Undertaking;

g) suits related to procedures issued by the employer regarding promotion, transfer and training;

h) Issues pertaining to reduction of workers.

2/ A conciliator shall endeavor to bring about an amicable settlement by all means as he considers appropriate.

3/ When a conciliator fails to settle a labour dispute within 30 days, he shall report same to the competent Authority together with his opinion, and shall serve copies of the report to the parties involved. Any one of the parties may submit the matter, other than those indicated under Sub-Article (1) (a) of this. Article to a Labour Relations Board. However, where the dispute under Sub-Article (1) (a) of this Article is related to those undertakings stipulated under Article 137(2) of this Proclamation, one of the parties may submit the case to an Ad Hoc Labour Relations Board.

144. Conciliation and Arbitration

1/ Notwithstanding the provisions of Article 142 of this Proclamation, parties to a dispute may agree to submit their case to arbitrators or conciliators, of their own choice for settlement in accordance with the appropriate law.

2/ If the parties fail to reach an agreement on the case submitted to conciliation under Sub-Article (1) of this Article or the party aggrieved by the decision of the arbitration may take the case to the Board or to the appropriate Court, as the case may be.

CHAPTER FOUR   THE LABOUR RELATIONS BOARD

145. Establishment of the Board

1/ One or more Permanent Labour Relations Board (hereinafter referred to as "Permanent Board") may be established in each Regional State, as may be necessary. However, the Ministry shall establish Permanent Labour Relations Board to entertain cases involving undertakings owned by the Federal Government which are situated in Addis Ababa and Dire Dawa city administration.

2/ Ad Hoc Labour Relations Board (hereinafter referred to as "Ad Hoc Board") may be established to hear and decide disputes that may arise on matters specified in Article 143 (1) (a) and in undertakings referred to in Article 137 (2) of this Proclamation. Similarly, the Ministry shall established Ad Hoc Board when ever necessary to entertain cases involving undertakings owned by the Federal Government which are situated in Addis Ababa and Dire Dawa city administration.

3/ Every Permanent or Ad Hoc Board shall be established under the Ministry or appropriate Authority.

4/ Notwithstanding to Sub-Article (3) of this Article as per sub article (1) and (2) of this article Ad Hoc and Permanent boards assigned to hear and decide disputes in respect of matters involving undertakings owned by the Federal Government located in Addis Ababa and Dire Dawa city administration shall be established and be accountable to the Ministry.

146. Composition of Permanent or Ad Hoc Board

1/ A Permanent or Ad Hoc Board appointed by the Ministry or appropriate Authority shall comprises of a chair person, two members who have the knowledge and skill on labour matters, four members out of which two represent trade unions and two represent employers' associations, and two alternate members one from each association.

2/ Employers Representatives shall be nominated from the most representative of Employers' Associations and workers representatives shall be appointed from the most representative of Trade Unions.

3/ The Ministry or the appropriate Authority shall assign a secretary and such other necessary staff to the Board.

4/ Members and alternate members of a board shall serve on part time basis without remuneration; provided, however, that the Ministry or the appropriate Authority shall fix standard fees for attendances at meetings of the Board.

5/ Members and alternate members of the Board shall be appointed for a term of three years; provided, however, that in making the initial appointments, the terms of one, two and three years, respectively, shall be specified so that in each subsequent year the terms of not more than one-third of the members and alternate members then serving shall expire in anyone calendar year.

6/ The Ministry or the appropriate Authority shall dismiss a member in case of neglect of duty or malpractice in office; and shall arrange for the appointment of a substitute for the remaining term.

147. Meeting Procedures of Permanent or Ad Hoc Boards

1/ In the absence of the Chairperson another member of the Board designated by him as acting Chairperson, shall preside over the meetings of the Board. Where no such member is designated, the member of the Board who is senior in terms of his service shall act as a Chairperson.

2/ In the absence of a member at any meeting of the Board, the Chairperson may designate an alternate member to replace the absentee at such meeting. Alternate member so designated shall be deemed a member for the meeting for which he is designated.

3/ Four members of the Board shall constitute a quorum at any meeting; provided, however, that a minimum of one member representing the workers side and another member representing the employers' side shall be present.

4/ Decision of the Board shall be taken by a majority vote of the members present. In case of a tie, the Chairperson shall have a casting vote.

5/ Each decision of the Board shall be signed by all members present.

6/ Minutes of meetings after approval by the Board shall be certified by the secretary and shall thereafter constitute the official record of the said meetings.

148. Powers of Permanent or Ad Hoc Board

1/ A Permanent Board shall have the following powers:

a) to entertain collective labour disputes except those in Sub-Article (1) (a) of Article 143; conciliate the parties; issue orders and render decisions;

b) to entertain and decide cases submitted to it by one of the disputing parties after the parties fail to reach an agreement in accordance with Sub- Article (3) of Article 143 of this Proclamation except on matters specified in Sub-Article (1) (a) Article 143 of this Proclamation;

c) to hear cases on prohibited actions referred to in Article 161 of this Proclamation;

d) to require any person or organization to submit information and documents required by it for the carrying out of its duties;

e) to require parties and witnesses to appear at its hearings;

f) to administer oaths or take affirmations of persons appearing before it and examine any such persons after such an oath or affirmation;

g) to enter the premises of any working place or undertaking during working hours in order to obtain relevant information, hear witnesses or to require the submission or documents or other articles for inspection from any person in the premises.

2/ An Ad Hoc Board shall have the power to entertain labour disputes on matters specified in Sub-Article 1 (a) of Article 143 of this Proclamation, to conciliate the parties and to give orders and decisions.

3/ Except in cases of urgency the person in charge of the premises or the undertaking shall be given reasonable advance notice before any entry in accordance with Sub-Article 1(g) of this Article.

4/ Orders and decisions handed down by a permanent or Ad Hoc Board shall be considered as any civil case decisions.

149. Rules of Procedure

A Permanent or an Ad Hoc board may adopt its own rules of evidence and procedure. In the absence of own procedure, the provisions of the Civil Procedure Code shall apply.

150. Hearings of cases

1/ Before disposing the case, a Permanent or An adhoc Board shall summon the parties concerned and provide them the opportunity to be heard. At least ten working days advance notice shall be given to the parties and the summons shall specify the date, time and place of the hearing.

2/ If any of the parties or any other person properly summoned fails to appear at the time and place, the Board may proceed with the hearing. If the failure to appear was not attributable to the person concerned, the Board shall grant that person another opportunity to appear before it.

3/ No appeal may be lodged solely against the Board's ruling in accordance with Sub-Article (2) of this Article.

4/ All deliberations of the Board shall be public unless the Board, for good cause, decides otherwise.

5/ A Permanent or an Ad Hoc board shall not be bound by the rules of evidence and procedure applicable to Courts of law and may apply any method as it thinks fit.

6/ Trade Unions, employers' Associations and other parties summoned to appear at a hearing may be represented by their duly authorized representatives or legal counsel. The Board may limit the number of such representatives who may actively participate in a hearing on behalf of any party.

151. Consideration of Matters

1/ The permanent or the Ad Hoc Board shall exert all possible effort to settle the disputes before it amicably, and to this end it shall employ and make use of all conciliatory means as it deems appropriate.

2/ The Board may, in appropriate circumstances, consider not only the interests of the parties before it but also the interest of the community of which they belong and may in such circumstances call up on the Government to intervene as an impartial advisor.

3/ In arriving at decision, the Permanent or Ad Hoc Board shall take into account the main merit of the case, and need not follow strictly the principles of substantive law followed by Civil Courts.

152. Decisions

1/ A Permanent or an Ad Hoc Board shall give render a decision within 30 days from the date when the claim is filed.

2/ Decisions of a Permanent or an Ad Hoc Board shall be made in writing and signed by the Board members who concur therein. Dissenting opinions, if any, shall also be made in writing and signed by the dissenting member.

3/ In every decision of a Board the decision shall contain the following:

a) The issue or dispute identified for decision;

b) The relevant testimony and evidence recorded together with their sources in the course of the proceedings;

c) The findings of the Board and the evaluation of the evidence which led the Board to make such findings;

d) The disposition of each issue or dispute;

e) The action to be taken on the basis of such decision.

4/ A copy of the decision of the Board shall be served to the parties concerned within five days from the date of the decision.

153. Effects of Decisions

1) Without prejudice to Article 155 of this Proclamation, any decision of a Permanent or an Ad Hoc Board shall have an immediate effect.

2) Where the decision of a Permanent or an Ad Hoc Board relates to working conditions, it shall be considered as the terms of the contract of employment between the employer and the worker, to whom it applies, and the contract shall be adjusted accordingly.

154. Finality of Board's Findings of Fact

All findings of facts made by a Board shall be final and conclusive.

155. Appeal

1/ In any labour dispute an appeal may be taken to the High Court by an aggrieved party on questions of law, within 30 days after the decision has been served to the parties.

2/ The High Court shall have the power to affirm, reverse or modify the decision of the Board.

3/ The High Court shall render its decision within 30 days from the date on which the appeal is submitted to it.

156. Offences against Permanent or Ad Hoc *Board*

1/ Whoever in the course of a board inquiry, proceeding or hearing in any manner disturbs deliberations shall be punishable with simple imprisonment not exceeding six months or with fine not exceeding Birr 1,000.

2/ Where the offence described in Sub-Article (1) of this Article is not committed openly or out of court session, the punishment, except in more serious cases, shall be a fine not exceeding Birr 500.

3/ Proceedings of the Board shall be considered quasi-judicial proceedings and the Board a competent judicial tribunal for the purpose of Article 449 of the Criminal Code, and violations thereof shall be punishable as provided there under.

4/ The Board may punish any person who committed any offence described in this Article.

157. Annual Report

A Permanent or an Ad Hoc board shall have the responsibility to submit to the Minister or competent authority annual report of its activities.

CHAPTER FIVE   STRIKE AND LOCK-OUT

158. General

1/ Workers shall have the right to strike to protect their interests in the manner prescribed in this Proclamation.

2/ Employers shall have the right to lock-out in the manner prescribed in this Proclamation.

3/ The provisions of Sub-Articles (1) and (2) of this Article shall not apply to workers and employers of undertakings referred to in Article 137(2) of this Proclamation.

159. Conditions to be Fulfilled

Prior to initiating a strike or lock-out partially or wholly the following steps shall be taken:

1/ The party initiating a strike or lock-out shall give advance notice to the other party indicating its reasons for taking the said action.

2/ Both parties shall make every effort to solve and settle their labour dispute in a mutually amicably manner.

3/ The strike to be taken by the workers shall have to be supported by simple majority of the workers concerned in a meeting in which at least two-third of the members of the trade union were present.

4/ Measures shall be taken to ensure the observance, by employers and workers, of safety regulations and accident prevention procedures in the undertaking

160. Procedure for Notice

1/ The notice under Article 159(1) of this Proclamation shall be given by the party initiating a strike or lock-out to the other party, and to the Ministry or the appropriate Authority.

2/ The notice specified in Sub-Article (1) of this Article shall be served 10 days in advance of taking action.

161. Prohibited Acts

1/ Without prejudice to the provision of Article 160 (1) of this Proclamation, a strike or lock-out shall be unlawful if initiated after a dispute has been referred to a Board or to a Court and 30 days have not elapsed before any order or decision is given by the Board or the prescribed period has elapsed before the Court has given decision.

2/ It shall be unlawful to resist or unduly delay the execution of an order or a decision of a Board or Court disposing, in whole or in part, a labour dispute or to take or continue to strike or to lock-out in protest to such order or decision of the Board or court; provided, however, that the strike or lock-out shall not be unlawful if initiated in order to ensure compliance with such order or decision.

3/ It is prohibited to conduct strike or lock-out accompanied by violence, threats of physical force or with any act which is illegal.

CHAPTER SIX
FEES

162. Exemption from Fees

1/ No service fees shall be levied in respect of cases submitted to conciliation and to a Labour Relations Board by any worker or Trade Union, employer or Employers' associations in accordance with Articles 142 and 148 of this Proclamation.

2/ No court fees shall be levied in respect of labour cases submitted to courts by any worker or trade union.

PART TEN
PERIOD OF LIMITATION AND PRIORITY OF CLAIMS

CHAPTER ONE PERIOD OF LIMITATION

163. Period of Limitation

1/ Unless a specific time limit is provided in this Proclamation or other relevant laws, an action arising from an employment relationship shall be barred after one year from the date on which the right becomes exercisable.

2/ Any claim by a worker to be reinstated shall be barred after three months from the date of termination of the contract of employment.

3/ Claim by a worker for payment of wage, over time or any other payment shall be barred after six months from the date it becomes due.

4/ Any claim by a worker or employer for any payment arising from termination of employment contract shall be barred unless an action is brought within six months from the date of termination of the contract of employment.

5/ The relevant law shall be applicable to the period of limitation which is not covered under this Proclamation.

164. Calculation of Period of Limitation

1/ Unless otherwise specifically provided for in this Proclamation, the period of limitation shall begin to run from the date following the date when the right may be exercised.

2/ Whenever the last date of a period of limitation falls on a non-working, it shall expire on the following working day.

165. Interruption of a Period of Limitation

A period of limitation shall be interrupted by:

1/ Any action taken before an authority responsible for the determination of labour disputes until a final decision is given;

2/ Any action taken before the competent authority responsible for the enforcement and implementation of this Proclamation until a final decision is given in writing;

3/ The written admission of the other parts as to the validity of claim; provided, however, that a period of limitation interrupted on such ground may not he interrupted for more than three times in the aggregate.

166. Waiver of Limitation

Any party may waive his right to raise a period of limitation as a defense; provided, however, that a waiver of such right made before the date of expiry of the period of limitation shall have no effect.

167. Discretion of the Competent Authority

1/ The organ responsible for the determination of labour disputes may accept an action after the expiry of a period of limitation if it ascertains that the delay is due to force majeure; provided, however, that such ground shall not be acceptable unless the action is brought within ten days from the date the force majeure ceases to exist.

2/ Without affecting the generality of the provisions of Sub-Article (1) of this Article, the following shall be considered as force majeure for disregarding a period of limitation:

a) Illness of the worker;

b) Transfer of the worker to a place out of his residence in fulfillment of job tasks;

c) Call of the worker for national service.

CHAPTER TWO   PRIORITY OF CLAIMS

168. Priority over other Debts

Any claim by a worker emanating from employment relations shall have priority over other payments or debts

169. Procedure of Payment of Claims

1/ In the event that the under taking is liquidated, execution officers or other persons authorized by laws or the Court to execute such liquidations hall have the duty to pay the claims referred to in Article 168 of this Proclamation with in thirty days following the decision of the competent authority.

2/ Where the claims are not satisfied within the time limit set forth in Sub-Article (1) of this Article due to lack of asset, they shall be paid as soon as the necessary resource are available.

170. Lien of Home Workers

Where an under taking is liquidated or ceases to operate, home workers may exercise alien on goods in their possession that they have produced for the under taking and such lien shall be of equal value with their claims. Such measure shall be deemed an action taken to enforce the right provided for in Article 168 of this Proclamation.

PART ELEVEN
Enforcement of Labour law

CHAPTER ONE Labour Administration

171. Powers of the Ministry

1/ The Ministry may issue directives necessary for the implementation of this Proclamation, in particular, with respect to:

a) Occupational safety, health and the protection of working environment;

b) Standards for working conditions;

c) Determination of hazardous jobs;

d) In consultation with the concerned organs, the type of works which are particularly hazardous or dangerous to the health and to the reproductive systems of women workers;

e) Types of works which require work permits for foreigners and, in general, the manner of giving work permits; conditions on which private employment agencies are to operate locally;

f) In consultation with other relevant organs, determine conditions of homework contracts, and the types of occupations in which apprenticeship need to be offered and other issues related thereto.

g) Procedures for registration of vacancies and job-seekers;

h) Procedure for the reduction of work force;

i) Determine undertakings required to arrange insurance coverage for the payment of employment injury benefits;

j) Procedures on the establishment of Permanent Advisory Board and the duties and responsibilities thereto;

k) Conditions for Private Employment Agency to participate in local Employment service;

l) Procedures on the requirements for the certification of private labour inspection service providers;

m) Procedures on the establishment of Occupational Safety and Health Committee in undertakings;

2/ The Ministry shall put in place an integrated labour administration system to initiate labour laws and policies, to coordinate, follow up and enforce their implementation, and to enhance employment service and a labour inspection service and establish a Permanent Advisory Board which consists of members representing Government, Employers' Associations and Trade Unions to advice the same.

3/ The appropriate Authority shall establish a Permanent Advisory Board consisting of members representing government. Employers' associations and Trade Unions that will advise it after studying and examining the implementation of labour laws and policies and the administration of employment services and labour inspection services.

SECTION ONE EMPLOYMENT SERVICE

172. General

Employment services shall include the following:

1/ Assisting persons who are capable and willing to work to obtain employment;

2/ Assisting employers in the recruitment of suitable workers for their job positions;

3/ Determining the manner in which foreign national are to be employed in Ethiopia;

4/ Cooperating with the concerned offices and organizations, in the preparation of training programmers;

5/ Conducting studies pertaining to the labour market;

6/ In collaboration with the concerned offices, conducting studies relating to the manner of improving vocational training at the country level and disseminating same to beneficiaries and implementing the employment policy properly.

173. Employment Exchange

Employment exchange shall include the following:

1/ Registration of job-seekers and vacancies; and

2/ Selecting from among the registered job-seekers and sending those who meet the requirements to compete for the positions notified by employers.

3/ Any job seeker who has attained the age of 15 years may up on presenting the necessary documents be registered by the organ delegated by the pertinent authority.

174. Conditions for the Private Employment Agencies to Participate in Provision of Local Employment Service

With the view to promote a comprehensive national employment service, private Employment Agencies can participate in the sector as per the Directive that will be issued by the Government.

175. Licensing of Private Employment Agencies

1/ Any person who desires to engage in private employment agency pursuant to this Proclamation shall acquire license from the Competent Authority.

2/ The appropriate Authority shall levy service charge prescribed by the regulation to be issued by the Council of Ministers for purposes of issuance, renewal of replacement of licenses.

176. Employment of Foreign Nationals

1/ any foreigner may only be employed in any type of work in Ethiopia where he possesses a work permit given to him by the Ministry.

2/ a work permit shall be given for an employment in a specific type of work for three years and shall be renewed every year; provided, however, that the Ministry may vary the three years limit as required.

3/ Where the Ministry ascertains that the foreigner is not required for the work, the work permit may be cancelled.

4/ The Ministry may, in accordance with the law, charge service fees for the issuance, renewal or replacement of work permit.

SECTION TWO LABOUR INSPECTION SERVICE

177. LABOUR INSPECTION SERVICE

Labour inspection service shall include the following activities:

1/ Ensuring the implementation of the provisions of this Proclamation, Regulations and directives issued in accordance with this Proclamation, other laws relating to labour relations, registered collective agreement, and the decisions and orders given by the authorities responsible to determine labour disputes;

2/ conducting studies and research, supervision, educating, and developing labour standards to ensure the enforcement of the provisions of this Proclamation and other laws regarding working conditions, occupational safety, health and working environment;

3/ preparation of list of occupational diseases and schedules of degrees of disablement;

4/ classifying dangerous occupations and undertakings;

5/ conducting studies and compiling statistical data relating to working conditions;

6/ preparing training programs to workers in order to prevent employment injuries;

7/ monitoring the construction of new undertaking, the expansion and renovation of existing undertakings and the erection of machineries to ensure the safety and health of workers;

8/ taking administrative measures with a view to implementing this Proclamation and regulations and directives issued in accordance with this Proclamation;

9/ taking appropriate measures to request the authorities responsible for determining labour disputes and the courts to enforce the provisions of this Proclamation and sanctions imposed by a labour inspection service in the course of its lawful activities;

10/ issuance of certificate of competence to private inspection service which desire to engage in workplace technical inspection, consultancy and training on the subject; and monitor their performance.

178. Power and Duty of Labour Inspectors

1/ The Minister or the appropriate Authority shall assign labour inspectors who are authorized to carry out the responsibilities of follow-up and supervision of the inspection service.

2/ In administering their responsibilities, labour inspector shall have an identity card issued by the Ministry or the appropriate Authority bearing an official seal.

3/ A labour inspector shall have the power to enter into, during any working hours without prior notice, any work place which he may think necessary to inspect in order to examine, test or enquire to ascertain observation of the provisions of Article 177 of this Proclamation and, this shall:

a) Interrogate any person alone or in the presence of witnesses;

b) check, copy or extract any paper, file or other documents;

c) take any sample of any matter in a workplace and to test it to ensure that it does not cause injury to workers;

d) ensure that the relevant notices are affixed at the appropriate place of work;

e) take picture of any worker, and measure, draw or test buildings, rooms, cars, factories, machineries or goods and copy and registered documents in order to ensure the safety and health of workers.

4/ Where a sample is taken in accordance with Sub-Article 3(c) of this Article, the employer shall be informed in advance and the manager or his representative shall have the right to be present at that occasion.

179. Measures to be taken by Labour Inspection

1/ Where a labour inspector finds that the premises, plant, machinery, equipment or material or the working methods of any undertaking constitute a threat to the health, safety or welfare of its workers, he shall instruct the employer to take the necessary corrective measure within a given period of time.

2/ Where the employer fails to take such steps within the given period after receiving instructions in accordance with Sub-Article (1) of this Article, the labour inspector shall issue an order requiring the employer:

a) that alteration in existing conditions which may be necessary to prevent the threat to the health, safety or well-being of the workers be completed within a stated period of time;

b) that any measure which may be necessary to prevent imminent danger to the safety, or health of the workers be taken immediately.

3/ Where the labour inspector is in doubt about the technical or legal danger of any particular case, he shall report same to the Minister or appropriate authority requesting that pertinent decision is given and orders issued accordingly.

180. Appeal

1/ Where an employer is aggrieved by an order given in accordance with Article 179 (1) and (2) of this Proclamation, it may appeal to the Competent Court with in five working days; provided, however, that there shall be no stay of execution of the order given by the labour inspector to avert an imminent danger pursuant to Article 179 (2) (b) of this Proclamation until decision is given on the appeal.

2/ Decision of the Court on the appeal lodged in accordance with Sub- Article (1) of this Article shall be final. Where an employer does not appeal within the time limit, the decision shall be executed.

181. Restriction on the Functions and Responsibility of Labour Inspectors

1/ Labour inspectors shall perform their duties diligently and impartially. They shall take into account any reasonable suggestions given to them by employers and workers.

2/ No labour inspector shall, at any time, whether during or after he left his employment, reveal any secrets of manufacturing, commercial or other working processes to third parties which may come to his attention in the course of his duties under this Proclamation.

3/ No labour inspector shall reveal to any person other than the concerned official the sources of any complaint brought to his attention concerning a defect or breach of legal provision and, in particular, he shall not make any indications to any employer or his representative that his inspection visit was made in response to a complaint filed with the labour inspection service.

4/ A labour inspector shall, in all cases, notify the employer of his visit to the premises of the undertaking unless he considers such notification may be prejudicial to the execution of his duties.

5/ No labour inspector shall inspect any undertaking of which he is an owner or in which he has an interest.

6 A labour inspector shall refrain from engaging or acting as a conciliator or an arbitrator in a labour dispute or collective bargaining.

182. Prohibited Acts

The following acts shall be deemed to constitute obstruction of a labour inspector in the performance of his duties:

1/ Preventing a labour inspect or from entering a work place or from staying in the premises;

2/ Refusing to let a labour inspector examine records or documents relevant for his tasks;

3/ concealing date relating to employment injury and the circumstance in which they occur;

4/ Any other conducts that delays or interferes with the exercise of the functions of a labour inspector.

183. Private Inspection Service

1/ Any person may conduct technical inspection, consultancy or training provided that it has been certified by the Ministry or the appropriate Authority to engage in occupations that demand special skill and technical qualifications.

2/ The Certificate of Competence indicated under Sub-Article (1) of this Article shall be issued by the Ministry or the appropriate Authority.

3/ The service charge to be levied in order to issue the certificate pursuant to Sub-Article (1) of this Article and other related issues shall be prescribed by Regulations of the Council of Ministers.

PART TWELVE
Administrative Measures and Miscellaneous Provisions

CHAPTER ONE   Administrative Measures

184. General

Without prejudice to the criminal liability; the administrative measures laid down from Article 185 up to 187 shall be applicable.

185. Measures Against Employer

1/ An employer who:

a) Causes workers to work beyond the maximum working hours set forth in this Proclamation or contravenes in any manner the provision relating to working hours;

b) In fringes the provisions of this Proclamation regulating weekly rest days, public holidays or leaves; or

c) contravenes the provisions of Article 19 of this Proclamation; shall by taking in to account its economic and organizational standing and the manner the fault was committed will be fined from Birr 5,000 up to Birr10,000 if the violation is for the first time, from Birr 10,000 up to Birr 15,000 if it is committed for the second time and from Birr 15,000 up to Birr 30,000 it is committed for the third time. Whereas if the act is committed more than three times may result closure of the under taking.

2/ An employer who:

a) fails to fulfill the obligations laid down in Article 12(5) of this Proclamation;

b) fails to keep records prescribed by this Proclamation or other legal instruments issued hereunder or failed to submit them in due time or when so requested;

c) violates the provisions of Article14(1) of this Proclamation; or

d) terminates a contract of employment in violation of the provisions of Article 26 (2) of this Proclamation; shall by taking in to account its economic and organizational standing and the manner the fault was committed will be fined from Birr 10,000 up to Birr 20,000 if the violation is for the first time, from Birr 20,000 up to Birr 40,000, if it is committed for the second time and from Birr 40,000—Birr 60,000, if it is committed for the third time. Whereas if the act is committed more than three times may result closure of the under taking.

186. Common Measures

1/ Any employer, employers' Association, a representative of an employer, a Trade Union or trade union leader who:

a) violates regulations and directives issued in accordance with this Proclamation pertaining to the safety of workers and commit an act which expose the life and health of a worker to a serious danger or does not accord special protection to women workers or young workers as provided for in this Proclamation;

b) violates Article 117 of this Proclamation;

c) contravenes the provisions of Article 161 of this Proclamation;

d) fails to comply with an order given by a labour inspector in accordance with this Proclamation or the provisions of other laws;

e) intentionally submits inaccurate information or declarations to pertinent organs; Shall be fined Birr 5,000 up to Birr 20,000; where the violation is for the first time, and a fine of Birr 20,000 up to Birr 40,000, if the violation is for second time, and a fine of up to Birr 70,000 if it is committed for the third time. Whereas if the act is committed more than three times may result closure of the under taking.

2/ taking in to account the economic and organizational standing of the undertaking or the trade union's general set up and the manner the violation was committed, any employer, trade union, trade union leader or a representative of an employer who violates the provisions Article 131 (2) or (4) of this Proclamation shall be fined up to Birr 5,000 up to Birr 20,000, where the violation is for the first time, and a fine of Birr 20,000 up to Birr 40,000 if the violation is for second time, and a fine of Birr up to Birr 70,000 where the violation committed more than twice.

187. Measures Against Private Employment Agency

1/ Any person who, without having obtained a license in accordance with this proclamation, or regulation, or directives issued pursuant to this proclamation and engages in providing employment exchange service in Ethiopia, shall he punishable with imprisonment for a term of not less than five years and not exceeding ten years and with a fine of Birr 100,000 (hundred thousand Birr).

2/ Any private employment agency which engages, while its license is suspended, in any employment exchange activity, shall be punishable with impressments for a term of not less than three years and not exceeding five years and with a line of birr 75,000 (seventy five thousand Birr).

3/ Any persona who commits an offense other than those stated under sub article (1) and (2) of this Article, by violating provision regulations or directives issued pursuant to this proclamation be punishable with imprisonment of upto two years or with a fine of upto Birr 75,000 (Birr seventy five thousand).

188. The Power to Institute Cases

Labour Inspectors shall have the power to file suits against violations committed the provisions of this Proclamation and regulations and directives issued here under to the courts having jurisdiction to try them.

CHAPTER TWO MISCELLANEOUS PROVISIONS

189. Period of Limitation

No proceedings of any kind referred to in this Proclamation shall be instituted where one year has elapsed from the date on which the fault was committed.

190. Transitory Provisions

Notwithstanding the provisions of Article 192 of this Proclamation:

1/ Regulation and directives issued pursuant to proclamation No. 377/2003 (as amended) shall remain enforce, in so far as they are not inconsistent with this Proclamation.

2/ Collective Agreements concluded pursuant to Proclamation No. 377/2003 (as amended) shall be deemed to have been concluded in accordance with this Proclamation and be governed by the provisions of this Proclamation.

3/ Trade Unions and employers association established in accordance with Proclamation No. 377/2003 (as amended) shall be deemed to have been established in accordance with this Proclamation.

4/ labour advisory board and labour tribunal board established in accordance with Proclamation No. 377/2003 (as amended) shall be deemed to have been established in accordance with this Proclamation.

5/ Labour disputes pending before any labour tribunal to settle labour dispute prior to the coming into force of this Proclamation shall be disposed in accordance with the previous Proclamation.

191. Determination of Degree of Disablement

Until such time the schedule determining the degree of disablement is issued pursuant to Article 102(1) of this Proclamation, the Medical Board shall continue its regular assessment of disability.

192. Repeal Laws

1/ The Labour Proclamation No. 377/2003; Proclamation No. 466/2005, Proclamation No. 494/2006 and proclamation 632/2009 are hereby repealed.

2/ No laws and practices shall, in so far as they are inconsistent with this Proclamation, have force or effect in respect of matters provided for in this Proclamation.

193. Effective Date

This Proclamation shall enter in to force on the date of its publication in the Federal Negarit

Gazette.

Done at Addis Ababa this 5th day of September, 2019

SAHILEWORK ZEWUDIE
PRESIDENT OF THE FEDERAL DEMOCRATIC
REPUBLIC OF ETHIOPIA

GROUP THREE
TAX LAWS AND REGULATIONS

TITLE SIX
FEDERAL TAX ADMINISTRATION PROCLAMATION
(Proclamation No. 983/2016)

FEDERAL NEGARIT GAZETTA
OF THE FEDERAL DEMOCRATIC REPUBLIC OF ETHIOPIA

22nd year No. 103
ADDIS ABABA 20th August, 2016

Issued under the Authority of the House of Peoples
Representatives of the Federal Democratic Republic of Ethiopia

PROCLAMATION No. 983/2016
FEDERAL TAX ADMINISTRATION PROCLAMATION

WHEREAS, it is necessary to enact a separate tax administration proclamation governing the administration of domestic taxes with a view to render the tax administration system more efficient, effective and measurable;

WHEREAS, it is believed that introducing the system of advance tax ruling helps to address the problem of prolonged pendency of taxpayers cases resulting from divergent interpretation of tax laws within the tax administration;

WHEREAS, it is necessary to establish a system for review of taxpayers' complaints on tax decisions which is accessible, well organized and capable of efficient disposition of cases;

NOW, THEREFORE, in accordance with Article 55 (1) and (11) of the Constitution of the Federal Democratic Republic of Ethiopia, it is hereby proclaimed as follows:

PART ONE
GENERAL

1. Short Title

This Proclamation may be cited as the "Federal Tax Administration Proclamation No. 983/2016".

2. Definitions

In the tax laws (including this Proclamation), unless the context otherwise requires:

1/ "Amended assessment" means an amended assessment made by the Authority under Article 28 of this Proclamation;

2/ "Appealable decision" means:

a) an objection decision;

b) any other decision of the Authority made under a tax law other than:

(1) a tax decision;

(2) a decision made by the Authority in the course of making a tax decision;

3/ "Approved form" has the meaning in Article 79 of this Proclamation;

4/ "Authority" means:

a) the Ethiopian Revenues and Customs Authority;

b) the Addis Ababa Revenue Bureau; and

c) the Dire Dawa Revenue Bureau;

5/ "Body" means a company, partnership, public enterprise or public financial agency, or other body of persons whether formed in Ethiopia or elsewhere;

6/ "Commission" means the Tax Appeal Commission established under Article 86 of this

Proclamation;

7/ "Company" means a commercial business organization established in accordance with the Commercial Code of Ethiopia and having legal personality, and includes any equivalent entity incorporated or formed under a foreign law;

8/ "Controlling member", in relation to a company, means a member who beneficially holds, directly or indirectly, either alone or together with a related person or persons:

a) 50% or more of the voting rights attaching to membership interests in the company;

b) 50% or more of the rights to dividends attaching to membership interests in the company; or

c) 50% or more of the rights to capital attaching to membership interests in the company;

9/ "Document" includes:

a) a book of account, record, register, bank statement, receipt, invoice, voucher, contract or agreement, or Customs entry;

b) a certificate or statement provided by a licensed tax agent under Article 22 of this Proclamation; or

c) any information or data stored on an electronic data storage device;

10/ "Estimated assessment" means an estimated assessment made by the Authority under Article 26 of this Proclamation;

11/ "Fiscal year" means the budgetary year of the Government of the Federal Democratic Republic of Ethiopia;

12/ "Jeopardy assessment" means a jeopardy assessment made by the Authority under Article 27 of this Proclamation;

13/ "Garnishee order" means a garnishee order issued by the Authority under Article 43 of this Proclamation;

14/ "International agreement" means an agreement between the Government of the Federal Democratic Republic of Ethiopia and a foreign government or governments, or an international organisation;

15/ "International organisation" means an organisation the members of which are sovereign states or governments of sovereign states;

16/ "Late payment interest" means late payment interest imposed under Article 37;

17/ "Licensed tax agent" means a tax agent licensed under Article 96 or Article 97 of this Proclamation;

18/ "Licensing authority" means any organ authorized under any law to issue a licence, permit, certificate, concession, or other authorisation;

19/ "Manager" means:

a) for a partnership, a partner or general manager of the partnership, or a person acting or purporting to act in that capacity;

b) for a company, the chief executive officer, a director, general manager, or other similar officer of the company, or a person acting or purporting to act in that capacity;

c) for any other body, the general manager or other similar officer of the body, or a person acting or purporting to act in that capacity.

20/ "Member", in relation to a body, means a person with membership interest in the body including a shareholder in a company or a partner in a partnership;

21/ "Membership interest", in relation to a body, means an ownership interest in the body including a share in a company or an interest in a partnership;

22/ "Ministry" or "Minister" means the Ministry of Finance and Economic Cooperation or the Minister of Finance and Economic Cooperation respectively;

23/ "Partnership" means a partnership formed under the Commercial Code and includes an equivalent entity formed under foreign law;

24/ "Penalty" means an administrative penalty for breach of a tax law imposed under Chapter Two of Part Fifteen of this Proclamation or under another tax law;

25/ "Penalty assessment" means an assessment of penalty made by the Authority under Chapter Two of Part Fifteen of this Proclamation;

26/ "Person" means an individual, body, government, local government, or international organisation;

27/ "Secondary liability" means a liability of a person (referred to as the "primary liability") that another person is personally liable for under Article 16 (4), 40 (3) (c), 41 (12), 42 (8), 43 (10), 46 (1), 47 (1), or 48 (1) of this Proclamation;

28/ "Self-assessment" means an assessment treated as having been made by a self-assessment taxpayer under Article 25 of this Proclamation;

29/ "Self-assessment declaration" means:

a) a tax declaration under the Federal Income Tax Proclamation;

b) a value added tax return under the Value Added Tax Proclamation;

c) a Customs entry to the extent that it specifies the value added tax or excise tax payable in respect of an import of goods;

d) an excise tax declaration under the Excise Tax Proclamation;

e) a turnover tax return under the Turnover Tax Proclamation;

f) an advance tax declaration under Article 23 of this Proclamation; or

g) a tax declaration specified as a self-assessment declaration under a tax law;

30/ "Self-assessment taxpayer" means a taxpayer required to file a self-assessment declaration;

31/ "Tax" means a tax imposed under a tax law and includes the following:

a) withholding tax;

b) advance payments of tax and instalments of tax payable under the Federal Income Tax Proclamation;

c) penalty;

d) late payment interest;

e) any other tax payable under the Federal Income Tax Proclamation;

32/ "Tax assessment" means a self-assessment, estimated assessment, jeopardy assessment, amended assessment, penalty or interest assessment, or any other assessment made under a tax law;

33/ "Tax avoidance provision" means the tax avoidance provisions of the:

a) Federal Income Tax Proclamation; and

b) Value Added Tax Proclamation;

34/ "Tax decision" means:

a) a tax assessment, other than a self-assessment;

b) a decision on an application by a self-assessment taxpayer under Article 29 of this Proclamation;

c) a determination under Article 40 (2) of this Proclamation of the amount of tax payable or that will become payable by a taxpayer;

d) a determination of a secondary liability or the amount of tax recovery costs payable;

e) a determination of late payment interest payable;

f) a decision to refuse an application for a refund under Article 49 or Article 50;

g) a determination of the amount of an excess credit under Article 49 of this Proclamation, the amount of a refund under Article 50 of this Proclamation, or the amount of a refund required to be repaid under Article 50 of this Proclamation; or

h) a determination of the amount of unpaid withholding tax under Article 92 (3) of the Federal Income Tax Proclamation;

35/ "Tax declaration" means the following:

a) a tax declaration required to be filed under the Federal Income Tax Proclamation;

b) a withholding tax declaration required to be filed under the Federal Income Tax Proclamation;

c) a value added tax return required to be filed under the Value Added Tax Proclamation;

d) a Customs entry to the extent that it specifies the value added tax or excise tax payable in respect of an import of goods;

e) a declaration required to be filed under the Excise Tax Proclamation;

f) a turnover tax return required to be filed under the Turnover Tax Declaration;

g) a tax declaration required to be filed by a taxpayer under this Proclamation;

36/ "Tax law" means:

a) this Proclamation;

b) the Federal Income Tax Proclamation;

c) the Value Added Tax Proclamation;

d) the Excise Tax Proclamation;

e) the Stamp Duty Proclamation;

f) the Turnover Tax Proclamation;

g) any other legislation (other than legislation relating to Customs) under which a tax, duty, or levy is imposed if the Authority has responsibility for the administration of the tax, duty, or levy;

h) any regulation or directive made under a law referred to in the above paragraphs;

37/ "Tax officer" means:

a) the Director General of the Authority;

b) the Deputy Generals of the Authority;

c) official or employees of the Authority appointed under the Ethiopian Revenue and Customs Authority Establishment Proclamation with responsibility for the administration and enforcement of the tax laws;

d) official or employees of the Tax Authorities of the Addis Ababa and Dire Dawa City Administrations;

e) when performing functions on behalf of the Authority:

(1) a member of the Ethiopian Federal police;

(2) an employee or official of the Ethiopian Postal Services; or

(3) an employee or official of Regional Tax Authorities;

38/ "Tax period", in relation to a tax, means the period for which the tax is reported to the Authority;

39/ "Tax recovery costs" means:

a) the costs of the Authority referred to in Article 30 (3) of this Proclamation incurred in recovering unpaid tax;

b) the costs of the Authority referred to in Article 41 (9) (a) of this Proclamation incurred in undertaking seizure proceedings;

40/ "Tax representative", in relation to a taxpayer, means an individual responsible for accounting for the receipt or payment of moneys or funds in Ethiopia on behalf of the taxpayer and includes the following:

a) for a partnership, a partner in the partnership or a manager of the partnership;

b) for a company, a director of the company;

c) for an incapable individual, the legal representative of the individual responsible for receiving income on behalf or, or for the benefit of, the individual;

d) for a taxpayer referred to in Article 40 of this Proclamation, the receiver in relation to the taxpayer under that Article;

e) for any taxpayer, an individual that the Authority has, by notice in writing to the individual, declared to be a tax representative of the taxpayer for the purposes of the tax laws;

41/ "Taxpayer" means a person liable for tax and includes the following:

a) for the income tax, a person who has zero taxable income or privilege of tax holiday or loss under Schedule 'B' or 'C' for a tax year;

b) for the value added tax, a person registered or who has the obligation to register for value added tax;

c) for the turnover tax, turnover taxpayer;

42/ "Unpaid tax" means tax that has not been paid by the due date or, if the Authority has extended the due date under Article 32 of this Proclamation, by the extended due date;

43/ "Withholding agent" means a person required to withhold tax from a payment under Part Ten of the Federal Income Tax Proclamation;

44/ "Withholding tax" means tax that is required to be withheld from a payment under Part

Ten of the Federal Income Tax Proclamation;

45/ any expression in the masculine gender includes the feminine.

3. Fair Market Value

1/ For the purposes of the tax laws and subject to Article 79 of the Federal Income Tax Proclamation, the fair market value of goods, an asset, service, or benefit at a particular time and place is the ordinary open market value of the goods, asset, service, or benefit at that time and place.

2/ If it is not possible to determine the fair market value of goods, an asset, service, or benefit under Sub-Article (1) of this Article, the fair market value is the consideration any similar goods, asset, service, or benefit would ordinarily fetch in the open market at that time and place, adjusted to take account of the differences between the similar goods, asset, service, or benefit and the actual goods, asset, service, or benefit.

3/ For the purposes of Sub-Article (2) of this Article, goods, an asset, service, or benefit is similar to other goods, asset, service, or benefit, as the case may be, if it is the same as, or closely resembles, the other goods, asset, service, or benefit in character, quality, quantity, functionality, materials, and reputation.

4/ If the fair market value of goods, an asset, service, or benefit cannot be determined under the preceding Sub-Articles of this Article, the fair market value shall be the amount determined by the Authority provided it is consistent with generally accepted principles of valuation.

5/ For the avoidance of doubt, the fair market value of goods, an asset, service, or benefit may be greater or lesser than the actual price charged for the goods, asset, service, or benefit.

6/ The Authority may issue a Directive for the purposes of determining the fair market value of any goods, asset, service, or benefit.

4. Related Persons

1/ For the purposes of the tax laws and subject to Sub-Article (2) of this Article, two persons are related persons when the relationship between the two persons is such that one person may reasonably be expected to act in accordance with the directions, requests, suggestions, or wishes of the other person, or both persons may reasonably be expected to act in accordance with the directions, requests, suggestions, or wishes of a third person.

2/ Two persons are not related persons solely by reason of the fact that one person is an employee or client of the other, or both persons are employees or clients of a third person.

3/ Without limiting the generality of Sub-Article (1) of this Article, the following are related persons:

a) an individual and a relative of the individual unless the Authority is satisfied that neither person may reasonably be expected to act in accordance with the directions, requests, suggestions, or wishes of the other;

b) a body and a member of the body when the member, either alone or together with a related person or persons under another application of this Article, controls either directly or through one or more interposed bodies 25% or more of the rights to vote, dividends, or capital in the body;

c) two bodies, if a person, either alone or together with a related person or persons under another application of this Article, controls, either directly or through one or more interposed bodies, 25% or more of the rights to vote, dividends, or capital in both bodies.

4/ The following are a relative of an individual:

a) the spouse of the individual;

b) an ancestor, lineal descendant, brother, sister, uncle, aunt, nephew, niece, stepfather, stepmother, or adopted child of the individual or spouse of the individual;

c) a parent of the adoptive child of the individual or spouse of the individual;

d) a spouse of any person referred to in paragraph (b) of this Sub-Article.

5/ The following are a spouse of an individual:

a) an individual who is legally married to the first-mentioned individual;

b) an individual who lives in an irregular union with the first-mentioned individual.

6/ An adopted child is treated as related to their adoptive parent in the first degree of consanguinity.

PART TWO
ADMINISTRATION OF THE TAX LAWS

5. Duty of the Authority

The implementation and enforcement of the tax laws shall be the duty of the Authority.

6. Obligations and Responsibilities of Tax Officers

1/ A tax officer shall exercise any power, or perform any duty or function, assigned to the officer for the purposes of the tax laws in accordance with the appointment of the officer under the Ethiopian Revenues and Customs Authority Establishment Proclamation and any delegation of powers or duties to the officer under Article 8 (3) of the Ethiopian Revenues and Customs Authority Establishment Proclamation.

2/ A tax officer shall be honest and fair in the exercise of any power, or performance of any duty or function, under a tax law, and shall treat each taxpayer with courtesy and respect.

3/ A tax officer shall not exercise a power, or perform a duty or function, under a tax law that:

a) relates to a person in respect of which the tax officer has or had a personal, family, business, pro-fessional, employment, or financial relationship;

b) otherwise involves a conflict of interest.

4/ A tax officer or any officer of the Ministry who is directly involved in tax matters shall not act as a tax accountant or consultant, or accept employment from any person preparing tax declarations or giving tax advice.

7. Duty to Co-operate

All Federal and State government authorities and their agencies, bodies, local government administrations, and associations, and non-government organisations shall have the duty to co-operate with the Authority in the enforcement of the tax laws.

8. Confidentiality of Tax Information

1/ Any tax officer shall maintain the secrecy of all documents and information received in his official capacity.

2/ The provision of Sub-Article (1) of this Article shall not prevent a tax officer from disclosing a document or information to the following:

a) another tax officer for the purpose of carrying out official duties;

b) a law enforcement agency for the purpose of the prosecution of a person for an offence under a tax law or the prosecution of a person for an offence relating to a tax law under any other law;

c) the Commission or a court in proceedings to establish a person's tax liability, or liability for penalty or late payment interest, or in a criminal case;

d) the competent authority of the government of a foreign country with which Ethiopia has entered an agreement providing for the exchange of information, to the extent permitted under that agreement;

e) the Auditor-General when the disclosure is necessary to the performance of official duties by the Auditor-General;

f) the Attorney General when the disclosure is necessary to the performance of its official duties;

g) the Regional Tax Authority when the disclosure is necessary to the performance of its official duties;

h) a person in the service of the Government in a revenue or statistical department or conducting research when the disclosure is necessary to the performance of official duties by the person and provided the disclosure does not identify a specific person;

i) any other person with the written consent of the person to whom the information relates;

j) an organ authorized by any law.

3/ A person receiving any information under Sub-Article (2) of this Article shall:

a) maintain the secrecy of the information except to the minimum extent necessary to achieve the object for which the disclosure was permitted;

b) return any documents reflecting the information to the Authority.

4/ In this Article, "Tax officer" includes:

a) a member or former member of the Advisory Board of the Authority;

b) a person employed or engaged by the Authority in any capacity including as contractor;

c) a former officer, employee, or contractor of the Authority.

PART THREE
TAXPAYERS

CHAPTER ONE   REGISTRATION

9. Registration of Taxpayers

1/ Subject to Sub-Articles (2) and (3) of this Article, a person who becomes liable for tax under a tax law shall apply to the Authority for registration unless the person is already registered.

2/ Sub-article (1) of this Article shall not apply to:

a) a non-resident if the only Ethiopian source income derived by the person is subject to Article 51 and Article 53 of the Federal Income Tax Proclamation;

b) an individual whose only income is subject to Article 64 (2) of the Federal Income Tax Proclamation.

3/ An employer shall apply for registration of an employee entering into employment with the employer unless the employee is already registered.

4/ Sub-article (3) of this Article shall not relieve the employee of the obligation to apply for registration under Sub-Article (1) of this Article should the employer fail to make the application for the employee.

5/ An application for registration shall be:

a) made in the approved form;

b) accompanied by documentary evidence of the person's identity, including biometric identifier, as may be specified in the Regulation;

c) made within 21 (Twenty-one) days of becoming liable to apply for registration or within such further period as the Authority may allow.

6/ In the case of an application made by an employer for an employee under Sub-Article (3) of this Article, the biometric identifier required under Sub-Article (5) (b) of this Article shall be provided by the employee.

7/ Subject to Sub-Article (10) of this Article, the obligation of a person to apply for registration under Sub-Article (1) of this Article shall be in addition to an obligation or option of the person to apply for registration for the purposes of a particular tax under another tax law.

8/ The Authority shall register a person who has applied for registration under Sub-Article (1) of this Article if satisfied that the person is liable for tax under a tax law and issue the person with a registration certificate in the approved form.

9/ If the Authority refuses to register a person who has applied for registration, the Authority shall serve the person with written notice of the refusal within 14 (Fourteen) days of the person filing the application for registration.

10/ When a person has applied for registration under Sub-Article (1) of this Article, the Authority shall use the information provided for the registration for the purposes of any other registration of that person required or permitted under a tax law for the purposes of a particular tax without the person being required to file any additional registration forms.

11/ Despite Sub-Article (10) of this Article, the Authority may request a person to provide any further information necessary to complete an additional registration of the person.

12/ The Authority may register a person who has failed to apply for registration as required under this Article and shall issue the person with a registration certificate in the approved form.

13/ The registration of a person under this Article shall take effect from the date specified on the person's registration certificate.

10. Notification of Changes

1/ A registered person shall notify the Authority, in writing, of a change in any of the following within 30 (Thirty) days of the change occurring:

a) the person's name, physical or postal address, constitution, or principal activity, or activities;

b) the person's banking details used for transactions with the Authority;

c) the person's electronic address used for communication with the Authority;

d) such other details as may be specified in a Directive issued by the Authority.

2/ The notification of changes under Sub-Article (1) of this Article by a registered person shall be treated as satisfying any obligation to notify the same changes in relation to a registration of the person for the purposes of a particular tax under another tax law.

11. Cancellation of Registration

1/ A person who ceases to be required to be registered for the purposes of all the tax laws shall apply to the Authority for cancellation of the person's registration.

2/ An application for cancellation of registration shall be made:

a) in the approved form; and

b) within 30 (Thirty) days of the person ceasing to be required to be registered for the purposes of all the tax laws or within such further time as the Authority may allow.

3/ An application by a person under Sub-Article (1) of this Article shall be treated as satisfying any obligation of the person to apply for cancellation of the person's registration for the purposes of a particular tax under another tax law.

4/ The Authority shall, by notice in writing, cancel the registration of a person who has applied under Sub-Article (1) of this Article when satisfied that the person has ceased all operations and is no longer required to be registered for the purposes of all the tax laws.

5/ A notice of cancellation of registration under Sub-Article (4) of this Article shall be served on the applicant within 30 (Thirty) days of receipt of the application and the Authority may conduct a final audit of the person's tax affairs within 90 (Ninety) days of service of the notice of cancellation of registration.

6/ If a person has failed to apply for cancellation of the person's registration as required under Sub-Article (1) of this Article, the Authority shall, by notice in writing to the person or the person's tax representative, cancel the registration of the person when satisfied that the person has ceased all operations and is no longer required to be registered for the purposes of all the tax laws, including when the person is a natural person who has died, a company that has been liquidated, or any other person that has ceased to exist.

7/ The cancellation of a person's registration under Sub-Article (4) or (6) of this Article shall include cancellation of any registration of the person for the purposes of a particular tax under another tax law.

8/ The cancellation of a person's registration shall take effect from the date specified in the notice of cancellation served on the person by the Authority.

9/ When the cancellation of the registration of a person involves cancellation of the person's registration for the purposes of a particular tax under another tax law, the person shall comply with any requirements relating to cancellation of that registration as specified under that other tax law.

CHAPTER TWO   TAXPAYER IDENTIFICATION NUMBER

12. Taxpayer Identification Number

For the purposes of identification, the Authority shall issue a number, to be known as a taxpayer identification number ("TIN"), in accordance with this Chapter to a taxpayer registered for the purposes of the tax laws and the taxpayer shall use the TIN as required under the tax laws.

13. Issue of a TIN

1/ The Authority shall issue a TIN to a taxpayer registered for the purposes of the tax laws under Article 9 of this Proclamation.

2/ A TIN shall be issued for the purposes of all tax laws and a tax payer shall have only one TIN at any time.

3/ The Authority issues a TIN to a taxpayer by serving the taxpayer with written notice of the TIN.

14. Use of a TIN

1/ A taxpayer who has been issued with a TIN shall state the TIN on any tax declaration, notice, or other document filed or used for the purposes of a tax law, or as otherwise required under a tax law, including supplying the TIN to a withholding agent in respect of payments made by the agent to the taxpayer.

2/ A tax payer applying for a licence to carry on a business or occupation shall be required to supply the taxpayer's TIN to the licensing authority.

3/ A taxpayer shall supply the taxpayer's TIN on a renewal of a licence referred to in Sub-Article (2) of this Article only if the taxpayer's TIN has changed since the original application of the licence.

4/ A licensing authority issuing a licence to carrying on a business or occupation shall not issue a licence to a taxpayer unless the taxpayer has supplied their TIN.

5/ A TIN is personal to the taxpayer to whom it has been issued and, subject to Sub-Article (6) of this Article, shall not be used by another person.

6/ The TIN of a taxpayer may be used by a licensed tax agent when:

a) the tax payer has given written permission to the licensed tax agent o use the TIN; and

b) the licensed tax agent uses the TIN only in respect of the tax affairs of the taxpayer.

15. Cancellation of a TIN

1/ The Authority shall, by notice in writing, cancel the TIN of a taxpayer when satisfied that:

a) the tax payer's registration has been cancelled under Article 11 of this Proclamation;

b) a TIN has been issued to the taxpayer under an identity that is not the taxpayer's true identity; or

c) the tax payer had been previously issued with a TIN that is still in force.

2/ The Authority may, at any time, by notice in writing, cancel the TIN issued to a taxpayer and issue the taxpayer with a new TIN.

CHAPTER THREE TAX REPRESENTATIVES

16. Obligations of Tax Representatives

1/ A tax representative of a taxpayer shall be responsible for performing any obligation imposed by a tax law on the taxpayer, including the filing of tax declarations and payment of tax.

2/ When there are two or more tax representatives of a taxpayer, each tax representative shall be jointly and severally liable for any obligations referred to in this Article but the obligations may be discharged by any of them.

3/ Except as provided otherwise under a tax law and subject to Sub-Article (4) of this Article, any tax that, by virtue of Sub-Article (1) of this Article, is payable by the tax representative of a taxpayer shall be recoverable from the tax representative only to the extent of the monies or assets of the taxpayer that are in the possession or under the control of the tax representative.

4/ Subject to Sub-Article (5) of this Article, a tax representative shall be personally liable for the payment of any tax due by the tax representative in that capacity when, while the amount remains unpaid, the tax representative:

a) alienates, charges, or disposes of any moneys received or accrued in respect of which the tax is payable;

b) disposes of or parts with any moneys or funds belonging to the taxpayer that are in the possession of the tax representative or which come to the tax representative after the tax is payable, when such tax could legally have been paid from or out of such moneys or funds.

5/ A tax representative shall not be personally liable for tax under Sub-Article (4) of this Article if:

a) the monies were paid by the tax representative on behalf of a taxpayer and the amount paid has a legal priority over the tax payable by the taxpayer; or

b) at the time the monies were paid, the tax representative had no knowledge, and could not reasonably be expected to know, of the taxpayer's tax liability.

6/ Nothing in this Article relieves a taxpayer from performing any obligation imposed on the taxpayer under a tax law that the tax representative of the taxpayer has failed to perform.

PART FOUR
DOCUMENTS

17. Record-keeping Obligations

1/ A taxpayer shall, for the purposes of a tax law, maintain such documents (including in electronic format) as may be required under the tax law and the documents shall be maintained:

a) in Amharic or English;

b) in Ethiopia; and

c) in a manner so as to enable the taxpayer's tax liability under the tax law to be readily ascertained.

2/ Subject to Sub-Article (3) of this Article or a tax law providing otherwise, a taxpayer shall retain the documents referred to in Sub-Article (1) of this Article for the longer of:

a) the record-keeping period specified in the Commercial Code; or

b) 5 (Five) years from the date that the tax declaration for the tax period to which they relate was filed with the Authority.

3/ When, at the end of the period referred to in Sub-Article (2) of this Article, a document is necessary for a proceeding under the Proclamation or any other law commenced before the end of the period, the tax payer shall retain the document until the proceeding and any related proceedings have been completed.

4/ When a document referred to Sub-Article (1) of this Article is not in Amharic or English, the Authority may, by notice in writing, require the taxpayer to provide, at the taxpayer's expense, a translation into Amharic or English by a translator approved by the Authority by the date specified in the notice.

5/ Notwithstanding the provisions of Sub-Article (1) to (4) of this Article the Transfer Pricing Directive to be issued by the Minister shall be applicable.

18. Inspection of Documents

A taxpayer required to maintain documents under a tax law shall make the documents available for inspection at all reasonable times by the Authority during the period specified in Article 17 of this Proclamation.

19. Receipts

1/ A taxpayer that has the obligation to maintain books of account shall register with the Authority the type and quantity of receipts before having such receipts printed.

2/ Any person operating a printing press engaged by a taxpayer to print receipts shall ensure that the type and quantity of receipts are registered with the Authority before printing the receipts.

3/ Any taxpayer that has an obligation to maintain books of account shall issue a receipt for any transaction.

4/ The Authority shall issue directives for the implementation of this Article.

20. Sales Register Machines

1/ The Council of Ministers shall issue Regulation on Sales Register Machines.

2/ The Regulation may provide for the following:

a) the obligatory use by taxpayers of sales register machines;

b) the conditions for the use by taxpayers of sales register machines;

c) the information required to be included on a receipt produced by a sales register machine;

d) the required features of sales register machines;

e) the process for suppliers to apply for accreditation of sales register machines and the reporting obligations of such suppliers;

f) the registration of a sales register machine sold to a taxpayer.

3/ For the purpose of this Article:

a) "Cash register machine" means a machine that uses a firmware that is installed in an electronic programmable read only memory chip and can record the sale of goods or services in lieu of a regular sales receipt;

b) "Point of sale machine" means a machine that is a computerised replacement for a cash register machine and having additional capability to record and track customers' orders and debit and credit card accounts, manage inventory, and perform similar functions;

c) "Sales register machine" means a cash register machine and a point of sale machine.

PART FIVE
TAX DECLARATIONS

21. Filing of Tax Declarations

1/ A taxpayer required to file a tax declaration under a tax law shall file the declaration in the approved form and in the manner provided for in the Regulation.

2/ Subject to Sub-Article (3) of this Article, the Authority may, by notice in writing, require a taxpayer to file by the due date set out in the notice:

a) a fuller declaration in relation to a tax declaration already filed; or

b) such other tax declaration as the Authority specifies in the notice.

3/ Sub-article (2) (a) of this Article shall not apply when the tax declaration already filed is a self-assessment declaration.

4/ The Authority shall not be bound by a tax declaration or information provided by, or on behalf of, a taxpayer and the Authority may determine a taxpayer's tax liability based on any reliable and verifiable sources of information available to the Authority.

5/ Subject to Sub-Article (6) of this Article and Article 82 of this Proclamation, a taxpayer shall sign a tax declaration filed by him and the tax declaration shall contain a representation by the taxpayer that the declaration, including any attached material, is complete and accurate.

6/ A taxpayer's tax representative or licensed tax agent shall sign the taxpayer's tax declaration and make the representation referred to in Sub-Article (5) of this Article when the taxpayer is:

a) not an individual;

b) an incapable individual; or

c) an individual who is otherwise unable to sign the declaration provided the taxpayer has provided the representative or tax agent with authority in writing to sign the declaration.

7/ When a tax declaration is signed by the taxpayer's tax representative or licensed tax agent, the taxpayer shall be deemed to know the contents of the declaration and shall be treated as having made the representation as to completeness and accuracy referred to in Sub-Article (5) of this Article.

22. Licensed Tax Agent Certification of Tax Declaration

1/ A licensed tax agent who prepares or assists in the preparation of a tax declaration of a taxpayer shall provide the taxpayer with a certificate, in the approved form, certifying that the tax agent has examined the documents of the taxpayer and that, to the best of his knowledge, the declaration together with any accompanying documentation, correctly reflects the data and transactions to which it relates.

2/ A licensed tax agent who refuses to provide a certificate referred to in Sub-Article (1) of this Article shall provide the taxpayer with a statement in writing of the reasons for such refusal.

3/ A licensed tax agent who prepares or assists in the preparation of a tax declaration of a taxpayer shall specify in the declaration whether a certificate under Sub-Article (1) of this Article or a statement under Sub-Article (2) of this Article has been provided to the taxpayer in relation to the declaration.

4/ A licensed tax agent shall keep a copy of certificates or statements provided to taxpayers under this Article for the period specified in Article 17 (2) of this Proclamation and shall, when required to do so by notice in writing from the Authority, produce the copy to the Authority.

23. Advance Tax Declarations

1/ A taxpayer who ceases to carry on any activity shall notify the Authority, in writing, of the cessation within 30 (Thirty) days of the date that the taxpayer ceased to carry on the activity.

2/ A taxpayer to whom Sub-Article (1) of this Article applies shall, within 60 (Sixty) days after the date that the taxpayer ceased to carry on the activity or within such lesser period as the Authority may require by notice in writing to the taxpayer:

a) file an advance tax declaration for the tax period in which the taxpayer ceased to carry on the activity and for any prior tax period for which the due date for filing has not arisen; and

b) pay the tax due under the advance tax declaration at the time of filing the declaration.

3/ If a taxpayer is about to leave Ethiopia during a tax period and the taxpayer's absence is unlikely to be temporary, the taxpayer shall, before leaving:

a) file an advance tax declaration for the tax period and for any prior tax period for which the due date for filing has not arisen by the time the taxpayer leaves; and

b) pay the tax due under the advance tax declaration at the time of filing the declaration or make an arrangement satisfactory to the Authority for the payment of the tax due.

4/ If, during a tax period, the Authority has reason to believe that a taxpayer will not file a tax declaration for the period by the due date, the Authority may, by notice in writing and at any time during the tax period, require:

a) the taxpayer or the taxpayer's tax representative to file an advance tax declaration for the tax period by the date specified in the notice being a date that may be before the date that the tax declaration for the tax period would otherwise be due; and

b) pay any tax payable under the advance tax declaration by the due date specified in the notice.

5/ If a taxpayer is subject to more than one tax, this Article shall apply separately for each tax.

6/ In this Article, "activity" means a business or any other activity giving rise to income subject to tax under a tax law, other than an activity giving rise to income subject to withholding tax as a final tax.

24. Tax Declaration Duly Filed

A tax declaration that is purported to be filed by or on behalf of a taxpayer shall be treated as having been filed by the taxpayer or with the taxpayer's consent unless the contrary is proved.

PART SIX
TAX ASSESSMENTS

25. Self-assessments

1/ A self-assessment taxpayer who has filed a self- assessment declaration in the approved form for a tax period shall be treated, for all purposes of this Proclamation, as having made an assessment of the amount of tax payable (including a nil amount) for the tax period to which the declaration relates being that amount as set out in the declaration.

2/ When a self-assessment taxpayer liable for income tax under Schedule 'B' or 'C' of the Federal Income Tax Proclamation has filed a self-assessment declaration in the approved form for a tax period and the taxpayer has a loss for the year, the taxpayer shall be treated, for all purposes of this Proclamation, as having made an assessment of the amount of the loss being that amount as set out in the declaration.

3/ When a self-assessment taxpayer has filed a value added tax return in the approved form for a tax period and the taxpayer's total input tax for the period exceeds the taxpayer's total output tax for the period, the taxpayer shall be treated, for all purposes of this Proclamation, as having made an assessment of the amount of the excess input tax for the period being that amount as set out in the declaration.

4/ A tax declaration in the approved form completed and filed electronically by a taxpayer is a self-assessment return despite the following:

 a) the form included pre-filled information provided by the Authority;

 b) the tax payable is computed electronically as information is inserted into the form.

26. Estimated Assessments

1/ When a taxpayer has failed to file a tax declaration for a tax period as required under a tax law, the Authority may, based on such evidence as may be available and at any time, make an assessment (referred to as a "estimated assessment") of:

 a) in the case of a loss under Schedule 'B' or 'C' of the Federal Income Tax Proclamation, the amount of the loss for the tax period;

 b) in the case of an excess amount of input tax under the Value Added Tax Proclamation, the amount of the excess input tax for the tax period;

 c) in any other case, the amount of tax payable (including a nil amount) for the tax period.

2/ The Authority shall serve a taxpayer assessed under Sub-Article (1) of this Article with notice, in writing, of an estimated assessment specifying the following:

 a) the amount of tax assessed, or loss or excess input tax carried forward, as the case may be;

 b) the amount assessed as penalty (if any) payable in respect of the tax assessed;

 c) the amount of late payment interest (if any) payable in respect of the tax assessed;

 d) the tax period to which the assessment relates;

e) the due date for payment of the tax, penalty, and interest being a date that is within 30 (Thirty) days from the date of service of the notice;

f) the manner of objecting to the assessment, including the time limit for lodging an objection to the assessment.

3/ The service of a notice of an estimated assessment under Sub-Article (2) of this Article shall not change the due date (referred to as the "original due date") for payment of the tax payable under the assessment as determined under the tax law imposing the tax, and late payment penalty and late payment interest remain payable based on the original due date.

4/ This Article shall apply only for the purposes of a tax that is collected by assessment.

5/ Nothing in this Article relieves a taxpayer from being required to file the tax declaration to which an estimated assessment served under this Article relates.

6/ A tax declaration filed by a taxpayer for a tax period after notice of an estimated assessment has been served on the taxpayer for the period is not a self-assessment declaration.

7/ The Authority may make an estimated assessment at any time.

8/ The Authority may issue directives for the implementation of this Article.

27. Jeopardy Assessments

1/ The Authority may, based on such evidence as may be available, make a "jeopardy assessment" of the tax payable by a taxpayer in the circumstances specified in Article 23 or Article 42 of this Proclamation for a tax period.

2/ Sub-article (1) of this Article applies only when:

a) the taxpayer has not filed a tax declaration for the tax period; and

b) the tax is collected by assessment.

3/ A jeopardy assessment:

a) may be made before the date on which the taxpayer's tax declaration for the period is due; and

b) shall be made in accordance with the law in force at the date the jeopardy assessment was made.

4/ The Authority shall serve a taxpayer assessed under Sub-Article (1) of this Article with notice, in writing, of the jeopardy assessment specifying the following:

a) the amount of tax assessed;

b) the amount assessed as penalty (if any) payable in respect of the tax assessed;

c) the tax period to which the assessment relates;

d) the due date for payment of the tax and penalty, which may be a date before the tax would otherwise be due for the tax period;

e) the manner of objecting to the assessment, including the time limit for lodging an objection to the assessment.

5/ The Authority may specify in a notice of a jeopardy assessment that the tax and penalty due are payable immediately.

6/ Nothing in this Article shall relieve a taxpayer from the requirement to file the tax declaration to which the jeopardy assessment served under this Article relates.

7/ A jeopardy assessment may be the subject of an amended assessment under Article 28 of this Proclamation so that the taxpayer is assessed in respect of the whole of the tax period to which the jeopardy assessment relates.

8/ A tax declaration filed by a taxpayer for a tax period after notice of a jeopardy assessment has been served on the taxpayer for the period is not a self-assessment declaration.

28. Amended Assessments

1/ Subject to this Article, the Authority may amend a tax assessment (referred to in this Article as the "original assessment") by making such alterations, reductions, or additions, based on such evidence as may be available, to the original assessment of a taxpayer for a tax period to ensure that:

a) in the case of a loss under Schedule 'B' or 'C' of the Federal Income Tax Proclamation, the taxpayer is assessed in respect of the correct amount of the loss for the tax period;

b) in the case of an excess amount of input tax under the Value Added Tax Proclamation, the taxpayer is assessed in respect of the correct amount of the excess input tax for the tax period;

c) in any other case, the taxpayer is liable for the correct amount of tax payable (including a nil amount) in respect of the tax period.

2/ Subject to a tax law specifying otherwise, the Authority may amend a tax assessment under Sub-Article (1) of this Article:

a) in the case of fraud, or gross or wilful neglect by, or on behalf of, the taxpayer, at any time; or

b) in any other case, within 5 (Five) years of:

(1) for a self-assessment, the date that the self-assessment taxpayer filed the self-assessment declaration to which the self-assessment relates;

(2) for any other tax assessment, the date the Authority served notice of the assessment on the taxpayer.

3/ When the Authority has served a taxpayer with notice of an amended assessment made under Sub-Article (1) of this Article, the Authority may further amend the original assessment to which the amended assessment relates within the later of:

a) the period specified in Sub-Article (2) (b) of this Article applicable to the original assessment; or

b) one year after the Authority served notice of the amended assessment on the taxpayer.

4/ In any case to which Sub-Article (3) (b) of this Article applies, the Authority shall be limited to amending the alterations, reductions, or additions made in the amended assessment to the original assessment.

5/ The Authority shall serve a taxpayer with notice, in writing, of an amended assessment made under this Article specifying the following:

a) the original assessment to which the amended assessment relates and a statement of reasons for making the amended assessment;

b) the amount of tax assessed, or loss or excess input tax carried forward, as the case may be;

c) the amount of penalty assessed (if any) under the amended assessment;

d) the amount of late payment interest (if any) payable in respect of the tax assessed;

e) the tax period to which the amended assessment relates;

f) the due date for payment of any additional tax, and penalty and interest, payable under the amended assessment, being a date that is not less than 30 (Thirty) days from the date of service of the notice;

g) the manner of objecting to the amended assessment, including the time limit for lodging an objection to the assessment.

6/ If an amount of additional tax is payable under an amended assessment, any late payment penalty and late payment interest payable in respect of the additional tax shall be computed from the original due date for payment of tax under the original assessment to which the amended assessment relates.

29. Application for Making an Amendment to a Self-assessment

1/ A taxpayer who has filed a self-assessment declaration may apply to the Authority for the Authority to make an amendment to the self-assessment.

2/ An application under Sub-Article (1) of this Article shall:

a) state the amendments that the taxpayer believes are required to be made to correct the self-assessment and the reasons for the amendments; and

b) be filed with the Authority within the period specified in Article 28 (2) (b) (1) of this Proclamation.

3/ When an application has been made under Sub-Article (1) of this Article, the Authority shall, in accordance with a Directive issued by the Authority, make a decision to amend the self-assessment or to refuse the application and such decision shall be made within 120 (One Hundred Twenty) days of the receipt of the application.

4/ If the Authority makes a decision to amend the self-assessment:

a) the amended assessment shall be made in accordance with Article 28 (1) of this Proclamation; and

b) notice of the amended assessment shall be served on the taxpayer in accordance with Article 28 (5) of this Proclamation.

5/ If the Authority makes a decision to refuse an application under Sub-Article (1) of this Article, the Authority shall serve the taxpayer with written notice of the decision.

PART SEVEN
COLLECTION AND RECOVERY OF TAX AND OTHER AMOUNTS

CHAPTER ONE   PAYMENT OF TAX AND OTHER AMOUNTS

30. Tax as a Debt Due to the Government

1/ Tax that is due and payable by a taxpayer under a tax law is a debt owed to the Government and shall be payable to the Authority.

2/ A taxpayer required to pay tax electronically by the Authority under Article 82 (2) of this Proclamation shall do so unless authorised by the Authority, by notice in writing, to use another method of payment.

3/ If a taxpayer fails to pay tax by the due date, the taxpayer shall be liable for any costs incurred by the Authority in taking action to recover the unpaid tax.

31. Secondary Liabilities and Tax Recovery Costs

1/ The Authority may serve a person liable for a secondary liability or tax recovery costs with notice of the amount of the liability payable by the person and the due date for payment.

2/ A reference in Parts Seven, Eight, Nine, and Ten, and Article 105 of this Proclamation:

a) to "tax", shall include a secondary liability and tax recovery costs;

b) to "unpaid tax", shall include an amount specified in paragraph (a) of this Sub-Article that is not paid by the due date; and

c) to "taxpayer", shall include a person liable for an amount specified in paragraph (a) of this Sub-Article.

3/ An amount of a secondary liability paid by a person shall be credited against the primary liability of the taxpayer to which the secondary liability relates.

32. Extension of Time to Pay Tax

1/ A taxpayer may apply, in writing, to the Authority for an extension of time to pay tax due under a tax law.

2/ When an application has been made under Sub-Article (1) of this Article, the Authority may, upon satisfaction that there is good cause and in accordance with a Directive issued by the Authority:

a) grant the taxpayer an extension of time for payment of the tax; or

b) require the taxpayer to pay the tax in such instalments as the Authority may determine.

3/ The Authority shall serve the taxpayer with written notice of the decision on an application under Sub-Article (1) of this Article.

4/ When a taxpayer permitted to pay tax by instalments under Sub-Article (2) (b) of this Article defaults in the payment of an instalment, the Authority may immediately take action to recover the whole balance of the tax outstanding at the time of default.

5/ The grant of an extension of time to pay tax or permission to pay tax due by instalments shall not prevent the liability for late payment interest arising from the original date the tax was due for payment.

33. Priority of Tax and Garnishee Amounts

1/ This Article applies to the following amounts:

a) withholding tax, value added tax, turnover tax or excise tax; and

b) an amount payable under a garnishee order.

2/ A person owing, holding, receiving, or withholding an amount to which this Article applies holds the amount on behalf of the Government and, in the event of the liquidation or bankruptcy of the person, the amount:

a) shall not form part of the person's estate in liquidation or bankruptcy; and

b) shall be paid to the Authority before any distribution of property is made.

3/ Despite any other law, withholding tax withheld by a person:

a) shall not be subject to attachment in respect of any debt or liability of the person;

b) shall be a first charge on the payment or amount from which the tax is withheld; and

c) shall be withheld prior to any other deduction that the person may be required to make from the payment or amount under an order of any court or any law.

34. Order of Payment

1/ When a taxpayer is liable for penalty and late payment interest in relation to a tax liability and the taxpayer makes a payment that is less than the total amount of tax, penalty, and interest due, the amount paid shall be applied in the following order:

a) first in payment of the tax liability;

b) then in payment of late payment interest;

c) then the balance remaining is applied in payment of penalty.

2/ When a taxpayer has more than one tax liability at the time a payment is made, the payment is applied against the tax liabilities in the order in which the liabilities arose.

35. Security for Payment of Tax

1/ When it appears to the Authority necessary to do so for the protection of the revenue, the Authority may require any taxpayer to give security in such amount and manner as the Authority considers appropriate:

a) for the payment of tax that is or may become due by the taxpayer; or

b) as a condition of the taxpayer claiming a refund of tax under a tax law.

2/ Security under this Article may be given by cash or bank guarantee and shall be subject to such conditions as the Authority may reasonably require.

3/ A taxpayer shall be liable to give security only if the Authority serves the taxpayer with a notice setting out:

a) the amount of the security required;

b) the manner in which the security is to be provided; and

c) the due date for providing the security.

4/ An amount of security that a taxpayer fails to provide as required under this Article shall be treated as unpaid tax of the taxpayer for the purposes of this Part.

36. Protection

1/ The provision of Sub-Article (2) of this Article shall apply to the following persons:

a) a withholding agent who has withheld tax from a payment under the Federal Income Tax Proclamation and paid the tax to the Authority;

b) a tax representative who has paid an amount to the Authority pursuant to Article 16 (1) of this Proclamation;

c) a receiver who has paid an amount to the Authority pursuant to Article 40 of this Proclamation; or

d) a person who has paid an amount to the Authority pursuant to a garnishee order.

2/ A person to whom this Article applies cannot be sued for payment of the amount paid on behalf a taxpayer to the Authority in accordance with the Tax Law.

CHAPTER TWO   LATE PAYMENT INTEREST

37. Late Payment Interest

1/ Subject to Sub-Article (8) of this Article, a taxpayer who fails to pay tax on or before the due date for payment shall be liable for late payment interest at the rate specified in Sub-Article (2) of this Article on the unpaid tax for the period commencing on the date the tax was due and ending on the date the tax was paid.

2/ The rate of late payment interest shall be the highest commercial lending interest rate that prevailed in Ethiopia during the quarter immediately before the commencement of the period specified in Sub-Article (1) of this Article increased by 15%.

3/ Late payment interest paid by a taxpayer under Sub-Article (1) of this Article shall be refunded to the taxpayer to the extent that the tax to which the interest relates is found not to have been payable.

4/ Late payment interest payable under this Article shall be in addition to any late payment penalty imposed under Article 105 of this Proclamation in respect of a failure to pay tax by the due date.

5/ Late payment interest payable under this Article shall be calculated as simple interest and shall be computed on a daily basis.

6/ The Authority may serve a taxpayer liable for late payment interest with a notice of the amount of interest payable by the taxpayer and the due date for payment.

7/ A notice of the amount of late payment interest payable by a taxpayer may be included in any other notice, including a notice of a tax assessment, issued by the Authority to the taxpayer.

8/ Late payment interest shall not accrue for the period between the date of notification and the date of payment on the following conditions:

a) the Authority notifies a taxpayer in writing of the taxpayer's outstanding tax liability under a tax law including in a tax assessment; and

b) the taxpayer pays the balance notified in full within the time specified in the notification including late payment interest payable up to the date of the notification.

9/ Late payment interest payable by a person in respect of withholding tax or a secondary liability payable by the person shall be borne personally by the person and shall not be recoverable from any other person.

10/ The total amount of late payment interest payable by a taxpayer shall not exceed the amount of the unpaid tax liability of the taxpayer.

11/ In this Article "tax" shall not include late payment interest.

CHAPTER THREE   RECOVERY OF UNPAID TAX

38. Enforcement of Tax Assessments

1/ Subject to Sub-Article (2) of this Article, a tax assessment served by the Authority on a taxpayer shall become final at the end of the objection period allowed under Article 54 of this

Proclamation if the taxpayer has not filed an objection to the assessment within that period.

2/ If a taxpayer has filed an objection to a tax assessment, the tax assessment shall become final on the later of:

a) if the taxpayer has not appealed the tax assessment to the Tax Appeal Commission, at the end of the appeal period in Article 88 of this Proclamation;

b) if the taxpayer has appealed the tax assessment to the Tax Appeal Commission, at the end of the appeal period to the Federal High Court in Article 57 of this Proclamation;

c) if the taxpayer has appealed the tax assessment to the Federal High Court, at the end of the appeal period to the Federal Supreme Court in Article 58 of this Proclamation; or

d) if the taxpayer has appealed the tax assessment to the Federal Supreme Court, when the Court renders its final decision.

3/ Nothing in Sub-Article (2) of this Article shall prevent the payment of tax in dispute in accordance with Article 56 (2) and Article 57 (3) of this Proclamation.

4/ A taxpayer who does not pay the tax due under a final assessment as determined under Sub-Articles (1) and (2) of this Article shall be in default.

39. Preferential Claim to Assets

1/ Subject to Sub-Article (2) of this Article, from the date on which tax becomes due and payable by a taxpayer under a tax law, and subject to any prior secured claims registered with the Registering Authority, the Authority has a preferential claim upon the assets of the taxpayer until the unpaid tax is paid.

2/ Subject to Sub-Article (7) of this Article, the priority for prior secured claims under Sub-Article (1) of this Article shall include the priority of banks in relation to secured claims and the priority of employees in relation to salary and wages, but shall not apply in relation to the taxes referred to in Article 33 (1) (a) of this Proclamation.

3/ When a taxpayer is in default in paying tax, the Authority may, by notice in writing, inform the taxpayer of the Authority's intention to apply to the Registering Authority to register a security interest in any asset owned by the taxpayer to cover the unpaid tax together with any costs incurred in recovery proceedings.

4/ If the taxpayer served with a notice under Sub-Article (3) of this Article fails to pay the tax specified in the notice within 30 (Thirty) days of service of the notice, the Authority may, by notice in writing, direct the Registering Authority that the asset specified in the notice, to the extent of the taxpayer's interest therein, shall be the subject of security for the amount of the unpaid tax specified in the notice.

5/ When the Authority has served a notice under Sub-Article (4) of this Article, the Registering Authority shall, without fee, register the notice of security as if the notice were an instrument of mortgage over, or charge on, as the case may be, of the asset specified in the notice and registration shall, subject to any prior mortgage or charge, operate while it subsists as a legal mortgage over, or charge on, the asset to secure the unpaid tax.

6/ Upon receipt of the whole of the amount of tax secured under Sub-Article (5) of this Article, the Authority shall serve notice on the Registering Authority cancelling the direction made under Sub-Article (4) of this Article and the Registering Authority shall, without fee, cancel the registration of the notice of security.

7/ The priority of banks in relation to secured claims in accordance with Sub-Article (2) of this Article applies only where the banks, before lending any amount, confirm that the taxpayer has a tax clearance certificate from the Authority.

40. Duties of Receivers

1/ A receiver shall notify the Authority, in writing, within 14 (Fourteen) days after the earlier of being appointed to the position or taking possession of an asset in Ethiopia of a taxpayer.

2/ The Authority shall determine the amount of unpaid tax owing by the taxpayer and the amount of tax that will become payable by the taxpayer whose assets are under the control of the receiver and shall notify the receiver, in writing, of that amount within 30 (Thirty) days of the Authority receiving a notice under Sub-Article (1) of this Article.

3/ Subject to Sub-Article (4) of this Article, a receiver:

a) shall not, without prior approval of the Authority, dispose of an asset of the taxpayer whose assets are under the control of the receiver until a notice has been served on the receiver under Sub-Article (2) of this Article or the 30 (Thirty) day period specified in Sub-Article (2) of this Article has expired without a notice being served under that Sub-Article;

b) shall set aside, out of the proceeds of sale of an asset, the amount notified by the Authority under Sub-Article (2) of this Article, or a lesser amount as is subsequently agreed to by the Authority; and

c) shall be personally liable to the extent of the amount required to be set aside for the tax payable by the taxpayer who owned the asset.

4/ Nothing in Sub-Article (3) of this Article prevents a receiver from paying the following in priority to the amount notified under Sub-Article (2) of this Article:

a) a debt that has a legal priority over the tax referred to in the notice served under Sub-Article (2) of this Article;

b) the expenses properly incurred by the receiver in the capacity as such, including the receiver's remuneration.

5/ When two or more persons are receivers in respect of a taxpayer, the obligations and liabilities under this Article apply jointly and severally to both persons but may be discharged by any of them.

6/ In this Article, "receiver" means a person who, with respect to an asset in Ethiopia of a taxpayer or deceased taxpayer, is any of the following:

a) a liquidator of a company;

b) a receiver appointed by a court or out of court;

c) a trustee for a bankrupt person;

d) a mortgagee-in-possession;

e) an executor of a deceased estate.

41. Seizure of Property

1/ Subject to Sub-Article (2) of this Article, the Authority may serve a notice on a taxpayer who has failed to pay tax by the due date stating the intention of the Authority to issue an order (referred to as a "seizure order") for the seizure of the property of the taxpayer if the unpaid tax is not paid within 30 (Thirty) days of service of the notice.

2/ If the Authority makes a finding that the collection of the tax owing by a taxpayer is in jeopardy, the Authority may immediately issue a seizure order.

3/ If the taxpayer has failed to pay the tax due within the time specified in a notice served under Sub-Article (1) of this Article or Sub-Article (2) of this Article applies, the Authority may issue a seizure order on the taxpayer and any person having possession of the taxpayer's property.

4/ A seizure order may be executed against any property of the taxpayer other than property that, at the time of execution of the order:

a) is subject to a prior secured claim of creditors;

b) is subject to attachment or execution under any judicial process; or

c) cannot be subject to attachment under the law of Ethiopia.

5/ If a seizure order has been issued in relation to a taxpayer or is about to be issued, the Authority may demand, by notice in writing, that any person having custody or control of documents containing evidence or statements relating to the property of the taxpayer exhibit the documents to the Authority.

6/ The Authority may request a police officer to be present during the execution of a seizure order and shall store the property seized in such manner as to ensure the security of the property.

7/ When the Authority has seized property of a taxpayer under this Article, the Authority shall serve a notice on the taxpayer:

a) specifying the seized property and the unpaid tax liability of the taxpayer;

b) stating that the Authority shall dispose of the property if the taxpayer does not pay the unpaid tax within the detention period specified in the notice.

8/ For the purposes of Sub-Article (7) (b) of this Article, the detention period is:

a) for perishable goods, the period that the Authority considers reasonable having regard to the condition of the goods;

b) for any other case, ten days after the seizure of the goods.

9/ If the taxpayer fails to pay the unpaid tax specified in the notice served under Sub-Article (7) of this Article by the end of the detention period, the Authority may sell the property by public auction and apply the proceeds as follows:

a) first towards the cost of taking, keeping, and selling the property as determined by the Authority;

b) then in payment of the unpaid tax liability of the taxpayer as specified in the notice served under Sub-Article (7) of this Article;

c) then in payment of any other unpaid tax liability of the taxpayer;

d) subject to Sub-Article (10) of this Article, the remainder of the proceeds, if any, are to be paid to the taxpayer within 45 (Forty-five) days of the sale of the property.

10/ With the written agreement of the taxpayer an amount referred to in Sub-Article (9) (d) of this Article may be carried forward for the payment of any future tax liability of the taxpayer under any tax law.

11/ When the proceeds of sale of the property under Sub-Article (9) of this Article are less than the total of the taxpayer's unpaid tax liability and the cost of taking, keeping, and selling the property as determined under Sub-Article (9) of this Article, the Authority may proceed under this Chapter Seven of this Proclamation to recover the shortfall.

12/ Any person who fails or refuses to surrender any property of a taxpayer that is the subject of a seizure order shall be personally liable to the Government for an amount equal to the value of the property not surrendered but not exceeding an amount equal to the taxpayer's unpaid tax liability together with the costs of the seizure determined under Sub-Article (9) (a) of this Article.

13/ The power to issue a seizure order under this Article may be exercised only by the Director General or a tax officer specifically authorised by the Director General to issue seizure orders.

14/ Any property seized under this Article shall be held and accounted for only by the Authority and the property shall not be transferred to or given over to any other Government agency for any purpose whatsoever.

15/ Seizure of property pursuant to this Article shall be made in an amount proportionate to the tax liability of the taxpayer.

42. Preservation of Funds and Assets Deposited with Financial Institutions

1/ This Article applies when the Authority has reasonable cause to believe that the collection of tax owing by a taxpayer is in jeopardy and there is urgency in the collection of the tax.

2/ When this Article applies, the Authority may serve an administrative order on a financial institution requiring the financial institution to:

a) block the accounts of the taxpayer;

b) freeze access to any cash, valuables, precious metals, or other assets of the taxpayer in a safe deposit box held by the financial institution; and

c) provide information relating to the accounts or contents of the safe deposit box.

3/ An order served on a financial institution under Sub-Article (2) of this Article shall specify the following the name, address, and TIN of the taxpayer to which the order applies.

4/ When an order has been served under Sub-Article (2) of this Article, the Authority may make an immediate jeopardy assessment of the tax payable by the taxpayer for the current and any prior tax year.

5/ The Authority shall obtain a court authorisation for the order within 10 (Ten) days of service of the notice of the order on the financial institution.

6/ If there is no court authorisation of the order within 10 (Ten) days of service of notice of the order, the order shall lapse.

7/ A financial institution served with an order under Sub-Article (2) of this Article shall comply with the order from the date of service until the date that the order expires according to its terms or lapses under Sub-Article (6) of this Article.

8/ A financial institution that, without reasonable cause, fails to comply with an order served on the financial institution under Sub-Article (2) of this Article shall be personally liable for the amount specified in the order.

43. Recovery of Unpaid Tax From Third Parties

1/ If a taxpayer is liable for unpaid tax, the Authority may serve an administrative order (referred to as a "garnishee order") on a payer in respect of the taxpayer requiring the payer to pay the amount specified in the order to the Authority, being an amount that does not exceed the amount of the unpaid tax.

2/ When a garnishee order requires a payer to deduct amounts from a payment of salary, wages, or other similar remuneration payable at fixed intervals to the taxpayer, the amount required to be deducted by the payer from each payment shall not exceed one-third of the amount of each payment of salary, wages, or other remuneration (after the payment of income tax).

3/ A garnishee order may be served on a payer in relation to an amount in a joint account only when:

a) all the holders of the joint account have unpaid tax liabilities; or

b) the taxpayer can withdraw funds from the account (other than a partnership account) without the signature or authorisation of the other account holders.

4/ A payer shall pay the amount specified in a garnishee order by the date specified in the order, being a date that is not before the date that the amount owed by the payer to the taxpayer becomes due to the taxpayer or held on the taxpayer's behalf.

5/ A payer who claims to be unable to comply with a garnishee order may notify the Authority, in writing and within 7 (Seven) days of receiving the garnishee order, setting out the reasons for the payer's inability to comply with the order.

6/ When a payer serves a notice on the Authority under Sub-Article (5) of this Article, the Authority shall, by notice in writing:

a) accept the notification and cancel or amend the garnishee order; or

b) reject the notification.

7/ The Authority shall, by notice in writing to the payer, revoke or amend a garnishee order when the taxpayer has paid the whole or part of the tax due or has made an arrangement satisfactory to the Authority for payment of the tax.

8/ The Authority shall serve the taxpayer with a copy of an order or notice served on a payer under this Article.

9/ The Authority shall credit any amount paid by a payer under this Article against the tax owing by the taxpayer.

10/ A payer who, without reasonable cause, fails to comply with a garnishee order shall be personally liable for the amount specified in the notice.

11/ This Article shall not apply to any amount that, under the law of Ethiopia, cannot be the subject of attachment.

12/ In this Article, "payer", in respect of a taxpayer, means a person who:

a) owes or may subsequently owe money to the taxpayer;

b) holds or may subsequently hold money, for or on account of, the taxpayer;

c) holds money on account of some other person for payment to the taxpayer;

d) has authority from some other person to pay money to the taxpayer.

44. Departure Prohibition Order

1/ This Article shall apply to a person when the Authority has reasonable grounds to believe that the person may leave Ethiopia without:

a) tax that is or will become payable by the person being paid; or

b) tax that is or will become payable by a body in which the person is a manager or Company in which the person is a controlling member being paid.

2/ When this Article applies, the Authority may issue an order (referred to as a "departure prohibition order") prohibiting the Person from leaving Ethiopia until:

a) the Person, Body, Company makes payment in full of the tax payable or that will become payable by the Person, Body or Company; or

b) an arrangement satisfactory to the Authority for payment of the tax referred to in paragraph (a) of this Sub-Article.

3/ A departure prohibition order shall specify the following:

a) the name, address, and TIN of the Person to which the order applies; and

b) the amount of tax that is or will become payable by the Person, Body or Company.

4/ A departure prohibition order issued under Sub-Article (2) of this Article shall expire after 10 (Ten) days from the date of issue unless a court of competent jurisdiction, on application by the Authority, extends the order for the period determined by the court.

5/ The Authority shall serve a copy of a departure prohibition order on the Person named in the order, but the non-receipt of a copy of the order shall not invalidate any proceedings under this Article.

6/ On receipt of a departure prohibition order in relation to a Person, the Head of National Intelligence and Security Service shall take such measures as may be necessary to comply with the order including the seizure and retention of the Person's passport, certificate of identification, or any other document authorising the taxpayer to leave Ethiopia.

7/ If the Person, Body or Company pays the tax specified in the departure prohibition order or makes a satisfactory arrangement for payment of the tax, the Authority shall issue the Person with a departure certificate and production of the certificate to an officer of National Intelligence and Security Service shall be sufficient authority for the officer to allow the Person to leave Ethiopia subject to other immigration requirements being satisfied.

8/ No proceedings, criminal or civil, may be instituted or maintained against the Government, or a tax, customs, National Intelligence and Security Service, police, or other officer for anything lawfully done under this Article.

9/ A departure prohibition order may be issued only by the Director General or a tax officer specifically authorised by the Director General to issue departure prohibition orders.

45. Temporary Closure of Business

1/ This Article shall apply when a taxpayer regularly fails to:

a) maintain documents as required under a revenue law; or

b) pay tax by the due date.

2/ When this Article applies, the Authority may notify the taxpayer, in writing, of the intention to close down part or the whole of the business premises of the taxpayer for a temporary period not exceeding 14 (Fourteen) days, unless the taxpayer pays the tax due, or maintains documents as required within a period of 7 (Seven) days of service of the notice.

3/ If a taxpayer fails to comply with a notice under Sub-Article (2) of this Article, or fails to maintain the required documents, the Authority may issue an order (referred as a "closure order") for the closure of part or the whole of the business premises of the taxpayer for a period not exceeding 14 (Fourteen) days.

4/ The Authority may, at any time, enter any premises described in a closure order for the purposes of executing the order and may require a police officer to be present while a closure order is being executed.

5/ The Authority shall affix, in a conspicuous place on the front of the premises that have been closed under a closure order, a notice in the following words:

"CLOSED TEMPORARILY FOR NOT COMPLYING WITH TAX OBLIGATIONS BY ORDER OF THE AUTHORITY UNDER ARTICLE 45 OF THE FEDERAL TAX ADMINISTRATION PROCLAMATION".

6/ The Authority shall immediately arrange for the reopening of the premises if:

(a) the Director-General or authorised officer is satisfied that the taxpayer has put into place sufficient measures to ensure that documents are properly maintained in the future;

(b) the taxpayer pays the tax due.

7/ A closure order may be issued only by the Director General or a tax officer specifically authorised by the Director-General to issue closure orders.

46. Transferred Tax Liabilities

1/ When a taxpayer (referred to as the "transferor") has an unpaid tax liability in relation to a business conducted by the taxpayer and the taxpayer has transferred all or some of the assets of the business to a related person (referred to as the "transferee"), the transferee shall be personally liable for the unpaid tax liability (referred to as the "transferred liability") of the transferor in relation to the business.

2/ Sub-article (1) of this Article shall not preclude the Authority from recovering the whole or part of the transferred liability from the transferor.

47. Tax Payable by a Body

1/ When a body fails to pay tax by the due date, every person who is a manager of the body at the time of the failure or was a manager within 6 (Six) months prior to the failure shall be jointly and severally liable with the body for the unpaid tax.

2/ Sub-article (1) of this Article shall not apply to a person when:

a) the failure by the body to pay tax occurred without the person's consent or knowledge; and

b) having regard to the nature of the person's functions and all the circumstances, the person has exercised reasonable diligence to prevent the body from failing to pay tax.

48. Liability for Tax in the Case of Fraud or Evasion

1/ A certified auditor, certified public accountant, or public auditor who:

a) aided, abetted, counselled, or procured a taxpayer to commit fraud resulting in a tax shortfall or to evade tax;

b) was in any way knowingly concerned in, or was a party to, fraud resulting in a tax shortfall or tax evasion committed by a taxpayer, shall be jointly and severally liable with the taxpayer for the amount of the tax shortfall or evaded tax resulting from the fraud or evasion.

2/ If a certified auditor, certified public accountant, or public auditors liable under Sub-Article (1) of this Article, the Authority shall report the conduct to:

a) the Institute of Certified Public Accountants, the Accounting and Auditing Board of Ethiopia, or other body having authority for the licensing of the person and request the Board to withdraw the person's licence to practice; or

b) the licensing authority responsible for issuing business licences.

3/ In this Article, "tax shortfall" has the meaning in Article 109 of this Proclamation.

PART EIGHT
CREDIT, REFUND, AND RELEASE FROM TAX LIABILITY

49. Credit for Tax Payments

1/ Where the total amount of tax credits allowed to a taxpayer for withholding tax or advance tax payments of the taxpayer for a tax year exceed the income tax liability of the taxpayer for the year, the Authority shall apply the excess in the following order:

a) first, in payment of any tax (other than withholding tax) owing by the taxpayer under the Federal Income Tax Proclamation;

b) then in payment of tax owing by the taxpayer under any other tax law;

c) subject to Sub-Article (2) of this Article and on application by the taxpayer by notice in writing, then refund the remainder, if any, to the taxpayer within 90 (Ninety) days of the date that the taxpayer filed the tax declaration for the year to which the tax credits relate.

2/ With the written agreement of the taxpayer an amount referred to in Sub-Article (1) (c) of this Article may be carried forward for the payment of any future tax liability of the taxpayer under any tax law.

3/ If the Authority fails to pay a refund to a taxpayer as required under Sub-Article (1) (c) of this Article, the taxpayer shall be entitled to interest for the period commencing from the end of the ninety period until the refund is paid.

4/ The rate of interest under Sub-Article (3) of this Article shall be the highest commercial lending rate that prevailed in Ethiopia during the quarter before the commencement of the period specified in Sub-Article (3) of this Article.

50. Refund of Overpaid Tax

1/ Subject to Sub-Article (2) of this Article, when a taxpayer has overpaid tax under a tax law (other than as specified in Article 49 of this Proclamation), the taxpayer may apply to the Authority, in the approved form, for a refund of the overpaid tax within three years after the date on which the tax was paid.

2/ This Article applies only when a refund of tax does not require the Authority to make an amended assessment.

3/ The Authority shall serve notice, in writing, to a taxpayer of the decision on an application by the taxpayer under Sub-Article (1) of this Article.

4/ When a taxpayer has made an application under Sub-Article (1) of this Article and the Authority is satisfied that the taxpayer has overpaid tax under the tax law, the Authority shall apply the amount of the overpayment in the following order:

a) first, in payment of any other tax (other than withholding tax) owing by the taxpayer under the tax law;

b) then in payment of tax owing by the taxpayer under any other tax law;

c) subject to Sub-Article (5) of this Article, then refund the remainder, if any, to the taxpayer within 45 (Forty-five) days of making the determination that the taxpayer is entitled to the refund.

5/ With the written agreement of the taxpayer an amount referred to in Sub-Article (4) (c) of this Article may be carried forward for the payment of any future tax liability of the taxpayer under any tax law.

6/ If the Authority has refunded tax under this Article to a taxpayer in error, the taxpayer shall, on notice of demand by the Authority, repay the amount erroneously refunded by the date specified in the notice.

7/ If a refund has been erroneously paid due to an error made by the taxpayer in claiming the refund, the taxpayer shall be liable to pay late payment interest at the rate specified in Article 37 (2) of this Proclamation computed for the period commencing on the date that the refund was erroneously paid and ending on the date that the refund was repaid.

8/ An amount of refund that a taxpayer is required to repay under Sub-Article (7) of this Article shall be treated as tax payable by a taxpayer for the purposes of this Proclamation.

51. Relief in Cases of Serious Hardship

1/ This Article applies if the Minister is satisfied that:

a) the payment of the full amount of tax owing by a taxpayer will cause serious hardship to the taxpayer due to natural cause, or supervening calamity or disaster, or in cases of personal hardship not attributable to the negligence or any failure on the part of the taxpayer; or

b) owing to the death of a taxpayer, the payment of the full amount of tax owing by the deceased taxpayer will cause serious hardship to the dependents of the deceased taxpayer.

2/ Subject to Sub-Article (3) of this Article, if this Article applies, the Minister may release the taxpayer or the executor of the estate of a deceased taxpayer wholly or in part from payment of the tax due and any late payment interest payable in respect of the tax due.

3/ The relief to be granted to a tax payer pursuant to Sub-Article (1) of this article shall be within the limits laid down by the regulation to be issued by the council of ministers.

4/ If a decision of the Minister to release a taxpayer or the executor of the estate of a deceased taxpayer from tax is based on fraudulent or misleading information, the tax liability released shall be reinstated and this Proclamation shall apply as if the taxpayer was never released from the liability to pay the tax.

5/ The Minister shall maintain a public record of each amount of tax and interest released under this Article together with the reasons thereof and the record of tax and interest released shall be reported to the Auditor General semi annually.

PART NINE
TAX DISPUTES

52. Statement of Reasons

When the Authority has refused an application made by a person under a tax law, the notice of refusal shall include a statement of reasons for the refusal.

53. Finality of Tax and Appealable Decisions

1/ Except in proceedings under this Part:

a) a tax or appealable decision shall be final and conclusive, and cannot be disputed in the Commission or a Court, or in any other proceedings on any ground whatsoever;

b) the production of a notice of a tax assessment or a determination, or a document certified by the Authority as a copy of a notice of a tax assessment or a determination shall be conclusive evidence of the due making of the assessment or a determination and that the amount and particulars of the assessment or a determination are correct; and

c) in the case of a self-assessment, the production of the original self-assessment declaration or a document certified by the Authority as a copy of such declaration shall be conclusive evidence of the contents of the declaration.

2/ When the Authority serves a notice of a tax assessment or a determination on a taxpayer electronically, the reference in Sub-Article (1) (b) of this Article to a copy of the notice of assessment or determination includes a document certified by the Authority identifying the assessment or determination and specifying the details of the electronic transmission of the assessment or determination.

3/ When a taxpayer has filed a self-assessment declaration electronically, the reference in Sub-Article (1) (c) of this Article to a copy of the declaration includes a document certified by the Authority identifying the declaration and specifying the details of the electronic transmission of the declaration.

4/ In this Article, "determination" means a decision referred to in paragraphs (b), (c), (d), (f), (g) or (h) of the definition of "tax decision" in Article 2 (34) of this Proclamation.

54. Notice of Objection to a Tax Decision

1/ A taxpayer dissatisfied with a tax decision may file a notice of objection to the decision, in writing, with the Authority within 21 (Twenty-one) days after service of the notice of the decision.

2/ When the tax decision objected to is an amended assessment, a taxpayer's right to object to the amended assessment shall be limited to the alterations, reductions, and additions made in it to the original assessment.

3/ A notice of objection shall be treated as validly filed by a taxpayer under Sub-Article (1) of this Article only when the following conditions are satisfied:

a) the notice of objection states precisely the grounds of the taxpayer's objection to the tax decision, the amendments that the taxpayer believes are required to be made to correct the decision, and the reasons for making those amendments;

b) when the objection relates to a tax assessment, the taxpayer has paid any tax due under the tax assessment that is not disputed by the taxpayer in the objection; and

c) if a tax payer prefers to pay the tax assessed on protest, after the tax in dispute is fully paid.

4/ When the Authority considers that a notice of objection filed by a taxpayer has not been validly filed, the Authority shall immediately serve written notice on the taxpayer stating the following:

a) the reasons why the objection has not been validly filed; and

b) that the objection will lapse unless a valid objection is filed by the later of:

(1) 21 (Twenty-one) days from the date of service of the notice of the tax decision to which the objection relates; or

(2) 10 (Ten) days from the date of service of the notice under this Sub-Article.

5/ The Authority shall serve written notice on the taxpayer when an objection shall be treated as lapsed under Sub-Article (4) of this Article.

6/ A taxpayer may apply, in writing and before the end of the objection period in Sub-Article (1) of this Article, to the Authority for an extension of time to file a notice of objection.

7/ When an application has been made under Sub-Article (6) of this Article, the Authority may allow an extension of time for a maximum of 10 (Ten) days from the end of the objection period in Sub-Article (1) of this Article when satisfied that:

a) owing to absence from Ethiopia, sickness, or other reasonable cause, the taxpayer was prevented from lodging the notice of objection within the period specified in Sub-Article (1) or (4) of this Article; and

b) there has been no unreasonable delay on the part of the taxpayer in lodging the notice of objection.

55. Making Objection Decisions

1/ The Authority shall establish a review department as a permanent office within the Authority to provide an independent review of objections validly filed under Article 54 of this Proclamation and make recommendations to the Authority as to the decision to be taken on an objection.

2/ The Authority shall issue a Directive specifying the procedures for reviewing an objection including hearings, and the basis for making recommendations to the Authority and the decision making procedure.

3/ If, in considering an objection to a tax assessment, the review department is of the view that the amount of tax assessed should be increased, the review department shall recommend to the Authority that the tax assessment be referred to the tax officer for reconsideration.

4/ After having regard to the recommendations of the review department, the Authority shall make a decision to allow the objection in whole or part, or disallow it, and the Authority's decision shall be referred to as an "objection decision".

5/ The Authority shall serve notice, in writing, of an objection decision on the taxpayer and take all steps necessary to give effect to the decision, including, in the case of an objection to a tax assessment, the making of an amended assessment.

6/ A notice of an objection decision shall contain a statement of findings on the material facts, the reasons for the decision and the right to appeal to the Commission.

7/ When the Authority has not made an objection decision within 180 (One Hundred Eighty) days from the date that the taxpayer filed notice of the objection, the tax payer may appeal to the Tax Appeal Commission within 30 (Thirty) days after the end of the 180 (One Hundred Eighty) days period.

56. Appeal to Tax Appeal Commission

1/ A taxpayer dissatisfied with an appealable decision may file a notice of appeal with the Tax Appeal Commission in accordance with Article 88 of this Proclamation.

2/ A notice of appeal to the Tax Appeal Commission in relation to an objection to a tax assessment shall be treated as validly filed by a taxpayer only if the taxpayer has paid to the Authority 50% of the tax in dispute under the tax assessment.

3/ The reference to "tax in dispute" in Sub-Article (2) of this Article shall not include penalty and late payment interest payable in respect of the disputed tax.

4/ The Tax Appeal Commission may issue a Directive providing for applications for an extension of time to file a notice of appeal under Sub-Article (1) of this Article.

57. Appeal to the Federal High Court

1/ A party to a proceeding before the Commission who is dissatisfied with the decision of the Commission may, within 30 (Thirty) days after being served with notice of the decision, file a notice of appeal to the Federal High Court.

2/ The Federal High Court may, on an application in writing by a party to a proceeding before the Tax Appeal Commission, extend the time for lodging a notice of appeal under Sub-Article (1) of this Article.

3/ A notice of appeal to the Federal High Court by a taxpayer in relation to an objection to a tax assessment shall be treated as validly filed only if the taxpayer has paid 75% of the tax in dispute under the assessment.

4/ An appeal to the Federal High Court shall be made on a question of law only, and the notice of appeal shall state the question of law that will be raised on the appeal.

5/ The Federal High Court shall hear the appeal and may:

a) decide to affirm the decision of the Commission;

b) decide to set aside the decision of the Commission:

(1) make a decision in substitution of the decision of the Commission; or

(2) remit the decision to the Commission or Authority for reconsideration in accordance with the directions of the Court; or

c) decide to dismiss the appeal; or

d) make any other decision the court thinks appropriate.

6/ The reference to "tax in dispute" in Sub-Article (3) of this Article means the tax determined by the Tax Appeal Commission to be payable that is disputed by the taxpayer in the notice of appeal, but does not include penalty and late payment interest payable in respect of the disputed tax.

58. Appeal to the Federal Supreme Court

1/ A party to a proceeding before the Federal High Court who is dissatisfied with the decision of the Federal High Court may, within 30 (Thirty) days after being served with notice of the decision, file a notice of appeal to the Federal Supreme Court.

2/ The Federal Supreme Court may, on an application in writing by a party to a proceeding before the Federal High Court, extend the time for lodging a notice of appeal under Sub-Article (1) of this Article.

59. Burden of Proof

In any proceeding under this Part in relation to a tax decision, the burden shall be on the taxpayer to prove that the tax decision is incorrect.

60. Implementation of Decision of Commission or Court

1/ The Authority shall, within 30 (Thirty) days after being served with notice of the decision of the Tax Appeal Commission, Federal High Court, or Federal Supreme Court, take such action, including serving the taxpayer with notice of an amended assessment, as is necessary to give effect to the decision.

2/ The time limit in Article 28 of this Proclamation for amending a tax assessment shall not apply to an amendment to give effect to a decision of the Tax Appeal Commission or a Court.

PART TEN
INFORMATION COLLECTION AND ENFORCEMENT

61. Tax Clearance

1/ A taxpayer may apply to the Authority, in the approved form, for a tax clearance certificate.

2/ The Authority shall issue a tax clearance certificate to a taxpayer within 14 (Fourteen) days of the taxpayer filing an application under Sub-Article (1) of this Article if satisfied that the taxpayer has fulfilled its obligations to pay tax under the tax laws as determined under a Directive issued by the Authority.

3/ If a taxpayer applying under Sub-Article (1) of this Article was not registered for tax for the preceding year or years, the Authority shall issue a tax clearance certificate to the taxpayer within 14 (Fourteen) days of the taxpayer lodging the application stating that the taxpayer is registered with the Authority.

4/ No Ministry, Municipality, Department or Office of the Federal or a State Government, or other Government body shall issue or renew any licence to a taxpayer, or allow the taxpayer to participate in a public tender, unless the taxpayer produces a tax clearance certificate.

5/ If the Authority refuses to issue a taxpayer with a tax clearance certificate, the Authority shall provide the taxpayer with notice of the decision within 14 (Fourteen) days of the taxpayer lodging an application under Sub-Article (1) of this Article.

62. Filing of Memorandum and Articles of Association

1/ A body shall file with the Authority a copy of the memorandum of association, articles of association, statute, partnership agreement, or other document of formation or registration within 30 (Thirty) days of the date of registration of the body.

2/ A body shall notify the Authority, in writing, of any change made to a document referred to in Sub-Article (1) of this Article within 30 (Thirty) days of the change being made.

63. Public Auditors

1/ Auditors shall file with the Authority the audit report of their clients within 3 (Three) months from the date of providing the report to their client.

2/ If an auditor fails to comply with Sub-Article (1) of this Article, the Authority shall notify the Accounting and Auditing Board of Ethiopia or Institute of Certified Public Accountants of Ethiopia of the failure and may request the Board or the Institute to withdraw the auditor's licence.

3/ In this Article, "auditor" means a certified auditor and a public auditor as defined under the Financial Reporting Proclamation.

64. Notification of Services Contract with Non-resident

1/ A person who enters into an Ethiopian source services contract with a non-resident shall notify the Authority, in the approved form, within 30 (Thirty) days of the earlier of the signing of the contract or the commencement of performance under the contract.

2/ In this Article, "Ethiopian source services contract" means a contract (other than an employment contract) under which the primary purpose is the performance of services, whether or not goods are also provided, which services give rise to Ethiopian source income.

65. Notice to Obtain Information or Evidence

1/ For the purposes of administering any tax law, the Authority may, by notice in writing, require any person whether or not liable for tax:

a) to furnish, by the time specified in the notice, such information relating to the person's or any other person's tax affairs as specified in the notice;

b) to present himself at the time and place designated in the notice to give evidence concerning the person's or any other person's tax affairs as specified in the notice;

c) to produce, by the time specified in the notice, all documents in the person's custody or under the person's control relating to the person's or any other person's tax affairs as specified in the notice.

2/ When a notice under Sub-Article (1) of this Article requires the production of a document, it shall be sufficient if the document is described in the notice with reasonable certainty.

3/ This Article shall have effect despite:

a) any law relating to privilege or the public interest with respect to the giving of information or the production of any documents (including in electronic format); or

b) any contractual duty of confidentiality.

66. Power to Enter and Search

1/ For the purposes of administering any tax law, the Authority:

a) shall have, at all times and without notice, full and free access to the following:

(1) any premises, place, goods, or property;

(2) any document;

(3) any data storage device;

b) may make an extract or copy of any document, including in electronic format, to which access is obtained under paragraph (a) of this Sub-Article;

c) may seize any document that, in the opinion of the Authority, affords evidence that may be material in determining the tax liability of a taxpayer and may retain the document for as long as the document may be required for determining a taxpayer's tax liability or for any proceeding under a tax law;

d) may, if a hard copy or copy on a data storage media of information stored on a data storage device is not provided, seize and retain the device for as long as is necessary to copy the information required.

2/ The powers in Sub-Article (1) of this Article may be exercised only by the Director General or a tax officer specifically authorised by the Director General to exercise such powers.

3/ A tax officer shall not enter or remain on any premises or place if, upon request by the owner or lawful occupier, the officer is unable to produce the Director General's written authorisation permitting the officer to exercise powers under Sub-Article (1) of this Article.

4/ The owner or lawful occupier of the premises or place to which an exercise of power under Sub-Article (1) of this Article relates shall provide all reasonable facilities and assistance to the Authority including:

(a) answering questions, either orally or in writing, relating to any document on the premises or at the place, whether on a data storage device or otherwise; or

(b) providing access to decryption information necessary to decrypt data to which access is sought under this Article.

5/ A person whose document or data storage device has been seized under Sub-Article (1) of this Article may examine it and make copies, including electronic copies of documents on a data storage device, at his own expense, during normal office hours and on such terms and conditions as the Authority may specify.

6/ The Director General or a tax officer authorised by Director General shall sign for any document or data storage device removed and retained under this Article.

7/ This Article shall have effect despite:

a) any law relating to privilege (including legal professional privilege) or the public interest with respect to access to premises or places, or the production of any property or document (including in electronic format); or

b) any contractual duty of confidentiality.

67. Implementation of Mutual Administrative Assistance Agreements

1/ The Minister may, on behalf of the Government, enter into, amend, or terminate a mutual administrative assistance agreement with a foreign government or governments.

2/ If there is any conflict between the terms of a mutual administrative assistance agreement having legal effect in Ethiopia and a tax law, the mutual administrative assistance agreement prevails.

3/ If a tax treaty or mutual administrative assistance agreement having legal effect in Ethiopia provides for exchange of information, or reciprocal assistance in the recovery of tax or the service of process, the Authority shall use the powers available under this Proclamation or any other law to meet Ethiopia's obligations under the treaty or agreement on the basis that a reference in this Proclamation or other law:

a) to "tax", includes a foreign tax to which the exchange of information or reciprocal assistance relates;

b) to "unpaid tax", includes an amount specified in paragraph (a) of this Sub-Article that has not been paid by the due date;

c) to "taxpayer", includes a person liable for an amount specified in paragraph (a) of this Sub-Article; and

d) to "tax law", includes the law under which a foreign tax specified in paragraph (a) of this Sub-Article is imposed.

4/ In this Article:

a) "international agreement" means an agreement between the Government of the Federal Democratic Republic of Ethiopia and a foreign government or governments;

b) "mutual administrative assistance agreement" means a tax information exchange agreement or other international agreement for mutual administrative assistance in relation to taxation matters;

c) "tax treaty" means an international agreement relating to the avoidance of double taxation and the prevention of fiscal evasion.

PART ELEVEN
ADVANCE RULINGS

CHAPTER ONE   PUBLIC RULINGS

68. Binding Public Rulings

1/ The Ministry may make a public ruling in accordance with Article 69 of this Proclamation setting out the Ministry's interpretation on the application of a tax law.

2/ A public ruling made in accordance with Article 69 of this Proclamation shall be binding on the Ministry and the Authority until withdrawn.

3/ A public ruling shall not be binding on a taxpayer.

69. Making a Public Ruling

1/ The Ministry shall make a public ruling by publishing the public ruling on the official website of the Ministry.

2/ A public ruling shall state that it is a public ruling and shall have a heading specifying the subject matter of the ruling by which it can be identified and an identification number.

3/ A public ruling shall have effect from the date specified in the public ruling or, when no date is specified, from the date the ruling is published on the official website of the Ministry.

4/ A public ruling sets out the Ministry's opinion on the application of a tax law in the circumstances specified in the ruling and is not a decision of the Ministry for the purposes of this Proclamation or any other law.

70. Withdrawal of a Public Ruling

1/ The Ministry may withdraw a public ruling, in whole or part, by publishing notice of the withdrawal on the official website of the Ministry and the withdrawal shall have effect from the later of:

a) the date specified in the notice of withdrawal; or

b) the date that the notice of withdrawal of the ruling is published on the official website of the Ministry.

2/ When legislation is passed, or the Ministry makes another public ruling that is inconsistent with an existing public ruling, the existing public ruling shall be treated as withdrawn to the extent of the inconsistency from the date of application of the inconsistent legislation or public ruling.

3/ A public ruling that has been withdrawn, in whole or part:

a) shall continue to apply to a transaction commenced before the public ruling was withdrawn;

b) shall not apply to a transaction commenced after the public ruling was withdrawn to the extent that the ruling is withdrawn.

CHAPTER TWO   PRIVATE RULINGS

71. Binding Private Rulings

1/ A taxpayer may apply to the Ministry for a private ruling setting out the Ministry's position regarding the application of a tax law to a transaction entered into, or proposed to be entered into, by the taxpayer.

2/ An application under this Article shall be in writing and:

a) include full details of the transaction to which the application relates together with all documents relevant to the transaction;

b) specify precisely the question on which the ruling is required; and

c) give a full statement setting out the opinion of the taxpayer as to the application of the relevant tax law to the transaction.

3/ Subject to Article 72 of this Proclamation, the Ministry shall, within 60 (Sixty) days of receipt of the application under this Article, issue a private ruling on the question to the taxpayer.

4/ If the taxpayer has made a full and true disclosure of all aspects of the transaction relevant to the making of a private ruling and the transaction has proceeded in all material respects as described in the taxpayer's application for the private ruling, the private ruling shall be binding on the Ministry and the Authority.

5/ A private ruling shall not be binding on a taxpayer.

6/ When a private ruling is inconsistent with a public ruling that is in force at the time that the private ruling is made, the private ruling shall have priority to the extent of the inconsistency.

72. Refusing an Application for a Private Ruling

1/ The Ministry may refuse an application by a taxpayer for a private ruling if any of the following applies:

a) the Authority or the Ministry, as the case maybe, has already decided the question that is the subject of the application in the following:

(1) a notice of a tax assessment served on the taxpayer;

(2) a public ruling made under Article 69 of this Proclamation that is in force;

(3) a private ruling published under Article 75 of this Proclamation that is in force.

b) the application relates to a question that is the subject of a tax audit in relation to the taxpayer, an objection filed by the taxpayer, or an application by the taxpayer under Article 29 of this Proclamation for an amendment to a self-assessment;

c) the application is frivolous or vexatious;

d) the transaction to which the application relates has not been carried out and there are reasonable grounds to believe that the transaction will not be carried out;

e) the tax payer has not provided the Ministry with sufficient information to make a private ruling;

f) in the opinion of the Ministry, it would be unreasonable to comply with the application, having regard to the resources needed to comply with the application and any other matters the Ministry considers relevant;

g) the making of the ruling involves the application of a tax avoidance provision.

2/ The Ministry shall serve the taxpayer with a written notice of a decision to refuse to make a private ruling under this Article.

73. Making a Private Ruling

1/ The Ministry shall make a private ruling by serving written notice of the private ruling on the taxpayer and the ruling shall remain in force for the period specified in the ruling or, if earlier, withdrawn under Article 74 of this Proclamation.

2/ The Ministry may make a private ruling on the basis of assumptions about a future event or other matter as considered appropriate.

3/ A private ruling shall state that it is a private ruling, set out the question ruled on, and identify the following:

a) the taxpayer;

b) the tax law relevant to the private ruling;

c) the tax period to which the ruling applies;

d) the transaction to which the ruling relates;

e) any assumptions on which the ruling is based.

4/ A private ruling sets out the Ministry's opinion on the question raised in the ruling application and is not a decision of the Ministry for the purposes of the Proclamation or any other law.

74. Withdrawal of a Private Ruling

1/ The Ministry may, for reasonable cause, withdraw a private ruling, in whole or part, by written notice served on the taxpayer and the withdrawal shall have effect from the date specified in the notice of withdrawal.

2/ When legislation is passed, or the Ministry makes a public ruling that is inconsistent with an existing private ruling, the private ruling shall be treated as withdrawn to the extent of the inconsistency from the date of application of the inconsistent legislation or public ruling.

3/ A private ruling that has been withdrawn:

a) shall continue to apply to a transaction of the taxpayer commenced before the ruling was withdrawn; and

b) shall not apply to a transaction of the taxpayer commenced after the ruling was withdrawn to the extent the ruling is withdrawn.

75. Publication of Private Rulings

1/ The Ministry shall publish a private ruling made under Article 73 of this Proclamation on the official website of the Ministry except that the identity of the taxpayer to whom the ruling relates and any confidential commercial information mentioned in the ruling shall not be indicated in the publication.

2/ Subject to Sub-Article (3) of this Article, any taxpayer may rely upon a ruling published under Sub-Article (1) of this Article as a statement binding on the Ministry and the Authority with respect to the application of the relevant tax law to the facts set out in the ruling and for the tax period covered by the ruling.

3/ When a private ruling has been withdrawn in accordance with Article 74 of this Proclamation, the Ministry shall immediately publish a notice of withdrawal on the official website of the Ministry stating that the ruling shall cease to be binding with effect from the date determined under Article 74 of this Proclamation.

CHAPTER THREE   OTHER ADVICE OF THE MINISTRY

76. Other Advice Provided by the Authority

No publication or other advice (oral or in writing) provided by the Ministry shall be binding on the Ministry or the Authority except a public ruling or private ruling binding under this Part.

PART TWELVE
COMMUNICATIONS, FORMS, AND NOTICES

77. Working Language

Amharic shall be the Federal language of the tax laws; and the Authority may refuse to recognise any communication or document that is not conducted in a Amharic.

78. Forms and Notice

1/ Forms, notices, tax declarations, statements, tables, and other documents approved or published by the Authority may be in such form as the Authority determines for the efficient administration of the tax laws and, except as required under a tax law, publishing of such documents on the official website of the Authority shall not be required.

2/ The Authority shall make the documents referred to in Sub-Article (1) of this Article available to the public at offices of the Authority and at any other locations, or by mail, electronically, or such other means, as the Authority may determine.

79. Approved Form

1/ A tax declaration, application, notice, statement, or other document shall be treated as filed by a taxpayer in the approved form when the document:

a) is in the form approved by the Authority for that type of document;

b) contains the information (including any attached documents) as required by the form; and

c) is signed as required by the form.

2/ The Authority shall immediately notify a taxpayer, in writing, when a tax declaration, application, notice, statement, or other document filed by the person is not in the approved form.

3/ The Authority may decide to accept a document that is not filed in the approved form if the document has been filed in a form that contains substantially the information required by the approved form for the document.

80. Manner of Filing Documents with the Authority

1/ A taxpayer required by the Authority under Article 82 (2) of this Proclamation to file a tax declaration, application, notice, statement, or other document with the Authority electronically shall do so unless authorised by the Authority by notice in writing to file the document in accordance with Sub-Article (2) of this Article.

2/ When Sub-Article (1) of this Article does not apply to a taxpayer, the taxpayer shall file a tax declaration, application, notice, statement, or other document with the Authority under a tax law by personal delivery or normal post.

81. Service of Notices

1/ A notice or other document issued, served, or given by the Authority under a tax law to a taxpayer shall be communicated in writing as follows:

a) by delivering it personally to the taxpayer or the taxpayer's tax representative or licensed tax agent, or, if no person can be found to accept service, by affixing the notice to the door or other available part of the taxpayer's place of business or residence in Ethiopia;

b) by sending it by registered post to the taxpayer's usual or last known place of business or residence in Ethiopia;

c) by transmitting it to the taxpayer electronically in accordance with Article 82 (3) of this Proclamation.

2/ When none of the methods of service specified in Sub-Article (1) of this Article are effective, service may be discharged by publication in any newspaper in which court notices may be advertised with the cost of publication charged to the taxpayer.

3/ The validity of service of a notice or other document under a tax law shall not be challenged after the notice or document has been wholly or partly complied with.

82. Application of Electronic Tax System

1/ Despite any other provisions of this Proclamation, the Authority may authorise the following to be done electronically through a computer system or mobile electronic device:

a) the lodging of an application for registration or for a TIN under a tax law;

b) the filing of a tax declaration or other document under a tax law;

c) the payment of tax or other amounts under a tax law;

d) the payment of a refund under a tax law;

e) the service of any documents by the Authority;

f) the doing of any other act or thing that is required or permitted to be done under a tax law.

2/ Subject to Sub-Article (4) of this Article, the Authority may direct that a taxpayer shall do anything referred to in Sub-Article (1) of this Article electronically through the use of a computer system or mobile electronic device.

3/ Subject to Sub-Article (4) of this Article, the Authority may do anything referred to in Sub-Article (1) of this Article electronically through the use of a computer system or mobile electronic device.

4/ Sub-articles (2) and (3) of this Article shall not apply to a taxpayer if the Authority is satisfied that the taxpayer does not have the capacity to receive or make communications or payments electronically.

5/ A taxpayer who files a tax declaration and pays tax electronically under this Article shall continue to do so unless otherwise authorised by the Authority.

83. Due Date for Filing a Document or Payment of Tax

If the due date for:

1/ filing a tax declaration, application, notice, statement, or other document;

2/ the payment of tax; or

3/ taking any other action under a tax law;

falls on a Saturday, Sunday, or public holiday in Ethiopia, the due date shall be the following business day.

84. Defect Not to Affect Validity of Notices

1/ This Article shall apply when:

a) a notice of a tax assessment or any other document has been served on a taxpayer under a tax law;

b) the notice is, in substance and effect, in conformity with, or is consistent with the intent and meaning of, the tax law under which the notice has been made; and

c) the tax payer assessed, intended to be assessed, or affected by the notice, is designated in the notice according to common intent and understanding.

2/ When this Article applies:

a) provided the notice of the tax assessment or other document has been properly served, the notice shall not be affected by reason that any of the provisions of the tax law under which the notice has been made have not been complied with;

b) the notice of the tax assessment or other document shall not be quashed or deemed to be void or voidable for want of form; and

c) the notice of the tax assessment or other document shall not be affected by reason of any mistake, defect, or omission therein.

3/ A tax assessment shall not be voided by reason of:

a) a mistake in the tax assessment as to the name of the taxpayer assessed, the description of any income or other amount, or the amount of tax charged;

b) any variance between the tax assessment and the duly served notice of the tax assessment; provided the mistake or variance is not likely to deceive or mislead the taxpayer assessed.

85. Correction of Errors

When a notice of a tax assessment or other document served by the Authority on a taxpayer under a tax law contains a clerical, arithmetic, or any other error that does not involve a dispute as to the interpretation of the law or facts of the case, the Authority may, for the purposes of correcting the mistake, amend the assessment or other document any time before the earlier of 5 (Five) years from the date of service of the notice of the tax assessment or other document.

PART THIRTEEN
TAX APPEAL COMMISSION

86. Establishment of Tax Appeal Commission

1/ The Tax Appeal Commission is hereby established to hear appeals against appealable decisions.

2/ The president of the Commission shall be appointed by the Prime Minister.

3/ The Commission shall be accountable to the Prime Minister.

87. Appointment of Members to the Commission

1/ The Prime Minister shall appoint such number of members to the Commission as the Prime Minister considers necessary having regard to the needs of the Commission.

2/ Subject to Sub-Article (3) of this Article, an individual may be appointed as a member to the Commission if the individual satisfies any one of the following:

a) the individual is a lawyer with significant experience in tax or commercial matters;

b) the individual is a member of the Institute of Certified Public Accountants with significant experience in tax matters;

c) the individual has previously been engaged as a tax officer with significant technical and administrative experience in tax matters;

d) the individual has special knowledge, experience, or skills relevant to the functions of the Commission.

3/ The following individuals shall not be appointed as a member of the Commission:

a) a currently serving tax officer or an individual who has ceased to be a tax officer for a period of less than two years;

b) an individual who has been liable for a penalty or convicted of an offence under a tax law relating to tax avoidance or evasion;

c) an individual who has been convicted of a crime of corruption under the Corruption Crimes Proclamation or any other law;

d) an individual who is an un discharged bankrupt.

4/ A member of the Commission:

a) may be appointed as either a full-time or part-time member;

b) shall be appointed for a term of 3 years and shall be eligible for re-appointment;

c) shall hold office on such terms and conditions, including in relation to remuneration and attendance fees, as the Prime Minister determines.

5/ The appointment of an individual as a member of the Commission shall terminate if:

a) the individual becomes employed or engaged as a tax officer;

b) the individual is liable for a penalty or convicted of an offence under a tax law relating to tax avoidance or evasion;

c) the individual is convicted of a crime of corruption under the Corruption Crimes Proclamation or any other law;

d) the individual becomes an un discharged bankrupt;

e) the individual resigns by notice in writing to the Prime Minister;

f) the individual's term of appointment comes to an end and the individual is not reappointed as a member of the Commission; or

g) the individual is removed by the Prime Minister, by notice in writing, for inability to perform the duties of office or for proven misconduct.

6/ No member of the Commission shall be liable to any action or suit for any act or omission done in the proper execution of the member's duties under this Part.

88. Notice of Appeal

1/ A person may appeal an appealable decision by filing a notice of appeal against the decision with the Commission in the approved form and within 30 (Thirty) days of service of notice of the decision.

2/ A notice of appeal shall include a statement of reasons for the appeal.

3/ The Commission may, on an application in writing and if good cause is shown, extend the time for lodging a notice of appeal under Sub-Article (1) of this Article.

4/ The Commission may issue a Directive specifying the procedure for dealing with applications for an extension of time to file a notice of appeal.

5/ In this Article, "approved form" means the form approved by the President of the Commission for notices of appeal.

89. Authority to File Documents with the Commission

1/ The Authority shall, within 30 (Thirty) days of being served with a copy of a notice of appeal to the Commission or within such further time as the Commission may allow, file with the Commission:

a) the notice of the appealable decision to which the notice of appeal relates;

b) a statement setting out the reasons for the decision if these are not set out in the notice referred to in paragraph (a) of this Sub-Article;

c) any other document relevant to the Commission's review of the decision.

2/ If the Commission is not satisfied with a statement filed under Sub-Article (1)(b) of this

Article, the Commission may, by written notice, require the Authority to file, within the time specified in the notice, a further statement of reasons.

3/ If the Commission is of the opinion that other documents may be relevant to an appeal, the Commission may, by written notice, require the Authority to file the documents with the Commission within the time specified in the notice.

4/ The Authority shall give the person appealing a copy of any statement or document filed with the Commission under this Article.

90. Proceedings of the Commission

1/ The President of the Commission shall serve as member of one of the panels of the Commission. The President of the Commission shall assign a member or members to the hearing of an appeal as the President considers appropriate having regard to the issues raised by the appeal.

2/ The Prime Minister may issue a Directive for the conduct of proceedings by the Commission.

3/ A member of the Commission who has a material, pecuniary, or other interest in any proceeding that could conflict with the proper performance of the member's functions shall disclose the interest to the President who must record the interest, and the member shall not take part in the proceeding.

4/ The President of the Commission may delegate authority to a Regional Tax Appeal Commission to hear any appeal under Article 88 of this Proclamation.

91. Decision of the Commission

1/ The Commission shall hear and determine an appeal and make a decision as set out in Sub-Article (5) or (7) of this Article.

2/ The Commission shall decide an appeal within 120 (One Hundred Twenty) days after the notice of appeal was filed.

3/ The President of the Commission may, by notice in writing to the parties to an appeal, extend the period for deciding the appeal for a period not exceeding 60 (Sixty) days having regard to the complexity of the issues in the case and the interests of justice.

4/ A failure by the Commission to comply with Sub-Article (2) or (3) of this Article shall not affect the validity of a decision made by the Commission on the appeal.

5/ If an appeal relates to a tax assessment, the Commission may make a decision to:

a) affirm, or reduce, or otherwise amend the tax assessment; or

b) remit the tax assessment to the Authority for reconsideration in accordance with the directions of the Commission.

6/ If, in considering an appeal relating to a tax assessment, the Commission is of the view that the amount of tax assessed should be increased, the Commission shall remit the tax assessment to the Authority in accordance with Sub-Article (5) (b) of this Article.

7/ If an appeal relates to any other appealable decision, the Commission may make a decision to affirm, vary, or set aside the decision, or remit the decision to the Authority for reconsideration in accordance with the directions of the Commission.

8/ The Commission shall serve a copy of the decision on an appeal on each party to the appeal within 7 (Seven) days of the making of the decision.

9/ The Commission's decision shall include the reasons for the decision and the findings on material questions of fact, and reference to the evidence or other material on which those findings were based.

10/ The decision of the Commission on an appeal shall come into operation upon the giving of the decision or on such other date as may be specified by the Commission in the notice of the decision.

11/ If the decision of the Commission is in favour of the taxpayer, the Authority shall take such steps as are necessary to implement the decision, including serving notice of an amended assessment, within 30 (Thirty) days of receiving notice of the decision under Sub-Article (8) of this Article.

92. Administration of the Commission

1/ The President of the Commission shall be responsible for managing the administrative affairs of the Commission.

2/ The Commission shall have a Registrar and such other staff as the President determines.

3/ The Registrar of the Commission shall have the power to do all things necessary or convenient to be done for the purpose of assisting the President under Sub-Article (1) of this Article and may act on behalf of the President in relation to the administrative affairs of the Commission.

93. Finances

1/ The budget of the Commission shall be allocated by the Government.

2/ The Commission shall keep complete and accurate books of account.

3/ The books of account and other financial documents of the Commission shall be audited by the Auditor-General or by an auditor designated by the Auditor-General.

94. Annual Report of the Commission

1/ The President of the Commission shall prepare a report of the affairs of the Commission for each fiscal year.

2/ A report under Sub-Article (1) of this Article for a fiscal year shall be submitted to the Prime Minister within three months after the end of the fiscal year.

PART FOURTEEN
LICENSING OF TAX AGENTS

95. Application for Tax Agent's Licence

1/ An individual, partnership, or company wishing to provide tax agent services may apply to the Authority, in the approved form, for licensing as a tax agent.

2/ In this Part, "tax agent services" means:

a) the preparation of tax declarations on behalf of taxpayers;

b) the preparation of notices of objection on behalf of taxpayers;

c) the provision of advice to taxpayers on the application of the tax laws;

d) representing taxpayers in their dealings with the Authority;

e) the transaction of any other business on behalf of taxpayers with the Authority.

96. Licensing of Tax Agents

1/ The Authority shall issue a tax agent's licence to an applicant under Article 95 of this Proclamation who is an individual when satisfied that the applicant is a fit and proper person to provide tax agent services.

2/ The Authority shall issue a tax agent's licence to an applicant under Article 95 of this Proclamation that is a partnership when satisfied that:

a) a partner in, or employee of, the partnership is a fit and proper person to provide tax agent services; and

b) every partner in the partnership is of good character and integrity.

3/ The Authority shall issue a tax agent's licence to an applicant under Article 95 of this Proclamation that is a company when satisfied that:

a) an employee of the company is a fit and proper person to provide tax agent services; and

b) every director, manager, and other executive officer of the company is of good character and integrity.

4/ The Regulation may provide guidelines for determining when a person is fit and proper to provide tax agent services.

5/ The Authority shall provide an applicant under Article 95 of this Proclamation with notice, in writing, of the decision on the application.

6/ A licence issued to a tax agent shall remain in force for three years from the date of issue and may be renewed under Article 97 of this Proclamation.

7/ The Authority may, from time to time, publish, in such manner as the Authority determines, a list of persons licensed as tax agents.

8/ A tax agent licence is a professional licence and a tax agent can carry on business as a tax agent only if the tax agent has been issued with a business licence.

97. Renewal of Tax Agent's Licence

1/ A tax agent may apply to the Authority for the renewal of the tax agent's licence.

2/ An application under Sub-Article (1) of this Article shall be:

a) in the approved form; and

b) filed with the Authority within 21 (Twenty-one) days of the date of expiry of the tax agent's licence or such later date as the Authority may allow.

3/ The Authority shall renew the licence of a tax agent who has applied under Sub-Article (1) of this Article if the tax agent continues to satisfy the conditions for licensing in Article 96.

4/ The renewal of a tax agent's licence shall be valid for three years from the date of renewal and can be further renewed in accordance with this Article.

5/ The Authority shall provide an applicant under Sub-Article (1) of this Article with notice, in writing, of the decision on the application.

98. Limitation on Providing Tax Agent Services

1/ Subject to Sub-Article (2) of this Article, no person, other than a licensed tax agent, shall, for a fee, provide tax agent services.

2/ Sub-Article (1) of this Article shall not apply to a person who is a licensed advocate acting in the ordinary course of his profession providing tax agent services other than services specified in Article 95 (2) (a) of the definition of "tax agent services".

99. Cancellation of Tax Agent's Licence

1/ A licensed tax agent shall notify the Authority, in writing, within 7 (Seven) days prior to ceasing to carry on business as a tax agent.

2/ A licensed tax agent may apply to the Authority, in writing, for cancellation of the tax agent's licence when the tax agent no longer wishes to be a licensed tax agent.

3/ The Authority shall cancel the licence of a tax agent when any of the following applies:

a) a tax declaration prepared and filed by the tax agent is false in any material particular, unless the tax agent establishes to the satisfaction of the Authority that this was not due to any wilful or negligent conduct of the tax agent;

b) the tax agent ceases to satisfy the conditions for licensing as a tax agent, or the Authority is satisfied that the tax agent has committed professional misconduct;

c) the tax agent has ceased to carry on business as a tax agent including, in the case of a company or partnership, when the company or partnership has ceased to exist;

d) the tax agent has applied for cancellation of the tax agent's licence under Sub-Article (2) of this Article;

e) the licence of the tax agent has expired and the agent has not filed an application for renewal of the licence under Article 97 of this Proclamation.

4/ The Authority shall serve notice, in writing, of a decision to cancel the licence of a tax agent.

5/ The cancellation of the licence of a tax agent shall take effect on the earlier of:

a) the date the tax agent ceases to carry on business as a tax agent; or

b) 60 (Sixty) days after the tax agent has been served with notice of the cancellation.

6/ Despite anything in any tax law, if the Authority is of the opinion that a person who is a licensed tax agent has committed professional misconduct, the Authority shall report the misconduct to:

a) the Institute of Certified Public Accountants, the Accounting and Auditing Board of Ethiopia, or other body having authority for the licensing of the person as an accountant, auditor, or lawyer, as the case may be; and

b) the licensing authority responsible for issuing business licences.

PART FIFTEEN
ADMINISTRATIVE, CRIMINAL PENALTIES, AND REWARDS

CHAPTER ONE   GENERAL PROVISIONS

100. General Provisions Relating to Administrative and Criminal Liabilities

1/ Where an act or omission entails both administrative and criminal liabilities at the same time, the person committing the offence shall not be relieved from criminal liability by the mere fact that he is held administratively liable.

2/ A taxpayer who is assessed for an administrative penalty or prosecuted for a criminal offence shall not be relieved from liability to pay any tax due.

CHAPTER TWO   ADMINISTRATIVE PENALTIES

101. Penalties Relating to Registration and Cancellation of Registration

1/ Subject to the other administrative penalties imposed by this proclamation, a person who fails to apply for registration as required under this Proclamation shall be liable for a penalty of 25% of the tax payable by the person for the period commencing on the date that the person was required to apply for registration and ending on the date that the person files the application for registration or the person is registered on the Authority's own motion.

2/ Where there is no tax payable by the tax payer mentioned in Sub-Article (1) of this article, the tax payer shall pay a penalty of Birr 1,000 (One Thousand Birr) for each month or part thereof from the day on which he should have been registered to the day of his actual registration.

3/ Where the penalty to be imposed pursuant to Sub-Article (1) of this article is less than the penalty to be imposed pursuant to Sub-Article (2) of this article, the penalty in Sub-Article (2) of this article shall apply.

4/ A person who, without reasonable excuse, fails to apply for cancellation of registration as required under this Proclamation shall be liable for a penalty of birr 1,000 (One Thousand Birr) for each month or part thereof for the period commencing on the date that the person was required to apply for cancellation of registration and ending on the date that the person files the application for cancellation or the person's registration is cancelled on the Authority's own motion.

102. Penalty for Failing to Maintain Documents

1/ Subject to Sub-Article (2) of this Article, a taxpayer who fails to maintain any document as required under a tax law shall be liable for a penalty of 20% of the tax payable by the taxpayer under the tax law for the tax period to which the failure relates.

2/ If no tax is payable by the taxpayer for the tax period to which the failure referred to in Sub-Article (1) of this Article relates, the penalty shall be:

a) birr 20,000 (Twenty Thousand Birr) for each tax year that the taxpayer fails to maintain documents for the purposes of the income tax; or

b) birr 2,000 (Two Thousand Birr) for each tax period that the taxpayer fails to maintain documents for the purposes of any other tax.

3/ Where the penalty to be imposed pursuant to Sub-Article (1) of this article is less than the penalty to be imposed pursuant to Sub-Article (2) of this article, the penalty in Sub-Article (2) of this article shall apply.

4/ Without prejudice to Sub-Articles (1), (2) and (3) of this Article, the licensing authority responsible for issuing business licences, shall on notification by the Authority, cancel the business licence of a taxpayer who fails to maintain documents for more than 2 years.

5/ A Category 'A' taxpayer who fails to retain documents for the period specified in Article

17 (2) shall be liable for a penalty of birr 50,000 (Fifty Thousand Birr).

6/ A Category 'B' taxpayer who fails to retain documents for the period specified in Article 33 (4) of the Federal Income Tax Proclamation shall be liable for a penalty of birr 20,000 (Twenty Thousand Birr).

103. Penalty in Relation to TINs

1/ A taxpayer who fails to state their TIN on a tax invoice, tax debit or credit note, tax declaration, or any other document as required under a tax law shall be liable for a penalty of birr 3,000 (Three Thousand Birr) for each failure.

2/ Except when Article 14 (6) of this Proclamation applies, a taxpayer shall be liable for a penalty of birr 10,000 (Ten Thousand Birr) if the taxpayer:

a) provides their TIN for use by another person; or

b) uses the TIN of another person.

3/ If the pecuniary advantage obtained by the taxpayer or another person as result of conduct referred to in Sub-Article (2) (a) or (b) of this Article exceeds birr 10,000 (Ten Thousand Birr) the penalty shall be equal to the pecuniary advantage obtained by the taxpayer.

104. Late Filing Penalty

1/ A person who fails to file a tax declaration by the due date shall be liable for a late filing penalty of 5 % of the unpaid tax for each tax period or part thereof to which the failure relates, provided that the penalty to be so imposed shall not exceed 25% of the unpaid tax.

2/ The penalty to which a tax payer is liable for non-filing of tax declaration for the first tax period or part thereof under Sub-Article (1) of this article shall not exceed 50,000 birr (Fifty Thousand Birr).

3/ For the purpose of this article, unpaid tax means the difference between the amount of tax that should have been entered in the tax declaration and the tax paid on the due date.

4/ The penalty to be imposed shall under no circumstance be less than the lowest of the following:

a) birr 10,000 (Ten Thousand Birr);

b) 100% of the amount tax that should have been entered in the tax declaration.

5/ Notwithstanding the provisions of this article, where the tax payer has no tax to pay for a tax period, he shall be liable for a penalty of birr 10,000 (Ten Thousand Birr) for each tax period to which the non-filing of tax declaration relates.

105. Late Payment Penalty

1/ A taxpayer who fails to pay tax by the due date shall be liable for the following late payment penalties:

a) 5% of the unpaid tax that remains unpaid at the expiration of one month or part thereof after the due date; and

b) an additional 2% of the amount of the unpaid tax for each month or part of a month thereafter to the extent that the tax remains unpaid.

2/ The amount of penalty assessed under this Article shall not exceed the amount of the tax liability to which it relates.

3/ Late payment penalty paid by a taxpayer shall be refunded to the taxpayer in accordance with Article 50 (4) of this Proclamation to the extent that the tax to which the penalty relates is found not to have been payable.

4/ This Article shall not apply when Article 106 of this Proclamation applies in relation to the unpaid tax.

106. Withholding Tax Penalties

1/ A person who fails to withhold tax or, having withheld tax fails to pay the tax to the Authority, as required under the Federal Income Tax Proclamation shall be liable for a penalty of 10% of the tax to be withheld or actually withheld but not transferred to the Authority.

2/ When Sub-Article (1) of this Article applies to a body and in addition to the penalty imposed under that Sub-Article, the manager of the body, chief accountant, or any other officer of the body responsible for ensuring the withholding and payment of withholding tax shall be liable for a penalty of birr 2,000 (Two Thousand Birr) each.

3/ When Article 92 of the Federal Income Tax Proclamation applies, both the supplier and purchaser shall be liable for a penalty of birr 20,000 (Twenty Thousand Birr) each.

4/ A person, who, with the intention of avoiding withholding tax under Article 92 of the Federal Income Tax Proclamation, refused to supply goods or services to a person who is obliged to withhold tax under that Article shall be liable for a penalty of birr 10,000 (Ten Thousand Birr).

107. Value Added Tax Penalties

1/ A person who fails to apply for registration as required under the Value Added Tax Proclamation shall be liable for a penalty of birr 2,000 (Two Thousand Birr) for each month or part thereof for the period commencing on the date that the person was required to apply for registration and ending on the date that the person files the application for registration or the person is registered on the Authority's own motion.

2/ In addition to the penalty imposed under Sub-Article (1) of this Article, a person to whom that Sub-Article applies shall also be liable for a penalty of 100% of the amount of value added tax payable on taxable transactions made by the person during the period commencing on the day on which the person was required to apply for registration and ending on the date that the person files the application for registration or the person is registered on the Authority's own motion.

3/ The imposition of penalty under Sub-Article (2) of this Article shall not relieve the person from liability for the value added tax payable on the taxable transactions made by the person during the period specified in that Sub-Article, but the amount of the value added tax payable is reduced by any turnover tax paid by the person on those transactions.

4/ A person who deliberately issues an incorrect tax invoice resulting in a decrease in the value added tax payable on a taxable transaction or an increase in the creditable value added tax in respect of a taxable transaction shall be liable for a penalty of birr 50,000 (Fifty Thousand Birr).

108. Failure to Issue Tax Invoice

Where a tax payer being required to issue tax invoice fails to do so, shall be liable for a penalty of birr 50,000 (Fifty Thousand Birr) for each transaction to which the failure to issue tax invoice relates.

109. Tax Understatement Penalty

1/ A taxpayer whose declared tax liability is less than the taxpayer's correct tax liability (the difference being referred to as the "tax shortfall") shall be liable for a penalty of 10% of the tax shortfall.

2/ The penalty under Sub-Article (1) of this Article shall be increased to 30% for the second application of the Article to the taxpayer.

3/ The penalty under Sub-Article (1) of this Article shall be increased to 40% for the third or subsequent application of the Article to the taxpayer.

4/ No penalty shall be imposed under this Article if the tax shortfall arose as a result of a self-assessment taxpayer taking a reasonably arguable position on the application of a tax law on which the Ministry has not issued ruling prior to the taxpayer filing their self-assessment declaration.

110. Tax Avoidance Penalty

If the Authority has applied tax avoidance provision in assessing a taxpayer, the taxpayer shall be liable for a tax avoidance penalty equal to double the amount of the tax that would have been avoided but for the application of the anti-tax avoidance provision.

111. Penalty for Failing to Comply with Electronic Tax System

1/ When a taxpayer required by the Authority under a tax law to file a tax declaration or pay tax electronically fails to do so, the Authority shall serve the taxpayer with notice in writing seeking reasons for the failure.

2/ A taxpayer who fails to provide adequate reasons to the satisfaction of the Authority for the failure to file a tax declaration or pay tax electronically within 14 (Fourteen) days of the date of service of the notice under Sub-Article (1) of this Article shall be liable for a penalty equal to birr 50,000 (Fifty Thousand Birr).

112. Tax Agent Penalties

A licensed tax agent shall be liable for a penalty of birr 10,000 (Ten Thousand Birr) if the tax agent fails:

1/ to provide a certificate or statement to their client as required under Article 22 of this Proclamation; or

2/ to keep certificates and statements provided to clients for the period specified in Article 22 (4) of this Proclamation; or

3/ to notify the Authority as required under Article 99 (1) of this Proclamation that the tax agent has ceased to carry on business as a tax agent.

113. Penalties Relating to Sales Register Machines

1/ Any person who has the obligation to use sales register machine shall be liable for a penalty of :

a) Birr 50,000 (Fifty Thousand Birr) if found using sales register machine or point of sales machine software not accredited or registered by the tax Authority;

b) Birr 50,000 (Fifty Thousand Birr) for carrying out transactions without receipt or invoice or for using any other receipt not generated by a sales register machine except at the time the machine is under repair or for any other justifiable reason;

c) Birr 100,000 (One Hundred Thousand Birr) if caused damage to or change of fiscal memory or attempts to cause damage to or change of fiscal memory;

d) Birr 25,000 (Twenty-five Thousand Birr) for obstructing inspection of the audit system of a sales register machine by officer of the Tax Authority or for failure to have annual machine inspections performed by a service centre;

e) Birr 25,000 (Twenty-five Thousand Birr) for not having a valid service contract with an authorized service centre for a sales register machine in use, or for using the sales register machine without connecting to the terminal, or for not keeping the inspection booklet besides the sales register machine, or for issuing refund receipts without properly recording the return of goods or customers' request for refund in the refund book;

f) Birr 10,000 (Ten Thousand Birr) for failure to inform the Tax Authority and the machine service center within three days of the termination of a sales register machine use due to theft or irreparable damage, or within four hours for failure to report machine malfunction due to any other causes;

g) Birr 50,000 (Fifty Thousand Birr) for failure to notify the Tax Authority the correct place of business the sales register machine is in use;

h) Birr 25,000 (Twenty-five Thousand Birr) for failure to notify the Tax Authority change of name or address or for failure to notify the Tax Authority and Service Center three days in advance in cases of termination of business;

i) Birr 10,000 (Ten Thousand Birr) for failure to put a conspicuous notice containing one or all the following information at a place where the machine is installed: -

(1) name of the machine user, trade name, location of trade, taxpayers' identification number, accreditation and permit numbers for the sales register machine;

(2) text stating that "in case of machine failure sales personnel must issue manual receipts authorized by the Tax Authority"; and

(3) text that reads "Do not pay if a receipt is not issued";

j) Birr 30,000 (Thirty Thousand Birr) for changing or improving a point of sales machine software by a person not accredited by the Tax Authority.

2/ Any person who is accredited and permitted for the supply of sales register machine or software shall be liable for a penalty of:

a) Birr 100,000 (One Hundred Thousand Birr) for failure to notify change of business address to the Tax Authority;

b) Birr 500,000 (Five Hundred Thousand Birr) for selling a sales register machine not accredited by the Tax Authority;

c) Birr 50,000 (Fifty Thousand Birr) for failure to get a machine registration code for each sales register machine from the Tax Authority or for not affixing the machine code stickers on a visible part of the machine;

d) Birr 100,000 (One Hundred Thousand Birr) for failure to notify to the Tax Authority in advance any change made to the sales register machine in use or for inserting or adding incorrect information or for omitting the correct information from the manual that guides the use of sales register machine;

e) Birr 50,000 (Fifty Thousand Birr) for failure to notify the Tax Authority in advance or for not being able to replace, within three days of the request made by a service center, sales register machine lost due to theft or sustained irreparable damage;

f) Birr 50,000 (Fifty Thousand Birr) for failure to keep information about service centers with which it has signed agreements or for failure to notify the Tax Authority about contracts terminated or newly entered agreements with service centers.

3/ Any Sales Register Machine Service Centre shall be liable for a penalty of:

a) Birr 20,000 (Twenty Thousand Birr) for failure to report to the Tax Authority within two days of change of the fiscal memory of a sales register machine;

b) Birr 20,000 (Twenty Thousand Birr) for failure to perform annual technical inspections on sales register machines that are under contract;

c) Birr 50,000 (Fifty Thousand Birr) for deploying every person not certified by the supplier and not registered by the Tax Authority.

114. Miscellaneous Penalties

1/ A taxpayer who fails to notify any change as required under Article 10 of this Proclamation shall be liable for a penalty of birr 20,000 (Twenty Thousand Birr).

2/ A body that fails to file a copy of its memorandum of association, articles of association, statute, partnership agreement, or other document of formation or registration, or any amendment to such document, with the Authority as required under Article 62 of this Proclamation shall be liable for a penalty of birr 10,000 (Ten Thousand Birr) for each month or part thereof that the document remains unfiled.

3/ A public auditor who fails to file an audit report with the Authority as required under Article 63 of this Proclamation shall be liable for a penalty of birr 10,000 (Ten Thousand Birr) for each month or part of a month that the document remains unfiled.

4/ The penalty provided for under Sub-Article (3) of this Article shall be in addition to any action taken by the Accounting and Auditing Board of Ethiopia in relation to the public auditor's licence.

5/ A person who fails to notify the Authority as required under Article 64 of this Proclamation shall be liable for a penalty of birr 1,000 (One Thousand Birr) for each day of default.

6/ A taxpayer who fails to provide details of transactions with related persons as required under Article 79 of the Federal Income Tax Proclamation shall be liable for a penalty of birr 100,000 (One Hundred Thousand Birr).

7/ Any person having the obligation to supply information fails to give any information requested by the authority, that person or the head of the organization, as appropriate, from which the information is sought shall be liable for a penalty of birr 5,000 (Five Thousand Birr).

115. Assessment of Administrative Penalties

1/ The Authority shall serve a person liable for an administrative penalty with notice of the penalty assessed.

2/ When the same act or omission may involve administrative penalties in relation to more than one tax, the penalties shall be aggregated after being assessed separately for each tax.

3/ A person liable for an administrative penalty may apply in writing to the Authority, for waiver of the penalty payable and such application shall include the reasons for the requested remission.

4/ The Authority may, upon application under Sub-Article (3) of this Article or on its own motion waive, in whole or in part, an administrative penalty imposed on a person in accordance with a Directive issued by the Authority.

5/ The Authority shall maintain a public record of each administrative penalty waived and report it to the Ministry on a quarterly basis.

CHAPTER THREE   TAX OFFENCES

116. Procedure in Tax Offence Cases

1/ A tax offence is a violation of the criminal law of Ethiopia and shall be charged, prosecuted, and appealed in accordance with Criminal Procedure Code of Ethiopia.

2/ Commission of an offence under this chapter violating various tax laws shall be construed as separate criminal act committed in contravention of such tax law and the penalty prescribed for each criminal act under the relevant provisions shall apply.

117. Offences Relating to TINs

1/ A person who:

a) obtains, or attempts to obtain, more than one TIN;

b) allows their TIN to be used by another person; or

c) uses the TIN of another person;

shall be punishable with a fine of birr 20,000 (Twenty Thousand Birr) and simple imprisonment for a term of one to three years.

2/ Sub-article (1) (a) of this Article applies separately to each TIN obtained or attempted to be obtained.

3/ Sub-article (1) (b) and (c) of this Article shall not apply when a TIN is used in the circumstances specified in Article 14 (6) of this Proclamation.

118. False or Misleading Statements and Fraudulent Documents

1/ A person who, with intent to defraud the Authority or recklessly:

a) makes a false or misleading statement to the Authority; or

b) omits without adequate reasons any detail which should have been included in a statement in such a manner that is likely to misled the Authority;

c) provides the Authority with fraudulent documents; shall be punishable with a fine of birr 50,000 (Fifty Thousand Birr) to 100,000 (One Hundred Thousand Birr) and rigorous imprisonment for a term of three to fifteen years.

2/ The reference in Sub-Article (1) of this Article to a statement made to the Authority by a person shall include a statement made by the person to another person with the knowledge or reasonable expectation that the person will pass on the statement to the Authority.

3/ Whosoever, with the intention to evade tax, engages in business in an agents capacity by obtaining a trade license in the name of a person who is not alive or whose address is not known or who does not have the legal capacity to give power of attorney or who does not benefit from the business or who does not exist, shall apart from being responsible for the tax liability of the business, be punishable under Sub-Article (1) of this article.

119. Fraudulent or Unlawful Invoices

1/ A person who:

a) prepares, produces, sells, or distributes fraudulent invoices; or

b) uses fraudulent invoices to reduce his tax liability or claim a refund;

shall be punishable with a fine of birr 100,000 (One Hundred Thousand Birr) and rigorous imprisonment for a term of seven to ten years.

2/ If the pecuniary benefit obtained by a person from a fraudulent invoice under Sub-Article (1) of this Article is greater than birr 100,000 (One Hundred Thousand Birr) the sanction under Sub-Article (1) shall be equal to the pecuniary benefit derived and rigorous imprisonment for a term of ten to fifteen years.

3/ A person who possesses, sells, leases, or otherwise supplies a machine, equipment, or software that is used in making, preparing, or printing fraudulent invoices shall be punishable with a fine of birr 200,000 (Two Hundred Thousand Birr) and rigorous imprisonment for a term of ten to fifteen years.

4/ Conviction for an offence under Sub-Article (3) of this Article shall not prejudice the confiscation of the machine, equipment, or software, and of the proceeds of the crime.

5/ A person who possesses, keeps, facilitates, or arranges the sale, or commissions the use of fraudulent invoices shall be guilty of an offence punishable by rigorous imprisonment for a term of three to five years.

120. General Offences Relating to Invoices

1/ Any tax payer with an obligation to issue a tax invoice, carrying out transaction without tax invoice shall be punishable with a fine of birr 25,000 (Twenty-five Thousand Birr) to 50,000 (Fifty Thousand Birr) and rigorous imprisonment for a term of three to five years.

2/ A person who understates a sales price by entering different amounts of the price in identical copies of the invoice for a single transaction shall be punishable with a fine of birr 100,000 (One Hundred Thousand Birr) and rigorous imprisonment for a term of five to seven years.

3/ If the actual price of the sale is greater than birr 100,000 (One Hundred Thousand Birr) the sanction under Sub-Article (2) of this Article shall be a fine equal to the highest of the prices specified on the invoices and rigorous imprisonment for term of seven to ten years.

4/ A person who provides or accepts an invoice for which there is no transaction shall be punishable with a fine of birr 100,000 (One Hundred Thousand Birr) to 200,000 (Two Hundred

Thousand Birr) and rigorous imprisonment for a term of seven to ten years.

5/ If the invoice to which Sub-Article (4) of this Article applies is for an amount in excess of birr 200,000 (Two Hundred Thousand Birr) the sanction under Sub-Article (1) of this Article shall be a fine equal to the amount stated on the invoice and rigorous imprisonment for a term of ten to fifteen years.

6/ Whosoever without authorization from the Authority prints tax invoices shall be punishable with a fine of birr 300,000 (Three Hundred Thousand Birr) to birr 500,000 (Five Hundred Thousand Birr) and with rigorous imprisonment from two to five years.

7/ A person found guilty and convicted under Sub-Article (6) of this Article for the second time, shall forfeit his printing machine and/or his business and his business license shall be cancelled.

121. Claiming Unlawful Refunds or Excess Credits

1/ A taxpayer who claims a refund or tax credit with intent to defraud the Authority using a falsified receipt or by employing any other similar method, shall be punishable with a fine of birr 50,000 (Fifty Thousand Birr) and rigorous imprisonment for a term of five to seven years.

2/ Conviction for an offence under Sub-Article (1) of this Article shall not relieve the taxpayer from the obligation to repay the refund under Article 50.

122. Value Added Tax Offences

1/ A person who has provided a tax invoice without being registered for value added tax shall be punishable with a fine of birr 200,000 (Two Hundred Thousand Birr) and rigorous imprisonment for a term of seven to ten years.

2/ A registered person who:

a) refuses to provide a tax debit note or tax credit note as required under the Value Added Tax Proclamation; or

b) provides a tax debit note or tax credit note otherwise than as allowed under the Value Added Tax Proclamation;

shall be punishable with a fine of birr 10,000 (Ten Thousand Birr) and simple imprisonment for a term of one year.

123. Stamp Duty Offences

1/ A person who:

a) executes or signs (other than as a witness) a document subject to stamp duty on which no stamp duty is paid; or

b) disguises or hides the true nature of a document with the intention of not paying stamp duty or paying a lower amount of stamp duty;

shall be punishable with a fine of birr 25,000 (Twenty-five Thousand Birr) to birr 50,000 (Fifty Thousand Birr) and rigorous imprisonment for a term of three to five years.

2/ A person who:

a) being authorised to sell stamps or stamped papers violates the Stamp Duty Proclamation or Regulation; or

b) sells or offers for sale stamps or stamped papers without authorisation;

shall be punishable with a fine of birr 5,000 (Five Thousand Birr) to birr 25,000 (Twenty-five Thousand Birr) and rigorous imprisonment for a term of three to five years.

124. Offences Relating to Recovery of Tax

1/ A receiver entrusted with the property of a tax payer failing to discharge his obligation under any tax law shall be punishable with a fine of birr 5,000 (Five Thousand Birr) and with simple imprisonment one year.

2/ A person who, after receipt of a seizure order under Article 41:

a) sells, exchanges, or otherwise disposes of the property that is the subject of the order;

b) hides, breaks, spoils, or damages the property that is the subject of the order; or

c) destroys, hides, removes, damages, changes, cancels, or deletes any documents relating to the property the subject of the order;

shall be punishable with simple imprisonment from two to three years.

3/ Subject to Sub-Article (5) of this Article, a person who fails to pay the amount specified in a garnishee order to the Authority shall be punishable with simple imprisonment from two to three years.

4/ A person who notifies the Authority under Article 43 (5) of this Proclamation is treated as being in compliance with a garnishee order served on the person until the Authority serves the person with a notice under Article 43 (6) of this Proclamation cancelling or amending the garnishee order or rejecting the person's notice under Article 43 (5) of this Proclamation.

5/ The conviction of a person for an offence under Sub-Article (3) of this Article shall not relieve the person of liability to pay the amount required to be paid under the garnishee order.

6/ A person who departs or attempts to depart from Ethiopia in contravention of a departure prohibition order shall be punishable with simple imprisonment from two to three years.

7/ A financial institution that fails to comply with order issued under Article 42 of this Proclamation shall be punishable by a fine equal to the tax that the Authority failed to collect as a result of the failure.

8/ If an offence under Sub-Article (7) of this Article was committed with the knowledge or as a result of negligence of the manager of the financial institution, the manager shall be punishable with simple imprisonment from two to three years.

9/ A person who, without the permission of the Authority, opens or removes the seal of premises that are the subject of a closure order under Article 45 shall be punishable with simple imprisonment from two to three years.

125. Tax Evasion

1/ Whosoever, with the intention to evade tax, conceals his income or fails to file a tax declaration or pay tax by the due date shall be punishable with a fine of birr 100,000 (One Hundred Thousand Birr) to 200,000 (Two Hundred Thousand Birr) and rigorous imprisonment for a term of three to five years.

2/ A withholding agent who withholds tax from a payment but fails to pay the withheld tax to the Authority by the due date with the intention to evade tax shall be punishable by rigorous imprisonment for a term of three to five years.

126. Obstruction of Administration of Tax Laws

1/ A person who obstructs or attempts to obstruct a tax officer in the performance of duties under a tax law shall be punishable with simple imprisonment for a term of one to three years.

2/ A person who obstructs or attempts to obstruct the administration of a tax law shall be punishable with a fine of not less than birr 10,000 (Ten Thousand Birr) and rigorous imprisonment for a term of three to five years.

3/ In this Article, the following and other similar actions constitute obstruction:

a) refusing to comply with a request of the Authority for inspection of documents, or the provision of reports or information relating to the tax affairs of a taxpayer, including a refusal to comply with a notice served on the person under Article 65 of this Proclamation;

b) non-compliance with a notice served on the person under Article 65 of this Proclamation requiring the person to attend and give evidence;

c) preventing the Director General or an authorised officer from exercising the right of access under Article 66 of this Proclamation;

d) refusing to provide reasonable assistance or facilities as required under Article 66 (4);

e) provoking a disturbance in an office of the Authority or impeding an employee of the Authority from performing their duties of employment.

127. Unauthorised Tax Collection

A person not authorised to collect tax under the tax laws who collects or attempts to collect tax, shall be punishable with fine of birr 50,000 (Fifty Thousand Birr) to 75,000 (Seventy-five Thousand Birr) and rigorous imprisonment for a term of five to seven years.

128. Aiding or Abetting a Tax Offence

A person who aids, abets, assists, incites, or conspires with another person to commit an offence under a tax law referred to as the "principal offence" shall be punishable by the same sanction as imposed for the principal offence.

129. Offences Relating to the Tax Appeal Commission

1/ A person who:

a) insults a member of the Commission in the exercise of his powers or functions as a member;

b) interrupts a proceeding of the Commission without authorisation;

c) creates a disturbance, or takes part in creating a disturbance, in or near a place where the Commission is sitting with the intent of disrupting the proceedings of the Commission; or

d) obstructs the function of the commission by whatever means;

shall be punishable with a fine of birr 500 (Five Hundred Birr) to 3,000 (Three Thousand Birr) or simple imprisonment for a term of six months to two years.

2/ A person who:

a) without reasonable excuse, refuses or fails to comply with a summons to appear before the Commission, or to produce any document or provide any information to the Commission;

b) without reasonable excuse, refuses to take an oath or fails to confirm to testify the truth before the Commission;

c) without reasonable excuse, refuses or fails to answer any question asked of the person during a proceeding before the Commission;

shall be punishable with a fine of birr 300 (Three Hundred Birr) to 3,000 (Three Thousand Birr) and simple imprisonment for a term of six months to two years.

3/ Whosoever, knowingly gives false or misleading evidence to the Commission, shall be punishable with a fine of not less than birr 50,000 (Fifty Thousand Birr) and with rigorous imprisonment from three to five years.

130. Offences by Tax Agents

Whosoever, without having a license to act as a tax agent, provides tax agent's services in contravention of Article 98 of this Proclamation shall be punishable by simple imprisonment for a term of one to three years.

131. Offences Relating to Sales Register Machines

1/ Any person who has the obligation to use sales register machine commits an offence:

a) if found using a sales register machine not accredited or registered by the Authority, shall be punished with rigorous imprisonment for a term of not less than three years and not more than seven years;

b) if he, except at the time the sales register machine is under repair, or other justifiable reason, carried out transactions without receipt or invoice or used any other receipt not generated by a sales register machine shall be punished with rigorous imprisonment for a term of not less than two years and not more than five years;

c) if caused damage or change to the fiscal memory of a sales register machine or attempts to cause damage or change to the fiscal memory shall be punished with rigorous imprisonment for a term of not less than three years and not more than five years.

2/ Any person who is accredited and registered to supply sales register machines commits an offence:

a) if sold a software or a sales register machine not accredited by the Tax Authority shall be punished with rigorous imprisonment for a term of not less than three years and not more than five years;

b) if failed to notify the Authority in advance any change made to the sales register machine in use, or if inserted incorrect information to or omitted the correct information from the manual that guides the use of sales register machine shall be punished with rigorous imprisonment for a term of not less than three years and not more than five years.

3/ Whosoever, without having a license to supply sales register machine or software, distributes sales register machine or software, shall be punishable with rigorous imprisonment from five to seven years.

4/ Any sales register machine service centre deploying a service personnel that is not certified by the supplier and/or not registered by the Authority, shall be punished with a fine of birr 50,000 (Fifty Thousand Birr) or simple imprisonment for a term of not exceeding one year.

5/ Any personnel of a sales register machine service centre commits an offence if, without the knowledge of the service centre and the Authority, dismantle or assemble a sales register machine, or if deliberately removed the seals on a sales register machine or changed parts of a sales register machine not reported to have any break down, or if committed any similar act and shall, upon conviction, be punished with a fine of not more than Birr 10,000 (Ten Thousand Birr) and simple imprisonment for a term of not less than one year and not more than three years.

6/ Any tax officer who, in violation of the rules and procedures of the use of sales register machines:

a) dismantles or assembles a sales register machine or approves its utilization without the presence of a service personnel or changes the machine registration code; or

b) knowingly or negligently fails to report to the Authority, within 24 (Twenty-four) hours, offences committed by the user, service centre or its personnel or supplier of a sales register machine;

commits an offence and shall, upon conviction, be punished with a fine of not more than Birr 5,000 (Five Thousand Birr) and rigorous imprisonment for a term of not less than one year and not more than three years.

132. Offences by Bodies

1/ When the person committing an offence under a tax law is a body, every person who is a manager of the body at the time the offence was committed shall be treated as having committed the same offence.

2/ Sub-article (1) of this Article shall not apply to a person where :

a) the offence was committed without the person's consent or knowledge; and

b) he has exercised due diligence and caution that a prudent person in his position is expected to take under similar circumstance.

133. Publication of Names

1/ The Authority may from time to time publish a list of the names of persons convicted by final decisions of court of law of an offence under a tax law on its website and through other mass media.

2/ A list published in accordance with Sub-Article (1) of this Article shall specify the following:

a) the name, picture, and address of the convicted person;

b) particulars of the offence as the Authority considers appropriate;

c) the tax period or periods during which the offence was committed;

d) the amount of tax not paid by the convicted person as a result of commission of the offence;

e) the amount, if any, of penalty assessed to the convicted person.

CHAPTER FOUR REWARDS

134. Reward for Verifiable Information of Tax Evasion

1/ If a person provides verifiable and objective information of tax evasion, through concealment, under-reporting, fraud, or other improper means, the Authority shall, in accordance with the directive to be issued by it, grant the person a reward of up to 20% of the amount of the tax evaded at the time the tax is collected by the Authority.

2/ A person shall not be entitled to a reward under Sub-Article (1) of this Article if:

a) the person participated in the tax evasion; or

b) the reporting of the tax evasion was part of the person's duties.

3/ The Authority shall provide details of a reward under this Article by Directive.

135. Reward for Outstanding Performance

1/ The Authority shall reward a tax officer for outstanding performance and a taxpayer for exemplary discharge of his tax obligations.

2/ The Minister shall provide details of a reward under this Article by Directive.

PART SIXTEEN
MISCELLANEOUS PROVISIONS

136. Power to Issue Regulations and Directives

1/ The Council of Ministers may issue Regulations necessary for the proper implementation of this Proclamation.

2/ The Minister may issue Directives necessary for the proper implementation of this Proclamation and Regulations issued under Sub-Article (1) of this Article.

137. Transitional Provisions

1/ This Proclamation shall apply to an act or omission occurring caused a tax decision made before its entry in to force.

2/ Notwithstanding Sub-Article (1) of this proclamation:

a) administrative penalties applicable to non-payment of taxes due before this proclamation becomes effective shall be assessed in accordance with the tax laws in force prior to this proclamation.

b) any case that has been pending in the tax appeal commission when this proclamation becomes effective shall be adjudicated in accordance with the tax laws in force prior to this proclamation, as if this proclamation were not enacted.

c) the existing tax complaint review committee and Tax Appeal Commission shall continue to function until such time as a new tax complaint review department and Federal Tax Appeal Commission is established in accordance with this proclamation.

d) If the period for the making of an application and appeal had expired before the commencement of this Proclamation, nothing in this Proclamation can be construed as enabling the application and appeal to be made under this Proclamation by reason only of the fact that a longer period is specified in this Proclamation.

3/ For the purposes of this Proclamation, if the Institute of Certified Public Accountants is not established at the commencement of this Proclamation, any reference in this Proclamation to the Institute shall be treated as a reference to the Accounting and Auditing Board of Ethiopia until the Institute is established.

4/ The Obligatory Use of Sales Register Machines Council of Ministers Regulation No. 139/

2007 shall continue to apply for the purposes of Article 20 of this Proclamation until replaced by new Regulation issued by the Council of Ministers.

138. Inapplicable Laws

Subject to the provisions of Article 137 of this proclamation, any law which is inconsistent with this proclamation shall not be applicable in respect of matters provided for in this proclamation.

139. Effective Date

1/ This Proclamation shall enter in to force on the date of its Publication in the Federal Negarit Gazette.

2/ Notwithstanding Sub-Article (1) of this Article, the provisions of Part Eleven and Part Fourteen of this proclamation shall begin to apply as from the date to be specified by the minister by notice to be published in a newspaper of wide circulation.

3/ Notwithstanding Sub-Article (1) of this Article, the provisions of part fourteen of this proclamation shall begin to apply as from the date to be specified by the authority by notice to be published in a newspaper of wide circulation.

Done at Addis Ababa, this 20th day of August, 2016.

MULATU TESHOME (DR.)
PRESIDENT OF THE FEDERAL DEMOCRATIC
REPUBLIC OF ETHIPOIA

TITLE SEVEN
COUNCIL OF MINISTERS FEDERAL TAX ADMINISTRATION REGULATION
(Council of Ministers Regulation No. 407/2017)

FEDERAL NEGARIT GAZETTE
OF THE FEDERAL DEMOCRATIC REPUBLIC OF ETHIOPIA

23rd Year No. 79
ADDIS ABABA 9th August, 2017

COUNCIL OF MINISTERS REGULATION NO. 407/2017 COUNCILS OF MINISTERS TAX ADMINISTRATION REGULATION

This Regulation is issued by the Council of Ministers pursuant to Article 5 of the Definitions of Powers and Duties of the Executive Organs of the Federal Democratic Republic of Ethiopia Proclamation No. 916/2015 and Article 136 of the Federal Tax Administration Proclamation No. 983/2016.

PART ONE
GENERAL

1. Short Title

This Regulation may be cited as "the Council of Ministers Federal Tax Administration Regulation No. 407/2017".

2. Definition

Unless the context requires otherwise, in this Regulation:

1) "Proclamation" means the Federal Tax Administration Proclamation No. 983/2016;

2) "Repealed Proclamation" means the Income Tax Proclamation No. 286/2002 (as amended), Mining Income Tax Proclamation No. 53/1993 and all amendments there to and Petroleum Operations Income Tax Proclamation No. 96/1986 and all amendments thereto.

3) A term used in this Regulation shall have the same meaning as in the Proclamation or the Federal Income Tax Proclamation No. 979/2016, as the case may be.

PART TWO
ADMINISTRATION OF TAX LAWS

3. Supply of Confidential Information

Without prejudice to Article 8(2) of the proclamation, the Authority shall provide a confidential document or information only when a written request is submitted to the Director General or his representative and the provision of the document or information is authorized.

PART THREE
REGISTRATION

4. Documentary Evidence of Identity

1/ An application for registration by an individual shall be accompanied by any of the following documentary evidence of identity:

a) the individual's current residence identity card or certified copy of the page of the Ethiopian or foreign current passport containing the individual's personal information; or

b) certified copy of the individual's current Ethiopian driver's licence; or

c) certified copy of the page of the individuals current foreign driver's licence containing personal information of the individual and to which the photograph of the individual is attached; or

d) certified copy of the individual's birth certificate;

2/ Notwithstanding the provision of Sub-Article (1) of this article, the Authority may require the applicant to submit such other evidence as it deems necessary.

3/ An application for registration by an incorporated company must be accompanied by the certificate of incorporation or registration of the company.

4/ An application for registration by a partnership must be accompanied by the partnership deed.

5/ An application for registration by any other body must be accompanied by the certificate of registration, or other document of formation or creation.

5. Biometric Information

1/ For the purposes of registration of an individual, the Authority may require an individual to submit biometric information so as to:

a) ensure the proper identification of the individual; or

b) counteract identity theft or fraud.

2/ In this Article, "biometric information", in relation to an individual, means biological data to authenticate the identity of the individual, and may include the following:

a) facial recognition;

b) fingerprint recognition;

c) vocal recognition;

d) iris or retina recognition.

PART FOUR
TAX REPRESENTATIVES

6. Tax Representative of a Non-Resident

1/ For a non-resident conducting business in Ethiopia through the activities of a person (referred to as the "agent") constituting a permanent establishment in Ethiopia of the non-resident under Article 4(4) of the Federal Income Tax Proclamation, the agent shall be a tax representative of the non-resident for the purposes of the Proclamation.

2/ The treatment of an agent as the tax representative of a non-resident under Sub-Article (1) of this Article shall be in addition to any other person treated as the tax representative of the non-resident under Article 2(40) of the Proclamation.

PART FIVE
HARDSHIP CASES

7. Limit to Remission of Tax Debt

The maximum amount of tax debt and late payment interest that the Minister may remit under Article 51 of the Proclamation shall be 10,000,000 (Ten Million) birr.

PART SIX
NOTICES AND PAYMENT OF TAX

8. Manner of Filing Documents and Paying Tax

Except as otherwise provided in the Proclamation or this Regulation, a person shall file a tax declaration or other document with the Authority and pay tax in the following manner:

1/ when Article 82(2) of the Proclamation applies, by electronic transmission or payment in accordance with the directions of the Authority under that Article; or

2/ in any other case, by personal delivery or post to an office of the Authority.

PART SEVEN
TAX APPEAL COMMISSION

CHAPTER ONE POWERS OF THE COMMISSION ON A HEARING

9. Powers of the Commission

1/ The Commission may:

a) take evidence on oath or affirmation;

b) subject to Article 11(2) of this Regulation, proceed in the absence of a party who has had reasonable notice of a hearing; or

c) adjourn a hearing from time to time.

2/ The President of the Commission may summon a person to appear before the Commission at a hearing to give evidence.

3/ A person summoned to appear as a witness before the Commission shall be entitled to be paid fees at such rates as are allowable for witnesses in the Federal High Court in accordance with the directive of the Commission.

CHAPTER TWO DECISION OF THE COMMISSION

10. Discontinuance, Dismissal, or Reinstatement of Appeal Application

1/ An appellant may discontinue or withdraw an appeal to the Commission at any time by filing written notice with the Registrar of the Commission and the Commission shall dismiss the appeal.

2/ If an applicant fails to appear in person or be represented at a hearing of the Commission, the Commission may dismiss the appeal.

3/ If an applicant fails to comply with the direction of the commission in relation to the appeal under consideration, the President may, on behalf of the Commission, dismiss the appeal.

4/ If the Commission has dismissed an appeal under Sub-Article (2) or (3) of this Article, the appellant may, within 30 days after receiving notification that the appeal has been dismissed, apply to the Commission for reinstatement of the appeal.

5/ If an application has been made under Sub-Article (4), the Commission may reinstate the appeal subject to any directions made by the President.

11. Agreement Between the Parties

If at any stage during an appeal, the parties agree in writing as to the terms of a decision of the Commission on the appeal or on a decision relating to part of the appeal:

1/ the Commission may make a decision in accordance with the terms of the agreement where the agreement relates to the terms of the decision of the Commission.

2/ the Commission may give effect to the terms of the agreement where the agreement reached relates to a decision on part of the appeal.

12. Decision to be Remitted to the Authority

1/ If, in accordance with Article 91 of the Proclamation, the Commission remits an appealable decision to the Authority for reconsideration, the Authority may, taking in to account the directions of the Commission:

a) affirm the appealable decision;

b) vary the appealable decision; or

c) set aside the appealable decision and make a new decision, including increasing a tax assessment when Article 91(6) of the Proclamation applies.

2/ When the Authority varies or sets aside an appealable decision in accordance with Sub-Article (1) of this Article, the decision as varied, or the new decision, shall be taken to be the appealable decision that is the subject of the appeal before the Commission and the appellant may either proceed with or withdraw the appeal.

13. Correction of Decision

1/ The Commission may alter the text of a decision or written statement of reasons for a decision if satisfied that there is an error in the text of the decision or the written statement of reasons.

2/ The altered text under Sub-Article (1) of this Article shall be treated as the decision of the Commission.

3/ For the purpose of this Article, an error in the text of a decision or statement of reasons includes:

a) a typographical or clerical error; or

b) any inconsistency between the decision and the statement of reasons.

CHAPTER THREE ADMINSTRATION OF THE COMMISSION

14. Place of Hearing

The hearings of the Commission shall take place at a location to be designated by the President of the Commission. Accordingly, the commission shall notify the parties the place of the hearing.

15. Costs

The Commission may make such order as it considers fair and reasonable regarding costs incurred by the parties in relation to the proceeding.

16. Filing of Documents with Commission

Any document required to be filed with the Commission shall be filed at the Registry of the Commission.

17. Address for Service of Documents

An appellant shall give the Registrar written notice of the appellant's address for service of any documents relating to the appeal.

PART EIGHT
LICENSING OF TAX AGENTS

18. Fit and Proper Person to Provide Tax Agent Services

1/ Subject to Sub-Articles (2) and (3) of this Article, an individual is a fit and proper person to provide tax agent services if the individual has:

a) aqualification of at least first degree in taxation, accounting, business, law, economics, management or other similar discipline; and

b) at least 2 years of full-time experience in the previous 5 years in Ethiopia:

(1) in providing tax agent services under the supervision of a licensed tax agent; or

(2) as a tax officer.

2/ The Authority may regard an individual as satisfying Sub-Article (1)(b)(1) of this Article if the individual has experience equivalent to that specified in Sub-Article (1)(b)(1) of this Article in another jurisdiction.

3/ The following individuals are not regarded as a fit and proper person to provide tax agent services:

a) an individual who could not discharge his debt or who is a judicially declared bankrupt;

b) an individual who has been found guilty of misconduct by a professional body;

c) an individual who has been convicted of a criminal offence relating to dishonesty and who has not been reinstated;

d) an individual who has an unsatisfactory tax compliance record including under the repealed Proclamation.

PART NINE
MISCELLANEOUS

19. Transitional Provisions

1/ The appointment of a person as a member of the Tax Appeal Commission established under the repealed Proclamation (referred to as the "former Commission") shall terminate once the Tax Appeal Commission established under the Proclamation (referred to as the "new Commission") comes into operation.

2/ A person to whom Sub-Article (1) of this Article applies shall be eligible for appointment as a member of the new Commission in accordance with Article 87 of the Proclamation.

3/ The reference in Article 87(3)(b) of the Proclamation to a "tax law" shall include the repealed Proclamation.

4/ If an appeal was filed with the former Commission and the appeal was not finalised before the former Commission ceased operations, the appeal shall be decided by the new Commission subject to any directions that the President of the new Commission may make.

20. Power to Issue Directives

The Minister may issue Directives for the proper implementation of this Regulation.

21. Effective Date

This Regulation shall enter in to force on the date of its publication in the Federal Negarit Gazette.

Done at Addis Ababa, on this 9th day of August 2017

Hailemariam Dessalegn
Prime Minister of the Federal
Democratic Republic of Ethiopia

TITLE EIGHT
COUNCIL OF MINISTERS REGULATION
ON THE FEDERAL INCOME TAX
(Council of Ministers Regulation No. 410/2017)

FEDERAL NEGARIT GAZETTE
OF THE FEDERAL DEMOCRATIC REPUBLIC OF ETHIOPIA

23rd Year No. 82
ADDIS ABABA 25th August, 2017

COUNCIL OF MINISTERS REGULATION No. 410/2017
COUNCIL OF MINISTERS REGULATION ON THE FEDERAL INCOME TAX

This Regulation is issued by the Council of Ministers pursuant to Article 5 of the Definitions of Powers and Duties of the Executive Organs of the Federal Democratic Republic of Ethiopia Proclamation No. 916/2015 and Article 99 of the Federal Income Tax Proclamation No. 979/2016.

SECTION ONE
GENERAL PROVISIONS

1. Short Title

This Regulation may be cited as the "Council of Ministers Federal Income Tax Regulation No. 410/2017".

2. Definition

Unless the context requires otherwise, in this Regulation:

1/ "Proclamation" means the Federal Income Tax Proclamation No. 979/2016;

2/ "Repealed Proclamation" means the Income Tax Proclamation No. 286/2002 (as amended), the Mining Income Tax Proclamation No. 53/1993 (as amended) and the Petroleum Operations Income Tax Proclamation No. 296/1986 (as amended);

3/ terms and phrases used shall have the same meaning as in the Proclamation or the Federal Tax Administration Proclamation No. 983/2016, as the case may be.

SECTION TWO
APPLICATION OF TERMS USED IN THE PROCLAMATION

3. Interest

An amount, however described, paid by a saving and credit association as the return on deposits with, or member's contributions to the association shall be treated as interest for the purposes of this Proclamation.

4. Permanent Establishment

1/ In determining whether a person exceeds the 183-day period specified in Article 4(2)(c) of the Proclamation, account shall be taken of a connected project of the person or of a related person.

2/ When a person operates a building site or conducts a project or activity referred to in Article 4(3) of the Proclamation, any connected activities conducted by a related person shall be added to the period of time during which the first-mentioned person has operated the building site or conducted the project or activities for the purpose of determining whether the 183-day period is exceeded.

5. Resident Individual

1/ Subject to Sub-Article (2) of this Article, in calculating the number of days an individual is present in Ethiopia for the purposes of Article 5(2)(c) of the Proclamation:

a) a part of a day that an individual is present in Ethiopia (including the day of arrival in, and the day of departure from, Ethiopia) shall count as a whole day of such presence;

b) the following days in which an individual is wholly or partly present in Ethiopia shall count as a whole day of such presence:

(1) a public holiday;

(2) a day of leave, including sick leave;

(3) a day in which the individual's activity in Ethiopia is interrupted because of a strike, lock-out, delay in the receipt of supplies, adverse weather conditions, or seasonal factors;

(4) days spent by the individual on holiday in Ethiopia before, during, or after any activity conducted by the individual in Ethiopia.

2/ A day or part of a day when an individual is in Ethiopia solely by reason of being in transit between two different places outside Ethiopia shall not count as a day present in Ethiopia.

6. Shares and Bonds

1/ The reference to "shares and bonds" in Article 59(7)(c) of the Proclamation includes any interest in shares or bonds, such as, in the case of shares, a right or option to acquire shares.

2/ A gain arising on disposal of an interest in a share in, or a bond issued by, a resident company shall be Ethiopian source income.

SECTION THREE
SCHEDULE "A" INCOME
SUB-SECTION ONE
FRINGE BENEFITS

7. Sub-Section One of Section Three Definition

1/ In this Section:

a) "employee share scheme" means an agreement or arrangement under which an employer company or a related company may allot shares to an employee of the employer company;

b) "household personnel" means a housekeeper, cook, driver, gardener, or other domestic assistant;

c) "market lending rate", in relation to a month, means:

(1) for a commercial bank, the lending rate on loans and rediscount facilities granted by the National Bank of Ethiopia to commercial banks that prevailed in Ethiopia during the month; or

(2) for any other person, the lowest lending interest rate of commercial banks that prevailed in Ethiopia during the month;

d) "related company", in relation to a company, means another company that is a related person in respect of the first-mentioned company;

e) "remote area" means a location that is thirty kilometers from an urban centre with a population of twenty thousand;

f) "services" include the use of property and the making available of any facility;

g) "vehicle" means a motor vehicle designed to carry a load of less than one tonne and fewer than nine passengers.

2/ In this Sub-section:

a) a reference to an "employer" includes a related person of the employer and a third party acting under an arrangement with an employer or a related person of the employer;

b) a reference to an "employee" includes a related person of the employee.

8. Fringe Benefits

1/ For the purposes of Article 12(1)(b) of the Proclamation and subject to this Article, benefits listed below which an employer provides to an employee are fringe benefits:

a) debt waiver;

b) household personnel;

c) housing;

d) discounted interest loan;

e) meal or refreshment;

f) private expenditure;

g) property or service;

h) an employee share scheme;

i) vehicle;

j) residual fringe benefit.

2/ A benefit is not a fringe benefit to the extent that, if the employee had acquired the benefit, the expenditure incurred by the employee in acquiring the benefit would have been incurred in deriving employment income.

3/ In determining whether a benefit is a fringe benefit and the value of a fringe benefit, any restriction on transfer of the benefit and the fact that the benefit is not otherwise convertible to cash are to be disregarded.

4/ The following benefits are not treated as fringe benefits for the purposes of the Proclamation or this Regulation:

a) a benefit that is exempted income under Schedule "E" of the Proclamation;

b) a benefit the value of which, after taking into account the frequency with which the employer provides similar benefits, is so small as to make accounting for it unreasonable or administratively impracticable in accordance with the directive to be issued by the Minister;

c) subsidy to a meal or refreshment provided in a canteen, cafeteria, or dining room operated by, or on behalf of, an employer solely for the benefit of employees and that is available to all non-casual employees on equal terms;

d) the provision of accommodation or housing to a non-managerial employee in a remote area if:

(1) the employee's usual place of employment is in the remote area; and

(2) it is necessary for the employer to provide the accommodation or housing to the employee in the remote area because the nature of the employer's business is such that the employee is likely to move frequently from one residential location to another or there is

insufficient suitable residential accommodation available in the remote area;

e) the provision of a mobile phone by an employer for use by an employee;

f) the payment by an employer of the cost of mobile phone calls made by an employee, including with a mobile phone provided by the employer;

g) tuition fees paid by an employer for the benefit of an employee for attendance at a course offered by a university, college, or other institution providing adult education courses;

h) the provision of the services of a security guard for the benefit of an employee;

i) the provision of food and beverage services by Hotels, Restaurants and other similar establishments for their employees;

j) the provision of uniforms and related work materials.

9. Debt Waiver Fringe Benefit

1/ The waiver by an employer of the obligation of an employee to pay or repay an amount owing to the employer is a debt waiver fringe benefit.

2/ The value of a debt waiver fringe benefit shall be the amount waived.

10. Household Personnel Fringe Benefit

The value of a household personnel fringe benefit for a month shall be the total employment income paid to the household personnel in that month for services rendered to the employee reduced by any payment made by the employee for such services.

11. Housing or Accommodation Fringe Benefit

1/ The value of a housing fringe benefit provided by an employer to an employee for a month when the employer owns the accommodation or housing shall be the fair market rent of the accommodation or housing for the month reduced by any payment made by the employee for the accommodation or housing.

2/ The value of a housing fringe benefit provided by an employer to an employee for a month when the employer leases the accommodation or housing shall be the rent paid by the employer for the accommodation or housing during the month reduced by any payment made by the employee for the accommodation or housing.

12. Discounted Interest Loan Fringe Benefit

1/ A loan provided by an employer to an employee is a discounted interest loan fringe benefit if the interest rate under the loan is less than the market lending rate.

2/ The value of a discounted interest loan fringe benefit for a month shall be the difference between the interest paid by the employee on the loan for the month, if any, and the interest that would have been paid by the employee on the loan for the month if the loan had been made at the market lending rate for that month.

13. Meal or Refreshment Fringe Benefit

The value of a meal or refreshment fringe benefit shall be the total cost to the employer of providing the meal or refreshment reduced by any amount paid by the employee for the meal or refreshment.

14. Vehicle Fringe Benefit

1/ A vehicle provided by an employer to an employee wholly or partly for the private use of the employee is a vehicle fringe benefit.

2/ Subject to Sub-Articles (3) and (4) of this Article, the value of a vehicle fringe benefit for a month shall be the amount calculated in accordance with the following formula:

$$\frac{(A \times 5\%)}{12}$$

Where: "A" is the cost to the employer of acquiring the vehicle or, if the vehicle is leased by the employer, the fair market value of the vehicle at the commencement of the lease. However, in case of a vehicle imported free of duty and taxes, the value of the vehicles' fringe benefit shall include the duty and taxes that would otherwise have been paid on the vehicle.

3/ From the value of a vehicle fringe benefit calculated under Sub-Article (2) of this Article the following shall be reduced:

a) any payment made by the employee for the use of the vehicle or for maintenance and running costs;

b) the proportion of the use of the vehicle (if any) by the employee in the conduct of employment;

c) the proportion of the month (if any) that the vehicle was not provided to the employee for private use.

4/ If an employer has held a vehicle for more than five years, the value of component "A" in the formula under Sub-Article (2) of this Article shall be 50% of the amount determined under Sub-Article (2).

5/ A reference in this Article to "a vehicle being provided to an employee for private use" includes a vehicle that is made available to an employee for private use even if the employee did not actually use the vehicle for a private use at any time.

15. Private Expenditure Fringe Benefit

1/ Subject to Sub-Article (3) of this Article, the payment of expenditure by an employer is a private expenditure fringe benefit to the extent that the expenditure gives rise to a private benefit to an employee.

2/ The value of a private expenditure fringe benefit shall be the amount of the expenditure treated as a private expenditure fringe benefit under Sub-Article (1) of this Article.

3/ This Article shall not apply to expenditure paid by an employer that is a fringe benefit under another Article in this section other than Article 18 of this Regulation.

16. Property or Services Fringe Benefit

1/ The transfer of property or provision of services by an employer to an employee is a property or services fringe benefit.

2/ Subject to Sub-Article (3) of this Article, the value of a property or services fringe benefit shall be:

a) if the employer supplies the property or services to customers in the ordinary course of business, 75% of the normal selling price of the property or services; or

b) in any other case, the cost to the employer of acquiring the property or services.

3/ The value of a property fringe benefit determined under Sub-Article (2) of this Article shall be reduced by any payment made by the employee for the property or services.

4/ For the purposes of Sub-Article (2)(a) of this Article, if the property or services fringe benefit is the provision of free or subsidised air travel by an employer that is an airline operator, the normal selling price is the standard economy fare for the flight provided by the employer.

17. Employees' Share Scheme Benefit

1/ The allotment of shares to an employee under an employee share scheme, including shares allotted as a result of the exercise of an option or right to acquire the shares, is an employee share scheme fringe benefit.

2/ The value of a right or option to acquire shares granted to an employee under an employee share scheme shall not be treated as a fringe benefit or otherwise included in employment income:

a) if the employee exercises the right or option, this Article applies to; or

b) if the employee disposes of the right or option, Article 59 of the Proclamation shall apply to the disposal on the basis that the right or option is a class "B" taxable asset.

3/ Subject Sub-Article (4) of this Article, the value of an employee share scheme fringe benefit shall be the fair market value of the shares at the date of allotment reduced by the employees' contribution for the shares.

4/ If shares allotted to an employee under an employee share scheme are subject to a restriction on the transfer of the shares, the employee is treated as having derived the employee share scheme benefit on the earlier of:

a) the time the employee is able to freely transfer the shares; or

b) the time the employee disposes of the shares.

5/ When Sub-Article (4) of this Article applies, the fair market value of the shares is determined at the time the employee share scheme benefit is derived as determined under this Sub-Article (4).

6/ In this Article, "employees contribution", in relation to shares allotted to an employee under an employee share scheme, means the sum of the consideration, if any, given by the employee:

a) for the shares; and

b) for the grant of any right or option to acquire the shares.

18. Residual Fringe Benefit

1/ A benefit provided by an employer to an employee not covered by another Article in this section is a residual fringe benefit.

2/ The value of a residual fringe benefit is the fair market value of the benefit determined at the time it is provided, as reduced by any payment made by the employee for the benefit.

19. Limitation of Tax Liability on Fringe Benefits

1/ Notwithstanding the provisions of this sub-section, the aggregate tax liability on fringe benefits shall under any circumstance not exceed 10% of the salary income of the employee.

2/ For the purpose of this Article "salary" doesn't include other employment related benefits.

SUB-SECTION TWO
FOREIGN EMPLOYMENT INCOME

20. Foreign Employment Income

1/ Article 93(1) of the Proclamation shall apply to a resident employee employed by a non-resident employer otherwise than as an employee of an Ethiopian permanent establishment of the non-resident.

2/ If a resident employee has derived foreign employment income for a calendar month on which the employee has paid foreign income tax, the employee shall be allowed a tax credit of an amount equal to the lesser of:

a) the foreign income tax paid; or

b) the employment income tax payable in respect of the foreign employment income calculated by applying the average rate of employment income tax applicable to the resident employee to the foreign employment income of the employee for the month.

3/ Article 45(3), (4), and (5) of the Proclamation shall apply for the purposes of the tax credit allowed under this Article on the basis that the reference to "business income tax" is a reference to "employment income tax" and the reference to "tax year" is a reference to the "calendar month".

4/ In this Article:

a) "average rate of employment income tax", in relation to a resident employee for a calendar month, means the percentage that the employment income tax payable by the employee for the month, before the allowance of any tax credit, is of the total employment income of the employee for the month;

b) "foreign employment income" means foreign income that is taxable under Schedule "A" of the Proclamation;

c) "foreign income tax" means income tax, including withholding tax, imposed by the government of a foreign country or a political subdivision of a government of a foreign country, but does not include a penalty, additional tax, or interest payable in respect of such tax;

d) "resident employee" means an employee who is a resident of Ethiopia.

SECTION FOUR
SCHEDULE "B" INCOME

21. Rental Payment Covering More Than One Year

If a lessor or sub-lessor to whom Article 15(5) of the Proclamation applies receives an amount of rental income for a period in excess of one year, the total amount of rental income received shall be treated as having been derived in the tax year in which it was received but the tax payable on the amount shall be calculated by prorating the rental income over the number of tax years to which the payment relates.

22. Lease of Business Assets

Income derived from the lease of a business, including goods, equipment, and buildings that are part of the normal operation of a business, shall be taxable under Schedule "C" of the Proclamation.

23. Depreciation of a Rental Building, Furniture, and Equipment

For the purposes of Article 15(7)(c) of the Proclamation, the deduction allowed for a tax year for depreciation of a rental building, furniture, and equipment shall be determined in accordance with Article 25 of the Proclamation and Sub-section Two of Section Five of this Regulation on the basis that:

1/ the rental building is a depreciable asset being a structural improvement to immovable property; and

2/ any furniture and equipment leased with the building are depreciable assets.

24. Rental Income Losses

1/ If the total rental income for a tax year of a taxpayer keeping records is exceeded by the deductions allowed to the taxpayer under Article 15(7)(c) of the Proclamation for the tax year, the amount of the excess shall be treated as a rental loss for the year.

2/ Article 26 of the Proclamation and Article 42 of this Regulation shall apply to a taxpayer who has a rental loss on the basis that the reference in those Articles to a "loss" is a reference to a "rental loss".

25. Foreign Rental Income

1/ If a resident taxpayer has foreign rental income for a tax year on which the taxpayer has paid foreign income tax, the taxpayer shall be allowed a tax credit of an amount equal to the lesser of:

a) the foreign income tax paid; or

b) the rental income tax payable in respect of the foreign rental income of the taxpayer calculated by applying the average rate of rental income tax applicable to the taxpayer to the net foreign rental income of the taxpayer for the tax year.

2/ Article 45(3), (4), and (5) of the Proclamation shall apply for the purposes of the tax credit allowed under this Article on the basis that the reference to "business income tax" is a reference to "rental income tax".

3/ In this Article:

a) "average rate of rental income tax", in relation to a resident of Ethiopia for a tax year, means the percentage that the rental income tax payable by the resident for the year, before the allowance of any tax credit, is of the taxable rental income of the resident for the year;

b) "foreign income tax" means income tax, including withholding tax, imposed by the government of a foreign country or a political subdivision of a government of a foreign country, but does not include a penalty, additional tax, or interest payable in respect of such tax;

c) "foreign rental income" means foreign income taxable under Schedule "B"; and

d) "net foreign rental income", in relation to a resident taxpayer for a tax year, means the total foreign rental income of the taxpayer for the year reduced by the deductions allowed under Article 15(7) of the Proclamation that relate to the derivation of that income.

26. Notification of Rental of New Building

For the purpose of Article 17(1) of the Proclamation, the period of notification of the completion or rental of new building shall be within one month of the earlier of the completion or rental of such building.

SECTION FIVE
SCHEDULE "C" INCOME
SUB-SECTION ONE DEDUCTIONS

27. Representation Expenditures

For the purposes of Article 27(1)(i) of the Proclamation, "representation expenditures" shall mean hospitality expenditures incurred by an employee in receiving guests from outside the business for the purposes of promoting and enhancing the business.

28. Deductibility of Interest Paid to a Foreign Lender

Interest paid to a foreign lender referred to in Article 23(2)(a)(2) of the Proclamation shall be deductible only if the borrower has provided the Authority with a copy of the letter of authorization to provide loan issued by the National Bank of Ethiopia to the foreigner lender.

29. Medical Expense Incurred for Employees'

Medical expense incurred by an employer for his employee including premium payments made under employees' health insurance scheme shall be deducted in accordance with Article 22(1)(a) of the Proclamation.

30. Food and Beverage Services Provided by Establishments Engaged in the Provision of Food and Beverage Services

1/ Expenditure incurred in the provision of food and beverage services by Hotels, Restaurants or other similar establishments for their employees shall be deducted in accordance with Article 22(1)(a) of the Proclamation.

2/ The limit to the deduction allowed pursuant to Sub-Article (1) of this Article shall be determined by a directive to be issued by the Minister.

31. Business Promotion Expenditure

The limit to the deduction of business promotion expenses incurred locally or abroad pursuant to Article 22(1)(a) of the Proclamation shall be determined by a directive to be issued by the Minister.

32. A Lessee Maintaining or Repairing or Improving a Business Asset at his own Expense

Expenditure incurred by a lessee of his own volition at variance with the terms of the contract concluded with the lessor in the maintenance or repair or improvement of the leased business asset shall be deducted from the business income of the lessee.

33. Charitable Donation

1/ A deduction allowed under Article 24(1) of the Proclamation for charitable donations shall apply to expenses incurred by the tax payer in the management of his own charitable activities.

2/ For the purpose of Article 24(1)(b) of the Proclamation, call by the government means call by the federal government or a regional state and includes a call by the Addis Ababa and Dire dawa city administrations.

3/ For the purpose of Sub-Article (1) of this Article "charitable donation" means a donation made in support of education, health, environmental protection or provided in the form of humanitarian aid other than for the tax payer's own employees.

34. Deduction allowed for Business Asset held under Capital Goods Lease Agreement

1/ Lease payment made for business asset held under capital goods lease agreement is deductible business expenditure from gross business income.

2/ A person realizing deduction under Sub-Article (1) of this Article shall not be entitled to depreciation on the asset.

35. Head Office Expense

Payment made by a permanent establishment doing business in Ethiopia to its parent non-resident body in reimbursement of actual expenses incurred by the parent non-resident body for the benefit of the permanent establishment shall be deducted to the extent that such expense was incurred in deriving, securing or maintaining business income.

SUB-SECTION TWO
DEPRECIATION DEDUCTION

36. Depreciation Deduction of Depreciable Assets and Business Intangibles

1/ Subject to Sub-Article (2) of this Article, a taxpayer may determine the depreciation deduction allowed under Article 25(1) of the Proclamation according to the straight-line method under Article 37 of this Regulation or the diminishing value method under Article 38 of this Regulation provided:

a) the taxpayer has used the same method of depreciation in its financial accounts prepared in accordance with financial reporting standards; and

b) the same method of depreciation is used by the taxpayer for all depreciable assets owned by the taxpayer.

2/ The following assets shall be depreciated only under the straight-line method:

a) a business intangible;

b) a structural improvement of immovable property.

3/ For the purposes of calculating the depreciation deduction in relation to a structural improvement of immovable property, the cost of the structural improvement shall not include the cost of the land on which the improvement is situated.

4/ No depreciation deduction shall be allowed for the cost of a depreciable asset or business intangible acquired by a taxpayer from a related person ("transferor") when the cost of the asset or intangible had been fully depreciated by the transferor.

37. Straight-line Depreciation

1/ Subject to Article 25(3) and (4) of the Proclamation, the depreciation deduction allowed to a taxpayer for a tax year in respect of a depreciable asset or business intangible under the straight-line method shall be calculated by applying the rate specified in Article 39 of this Regulation against the cost of the asset.

2/ The total deductions allowed, or that would be allowed but for Article 25(4) of the Proclamation, to a taxpayer in respect of a depreciable asset or business intangible to which this Article applies for the current tax year and all previous tax years shall not exceed the cost of the asset.

38. Diminishing Value Depreciation Deduction

1/ Subject to Article 25(3) and (4) of the Proclamation, the depreciation deduction allowed to a taxpayer for a tax year in respect of a depreciable asset under the diminishing value method shall be calculated by applying the rate specified in Article 39 of this Regulation against the net book value of the asset at the beginning of the year.

2/ If Article 25(4) of the Proclamation applies to a depreciable asset for a tax year, the net book value of the asset shall be calculated on the basis that the asset has been used in that year solely to derive business income.

3/ If the balance of a depreciable asset of the taxpayer is not more than two thousand Birr, the amount shall be fully deducted in the tax year to which the balance corresponds.

39. Rates of Depreciation Deduction

1/ The rates of depreciation applicable to a depreciable asset are specified in the following table based on the following categories:

Depreciable Asset	Straight-line Rate
Computers, software, and data storage equipment	20%
Greenhouses	10%
Structural improvement on immovable property other than a greenhouse	5%
Any other depreciable asset	15%
Depreciable asset used in mining and petroleum development operations	25%

2/ The rate of depreciation applicable to a business intangible shall be:

a) for preliminary expenditure, 25%;

b) for a business intangible with a useful life of more than 10 years, other than a business intangible referred to in paragraph (a), 10%; or

c) for any other business intangible, 100% divided by the useful life of the intangible.

3/ In this Article, "preliminary expenditure" means expenditure referred to in paragraph (4) of the definition of "business intangible" in Article 25(7)(a) of the Proclamation incurred by a taxpayer before the commencement of a business.

40. Depreciation allowed on a Building used Partially as a Business Asset

Depreciation on a building used partially as a business asset shall be allowed only in proportion to the portion of the property used as a business asset.

41. Repairs and Improvements

1/ Subject to Sub-Article (2) of this Article, a taxpayer shall be allowed a deduction for a tax year for the cost of a repair or improvement made to a depreciable asset during the year.

2/ The amount of the deduction allowed under Sub-Article (1) of this Article shall not exceed twenty percent of the net book value of the asset at the end of the tax year.

3/ If the cost of a repair or improvement made to a depreciable asset during the year exceeds twenty percent of the net book value of the asset, the whole cost of the repair or improvement shall be added to the net book value of the asset.

SUB-SECTION THREE
LOSS CARRY FORWARD

42. Loss Carry Forward

1/ If a taxpayer has a loss carried forward under Articles 26, 38 or 46 of the Proclamation for more than one tax year, the loss of the earliest year shall be deducted first.

2/ A loss may be carried forward only if the taxpayer's books of account showing the loss are audited and acceptable to the Authority.

3/ Despite Sub-Article (2) of this Article, a taxpayer may carry a loss forward if:

a) the taxpayer has submitted books of account to the Authority showing that the loss has been audited by external auditors; and

b) the Authority has failed to audit the taxpayer's books of account before the due date for filing the taxpayer's tax declaration for the next following tax year.

4/ Nothing in Sub-Article (3) of this Article prevents the Authority from subsequently auditing the loss and serving the taxpayer with a notice of amended assessment in relation to the loss in accordance with Article 28 of the Federal Tax Administration Proclamation.

43. Loss Carry Backward

For the purpose of Article 32 of the Proclamation, loss sustained in the performance of a long-term contract may be carried backward until the loss is fully deducted.

SUB-SECTION FOUR
FOREIGN CURRENCY EXCHANGE
GAINS AND LOSSES

44. Foreign Currency Exchange Gains and Losses

1/ A foreign currency exchange gain derived by a taxpayer shall be included in business income.

2/ Subject to Sub-Article (3) of this Article, if a taxpayer incurred a foreign currency exchange loss during a tax year, the loss shall be offset against a foreign currency exchange gain derived by the taxpayer during the year subject to the following:

a) the unused amount of a loss can be carried forward indefinitely for offset against foreign currency exchange gains until fully offset;

b) the taxpayer has substantiated the amount of the loss to the satisfaction of the Authority.

3/ Sub-article (2) of this Article shall not apply to a foreign currency exchange loss incurred by a financial institution and the amount of the loss shall be allowed as a deduction provided the financial institution has substantiated the amount of the loss to the satisfaction of the Authority.

4/ A taxpayer derives a foreign currency exchange gain or incurs a foreign currency exchange loss when the gain or loss is realised.

5/ In determining whether a taxpayer has derived a foreign currency exchange gain or incurred a foreign currency exchange loss in respect of a foreign currency transaction, account must be taken of the taxpayer's position under a hedging contract entered into by the taxpayer or by a related person in relation to the transaction.

6/ In this Article:

a) "debt obligation" means an obligation to make a payment of money to another person, including accounts payable and the obligations arising under promissory notes, bills of exchange, and bonds;

b) "foreign currency exchange gain" means a gain attributable to currency exchange rate fluctuations derived in respect of a foreign currency transaction;

c) "foreign currency exchange loss" means a loss attributable to currency exchange rate fluctuations incurred in respect of a foreign currency transaction;

d) "foreign currency transaction" means any of the following transactions entered into in the conduct of a business to derive business income:

(1) a dealing in a foreign currency;

(2) the issuing of, or obtaining a debt obligation, denominated in foreign currency; or

(3) any other dealing in which foreign currency is denominated.

e) "hedging contract" means a contract entered into by a person for the purpose of eliminating or reducing the risk of adverse financial consequences that might result for the person under another contract from currency exchange rate fluctuations.

SUB-SECTION FIVE
BANKS AND INSURANCE COMPANIES

45. Loss Reserve of Banks

A bank shall be allowed a deduction for a tax year for eighty percent of its loss reserve for the year, provided that the amount of the reserve has been calculated in accordance with the prudential requirements prescribed by the National Bank of Ethiopia and is consistent with financial reporting standards.

46. Reserve for Unexpired Risks of General Insurance Companies

1/ Subject to Sub-Article (2) of this Article, an insurance company carrying on the business of general insurance shall be allowed a deduction for a tax year of the balance of its reserve for unexpired risks as at the end of the year provided the amount of the reserve has been calculated in accordance with financial reporting standards.

2/ If an insurance company is a non- resident company carrying on business through a permanent establishment in Ethiopia, the deduction allowed under Sub-Article (1) of this Article shall be limited to the balance of the company's reserve for unexpired risks in Ethiopia.

3/ The business income of an insurance company carrying on the business of general insurance for a tax year shall include the amount of the company's reserve for unexpired risks deducted in the previous tax year under Sub-Article (1) or (2) of this Article, as the case may be.

4/ In this Article, "general insurance" means all insurance other than life insurance as defined in the Commercial Code.

47. Taxable Income from Life Insurance Business

1/ The taxable income of an insurance company from the conduct of the business of life insurance for a tax year shall be calculated according to the following formula:

$$(A+B+C+D)-(E+F+G+H)$$

where:

"**A**" is the life insurance premiums derived by the company during the year but not including premiums returned to policy holders during the year;

"**B**" is investment income derived by the company during the year relating to the business of life insurance;

"**C**" is the amount of any previously deducted reserves for life policies cancelled during the year;

"**D**" is any other income derived by the company during the year relating to the life insurance business;

"**E**" is underwriting expenses incurred by the company during the year in the conduct of life insurance business, including commissions paid, reinsurance premiums, risk analysis costs, Government charges on the policy, and operating expenses;

"**F**" is the additions to life policy reserves, including the initial reserve on new life policies issued during the year;

"**G**" is the amount of claim payments under life policies made in excess of the sum of reserved amounts and income earned on the reserved amounts in relation to life policies paid out during the year; and

"**H**" is any other deductible expenditure incurred by the company during the year in relation to the life insurance business.

2/ If a company conducts the business of life insurance and some other business including the business of general insurance, the taxable income of the company from the conduct of the life insurance business shall be calculated separately from the taxable income from other business of the taxpayer.

3/ In this Article, "life insurance" has the meaning given to the term in the Commercial Code.

SUB-SECTION SIX
MICRO ENTERPRISES

48. Obligation of Micro Enterprises to Maintain Books of Account

For the purpose of Article 82 of the Proclamation, micro enterprises shall be treated as individual and the obligation to maintain books of account shall apply to such enterprises on the basis of their annual turnover.

SUB-SECTION SEVEN
CATEGORY "C" TAX PAYERS

49. Presumptive Business Tax of Category "C" Tax Payers

1/ The presumptive business tax to be paid by category "C" tax payers shall be calculated in accordance with the SCHEDULE attached to this Regulation.

2/ The annual taxable income of a tax payer shall be assessed in accordance with the maximum annual turnover in the income bracket within which the annual gross income of the tax payer falls.

3/ The Minister shall revise the schedule in accordance with which the tax to be paid by category "C" tax payers is assessed at least every three years.

4/ If a tax payer who is the owner of a vehicle, drives the vehicle he uses in the business of rendering transport service, the employment income tax that the driver would have paid had the owner employed such driver, shall be included in calculating the tax payable by the owner of the vehicle.

SECTION SIX
SCHEDULE "D" INCOME

50. Income from Casual Rental of Asset

For the purpose of Article 58 of the Proclamation "income derived from casual rental of asset" means gross income derived by a person who is not engaged in the regular business of rental of movable or immovable asset.

51. Repatriated Profit of a Permanent Establishment

1/ The tax under Article 62 of the Proclamation on the repatriated profit of a non-resident body conducting business through a permanent establishment in Ethiopia shall be imposed by reference to the body's tax year.

2/ The repatriated profit of a body for a tax year shall be calculated in accordance with the following formula:

$$A+(B-C)-D$$

where:

"**A**" is the total cost of assets, net of liabilities, of the permanent establishment at the commencement of the tax year;

"**B**" is the net profit of the permanent establishment for the tax year calculated in accordance with the financial reporting standards;

"**C**" is the business income tax payable on the taxable income of the permanent establishment for the tax year; and

"**D**" is the total cost of assets, net of liabilities, of the permanent establishment at the end of the tax year.

3/ In calculating the repatriated profit of a permanent establishment for a tax year, the total cost of assets of the permanent establishment at the end of a tax year shall be the total cost of assets at the commencement of the next following tax year.

52. The Effect of Adjustment of Business Profit on Paid out Dividends

The fact of a business profit declared by a body being less than the adjusted business profit of the body by the authority in accordance with the finding of a tax audit, shall not affect the tax on dividend distributed to shareholders on the basis of the profit declared by that body.

53. Capital Gains Tax Payable on the Disposal of Certain Investment Assets by Donation

1/ For the purpose of Article 59 of the Proclamation, tax payable on a capital asset disposed by donation shall be calculated on the difference between the original cost of the asset and the cost of the asset at the time of disposal by donation.

2/ The receiver of donation shall be liable to pay tax on a capital asset disposed by donation.

SECTION SEVEN
EXEMPT INCOME

54. Exempt Income

1/ The following items of income are exempt from income tax:

a) employment income of not exceeding five years paid to expatriate professionals recruited for transfer of knowledge by investors engaged in export business in accordance with a directive to be issued by the Minister;

b) income from employment received by unskilled employee working for the same employer whether continuously or intermittently for not more than thirty (30) days within any twelve-month period; provided, however, that the tax payable on income from employment received by a casual employee working intermittently for the same employer for more than thirty (30) days within twelve months period shall be calculated only on the income received by that employee from the last employment;

c) for the purpose of the exemption under paragraph (b) of this Sub-Article "unskilled employee" means an employee who has not received vocational training, does not use machinery or equipment requiring special skill, and who is engaged by an employer for a period aggregating not more than thirty (30) days during a calendar year.

2/ The exemption accorded under Article 65(1)(a)(1) of the Proclamation to an amount paid by an employer to cover the cost of medical treatment of an employee shall include premium payments made by an employer on behalf of an employee under employees' medical insurance scheme.

SECTION EIGHT
ASSETS

55. Disposal and Acquisition of Asset

For the purpose of depreciation and capital gain tax, when a registerable asset is transferred by sale, exchange or gift, the transferor is treated as having disposed of the asset and the transferee is treated as having acquired the asset at the time the contract of sale, exchange or gift is registered by an entity empowered to exercise the function of the notary.

56. Cost

1/ The cost of a class "A" taxable asset provided in the Proclamation shall be adjusted for inflation as determined under a directive issued by the Minister.

2/ If the acquisition of an asset by a taxpayer is the derivation of an amount that is:

a) included in the income of the taxpayer subject to tax under the Proclamation, the cost of the asset is the amount so included plus any amount paid by the taxpayer for the asset; or

b) exempt income, the cost of the asset is the exempt amount plus any amount paid by the taxpayer for the asset.

57. Transfer of share

If a share that a non-resident person transfers is related directly or indirectly with an asset in Ethiopia, such share shall be treated as having been transferred in Ethiopia.

SECTION NINE
ADMINISTRATIVE AND PROCEDURAL RULES

58. Books of Account to be kept by Category "B" Tax Payers

1/ The Authority shall determine by directive the documents that category "B" tax payers shall be required to submit together with their simplified books of account.

2/ Category "B" taxpayers may voluntarily account on accrual basis provided that they comply with the requirements set under financial reporting standards.

59. Books of Account and Documents to be Kept by Category "C" Tax Payers

1/ For the purpose of Article 82(3) of the Proclamation, Category "C" tax payers may keep book of accounts that Category "B" tax payers are required to maintain. The tax of Category "C" tax payers maintaining books of account shall be assessed in accordance with such books of account as are acceptable to the Authority.

2/ Notwithstanding the provision of Sub-Article (1) of this Article, a Category "C" tax payer employing a worker shall keep documents showing any amount of employment income paid to the employee and any amount withheld in tax from such income.

60. Payment of Tax by Category "C" Tax Payers

1/ For the purposes of Article 49 of the Proclamation, Category "C" tax payers shall pay tax in accordance with turn over based standard presumptive business tax or indicator based presumptive business tax methods.

2/ Category "C" taxpayers engaged in the business of transport service shall pay the withholding tax from employment income together with their business income tax.

61. Non- Applicability of Withholding Tax

For the purpose of Article 92 of the Proclamation, the Minister shall specify by a directive:

1/ the type of services to which withholding tax shall not apply;

2/ persons to whom the obligation to withhold tax shall not apply.

62. Withholding of Tax from Domestic Payments

1/ A withholding agent required to withhold tax under Article 92 of the Proclamation shall issue a serially numbered official receipt to the recipient of the payment from which tax is to be withheld under that Article.

2/ If the withholding agent is a Government agency, the receipts referred to in Sub-Article (1) of this Article shall be authenticated by the Ministry.

3/ Article 19 of the Federal Tax Administration Proclamation shall apply to receipts referred to in Sub-Article (1) of this Article issued by a withholding agent other than a Government agency.

63. Requirement to provide Trade License to a Withholding Agent

Apart from the requirement of Tax Identification Number (TIN) laid down in Article 92 Sub-Article (4) of the Proclamation, a tax payer shall also be required to submit his trade license.

64. The Liability of a Withholding Agent

1/ Article 97(3) of the Proclamation shall not apply where a withholding agent required to withhold and transfer tax to the Authority under the Proclamation presents evidence to the tax authority that the principal tax payer has paid the tax, notwithstanding that the withholding agent has failed to withhold and transfer the tax.

2/ The provision of Sub-Article (1) of this Article does not preclude the penalty imposed under Article of 106(1) of the Tax Administration Proclamation.

65. Delayed Submission of Books of Account

1/ Books of account shall not be rejected by more reason of late submission.

2/ The provision of Sub-Article (1) of this Article shall:

a) not apply where the tax has been assessed by estimation because of non-filing of tax return;

b) not preclude the penalty imposed under article 102 of the Tax Administration Proclamation.

66. Income Derived after Ceasing of Business

For the Purpose of Article 74 of the Proclamation, the Tax Authority shall issue a directive on the procedure of payment of tax by a tax payer deriving income after ceasing business.

SECTION TEN
MISCELLANEOUS

67. Pooled Depreciable Assets

1/ A taxpayer who has a positive balance in a depreciation pool at the commencement of the Proclamation shall continue to depreciate the balance of the pool in accordance with repealed Proclamation.

2/ If a taxpayer to whom Sub-Article (1) of this Article applies disposes of a depreciable asset in a depreciation pool, the consideration for the disposal shall reduce the depreciation base of the pool.

3/ If, as a result of a disposal a depreciable asset referred to in Sub-Article (1) of this Article, the depreciation base of a depreciation pool is a negative amount:

a) the negative amount is included in business income; and

b) the pool is treated as closed and any assets remaining in the pool are treated as fully depreciated.

4/ A taxpayer who has acquired a depreciable asset on or after the commencement of the Proclamation shall depreciate the asset in accordance with Article 38 of this Regulation and the cost of the asset shall not be added to a depreciation pool referred to in Sub-Article (1) of this Article.

68. Business Loss Carried Forward

1/ A taxpayer who has a business loss under the repealed Proclamation that has not been fully deducted under the repealed Proclamation shall continue to be deducted in accordance with the repealed Proclamation.

2/ Any loss incurred under the repealed Proclamation shall not be taken into account for the purposes of Article 26(4) of the Proclamation.

69. Exemptions under Directives

An exemption provided for in a Directive issued by the Minister prior to the commencement of the Proclamation shall remain in force until the earlier of:

1/ the date that the Directive lapses according to its terms; or

2/ the date that the Minister repeal the Directive.

70. Repealed and Inapplicable Laws

1/ The Income Tax Regulation No. 78/2002 (as amended) are repealed by this Regulation.

2/ The repealed Regulation shall continue to apply for tax years preceding the effective date of this Regulation.

71. Effective Date

This Regulation shall apply on income derived as of 8th day of July, 2016.

Done at Addis Ababa, this 25th day of August 2017.

HAILEMARIAM DESSALEGN
PRIME MINISTER OF THE FEDERAL
DEMOCRATIC
REPUBLIC OF ETHIOPIA

Schedule (Omitted)

GROUP FOUR
INDUSTRIAL PARK CODE

TITLE NINE
A PROCLAMATION ON INDUSTRIAL PARKS
(Proclamation No. 886/2015)

FEDERAL NEGARIT GAZETTE
OF THE FEDERAL DEMOCRATIC REPUBLIC OF ETHIOPIA

21st Year No. 39
ADDIS ABABA 9th April, 2015

PROCLAMATION NO. 886/2015
A PROCLAMATION ON INDUSTRIAL PARKS

WHEREAS, it is necessary to accelerate the economic transformation and development of the country through the establishment of Industrial Parks in strategic locations to promote and attract productive domestic and foreign direct investment thereby upgrading industries and generate employment opportunity;

RECOGNIZING, the need to enhance export promotion, protection of environment and human wellbeing, economical land use and establishing and expanding planned urban centers;

RECOGNIZING, the paramount importance of legislation in respect of establishment development, operation, management and regulation of Industrial Parks;

NOW, THEREFORE, in accordance with Article 55 (1) of the Constitution of the Federal Democratic Republic of Ethiopia, it is hereby proclaimed as follows:

PART ONE
GENERAL

1. Short Title

This Proclamation may be cited as the "Industrial Parks Proclamation No. 886/2015".

2. Definition

In this Proclamation, unless the context otherwise requires:

1/ "Industrial Park" means an area with distinct boundary designated by the appropriate organ to develop comprehensive, integrated, multiple or selected functions of industries, based on a planned fulfillment of infrastructure and various services such as road, electric power and water, one stop shop and have special incentive schemes, with a broad view to achieving planned and systematic, development of industries, mitigation of impacts of pollution on environment and human being and development of urban centers, and includes special economic zones, technology parks, export processing zones, agro-processing zone, free trade zones and the like designated by the Investment Board;

2/ "asset" means any movable or immovable property as well as intangible property rights and interests relating to Industrial Park owned by public, public-private or private entities;

3/ "land" means any land designated for Industrial Park;

4/ "developed land" means land furnished with infrastructures such as road, water, power, telephone, dray and liquid sewerage discharging facilities, air pollution mitigation facilities and other important infrastructures;

5/ "lease" means a system of land tenure by which the right of use of industrial park land is acquired under a contract of a definite period;

6/ "commencement of development" means:

a) in the case of industrial park developer, the construction of the foundation works of infrastructures such as road, water, power, telephone, dray and liquid sewerage treatment facilities and other important infrastructures as well as foundation works of buildings;

b) in the case of industrial park enterprise, the construction of at least the foundation or erection of re-enforcement bars to cast columns of the permitted construction or building on the industrial park land;

7/ "sub-lease" means a transfer of parcel of developed industrial park land to industrial park enterprise by the industrial park developer or industrial park operator which has been possessed through allocation or lease;

8/ "investment" means expenditure of capital in cash or in kind or in both by an industrial park developer, industrial park operator or industrial park enterprise, as the case may be, to establish a new or to expand or upgrade industrial park, industrial park operation and industrial park enterprises within the industry park in accordance with the permit issued or agreements concluded;

9/ "corporation" means the Industrial Park Development Corporation established under Council of Ministers Regulation 326/2014;

10/ "industrial park developer" means any profit making public, public-private or private developer including the Corporation engaged in designing, constructing or developing industrial parks in accordance with Investment Proclamation and Investment Regulations, industrial park developer permit and industrial park developer agreement;

11/ "industrial park operator", means any profit making enterprise that operates, maintains or promotes industrial park in accordance with the Investment Proclamation and Investment Regulation, the industrial park operator permit and industrial park operator agreement and, includes the Corporation;

12/ "industrial park enterprise" means a public, private or public-private enterprise owned by Ethiopians, foreigners or jointly and possess developed land under the industrial park through sub-lease or by renting or building a factory within the industrial park to engage in manufacturing activity or in service provision for profit making in accordance with Investment Proclamation and Investment Regulation, industrial park enterprise permit and industrial park enterprise agreement;

13/ "Investment Proclamation" and "Investment Regulation" means the Investment Proclamation No. 769/2012 (as amended) and Investment Incentives and Investment Areas Reserved for Domestic Investors Council of Ministers Regulations No. 270/2012 (as amended);

14/ "agreement" means, as the case may be, an agreement concluded between:

a) the Commission and industrial park developer to design, construct, develop or to provide other services within the industry park;

b) the industrial park developer and industrial park operator to operate, maintain, promote or provide other specialized support services within the industrial park;

c) the industrial park developer or industrial park operator and industrial park enterprise;

15/ "industrial park resident" means a natural person granted a certificate of industrial park residence by the Commission in order to reside within the residential area of the industrial park;

16/ "Government" means the Government of the Federal Democratic Republic of Ethiopia or Regional government;

17/ "region" means any state referred to under Article 47 (1) of the Constitution of the Federal Democratic Republic of Ethiopia and includes Addis Ababa and Dire Dawa City administrations;

18/ "Board" and "Commission" means the Board or the Commission established under the Ethiopian Investment Board or the Ethiopian Investment Commission Establishment Council of Ministers Regulation No. 313/2014, respectively;

19/ "competent authority" means any federal, regional or city administration government organ having regulatory powers and duties over particular subject matters or geographic areas in respect of Industrial Parks;

20/ "investment permit" means a permit issued by the Commission for Industrial Park Developer, Industrial Park Operator or Industrial Park Enterprise to carry out industrial park development related activities as an investor;

21/ "customs territory" means the territory of Ethiopia in which the conventional customs laws relevant to the Industry Park of the country are applicable;

22/ "industrial park customs controlled area" means an area that is part of the industrial park where customs has the power to control but deemed to fall outside the customs territory;

23/ "applicable law" means any proclamation, regulations or directives applicable within Industrial Park supplementing or being interpreted in light of this Proclamation and the Industrial Park Regulation;

24/ "Regulation" means the Regulations issued by the Council of Ministers to implement this Proclamation;

25/ "tripartite modality" means the arrangement by which the Ministry of Labor and Social Affairs, Employers of Industrial Park Developer, Industrial Park Operator or Industrial Park Enterprise and employees' representatives address labor issues through constructive consultations;

26/ "basic utilities" means industrial park related utility such as water, electric power, telephone, gas and other similar utilities specified in the regulation;

27/ "person" means any natural or juridical person;

28/ any expression in the masculine gender includes the feminine.

3. Scope of application

The provisions of this Proclamation shall, uniformly in the territory of Ethiopia, apply to the federal industrial park activities or activities undertaken in connection with them as well as to any person conducting any activity in the federal industrial park.

4. Objectives

This Proclamation shall have the following objectives:

1/ regulating the designation, development and operation of Industrial Park;

2/ contributing towards the development of the country's technological and industrial infrastructure;

3/ encouraging private sector participation in manufacturing industries and related investments;

4/ enhancing the competitiveness of the country's economic development; and

5/ creating ample job opportunities, and achieve sustainable economic development.

PART TWO
RIGHTS AND OBLIGATIONS OF INDUSTRIAL PARK DEVELOPER AND INDUSTRIAL PARK OPERATOR

5. Rights of an Industrial Park Developer

Any Industrial Park Developer shall have the right to:

1/ design, construct, develop, exploit industrial park and provide services;

2/ sub-lease developed industrial park land;

3/ rent or sell to industrial park enterprises his immovable assets, buildings and rooms built within the industrial parks in accordance with the proportion specified in the regulation for manufacturing, office, residential and other services;

4/ enter into sub-lease agreement for the development, operation and promotion of industrial park land;

5/ operate, maintain and promote industrial park in accordance with industrial park development agreement;

6/ employ Ethiopian citizens and foreigners in accordance with the regulation;

7/ participate in financial markets in order to obtain loan, fund guarantees and other financial resources in the manner provided for in the Regulations issued pursuant to this Proclamation and other applicable laws;

8/ provide service to industrial park enterprises engaged within the industrial parks, in accordance with the commission agreements reached with the utility suppliers, collect charges and fees; the details shall be specified in the regulation;

9/ enjoy tax and customs duty exemptions and other incentives granted under applicable laws.

6. Obligations of an Industrial Park Developer

Any industrial park developer shall have the obligation to:

1/ construct immovable property with the industrial park, on-site infrastructure, office space and other facilities for the Commission's one-stop shop use and for the Revenues and Customs Authority as may be required by the permit and the Industrial Park Developer or Industrial Park Operator Agreement;

2/ facilitate conditions necessary for the participation of domestic training institutions in the design works of industrial park development;

3/ commence development within the period specified in the industrial park development agreement;

4/ adhere to the performance requirements for the phased development of the Industrial Park as well as any financial obligations and time schedule for capital and debt financing, specified in the permit;

5/ produce document envisaging their financial source trustworthiness;

6/ shall not transfer the un-developed industrial park land in any manner to third party;

7/ comply with any other obligations specified in this Proclamation, the Regulation, environmental protection legislation and other applicable laws, and the permit;

8/ replace expatriate personnel or professional by Ethiopian nationals by transferring required knowledge and skills through specialized trainings.

7. Rights of an Industrial Park Operator

Any Industrial Park Operator in the Industrial Park shall have the right to:

1/ transfer on sub-lease developed industrial park land and let or sub-let immovable assets, provide utilities and other services, on behalf of the industrial park developer, provide basic service and other service with charge;

2/ operate, manage, maintain and promote the Industrial Park in accordance with the industrial park operatorl's agreement;

3/ employ both Ethiopian and foreign nationals in accordance with the Regulation;

4/ use such other rights provided for in this Proclamation, regulation and other applicable laws.

8. Obligations of an Industrial Park Operator

Any Industrial Park Operator in the Industrial Park shall have the obligation to:

1/ adhere to this Proclamation, the Regulations, and the permit terms;

2/ in accordance with industrial park permit, operate, maintain and promote the industrial park and keep its assets and utilities in operational condition;

3/ maintain readily available office space and facilities for one-stop shop and customs service;

4/ refrain from transferring the un-developed industrial park land in any manner to third party, with the exception of the Corporation's transfer of industrial land to other industrial park developer;

5/ link domestic manufacturing enterprises with industrial park enterprises in order to develop their technological capacities and to benefit them from international market;

6/ comply with the social and environmental as well as any other obligations as provided for in this Proclamation, the Regulation, applicable laws, its permit or agreement;

7/ replace expatriate personnel or professional by Ethiopian nationals by transferring required knowledge and skills through specialized trainings.

PART THREE
INDUSTRIAL PARK ENTERPRISE AND INVESTMENT

9. Rights of Industrial Park Enterprise

Any Industrial Park Enterprise shall have the right to:

1/ may obtain Industrial Park Permit in order to carry out investment activities within Industrial Park. The manner of submission of application for Permit, the requirements thereof and the making of decision thereon shall be specified in the Regulation;

2/ obtain tax, customs duty and other incentives as provided in applicable laws, upon obtaining the permit indicated in Sub-Article 1 of this Article;

3/ freely exercise investment activities in accordance the terms and conditions of the permit, excluding those endangering public order, moral, safety and security as well as human and animal health and plant life; the details shall be defined in the Regulations;

4/ acquire land on a sub-lease basis and possess, sell own buildings, rent other immovable assets, export out of the Country, import into any industrial parks, sell in the industrial park customs controlled area goods and services pursuant to customs treatment specified in this Proclamation and other applicable laws.

10. Obligation of the Industrial Park Enterprise

Any Industrial Park Enterprise shall have the obligation to:

1/ commence development within the period specified in the industrial park enterprise permit and agreement;

2/ carry out the investment activities specified in the permit;

3/ allow entrepreneurship trainings of the technical and vocational education and trainings, collaboration trainings and that of higher education;

4/ comply with its obligations set forth in this Proclamation and the Regulation in general and the environmental, social and employer obligations in particular contained therein and in other applicable laws;

5/ replace expatriate personnel or professional by Ethiopian nationals by transferring required knowledge and skills through specialized trainings.

11. Administrative Measures of the Board against Speculation

1/ In the event that an Industrial Park Developer or an Industrial Park Operator transfers on lease or sub-lease basis the land it acquired in violation of the terms of the respective Industrial Park permits and the agreements or Proclamation and the Regulation without the prior approval of the Board administrative measure, shall be taken in accordance with directives issued by the Board.

2/ The provision of Sub-Article (1) of this Article shall have no implication with respect to sub-lease agreement reached between industrial park enterprise and the industrial park developer or industrial park operator on developed parcel of land within the industrial park development site.

3/ For the purpose of implementing this provision, the Board shall keep track of the annual fair market lease value of all Industrial Park land.

12. Business Registration and Compliance

1/ Any prospective Industrial Park Developer, Industrial Park Operator or Industrial Park Enterprise shall submit the following documents to the Commission in relation to its establishment and registration:

a) an application form duly signed by the owner or agent of the prospective Industrial Park related investor;

b) notarized memorandum and Articles of associations;

c) if a branch, documents ascertaining the registration and legal personality of the parent company in the country of origin.

2/ The industrial park developer, industrial park operator or industrial park enterprise registered pursuant to Sub-Articles (1) of this Article shall acquire legal personality.

3/ The details pertaining to Industrial Park business registration and related operating approvals and licensing, reporting, inspections, bankruptcy and liquidation envisaged under this Proclamation shall be specified in the Regulation.

PART FOUR
INDUSTRIAL PARK WORK PERMITS AND RESIDENCE

13. Industrial Park Expatriate Entry, Work Permits and Residency

1/ Any industrial park developer, industrial park operator or industrial park enterprise may hire expatriate personnel for its top management, supervisory, training or other technical functions.

2/ The entry, work permit and certificate of residency of expatriate personnel and their dependents shall be expedited through a coordinated function of the Commission as part of one-stop shop or Department for Immigration and Nationality Affairs and the Ministry of Labor and Social Affairs; the modalities of which shall be specified in the Regulations.

14. Eligibility for a Certificate of Industrial Park Residency

1/ Any natural person, whether an Ethiopian or foreign national, may become an industrial park resident subject to meeting the requirements as specified in the Regulation.

2/ The classification and issuance of industrial park residence permit and work permit shall be specified in the regulation.

15. Industrial Park Resident Rights

An industrial park resident shall have the right to:

1/ live and reside in the area designated for the duration specified in the Certificate of Residency;

2/ import personal effects free from customs duties, and other charges while staying in industrial park; the details of which shall be specified in the Regulation;

3/ establish community committees for better understanding of Industrial Park Developer and Industrial Park Operator in respect of facilities and services;

4/ transfer his personal effects to the other industrial park residents; the details of which shall be specified in the Regulation;

5/ enjoy such other rights to be specified in the Regulation.

16. Industrial Park Resident Obligations

An industrial park resident has the obligation to:

1/ unless otherwise provided under this Proclamation, pay all applicable customs duties, tariffs, taxes and other appropriate charges for any imported goods;

2/ pay personal income tax and other taxes in accordance with applicable laws;

3/ respect obligation provided in other laws.

17. Speculation by Industrial Park Residents Administrative Measures of the Commission

In the event an industrial park resident transfers its industrial park immoveable property to a third party in violation of the terms of the Certificate of Industrial Park Residency, this Proclamation or the Regulation, the Commission may take the following administrative measures:

1/ revoke the certificate of Industrial Park Residency;

2/ cause return of assets which have been received from industrial park developer or industrial park operator while he was resident;

3/ impose on the industrial park resident the payment of rents on such assets, for a period of up to 30 days.

18. Revocation of Certificate of Industrial Park Residency

1/ The Commission may, subject to providing 90 days prior notice and due process safeguards, especially after administrative hearing, revoke certificate of Industrial Park Residency for the following reasons:

a) if the industrial park resident fails to meet the requirements of this Proclamation, the Regulation, operating rules and procedures, certificate of Industrial Park Residency or any other applicable law; or

b) if the certificate of industrial park residency is obtained through misrepresentation or by provided false information or declaration;

2/ The revocation certificate of industrial park residency entails cessation of entitlement to any rights by the Resident; and the ceased immovable property shall revert to the Industrial Park Developer or Industrial Park Operator as the case may be.

3/ The resident whose industrial park resident certificate has been revoked or who leaves the park may sell his personal effects upon payment of customs duties and taxes.

4/ The Commission may also impose further administrative measures as specified in the Regulation.

PART FIVE
GUARANTEES AND PROTECTION, AND NATIONAL TREATMENT

19. National Treatment

Without prejudice to the provisions of other applicable laws of the country with respect to a foreign investor, any foreign investor individually or jointly with Ethiopian may participate as Industrial Park Developer, Industrial Park Operator or Industrial Park Enterprise.

20. Guarantee and Protection

1/ No Industrial Park investments may be expropriated unless otherwise required for public purpose, and subject to prompt payment of adequate compensation.

2/ The compensation shall be paid in any convertible currency in the international financial markets if the investor is foreign investor.

3/ Any unlawful expropriation shall entitle the Industrial Park Developer, Industrial Park

Operator or Industrial Park Enterprise to the restitution of its assets or investment together with reasonable interest rate calculated as of the time the unlawful expropriation until restitution of such property.

4/ The provisions of appropriate law shall be applicable with respect to manner of expropriation and what constitutes unlawful expropriation, compensation and restitution.

21. Applicable Foreign Exchange Rules

Any Industrial Park Developer or Industrial Park Operator or Industrial Park Enterprise subject to the laws of the country, shall:

1/ be entitled to borrow funds from banks abroad and domestic financial institutions;

2/ be allowed to list its stocks, bonds and other securities on foreign security markets;

3/ have the right to make remittances, in accordance with paragraph (a) to (g) of Sub-Article (1) of Article 26 of the Investment Proclamation No. 769/2012, in a convertible foreign currency at the prevailing rate of exchange on the date of remittance; details of which shall be specified in the regulation.

PART SIX
ACCESS TO LAND AND ENYJRONMENTAL PROTECTION

22. Acquisition of Industrial Park Land Moveable and Immoveable Asset

1/ The industrial park developer may possess industrial park land through lease system and transfer developed industrial park land through sub-lease.

2/ The industrial park operator may possess and administer, upon approval by the Board, the industrial park land which he has acquired through agreement from industrial park developer.

3/ The industrial park enterprise may possess land within the industrial park land which he has obtained through agreement from industrial park developer or industrial park operator upon approval and issuance of investment permit by the Commission.

4/ The restrictions in terms and tenure of land and use of urban or rural land and bidding system shall not apply on industrial park land.

5/ The details regarding industrial park land site registration, plot leasing, sub-leasing, site development, construction, safety and supply of utilities shall be specified in the Regulation.

6/ Any Industrial Park Developer, Industrial Park Operator or Industrial Park Enterprise has the right to mortgage its developed land, other immovable or movable asset, which commensurate to the development invested on the land, in order to obtain loan from financial institutions; the details of which shall be specified in the Regulations.

7/ The industrial park developer or industrial park operator may not, except to an industrial park enterprise, transfer a leased and developed industrial park land to third parties without a written permission of the Board.

23. Building Norms

Notwithstanding the provisions of other laws, norms or standards in respect of development of Industrial Park land, infrastructure and the construction of Industrial Park building and structures, shall be specified in the Regulations in order to ensure proper project design, planning, construction, management of Industrial Park, land development, management and related project supervision and quality control.

24. Environmental Regulations

1/ The federal and regional environmental legislations shall apply within industrial parks.

2/ The Ministry of Environment and Forest shall establish an office within industrial parks for the application, supervision, protection and enforcement of environmental norms, standards, safeguards, management and mitigation plans within the Industrial Parks.

3/ The details regarding environmental obligations of an Industrial Park shall be specified in the Regulation.

25. Industrial Park Designation and Modification

1/ An industrial park shall be designated by the Board.

2/ The Board in designating the Industrial Parka shall consider:

a) the nature of the proposed project;

b) the intended size and perimeter of the proposed Industrial Parks;

c) clearance from encumbrance, proximity to industrial inputs and infrastructure, conduciveness to become population center and the nature of project including availability of medical and recreational center;

d) compatibility with master plan, land use and the like.

3/ the details of designation procedures shall be specified in the Regulations;

4/ any modification to and revocation of an Industrial Park shall be determined by the Board.

26. Requirements for Selection of Industrial Park Developer

The selection of industrial park developer shall be effected in accordance with the regulation.

27. One-Stop Shop

1/ The services provided by competent authorities in any Industrial Park shall be offered through One-Stop Shop in an efficient and streamlined manner.

2/ The Commission shall provide one-stop shop service within the industrial parks; bring into line other competent organs and co-ordinate their day-to-day functions.

3/ The competent authorities shall maintain their mandates in the course of discharging their specific functions in the one-stop shop.

4/ Details relating to one-stop shop services shall be specified in the Regulation.

28. Labor Affairs

1/ Labor Proclamation No 377/2003 (as amended) shall be applicable in any Industrial Park;

2/ Without prejudice to Sub-Article (1) of this Article labor contract may be negotiated between the employer and employee taking into account the Industrial Park's peculiar feature;

3/ The Ministry of Labor and Social Affairs shall establish the rules and procedures on labor issues in consultation with the Ministry of Industry on the basis of tripartite modality the details of which shall be specified in the Regulation;

4/ The Ministry of Industry shall organize technical and vocational training program in collaboration with the concerned government entities and Industrial Park Developer (operator) whenever necessary;

5/ The Ministry of Industry shall facilitate technology transfer and skills development in general and domestic manufacturing sector capacity building in particular mainly through clustering and other best practice approaches.

PART SEVEN
REGULATORY ORGANS AND GRIEYANCE PROCEDURE

29. Regulatory Organs

1/ The Board shall designate and oversee the administration and supervision of Industrial Parks.

2/ The Board shall decide on complaints submitted by any Industrial Park Developer, Industrial Park Operator or Industrial Park Enterprise challenging decision given by the Commission.

3/ The manner in which the Board exercises its regulatory mandate shall be specified in the Regulation.

4/ The Ministry of Industry shall ensure and supervise that the industrial park enterprise are provided with assistance such as extension services, technology, inputs and marketing and method of manufacturing.

5/ The Commission, in addition to exercising its mandates under Investment Proclamation No. 769/2012 (as amended), shall issue permits to Industrial Park Developer, Industrial Park Operator or Industrial Park Enterprise; conclude agreements with industrial park developer and industrial park operator.

6/ The detail functions of the Board and the Commission provided for in this Article shall be specified in the Regulation.

30. Issuance of Reprimand, Suspension and Revocation of Permit

1/ The Board shall:

a) issue reprimand to industrial park developer or industrial park operator, so as to take rectification measure within the time limit specified in the regulations, if he violates the conditions set out in the permit, the regulations or directives issued for the implementation of this Proclamation or any other applicable law;

b) suspend the industrial park developer or industrial park operator pursuant to the time limit specified in the regulations, until the rectification measure is taken, if he fails to take rectification measure pursuant to paragraph (a) of this Article.

2/ Where an industrial park developer or industrial park operator fails to take rectification measure pursuant to paragraph (b) of Sub-Article (1) of this Article and if one of the following causes materialized, the Board may revoke the permit:

a) declared bankrupt;

b) provided that permit is given on the basis of false information or misrepresentation;

c) fails to develop the land or to administer the industrial park, as the case may be, in accordance with agreement;

d) notifies to an appropriate organ termination of its activities.

3/ Upon revocation of the permit, the land possessed by such permit holder shall be reverted to the entity that leased the same.

4/ The revocation of the permit shall entail termination of the industrial park development or industrial park operation agreement.

5/ The Commission may:

a) issue reprimand to industrial park enterprise, so as to take rectification measure within the time limit specified in the regulations, if he violates the conditions set out in the permit, the regulations or directives issued for the implementation of this Proclamation or any other applicable law;

b) suspend the industrial park enterprise in accordance the time limit specified in the regulations, until the rectification measure is taken, if he fails to take rectification measure pursuant to paragraph (a) of this Article.

6/ Where an industrial park enterprise fails to take rectification measure pursuant to paragraph (b) of Sub-Article (5) of this Article and if one of the following causes materialized, the Commission may revoke the permit:

a) declared bankrupt;

b) proved that permit is given on the basis of false information or misrepresentation;

c) fails to develop the land in accordance with the agreement;

d) voluntarily notifies to appropriate organ the termination of its activities.

7/ The revocation under this Article shall deprive the permit holder from the rights provided under this Proclamation.

31. Complaint Handing

1/ Any industrial park developer, industrial park operator, industrial park enterprise or industrial park resident shall have the right to lodge complaints to the Commission against measures taken by any competent authority.

2/ Any such complaint may be lodged with the Commission within 30 days of the taking of the measure in question.

3/ The Commission shall deliver its decision on the complaint submitted to it within 30 days.

4/ The Board shall entertain complaint lodged against the decision of the Commission if it is lodged within 30 days and shall give its decision within 30 days.

5/ An aggrieved party by the decision of the Board may appeal within 30 days of receipt of the decision to a court having jurisdiction.

6/ Details regarding the manner of lodging of complaints and rendering of decision shall be specified in the Regulation.

PART EIGHT
MISCELIANEOUS PROVISIONS

32. Powers to Issue Regulation and Directive

1/ The Council of Ministers may issue regulation with respect to incentive package applicable to industrial parks and other regulations necessary.

2/ The Board may issue directives necessary for the implementation of this Proclamation and the regulation issued pursuant to Sub-Article (1) of this Article.

33. Transitory Provision

1/ Any existing industrial zone or information technology park, shall be presumed as industrial park upon entry into force of this Proclamation provided they meet the designation criteria and be governed by this Proclamation.

2/ The prior:

a) agreements entered into by the Government with the industrial zone, industrial park developer or with the industry park operator;

b) incentives given by the Government to the industry zone, industry park developer, industry park operator or industry park enterprise; shall continue to be applied.

3/ Any prior application in respect of the development and operation of industrial development zones or industrial parks shall be deemed pending before the Commission pursuant to this Proclamation and regulations issued hereunder.

4/ The Industrial Parks Development Corporation shall be presumed as established pursuant to this Proclamation.

34. Inapplicable Laws

No proclamation, regulation, directive or customary practice, inconsistent with this Proclamation shall have force and effect, in respect of matters provided for in this Proclamation.

35. Effective Date

This Proclamation shall enter into force on the date of Publication in the Federal Negarit Gazette.

Done at Addis Ababa, this 9th day of April, 2015.

MULATU TESHOME (Dr.)
PRESIDENT OF THE FEDERAL DEMOCRATIC
REPUBLIC OF ETHIOPIA